Social History of the
United States

Titles in ABC-CLIO's
Social History of the United States

Social History of the United States
The 1910s

Gordon Reavley

Series Editors
Daniel J. Walkowitz and Daniel E. Bender

A B C  C L I O

Santa Barbara, California   Denver, Colorado   Oxford, England

For Chris, without whose enduring support and inspiration this would have been so much less.

Copyright 2009 by ABC-CLIO, Inc.

Library of Congress Cataloging-in-Publication Data

Reavley, Gordon.
  Social history of the United States : the 1910s / Gordon Reavley.
    p. cm. — (Social history of the United States)
  Includes bibliographical references and index.
  ISBN 978-1-85109-894-1 (hard copy : alk. paper) — ISBN 978-1-59884-127-5 (set)
  EISBN 978-1-85109-896-5 (ebook)
  1. United States—Social conditions—1865–1918. I. Title.
  HN64.R293 2009
  306.97309'041—dc22   2008016623

12 11 10 09   1 2 3 4 5

Production Editor: Anna A. Moore
Production Manager: Don Schmidt
Media Editor: Julie Dunbar
Media Resources Manager: Caroline Price
File Management Coordinator: Paula Gerard

This book is also available on the World Wide Web as an eBook.
Visit www.abc-clio.com for details.

ABC-CLIO, Inc.
130 Cremona Drive, P.O. Box 1911
Santa Barbara, California 93116–1911

This book is printed on acid-free paper ∞
Manufactured in the United States of America

Contents

Contents

Series Introduction

Ordinary people make history. They do so in ways that are different from the ways presidents, generals, business moguls, or celebrities make history; nevertheless, the history of ordinary people is just as profound, just as enduring. Immigration in the early decades of the 20th century was more than numbers and government policy; it was a collective experience of millions of men, women, and children whose political beliefs, vernacular cultural expression, discontent, and dreams transformed the United States. Likewise, during the Great Depression of the 1930s, President Franklin Delano Roosevelt advanced a broad spectrum of new social policies, but as historians have argued, ordinary Americans "made" the New Deal at the workplace, at the ballot box, on the picket lines, and on the city streets. They engaged in new types of consumer behavior, shifted political allegiances, and joined new, more aggressive trade unions. World War II and the Cold War were more than diplomatic maneuvering and military strategy; social upheavals changed the employment patterns, family relations, and daily life of ordinary people. More recently, the rise of the Christian Right in the last few decades is the expression of changing demographics and emerging social movements, not merely the efforts of a few distinct leaders.

These examples, which are drawn directly from the volumes in this series, highlight some of the essential themes of social history. Social history shifts the historical focus away from the famous and the political or economic elite to issues of everyday life. It explores the experiences ordinary Americans—native-born and immigrant, poor and rich, employed and unemployed, men and women, white and black—at home, at work, and at play. In the process, it focuses new attention on the significance of social movements, the behavior and meanings of consumerism, and the changing expression of popular culture.

In many ways, social history is not new. American historians early in the 20th century appreciated the importance of labor, immigration, religion, and urbanization in the study of society. However, early studies shared with political history the emphasis on leaders and major institutions and described a history that was mostly white and male—in other words, a history of those who held power. Several cultural shifts combined to transform how social history was understood and written in the last half of the 20th century: the democratization of higher education after World War II with the GI Bill and the expansion of public and land grant universities; the entry of women, children of immigrants, and racial minorities into the universities and the ranks of historians; and the social movements of the 1960s. Historians created new subjects for social history, casting it as "from the bottom." They realized that much was missing from familiar narratives that stressed the significance of "great men"—presidents, industrialists, and other usually white, usually male notables. Instead, women, working people, and ethnic and racial minorities have become integral parts of the American story along with work, leisure, and social movements.

The result has not simply been additive: ordinary people made history. The story of historical change is located in their lives and their struggles with and against others in power. Historians began to transform the central narrative of American history. They realized that—in the words of a popular 1930s folk cantata, "Ballad for Americans"—the "'etceteras' and the 'and so forths' that do the work" have a role in shaping their own lives, in transforming politics, and in recreating economics. Older themes of study, from industrialization to imperial expansion, from party politics to urbanization, were revisited through the inclusion of new actors, agents, and voices. These took their place alongside such new topics as social movements, popular culture, consumption, and community. But social history remains socially engaged scholarship; contemporary social issues continue to shape social historians' research and thinking. Historians in the 1970s and 1980s who focused on the experiences of working people, for instance, were challenged by the reality of deindustrialization. Likewise, historians in the 1990s who focused on popular culture and consumer behavior were influenced by the explosion of consumerism and new forms of cultural expression. Today's historians explore the antecedents to contemporary globalization as well as the roots of conservatism.

The transformation of the questions and agendas of each new era has made it apparent to historians that the boundaries of historical inquiry are not discrete. Social history, therefore, engages with other kinds of history. Social history reinterprets older narratives of politics and political economy and overlaps both areas. Social historians argue that politics is not restricted to ballot boxes or legislatures; politics is broad popular engagement with ideas about material wealth, social justice, moral values, and civil and human rights. Social historians, naturally, remain interested in changing political affiliations. They have, for example, examined the changing political allegiances of African Americans during the 1930s and the civil rights movement of the 1960s. So too have they examined the relationship of socialist and communist parties to working-class and immigrant communities. At the same time, social historians measure change by looking at such issues as family structure, popular culture, and consumer behavior.

For the social historian, the economy extends far beyond statistical data about production, gross domestic product, or employment. Rather, the economy is a lived experience. Wealthy or poor, Americans have negotiated the changing reality of economic life. Social historians ask questions about how different groups of Americans experienced and resisted major economic transformations and how they have grappled with economic uncertainty. The Great Depression of the 1930s, for example, left both urban workers and rural farmers perilously close to starvation. During the 1970s and 1980s, factories in the Rust Belt of the Midwest and Northeast shuttered or moved, and many Americans began laboring in new parts of the country and working new kinds of jobs, especially in the service sector. Americans have also grappled with the unequal distribution of wealth; some people advanced new ideas and engaged with emerging ideologies that challenged economic injustice, but others jealously guarded their privilege.

As social history has broadened its purview, it has transformed our sense of how historical change occurs. Social history changes our conception of chronology; change does not correspond to presidential election cycles. Social history also changes how we understand sources of power; power is constituted in and challenged by diverse peoples with different resources. Social historians, then, look at the long history of the 20th century in the United States and examine how the terrain has shifted under our feet, sometimes slowly and sometimes dramatically and abruptly. Social historians measure change in complex ways, including but also transcending demographic and geographic expansion and political transformation. How, for example, did the institution of the family change in the face of successive waves of immigration that often left spouses and children separated by national borders and oceans? Or during years of war with rising rates of women's wage and salary employment? Or following moralist reaction that celebrated imagined traditional values, and social movements that focused on issues of sexuality, birth control, homosexuality, and liberation? Historical change can also be measured by engagement with popular culture as Americans shifted their attention from vaudeville and pulp novels to radio, silent films, talkies, television, and finally the Internet and video games. The volumes in this series, divided by decades, trace all these changes.

To make sense of this complex and broadened field of inquiry, social historians often talk about how the categories by which we understand the past have been "invented," "contested," and "constructed." The nation has generally been divided along lines of race, class, gender, sexuality, and ethnicity. However, historians have also realized that analysts—whether in public or professional discourse—define these "categories of analysis" in different ways at different moments. Waves of immigration have reconfigured understandings of race and ethnicity, and more recent social movements have challenged the meanings of gender. Similarly, to be working class at the dawn of the age of industry in the 1900s meant something very different from being working class in the post-industrial landscape of the 1990s. How women or African Americans—to cite only two groups—understand their own identity can mean something different than how white men categorize them. Social historians, therefore, trace how Americans have always been divided about the direction of their lives and their nation, how they have consistently challenged and rethought social and cultural values and sought to renegotiate relationships of power, whether in the family, the workplace, the university, or the military. Actors do this armed with differing forms of power to authorize their view.

To examine these contestations, social historians have explored the way Americans articulated and defended numerous identities—as immigrants, citizens, workers, Christians, or feminists, for example. A post–World War II male chemical worker may have thought of himself as a worker and trade unionist at the factory, a veteran and a Democrat in his civic community, a husband and father at home, and as a white, middle-class homeowner. A female civil rights worker in the South in the 1960s may have seen herself as an African American when in the midst of a protest march or when refused service in a restaurant, as working class during a day job as a domestic worker or nurse, and as a woman when struggling to claim a leadership role in an activist organization.

Social historians have revisited older sources and mined rich new veins of information on the daily lives of ordinary people. Social historians engage with a host of materials—from government documents to census reports, from literature to oral histories, and from autobiographies to immigrant and foreign-language newspapers—to illuminate the lives, ideas, and activities of those who have been hidden from history. Social historians have also brought a broad "toolbox" of new methodologies to shed light on these sources. These methodologies are well represented in this series and illustrate the innovations of history from the bottom up. These volumes offer many tables and charts, which demonstrate the ways historians have made creative use of statistical analysis. Furthermore, the volumes are rich in illustrations as examples of the new ways that social historians "read" such images as cartoons or photographs.

The volumes in this series reflect the new subject matter, debates, and methodologies that have composed the writing of the United States' 20th-century social history. The volumes have unique features that make them particularly valuable for students and teachers; they are hybrids that combine the narrative advantages of the monograph with the specific focus of the encyclopedia. Each volume has been authored or co-authored by established social historians. Where the work has been collaborative, the authors have shared the writing and worked to sustain a narrative voice and conceptual flow in the volume. Authors have written the social history for the decade of their expertise and most have also taught its history. Each volume begins with a volume introduction by the author or authors that lays out the major themes of the decade and the big picture—how the social changes of the era transformed the lives of Americans. The author then synthesizes the best and most path-breaking new works in social history. In the case of the last three volumes, which cover the post-1970 era, scholarship remains in its relative infancy. In particular, these three volumes are major original efforts to both define the field and draw upon the considerable body of original research that has already been completed.

The ten volumes in the series divide the century by its decades. This is an avowedly neutral principle of organization that does not privilege economic, political, or cultural transformations; this allows readers to develop their own sense of a moment and their own sense of change. While it remains to be seen how the most recent decades will be taught and studied, in cases such as the 1920s, the 1930s, and the 1960s, this decadal organization replicates how historians frequently study and teach history. The Progressive Era (ca. 1890–1920) and postwar America (ca. 1945–1960) have less often been divided by decades. This highlights the neutrality of this division. In truth, all divisions are imposed: we speak of long decades or short centuries, and so forth. When historians teach the 1960s, they often reach back into the 1950s and ahead into the 1970s. The authors and editors of these volumes recognize that social processes, movements, ideas, and leaders do not rise and fall with the turn of the calendar; therefore, they have worked to knit the volumes together as a unit.

Readers can examine these texts individually or collectively. The texts can be used to provide information on significant events or individuals. They can provide an overview of a pivotal decade. At the same time, these texts are designed to allow readers to follow changing themes over time and to develop their own sense of chronology. The authors regularly spoke with one another and with the series editors to establish the major themes and subthemes in the social history of the century and to sustain story lines across the volumes. Each volume divides the material into six or seven chapters that discuss major themes such as labor or work; urban, suburban, and rural life; private life; politics; economy; culture; and social movements. Each chapter begins with an overview essay and then explores four to six major topics. The discrete essays at the heart of each volume give readers focus on a social movement, a social idea, a case study, a social institution, and so forth. Unlike traditional encyclopedias, however, the narrative coherence of the single-authored text permits authors to break the decade bubble with discussions on the background or effects of a social event.

There are several other features that distinguish this series.

- Many chapters include capsules on major debates in the social history of the era. Even as social historians strive to build on the best scholarship available, social history remains incomplete and contested; readers can benefit from studying this tension.

- The arguments in these volumes are supported by many tables and graphics. Social history has mobilized demographic evidence and—like its sister field, cultural history—has increasingly turned to visual evidence, both for the social history of media and culture and as evidence of social conditions. These materials are not presented simply as illustrations but as social evidence to be studied.

- Timelines at the head of every chapter highlight for readers all the major events and moments in the social history that follows.

- A series of biographical sketches at the end of every chapter highlights the lives of major figures more often overlooked in histories of the era. Readers can find ample biographical material on more prominent figures in other sources; here the authors have targeted lesser known but no less interesting and important subjects.

- Bibliographies include references to electronic sources and guide readers to material for further study.

- Three indices—one for each volume, one for the entire series, and one for all the people and events in the series—are provided in each volume. Readers can easily follow any of the major themes across the volumes.

Finally, we end with thanks for the supportive assistance of Ron Boehm and Kristin Gibson at ABC-CLIO, and especially to Dr. Alex Mikaberidze and Dr. Kim Kennedy White, who helped edit the manuscripts for the press. But of course, these volumes are the product of the extraordinary group of historians to whom we are particularly indebted:

The 1900s: Brian Greenberg and Linda S. Watts
The 1910s: Gordon Reavley
The 1920s: Linda S. Watts, Alice L. George, and Scott Beekman
The 1930s: Cecelia Bucki
The 1940s: Mark Ciabattari
The 1950s: John C. Stoner and Alice L. George
The 1960s: Troy D. Paino
The 1970s: Laurie Mercier
The 1980s: Peter C. Holloran and Andrew Hunt
The 1990s: Nancy Cohen

Daniel J. Walkowitz, Series Editor
Daniel E. Bender, Series Associate Editor

Volume Introduction

AMERICA AT THE CROSSROADS

Now this is nothing short of a new social age, a new era of human relationships, a new stage-setting for a new drama of life.
—Woodrow Wilson, 1912

In many ways, Americans in the Progressive era enjoyed benefits unimagined by their antecedents: new technologies; an unparalleled diversity of consumer merchandise; greater disposable income; increased leisure, and an almost bewildering choice of activities, from the liberating environment of dance halls to cinema; the introduction of the Ford Model T, which liberated Americans in the country and the city; increased employment options; and the gradual reordering of traditional social hierarchies. Americans, however, increasingly lived in an interdependent and urbanized country, one that was reshaped between the 1870s and the 1920s by the interwoven mechanisms of industrialization, bureaucratization, urbanization, and immigration. Because immense, indifferent corporations produced the majority of the material benefits enjoyed by those Americans whose circumstances were transformed by industrial capitalism, many had misgivings about individuals' loss of control over their lives. As growing numbers of people worked for corporations, their jobs and, by extension, their security depended on the corporations' endeavours, whereas their own efforts and capabilities appeared less important. Wilson observed that "there is a sense . . . (that) the individual has been submerged . . . that most men are the servants of the corporations." (Diner, 1998, preface)

Moreover, many critics had reached the inescapable conclusion that the gap between rich and poor, and even that between the better off and the disadvantaged, was more apparent than it was in any previous era. As corporate America and a market economy expanded, concerns were raised that industrialization had brought wage slavery in its wake and that laborers now entirely reliant on capital had relinquished control over their lives, whereas increasing numbers of single women in employment threatened established notions of female subordination. As the number of smaller businesses declined and subsequent conflicts between capital and labor intensified anxieties over wage slavery, repercussions were probably inevitable. This backlash (i.e., redress for the suspected profligacy of capital) characterized America from around 1890 to the beginning of World War I. Several opposing narratives emerge from contemporary accounts during this period: Those that concentrate on attempts by reformers and government to curb the effects of business and moderate the social consequences by extending the function and sphere of government. Narratives that contend that because corporate capitalism was responsible for the material advances in people's lives, business should both drive and control politics and reform. There are also others that assert that the corporate and bureaucratic transformation of the era bred both corporate capitalists as well as a new professional class who, along with reformers, surmised that modern scientific expertise, when applied to government policy, could mold social processes. Along with these accounts (that is, businessmen whose priority was the maximization of profit, scientists who invested their faith in expertise, and reformers attempting to effect change by education and legislation) are those that examine the responses and behavior of those affected by the transformation of America— the ordinary people.

Whatever their background (e.g., immigrant, laborer, farmer, scientist, African American, or white collar worker, and these categories might overlap), Diner contends that most Americans in the 1910s shared common aspirations: "economic security, personal autonomy, and social status." (1998, 9) It is clear, however, in attempting to realize those aspirations, such factors as race, gender, economic status, place of origin, and so on restricted the options available to people. Moreover, priorities differed within those three categories (e.g., social status would be less important than economic security for a migrant laborer). Although individuals strived to achieve those three goals, the decade was also characterized by the efforts of groups (e.g., corporate leaders, workers, farmers, reformers, or women) to procure the advantage or just to maintain their position against a background of institutional and political change.

By 1910, it was clear that the United States was indeed in a new social age as well as at some sort of crossroads. The beginning of the decade was one in which America attempted to contend with the full impact of a modern nation, modern, as Keller observes, "in its scale, diversity, and complexity." (1994, x) The crossroads appears to be a choice between whether the era can be understood as one in which a modern state materialized, or, as Keller argues, an era overshadowed by a confrontation between new concerns and the established order. The first part of the decade is commonly termed the "Progressive Era," a period in which a Progressive movement attempted to rein in the power of big business, to cleanse politics and encourage a more reactive attitude to the people, and to expand the role of government in order to defend the public interest and alleviate social and economic hardship.

This broad summary, however, obscures the reality that there is little coherence among those who advocated reform regarding their aims and motives and some divergence in their priorities and policies.

There is now some consensus among historians, including Richard Hofstadter, Samuel P. Hays, and Gabriel Kolko, that the economic conditions and moral imperatives of an earlier age seemed preferable to some. They would contend that in some reforms, the interests of the few held sway over the concerns of the many and that business interests were the beneficiaries, rather than the prey, of Progressives. Thompson believes that the period can be characterized as "the triumph of conservatism" when the "political capitalism that distinguished modern America was formed." (1979, 6)

Two issues emerge from these revisionist perspectives: whether there was anything sufficiently unified about the Progressives' program, rationale, and social configuration to support the term *Progressive movement,* and how, if at all, was the history of the early 20th century formed by the endeavors of the movement. As Thompson asks, "in other words, what, if anything, was distinctively progressive about the 'Progressive Era?'" (1979, 6) It is also difficult to establish the identity of Progressives. Because the Progressive Party itself was essentially the means by which Roosevelt hoped to campaign successfully for the presidency, advocates of progressive reforms cannot be defined by their allegiance to a particular political party. Moreover, reformers' objectives are broadly ahistorical and cannot be restricted to any one era, whereas some historians describe nearly everyone engaged in changing laws or institutions in the period up to 1914 as "Progressive." Nevertheless, the sometimes uneasy, temporary, and contingent alliances were enabled by a public climate broadly responsive to reform initiatives. This is the mood that appears to characterize the "Progressive Era." That the era can be described as both shallow and ephemeral and that the motives and aims were so diverse can, in part, explain the limited realization of reformers' aspirations.

Despite improvements in many people's material lives, they, and reformers as well, were perhaps justified in their concerns regarding life in modern America. By 1914, 23 million immigrants had entered the country, and around 15 percent of the population had been born overseas by 1920. An additional 25 percent were children of at least one immigrant parent. Americans were concerned both by the scale of immigration as well as its character (Jewish, Catholic, and Orthodox newcomers from eastern, central, and southern Europe, rather than the northern Europeans of the previous century). Progress, it seemed, came at a price, and that price was most visible in the cities. New immigrants tended to settle in the large industrial cities of the Northeast. More than two-thirds of the inhabitants of most large cities were either born overseas or were first- or second-generation immigrants by 1910, whereas that figure approached 75 percent in New York, Boston, and Chicago. Fire and disease were common in the over-crowded tenements, workshops, and factories, and the cities' basic services (e.g., streets and sewers) were simply not equipped to deal with the massive influx of immigrants and migrants. Political machines, usually under the control of a "boss," were vulnerable to corruption, and valuable franchises for public services were frequently bestowed on private enterprises.

A defining characteristic of Progressivism can be seen in the critical responses by a number of reformers and writers to the negative consequences of such rapid economic development. Muckraking articles exposing instances of political corruption, financial deception, and profiteering began to appear in the popular magazines of the early century. Some wrote of the scope and nature of urban deprivation, whereas others still advocated reforms. All seemed united in their desire to challenge the creed of laissez-faire. Thus, the urban environment became the focus of reform efforts, which had at its heart the shared belief that such reforms would be instrumental in shaping the moral order and destiny of the cities.

The belief in democracy was central to Progressivist philosophy—government by the people—but it was also more than that, as can be discerned in Weyl's 1912 call for "a new social spirit" that combined collaboration with philanthropy. (Thompson, 1979, 16) Some of this rhetoric was articulated in language that recalled religious revivalism. A significant proportion of reformers followed the doctrine of the Social Gospel, believing that the Christian principles of equality, brotherhood, and obligation to humankind should be put into practice. In matters of social reform, then, Progressives prioritized the common good rather than the individual good.

This emphasis on the collective, however, could result in a certain equivocation in their outlook regarding organized labor—this despite Progressives' endorsement of economic equality. In a decade defined by labor unrest, most people tended to support workers rather than employers, but there was also a general feeling that unions were less than selfless. For example, the American Federation of Labor (AFL) was criticized for its apparent disinterest in the vast pool of unorganized workers, its hostility towards immigrants, and the reluctance of its leaders to support social welfare legislation. It was inevitabe, perhaps, that some writers felt more empathy toward the Industrial Workers of the World (IWW), whose reputation as a mouthpiece for foreign-born workers and those disdained by the AFL gained the organization some considerable support during the decade.

To confront the problems of unequal distribution of wealth and to implement such measures as the elimination of child labor, the minimum wage and working-time legislation, compulsory accident insurance, sickness benefits, and improvements to public health and municipal services, Progressives advocated a graduated income tax, which was introduced in 1913. For example, reforms relating to child labor or reductions in hours for women were frequently the result of agitation by reformers involved with settlement houses. More than 400 of these houses had been established by 1910 in deprived urban areas by largely middle class, educated women, who were unable to enter professions from which they were largely excluded, to alleviate conditions for mainly immigrant populations.

The emphasis on efficiency went hand in hand with the process of modernization that swept through America during the 1910s. In 1911, Frederick W. Taylor described how his doctrine of scientific management could equally be applied in the home, on the farm, and in churches, government departments, and universities. This initiative was part of the growing professionalization of middle America's salaried employees. By 1910, easily the most rapidly increasing economic group was that which included employees above laborers and artisans, from clerks to engineers and from teachers to accountants. By no means were all the advocates of efficiency altruistic reformers; business enthusiastically adopted the doctrine as one more way of maximizing profits.

A tendency that emphasized the values of an earlier age ran parallel and counter to the belief in efficiency and technological progress. This retrogressive aspect of Progressivism attracted those with traditional moral principles who, like those of a more liberal disposition, advocated eliminating political corruption and ridding business of chicanery. It also appealed to those whose agenda was people's private lives, however, who saw the city as the locus of evil and advocated the prohibition of alcohol and prostitution. Hofstadter believes this virtuous aspect of Progressivism was led by men—frequently, "the old gentry, merchants of long standing, the small manufacturers, the established professional men"—whose lives had not been diminished by a reduction in their means, "but through the changed pattern in the distribution of deference and power" (Hofstadter, 1955, 135), outshone by the newly rich.

Much of the initiative behind the desire to uphold traditional standards and ethics stemmed from nativist anxieties regarding the changing structure of the population and was most evident in the campaign to limit immigration. In part, these impulses—similar to those that arose in the campaign to prohibit alcohol—can be viewed as part of the dichotomy between the values of rural, small town America and those of the cities. It is clear, however, that their roots also lie in class, ethnic, and religious concerns. Although both impulses can be viewed as Progressive, they represent a renunciation of the ideology of laissez-faire. Both initiatives attracted social workers and reformers, but they, and such others as the campaigns to reform saloons and prostitution, also interested many whose agenda was far from Progressive.

Not all attempts to rekindle traditional standards were grounded in nativist bigotry, however. For example, the appeal of efforts to excise corruption from business lay in people's moral opposition to the practices of capital. Immigration restriction could also be defended as part of labor's belief that unrestricted immigration held down wages. Many reformers who felt unable to support restricted entry nevertheless endorsed initiatives to Americanize newcomers. There were some, though (e.g., those who espoused the spurious "scientific" theory of eugenics), who throughout the decade coupled a belief in Progressive reform with nativist opinions that bordered on racism.

Although many reforms in the decade came about because of tireless campaigning by not a few altruistic reformers, it is evident that some were the result of self-interest (e.g., the establishment of the Federal Trade Commission, a body that was generally favorably disposed to the interests of large corporations). Advocacy for social and political reforms might logically be expected to come from those who would gain the most from them (the urban working class); however, until recently when the significance of support by urban political machines (which benefited considerably from working-class votes) for local reform initiatives has been emphasized, there was little evidence that urban wage earners contributed much to the reform impulse during the decade. There are several explanations for this: many reformers came from resolutely middle-class backgrounds, whereas the heterogeneous nature of the many ethnic communities that comprised the urban working class seemed to preclude any united or cooperative reform initiative.

Although it is true that the Socialist Party amassed much of its support from the working class and from immigrants, the 6 percent that Eugene Debs acquired in the 1912 presidential election was the highest percentage that party ever achieved. Organized labor was generally weak and was largely hesitant and cautious in its attitude to politics and reform. In 1910, less than 6 percent of labor was unionized, and its leaders—conspicuously, Samuel Gompers of the AFL—were disinclined to endorse any reform initiatives unlikely to benefit unions specifically.

This emphasis on reform might suggest that such activities overshadowed all features of life in the decade, or that everything achieved under the heading of reform amounted to change for the better. By any interpretation, increased segregation and discrimination against minorities, the brutal quelling of strikes, urban and rural poverty, and other features of life in the decade could not be described as "progressive." Against this background, America's entry into the war in 1917 aggravated tensions and heightened social problems. Exhibitions of patriotism and an impressive mobilization program failed to mask some uncomfortable realities: that business grew ever richer (total profits increased from under $4 billion in 1914 to $10 billion in 1917) and that government introduced some of the harshest measures against perceived dissent yet experienced in America.

Despite government entreaties, largely because of labor shortages caused by drastically reduced immigration and the mobilization of several million men, production in most industries did not increase. Many workers exploited the buoyant labor market by changing jobs more often. They also struck in record numbers. Actual numbers for strikes vary, with some sources putting the figure for 1917 at 4,450 and for 1918 at 3,353 (Hacker and Zahler, 1952, 195), whereas Diner (1998, 239) estimates that there were more than 6,000 during the 19 months of war. There is similar dissent regarding the extent of increases in union membership, but, as Diner observes, it is evident that some workers did use the war to bring about increased "economic security and autonomy." (1998, 237)

Although the war provided employment for around 1 million additional women, they were often seen as cheap labor, competing with men for their own jobs. Nevertheless, middle class women whose employment options had been decidedly limited before the war discovered that some male-dominated professions like medicine and the law were suddenly open to them.

The armistice ended any temporary advantage secured by men and women workers as government agencies were peremptorily broken up and business introduced measures to reverse any gains in wartime wages and union benefits, provoking still more strikes and disputes. Although widespread strikes continued into 1919—including a general strike in Seattle and, in the case of U.S. Steel, on an unprecedented scale—the government extended an already repressive program aimed at eliminating radicals (the so-called Red Scare). Farmers also suffered in the aftermath of World War I. A combination of high debt, the reduction of postwar relief measures, and complacency bred by artificially high prices meant that many were particularly badly affected in the depressed economic climate, a situation that was only to worsen in the next decade.

With the outbreak of war, the source of cheap immigrant labor dried up, and along with women, African Americans exploited increased employment opportunities. The Great Migration from the rural South to the industrial North provided American industry with a ready alternative, but like their predecessors in the prewar era, African Americans were forced to endure lower wages and worse conditions—as well as segregation and discrimination—than their white counterparts. Despite a national decline in female domestic service in the war years, the majority of northern African American women went into service, largely replacing white women who had moved into the factories. If African Americans hoped that opportunities opened up by wartime labor shortages would lead to any lasting improvement, however, they were to be disappointed.

As Americans returned from the war and immigration resumed, industry was unable to absorb large numbers of African American migrant workers. Because most African Americans could not return to the South, they were forced into the lowest-paid jobs or into unemployment. Cities with inadequate municipal services, poor-quality housing, and swelled by both immigrants and southern migrants became breeding grounds for racial tensions as African Americans were forced into ghettos. Tensions predictably erupted into outright violence in dozens of cities from East St. Louis to Chicago. The majority of African Americans who remained in the South had to suffer increased racial discrimination and segregation, and, in the worst cases, lynchings. The Great Migration turned violence against African Americans into a national, and not just a southern, symptom of racism.

If workers failed to capitalize on wartime gains, many of the advantages achieved by business were retained; corporate hegemony, concentration, and consolidation increased—with inevitable reductions in competition—as highly organized, standardized mass production methods were adopted across the manufacturing sector.

America's participation in the war also provided a platform, as well as a "laboratory," for the two polar opposites of Progressivism (liberal versus conservative). Control proved more durable than liberal hopes, and the stringent measures of wartime America remained in force afterwards. Mechanisms, some of which were voluntary, that were introduced ostensibly because of the emergency obscured a more authoritarian, prohibitive, and widespread program.

Although there were some exceptions (e.g., Jane Addams remained resolutely opposed throughout), America's entry into the war was generally welcomed by most reformers and intellectuals. The majority believed that federal direction and control and a unified effort could act for the common good. Their optimism initially seemed justified. For example, regulation and organization of the economy, resolution of labor disputes, and some social reforms related to child labor seemed to warrant reformers' enthusiasm. Moreover, patriotism provided a means whereby some reformers could justify their concerns regarding alcohol and prostitution and have measures originally aimed at the military more widely endorsed.

Even after the Armistice, reformers remained positive when such long-term objectives as women's suffrage and Prohibition were achieved. Soon, however, the impulse for progressive social engineering was conclusively reversed as federal agencies were disbanded, industrial disputes and violence increased, racial tensions escalated, and suppression of dissent and radicalism grew to unprecedented levels. Some Progressive reformers acknowledged that they had overestimated people's ability to work collectively during the conflict and that the government in which they had placed so much faith had, in fact, served the interests of those they were intended to rein in.

It now seems debatable whether there was a Progressive movement. Notwithstanding specific ad hoc alliances between groups with shared reform agendas, there seems little sense that there was anything unified about the Progressives. Moreover, within one group, there might be a mix of motives: altruistic *and* disciplinarian, for example. Despite the widespread attraction of certain reform measures, however, the often-disparate constituents drawn to Progressivism ultimately proved to be too unstable to last. Neither does there seem to have been a Progressive era. Many of the reforms and concerns commonly associated with Progressivism (e.g., antitrust tendencies, the maintenance of traditional American standards, and adjustment to the requirements of a convoluted industrial society) can be discerned both before and after the decade.

The thing that did seem to characterize the decade and to set it apart from any other was a public sentiment that was broadly responsive to a reform agenda. In an era of profound social change, a shared—but perhaps illusory—sense of purpose among reformers who shared little else was assisted by the rhetoric of leaders from Wilson on down. Although many reforms can be projected both backwards and forwards, the public sentiment that seemed responsive to social reform was largely finished by 1914, despite optimism among reformers that wartime reforms would be maintained afterwards.

Any analysis of the decade confronts a further problem: the reforms took place in a period of general affluence. This can be explained in part by examining the conditions—the response to widespread industrialization and urbanization —that gave rise to a desire for reform. The Progressive era represents a period of recovery after the 1890s, and it is possible that the public would be more sympathetic to collective and altruistic reforms when their own security was largely assured. There is also a sense that at least some of the sentiment was generated by concerns that many of the problems were a direct result of conditions in the cities, unrestricted immigration, racial conflict, and so on, and that left un-checked, the result would be class conflict at the least and revolution at worst.

The relatively limited success of many reforms can perhaps be attributed to the inherent conservatism of vested interests and established institutions. Issues apparently at the heart of Progressive ideology were left more or less unchanged or even worse at the end of the decade. For example, Thompson believes that the distribution of income actually became more inequitable, not less. (1979, 40) Most Americans, it seems, left the decade unconvinced that there was any viable alternative to the free market, and Progressives were forced to acknowledge that they entered the 1920s under rules established by industrial capitalism.

References and Further Readings

Diner, Steven A. 1998. *A Very Different Age: Americans of the Progressive Era*. New York: Hill and Wang.

Hacker, Louis M., and Helene S. Zahler. 1952. *The United States in the 20th Century*. New York: Appleton-Century-Crofts.

Hofstadter, Richard. 1955. *The Age of Reform: From Bryan to F.D.R.* New York: Vintage Books.

Keller, Morton. 1994. *Regulating a New Society: Public Policy and Social Change in America, 1900–1933.* Cambridge, MA: Harvard University Press.

Thompson, J. A. 1979. *Progressivism.* Durham, UK: British Association for American Studies.

Issues of the 20th Century

Social Reforms

OVERVIEW

The transition between the Gilded Age and the Progressive era is marked by enormous contrasts as America was transformed from a largely agricultural economy and a rural environment to a highly industrialized and urbanized nation. The chasm between rich and poor was more marked than at any time in the country's history, and a diverse and broad coalition of reformers evolved to address these social problems as the inequalities, deprivation, poor working and living conditions, and social divisions became more evident.

Reformers' aims were widespread and frequently contradictory. Nevertheless, most shared common beliefs that shaped their activities in the 1910s. They believed that the environment shaped behavior; poor conditions fostered poor character and poor character led to a socially debilitating society. To ensure both moral and political order, the urban environment became the focus of their reform efforts. Reformers in the Progressive era realized that urban deprivation affected more than the slum dwellers. In an effort to make urban life more equitable and more moral, reformers borrowed from the scientific professions, such as medicine, employed their training, and applied their knowledge to social problems.

Many were followers of the Social Gospel, which held the core belief that the Christian ethos of brotherhood, equality, and responsibility for humankind had to be put into practice. Despite the climate of reform, there were some who felt

1

that changes in America were both undesirable and unsought. The many religious fundamentalists strongly resisted any reconciliation with empirical science, especially Darwinian theories of evolution. The majority of reformers, however, were convinced that education was the most powerful instrument for social change. This broad coalition of reformers, who were mainly urban, American-born, middle-class, and educated, sought to eradicate slum housing and improve the urban environment; provide parks and playgrounds in the cities; improve public health and provide adequate sewerage and water supplies; eliminate urban vice and corruption; galvanize politicians to enact laws against prostitution, brothels, and alcohol; prosecute corrupt officials; reform working conditions; curb the power of big business; and develop settlement houses to assist the poor and to help assimilate immigrants. There was a shared belief at the heart of the Progressive reform movement that reform would be central in shaping the moral order and destiny of the cities.

TIMELINE

1910   The Mann Act passed, making it an offense to transport a woman across a state line for immoral purposes.

1911   Wisconsin becomes the first state to pass a Workmen's (later, Worker's) Compensation Act, guaranteeing injury compensation as a legal right.

1912   President Taft creates the Children's Bureau following calls by such social reformers as Jane Addams and Lillian Wald for a federal agency to assist in the protection of children living in poverty.

Massachusetts becomes the first state to enact a minimum wage law, establishing a wage commission that recommended voluntary minimum wage rates based on what commission members decided was the most appropriate combination of a living wage for employees and the financial state of the employer's business. During the decade, Massachusetts was followed by 15 other states, but there was no national minimum wage until the New Deal.

Theodore Roosevelt forms the Progressive Party following a split in the Republican Party in the 1912 presidential election, after losing the nomination to Taft.

Progressive Party becomes the first national political party to adopt a woman suffrage plank.

1913	Seventeenth Amendment provides for the direct election of U.S. senators.
	U.S. Department of Labor established to promote the welfare of wage earners and to improve working conditions.
	The first major reduction in tariffs occurred under the Underwood Tariff Bill. The average tariff was reduced from 41 percent to 27 percent, whereas some 100 items became free of tariff. To substitute for the lost revenue, a graduated income tax was introduced, the first such income tax in U.S. history.
1914	National Federation of Women's Clubs formally endorses the suffrage campaign.
1915	Federal Trade Commission established to prevent monopolies and unfair trade practices.
	Following the outbreak of World War I, Women's Peace Party founded by Jane Addams, Sophonisba Breckinridge, and other reformers to bring about an end to the conflict.
1916	The Adamson Eight-Hour Act, the first federal law regulating the hours of work in private companies, brought in to prevent a national railroad strike.
	The Keating-Owen Act passed by Congress—raises the minimum age of workers to fourteen, enforces an eight-hour working day, and prohibits the interstate commerce of goods manufactured by underage children. Subsequently declared unconstitutional in 1918.
	Mary Dennett, Clara Gruening Stillman, and Jessie Ashley found the National Birth Control League in order to repeal the laws prohibiting contraceptives in the U.S. mails. Disbanded in 1919 and reconstituted as the Voluntary Parenthood League.
	Margaret Sanger opens first birth control clinic, Brooklyn, New York City, publishing *What Every Girl Should Know* the same year and *What Every Mother Should Know* in 1917.
	Jeannette Rankin becomes the first woman to be elected to the House of Representatives.
1917	The Eighteenth Constitutional Amendment proposed, prohibiting the manufacture, sale, or importation of alcohol across America.

National Conference of Social Work, formerly the National Conference of Charities and Corrections, founded.

1918   By 1918, all states had enacted legislation requiring children to attend at least elementary school.

1919   The Eighteenth Constitutional Amendment approved, having been ratified by 36 states.

International Labor Organization founded, with protection of workers from sickness, disease, and occupational injury as one of its major goals.

PARKS, PLAYGROUNDS, AND CHILDREN

Getting Kids off the Streets

Born out of need, the movement for parks and playgrounds was part of a much broader reforming initiative in Progressive era urban America. Cities in the early 20th century were transitional places, not quite fully modern and still slightly primitive. Even though cities were clearly the engine of commerce and industry, they were nevertheless dark, dirty, and crowded places, especially in the neighborhoods of millions of migrants and immigrants. Despite the optimism of reformers regarding its social and moral advantages, housing reform was an enormous and highly complex project, and it is, perhaps, unsurprising that many urban reformers sidestepped a direct offensive on tenements and urban ghettos to focus on other potentially more productive and achievable schemes. Two such were the municipal park and the urban playground.

Urban children always played where they discovered space, and that space was frequently of their own making. Public roads, streets, and alleys made dangerous playgrounds, and as such, they were exciting places. At best, children disrupted businesses, whereas at worst they were injured. Nevertheless, urban children were remarkably resilient and determined to adapt their environment to their needs. Urban space was a "commodity" subject to keen bargaining. Once school let out and after dinner, children poured from the tenements into the street, and in the process, they helped shape the city as children's play and street games provided the soundtrack of urban life in the Progressive era.

Because they were frequently viewed as disruptive and "in the way" in overcrowded tenements where they were simply told to go out and play, urban children colonized the streets. Neither inside (the home, which was under adult jurisdiction and where there was little space for play) nor outside (the street) was under children's control or design; however, outside children could create their own world, with their own rules. In urban America, the street was all things to

Boys play checkers in the street in New York City, ca. 1908–1915. (Library of Congress)

all people: a place of commerce for the street vendor, a place of transportation, and, above all else, a place of constant movement. The street thus became home for urban youth, particularly immigrants, who played, invented or adapted games, or simply hung out. In the anonymous streets of big cities, children were free to be themselves and there, ignored by adults, a children's world was born.

Although children might have claimed the street as theirs, it was at best always a shared space, too valuable to be owned by any one group. Market, political arena, social gathering point, and thoroughfare, the streets were chaotic and conflicted. Children came into conflict with adults as urban children developed their own rules of play. Those rules were frequently in opposition to those of adults. Whether they ignored signs, used stoops for play, or stole from street vendors, children rebelled both because they resented adult intrusion in their world of play and because they claimed a right to exist in urban America.

Although some adults or older children kept a watchful eye on neighborhood children, buildings and streets were nevertheless dangerous places and many children became accident victims during the Progressive era. Moreover, children interrupted the commerce of the city and the combination of a genuine concern for their well being and hard-nosed economic pragmatism drove reformers to demand supervised urban spaces specifically designed for children—the safety

Skelly

Skelly, one of a number of street games played by urban children, is an example of adaptive play. Traffic, noise, and dirt made urban streets ill-suited for youthful play. Nevertheless, youngsters learned to take found material and detritus and turn it into toys and games. Skelly was known by different names in the many urban neighborhoods of the era and is a perfect example of the street games played by urban, immigrant children.

The game consisted of bottle caps as playing pieces and a board drawn in chalk on the street or sidewalk. Players flicked the caps between thumb and forefinger to skim the piece along the ground into squares, numbered one through thirteen, on the board. A skull and crossbones (a skeleton) marked the center, hence the name. Like sidewalk shuffleboard, players aimed to place their pieces in the numbered boxes to gain points and to knock their opponent's pieces out of boxes. Skilled players learned to search for the perfect materials to weight down the caps, and debates concerning the relative merits of tar, wax, coins, or any other materials could be heard in the streets. In many neighborhoods, skelly was more popular than marbles because players flicked sideways and there was less risk of scraping their knuckles; moreover, caps were more controllable than were marbles.

Skelly was the perfect urban street game both because it required no purchases and relied on the street as the game board and because it was a public, rather than a private, game.

of the parks and playgrounds where children could be children and business could continue uninterrupted.

Parks

The initiative to provide parks and playgrounds emerged from a desire to incorporate a slice of nature into the new urban wastelands as a restorative to modern life. As cities grew and slum areas became more crowded with immigrants, the shortcomings of providing only one municipal park were evident. However large and imposing examples like New York's Central Park were, they were often some distance from where the masses lived, so efforts became concentrated on the creation of park systems that were to include small neighborhood parks in crowded areas. Following the examples of Kansas City, Boston, Chicago, and New York, a park commission with a network of parks was either provided or under development in almost every large urban area by 1920.

Just as early advocates of tenement reform had believed their efforts incorporated a significant moral aspect, so too did the reformers who promoted the

Organized Sports

Progressive reformers were as concerned by social control as they were in socialization; therefore, they took a close interest in team sports and organized play. This was particularly true for advocates of children's reform, but for such employers as the Ford Motor Company, who also established sports teams, the logic behind this policy had two purposes. First, it created an organized leisure activity that was in marked contrast to the street corner or the saloon and was thus hygienic and morally uplifting. In addition, it fostered a team spirit that bound the players together in ways that could break down ethnic or old world communal ties and thereby assist in the process of Americanization and assimilation considered essential for employees.

Organized play (e.g., baseball leagues for older males) took many forms. G. Stanley Hall, the noted Progressive era reformer, believed that boys required special guidance through their "primitive" stages and that unless they were allowed to experience this phase in a controlled manner, eradicating it from their systems, they would not be able to participate in society as responsible adults. For Hall and other reformers, therefore, sports were important. On a team, boys learned the rules, helped teammates, and stayed competitive while remaining good sports, developing physical skills, and finding an acceptable outlet for teenage aggression. Reformers, motivated by the desire to provide children alternatives to the influences of the streets, their working-class families, and their ethnic communities, hoped to inculcate them into supervised play, whether in team sports or supervised playgrounds, creating an initiative that was at its core part of a broader effort to Americanize immigrant youth.

Although many working-class immigrant children did play in the parks and on teams, they did not always adhere to the rules. Because children sensed what reformers wanted and because they felt safer close to home and the familiar, they tended to play in neighborhood playgrounds or parks that were populated mainly by children from similar ethnic backgrounds. Since urban children tended to remain in ethnic or neighborhood groups, there was less association with other children from outside those groups and tensions and conflicts frequently arose.

Organized sports also meant that such public space as parks had to have specific uses, so certain areas became ball fields, thus ending their use as open play areas.

provision of parks. Earlier reformers, such as Frederick Law Olmstead, the landscape designer and winner of the competition for New York's Central Park, had contended that urbanization "posed social and moral hazards all the more hazardous for being intermingled with positive social gains" (Boyer, 1978, 237), and that the natural counter to the absence of occasions for contemplation and rest was "direct action" by city authorities to provide parks where social control would be emphasized. This articulation of "enlightened moral sentiment" (Boyer, 1978,

239) was espoused by reformers in the early 20th century, who also believed that parks would foster the moral growth of urban residents. In 1917, C. Walker Hayes, writing in *Social Hygiene,* quoted—apparently uncritically—a park superintendent who believed that a larger budget would enable him to reduce city prostitution by 98 percent. (Ibid.)

Although the notion of parks as a natural antidote to the morally corrosive effects of urban life remained at least partly influential well into the 20th century, a rather different perspective was evident by the second decade. Proponents believed that it was no longer sufficient to create a green retreat in the city and then do little else other than observe its beneficial effects. The park had to be managed and administered, they believed, in order to operate as an agent of social control. Although the park could act as a restorative, the mere existence of nature and leisure was insufficient in itself, so human assistance in the form of organized activities and professionals who would interpret nature for the masses was required. Reformers argued that community activities would thus engender "a spirit of neighborliness." (Boyer, 1978, 240)

These ideas reached what was possibly their ultimate expression in 1916 with the publication of *Parks: Their Design, Equipment, and Use* by landscape architect George Burnap. Burnap, who shared Olmstead's views regarding the moral significance of parks, went further in his belief that every aspect of park design—from its architectural elements to the paths and plants—should literally and unequivocally echo the social principles of its planners and managers and, moreover, epitomize the authority of the city over its residents. Burnap was less concerned with the idea of the park as a retreat from urban tensions or in nature as a moral antidote than he was in consciously modeling the park as a social creation. He believed that these public spaces should articulate the class realities of urban-industrial society. To this end, he contended that park design should be determined by the social properties of different urban classes. Parks in areas where slums predominated, for example, should be sufficiently open to permit workers to escape the overcrowded tenements with good-quality landscaping to encourage workers to aspire to something better. Parks for the middle classes should be restrained and orderly, whereas the upper classes were allowed a greater degree of flexibility. These suppositions and prescriptions were clearly expressed in contemporary urban social control texts and faithfully applied in parks throughout the decade.

City Space: Creating Playgrounds

The advocates of the playground movement were even more confident than those Progressives who promoted the park as the agent of social control through environmental practice. Evangelists proclaimed that the simple attributes of the playground—the slides, swings, and sandboxes—would nurture a new urbanite:

Boys wrestle for the basketball on the Carnegie playground in New York City, August 1911. (Library of Congress)

moral, diligent, and socially accountable. Building on other urban reform schemes at the turn of the century, Progressive reformers established small playgrounds in a few cities in the East. The movement gained ground slowly at first, but the lead of the tireless "father of American playgrounds," Joseph Lee, and his collaborators, Luther H. Gullick and Henry Stoddard Curtis, in forming the Playground Association of America proved instrumental in encouraging others to take up the cause.

Chicago budgeted some $15 million to establish around 30 playgrounds and recreation centers in immigrant neighborhoods during the early 1900s. Almost 500 cities across America had adopted the reforms by 1917. Reformers were not merely interested in providing fun for the young urban poor, nor were their social visions confined to improved physical health resulting from fresh air and exercise. Like other urban reformers, they believed that playgrounds would shape a firm, collective urban moral structure. Nevertheless, playgrounds were complicated urban spaces. Reformers would have to purchase land or convince municipal governments to do so, the site would have to be developed, and staff needed to be found for the newly designed space. Capitalizing on the desire to Americanize children through supervised play, reformers approached such businessmen as John D. Rockefeller and J. P. Morgan, who were known to have sympathies in this area. They also lobbied local governments to establish and maintain playgrounds in crowded urban neighborhoods. The initiatives to create municipal playgrounds led reformers into the realm of city planning and zoning laws, and reformers came to realize that these laws could revitalize neighborhoods, create recreational space, and instill in neighbors a sense of pride and ownership in their neighborhood.

Play and Urban Street Games

Children are adept at using their imaginations, adapting what they discover to find something of interest to occupy their time. In the cities of Progressive era America, street games were as numerous as the neighborhoods of each city. Because each street was different, often with different ethnic mixes, each block might have different rules for the same game, so knowing the local rules and custom of play was a sign of fitting in and belonging. Games ranged from versions of baseball, tag, and jacks, to games that more resembled gambling than innocent street pastimes. Although children might have been warned in school or at home that gambling was wrong, in the streets gambling was a common activity. Craps, a dice game, and pitching pennies, which involved tossing pennies against a wall, were popular street games.

Children would divide the block in an organized way. Girls would typically occupy the stoop, where they watched their brothers, jumped rope, chatted, played potsies, and occasionally joined the boys in a game such as ring-a-levio. The middle of the street belonged to the boys, who played variations of games with a ball and a bat, played marbles, and jumped various dangerous objects. Older boys occupied the street corners, playing craps, pitching pennies, and generally waiting for some excitement to happen. For boys, any variation on baseball was the big game, but because street children had no money for equipment, they had to play games with the most rudimentary tools. A rubber ball and a broom handle that deputized for a bat were the basic requirements, whereas manholes became bases, as did carts, fire hydrants, or any other object that was at hand and semi-permanent.

Games were temporarily stopped for traffic—a timeout—and children scoured the streets in a constant search for discarded items that could be used for play. Whether what they found was of use seldom mattered because the hunt became the game. In immigrant neighborhoods where large families were the norm, children found friends to play with in the same way that they discovered implements—they made use of what was there. When looking for playmates, children tended to stick to the immediate neighborhood. As the average tenement building in New York City housed 16 families, each with five or six children, there was no shortage of choice. Geographical proximity, rather than racial, ethnic, or religious considerations, tended to determine the organization of both playgroups and gangs, and children played with others who would not have been welcome in their own homes. There were different rules on the street, however, so gangs and groups were often mixed in terms of both age and ethnicity. Territory became all-important and fighting between groups, which was often intense, was usually undertaken to protect precious urban space. Contemporary photographs of urban gangs show how these groups functioned as familiar stand-ins (for parents, teachers, or community leaders), protecting, teaching, and socializing children in the tough rules of the streets.

Social Control and Organized Play

In their enthusiasm to improve the lives of those that the middle-class reformers saw as the underprivileged of the city, they too often sought to control the lives of those they sought to help, believing that the poor were incapable of helping themselves. Seeing urban America as unordered, and children's play as chaotic, dangerous, and anarchistic, reformers thought they would provide logic and order, and in the process reform America. Urban children's play, they believed, was simply not American play. These reformers also believed that children would become Americans only through their guidance and through answers derived from scientific research. To counteract the failures of the chilren's own parents and earlier attempts at reform, professionals would properly supervise children. To bring order out of chaos, rules on play would be imposed. Organized little leagues, with uniform rules of play, replaced unruly stickball games. Supervised playgrounds supplanted street games. Above all, sportsmanship was emphasized.

Even though these may have been worthwhile values for children to learn and few would have denied that safer play areas were needed, there was a clear lack of trust in those they were attempting to help underlying many of the reformers' efforts. The Progressive era can be characterized as a search for order and nowhere is this more evident than in the movement to reform or save children. Because many reformers felt that the street, the neighborhood, and children's friends were a negative influence, they established clubs for boys and girls in an effort to create an alternate, healthy community to inculcate middle-class values into working-class children. Reformers, though, were frequently surprised that their efforts did not result in automatic success. The rules of geography, the sense of community, and contempt for the controlling influence of some reformers all kept children from venturing too far from home, no matter how impressive the facilities.

Younger children were particularly reluctant to visit a playground that was more than two blocks from home, and even older children would not go to a playground further than half a mile away on a regular basis. Reformers were disappointed to find that children and their mothers preferred the streets below

New York tenement house with children in front, 1910. Photo attributed to Lewis Hine. (Library of Congress)

their tenements to the parks and playgrounds. Some deliberately chose the street because they had more control over it, whereas others felt more comfortable on the street because it was safely ensconced in their familiar ethnic neighborhood.

The language of social control suffuses the literature of the movement. Reformers seemed convinced that anything spent on play facilities would reap dividends in nurturing the moral nature of children, promoting civic cohesion and providing the "social training and discipline" (Boyer, 1978, 243) needed without delay among immigrant communities. Blunter still was the reformer who, in 1911, contended that reforms were necessary because they would give urban children "new social notions, and a better standard of what is acceptable to those 'higher up.'" (Ibid.) The solution to what such reformers as Curtis perceived as the "overstimulation" of the pace of urban life was not further repression; rather, it was the creation of a different environment (i.e., the playground, where children would be productively occupied in the hours when they were beyond the watchful eye of parents and teachers).

Rifts opened up between the leaders of the park movement and playground advocates, who argued that the emphasis on natural landscapes in parks placed strict limitations on children's play. There was occasional sniping at such purely sectarian initiatives as Sunday schools or the YMCA because they excluded, for example, Catholic or Jewish children. Nevertheless, the playground movement attracted widespread support from other urban reformers, such as Jacob Riis, who believed that the playground was high among the "wholesome counter-influences to the saloon, street gang, and similar evils." (Boyer, 1978, 245)

Considerable emphasis was placed on the importance of providing adequate adult supervision on playgrounds. This was symptomatic of a broader programmatic and philosophical shift in the playground movement and paralleled similar changes in the park movement. Unlike earlier advocates who believed that the function of the authorities was merely to supply such diversions as sandboxes and swings, along with a safe and agreeable environment, and that children should be left to play freely and spontaneously, later proponents dismissed this view as ingenuous and potentially damaging. Reformers asserted that activities had to be funneled in a positive direction and that the moral worth of play-grounds depended on the participation of someone to act as guide. As in other aspects of Progressive reform, the notion of expertise became central to the potential success of playgrounds. In many cities, professional playground man-agers were recruited. In 1918, Cleveland mayor Newton D. Baker, writing in *Social Hygiene,* recounted his realization that wholesome play meant supervised play, "and so we began to train experts." (Boyer, 1978, 248)

These "experts" were advised to praise children's tendencies toward self-sacrifice for the benefit of the team and, similarly, to criticize and even exclude the child from organized play when necessary. In this way, the bedrock of "co-operation, politeness, and good morals" (Boyer, 1978, 250) would have been laid. These traits would in turn influence the family and, eventually, society it-self. In playground competitions, children were marked partly on their conduct and were heard warning parents not to say anything critical in case they lost points. Reformers also believed that these social control mechanisms could be extended to such other forms of urban leisure as dance halls, movie theaters, and vaudeville—a comprehensive program of "direct and indirect control of leisure"—and that, by extension, this would include the "care of the morals of adults as well." (Boyer, 1978, 250–251)

This significant and optimistic investment in playgrounds mirrored the dom-inant environmentalism of the era and the notion that these tactics could influ-ence children—untainted yet by the vices associated with urban life—for the better. In this sense, children were the constantly renewable source of the city's potential for the moral transformation of its most moldable residents through the transfiguration of the physical environment. By the end of the decade, how-ever, the ambitions behind this social vision were in decline. Nevertheless, for a while in the Progressive era, parks and playgrounds symbolized reformers' dreams of an America transformed by social engineering.

TEMPERANCE, MORALITY, AND RELIGION

America's Growing Cities

Since the first census of the United States in 1790, the country changed from one that was predominantly rural—almost 95 percent of the population—to one that, at the beginning of the 20th century, was overwhelmingly urban. These changes brought with them profound concerns about the effects that urbanization and industrialization would have on both rural and urban communities. Indeed, around the time of the first census, "Thomas Jefferson believed that a nation of large cities would inevitably become corrupt" (Gardner in Goldfield, 2007, 592), and his vision for the nation was one of self-sufficient farmers in an agri-cultural land. By the early 20th century, the majority of growth took place in the

Blue Laws

"Blue laws" refer to legislation that regulates public and private conduct, especially that which relates to observance of the Sabbath. The term originates in the rigid religious prescriptions of 17th-century New England, which declined after the Revolution and were revived with the growth of the prohibition movement in the late 19th and early 20th centuries. Other legislation relating to retail sales (e.g., of tobacco), secular amusements, and "unnecessary" work, as well as strict local censorship of various entertainments, was brought in to enforce moral standards. In the early 20th century, blue laws frequently applied to the sale of alcohol. They were upheld by the courts despite their original religious meaning on the basis that their observance had become secular and that they promoted Sunday as a day of rest and relaxation.

Under blue laws, some activities were only prohibited during certain hours, although there were usually exceptions in certain areas of commerce (e.g., sales in grocery and drug stores, which could remain open for the sale of emergency medical goods, where customers could buy certain groceries and housewares). Despite exceptions, there were frequent anomalies (e.g., in Texas, blue laws prohibited the sale of pots, pans, and washing machines on Sundays). In some cases, the laws were established or remained in force with the support of those affected so that they were permitted a day off each week unconcerned that their competitors would remain open. Most states during the decade prohibited the sale of alcohol, with some permitting sales only after noon on the basis that people should attend church on Sunday mornings.

By 1910, there were still numerous laws protecting the Sabbath, especially in the southern and midwestern states. Legislation targeted such various groups as saloon owners, Jews, and nonreligious people. As part of an effort to enforce religious observance and church attendance, the laws frequently carried penalties for failure to observe them, and there are many documented cases of people arrested for playing cards, undertaking "unnecessary" work, and even mending machinery. There is no evidence to support the assertion that blue laws were originally printed on blue paper; rather, it is thought that the term is a derogatory reference to rigid moral codes and those who originally observed them—"bluenoses."

industrial heartland of the Northeast and Midwest. The census data in Table 1.1 shows population numbers and percentages in the decades between 1900 and 1920.

Because of increasing fragmentation, the U.S. Census Bureau in 1910 added its first metropolitan classification, the "Metropolitan District," an attempt to quantify the full extent of urban growth at a time that areas close to large cities were growing faster than urban centers. The majority of the population lived in urban locations by 1920, and although more than 50 percent of the population

The Preacher as Reformer

Although many Progressive era reformers emerged from a scientific, sociological, or academic and humanitarian background—and applied the doctrines and practices of those disciplines in their reform activities—there were others who came from a less formal environment. Even though an urban, educated middle class accepted the scientific, efficiency-based and technocratic reform agendas, many in the lower middle class and among the rural population were less sanguine about the changes. Flamboyant lay preacher and revivalist Billy Sunday was typical of those who appealed to this constituency. He used his revivalist platform to condemn Darwinism and supported Prohibition.

Sunday was immensely popular between 1905 and 1920, attracting massive crowds to his urban crusades. He utilized many elements of modern, professional public relations and developed an extensive team of "experts." Although he was a source of embarrassment to a more modern clergy and their better-educated parishioners who considered his theology and social theory reactionary and bigoted, he was highly conscious of the changing social climate. For Sunday, the most important social issue of the era was Prohibition, a reform that exercised church liberals and political progressives alike. While exploiting public concerns regarding political corruption, he contended that his revivals mobilized respectable people to ally themselves with reform movements, overthrow the bosses, and elect reform administrations. Many church leaders in the Midwest supported Sunday, believing that he would shortcut administrative procedures and assist in reforming their cities. A 1914 Pittsburgh newspaper headline—"What Years of Reform Work Could Not Do, He Has Wrought in a Few Short Weeks"—reinforced this view.

Nevertheless, Sunday was a controversial and ambiguous figure, seeing no reason why the church should encourage people to spend time on "social service." He argued that the efforts to mobilize Protestant ministers toward social action were wrong-headed, believing instead that the solution to poverty and crime was the conversion of people to the Protestant ethic. He was also an advocate for "100 percent Americanism" and was in favor of deporting "dangerous aliens" and restricting aliens. Despite being out of touch with the prevailing climate of social reform, his views did reflect and represent those of many Americans who went along with his concerns that the changes of the era would lead to a decline in America's standards, values, and institutions.

was resident in urban areas by then, the Northeast had crossed that barrier forty years earlier. By 1920, more than 75 percent of those in the Northeast lived in urban areas, whereas the Midwest and the West crossed the 50 percent threshold in 1920. The South lagged behind, however, with only 28.1 percent. The census shows that although the rural population increased in these decades, the *percentage* of rural dwellers actually fell, from 54.4 percent in 1910 to 48.8 percent in 1920. (Gardner in Goldfield, 2007, 592)

Table 1.1. Population in Urban and Rural Areas in the United States, 1900–1920

			Urban		Rural	
Census Year	US Total Population	Number of Urbanized Areas of 50,000 or more	Urbanized Area— Central City Population	Urbanized Area— Fringe Population	Non-Urbanized Area— Urban Population	Rural Population
1900	76,212,168	65	16,766,830	1,942,831	11,505,171	45,997,336
1910	92,228,496	90	23,932,711	3,260,551	14,870,739	50,164,495
1920	106,021,537	116	31,691,083	4,976,698	17,585,501	51,768,255

	Urban			Rural
	Urbanized Areas			
Census Year	Percentage in Urbanized Area— Central City	Percentage in Urbanized Area— Fringe	Non-Urbanized Area Urban Percentage	Rural Percentage
1900	22.0	2.5	15.1	60.4
1910	25.9	3.5	16.1	54.4
1920	29.9	4.7	16.6	48.8

Source: Adapted from Gardner, 2007, 593.

Progressive reform began in the large cities of the East and Midwest and the mainly agricultural states of the Midwest and parts of the South. As Wiebe shows, the urban faction led the rural "by priority, complexity, and sophistication." (Wiebe, 1967, 166) As Boyer (1978, ix) observes, although the reforms associated with morality like Prohibition and the antiprostitution crusades frequently emerged because of the concerns of those who were firmly established in the Protestant moral tradition, they often worked outside the framework of organized religion. Moved by what they perceived as the debilitating effects of the city, these men and women played a part in shaping the moral order of the cities. Their strategies were influenced in part by the heightened urban reform climate of the 1890s, but where the reformers of that decade focused on reforming individuals or families, Progressive era reformers insisted that urban moral destiny was to be most conclusively influenced by a broad program of governmental strength and targeted at an elemental reorganization of the urban environment.

Immorality: The Saloon and the Brothel

Among the many moral reforms of the Progressive era, two stand out. The first was the 1910 Mann Act, which made it a federal offense to transport a woman across a state line for "immoral purposes" and was intended to reduce or even eliminate the prevalence of prostitution, brothels, and the perceived "white slave traffic" of the pre–World War I period. The second was the constitutional amendment (the Eighteenth Amendment) that prohibited the manufacture, sale, or importation of alcohol across America. Although the amendment was ratified in 1919, as a sop to liquor interests, enforcement only began a year later.

Although the origins of both these measures against the twin "evils" of liquor and prostitution lie in the 19th century, they were central to the Progressive era reform agenda of the 1910s because there seemed little hope of achieving the moral and decontaminated city without them. Before the successful enactment of the measures, both had been the subject of reformist activities; the Women's Christian Temperance Union had campaigned during the 1870s, whereas there were strenuous efforts to raise the legal age of consent in the 1890s. Initiatives included national temperance conventions and "purity" congresses, and the Anti-Saloon League (ASL) and the American Purity Alliance were both established. Despite reformers' efforts, saloons and brothels in the cities' red light districts continued to proliferate in the early years of the 20th century, and per capita consumption of alcohol rose.

For many reformers, the twin evils embodied the seductive and ultimately degenerative attraction of the city. Concentrating their efforts into highly targeted aims and diligently worked-out strategies, and supported by many small contributors as well as such eminent ones as John D. Rockefeller, Jr., the ASL was instrumental in organizing the campaign. Believing that piecemeal measures would be ineffective, the League focused their efforts on legal prohibition and targeted the cities, beginning in counties and smaller towns before subsequently moving on to the states. There, the League lobbied legislatures and mobilized public opinion, and, because cities were underrepresented in state legislatures, urban America was gradually isolated. Toward the end of the campaign, thousands of ASL speakers promoted antiliquor legislation in Protestant churches, whereas masses of propaganda leaflets were printed by ASL presses and editorials appeared in the ASL journal, *American Issue.*

Both of these issues encapsulated deep fears among the public concerning the long-term implications of unchecked urban expansion. The social-control crusades can be seen as one aspect of a much wider Progressive reform initiative, and throughout the decade, the emphasis shifted from moral entreaties to the individual (which assumed that the reformer and the citizen had values and standards in common) to a belief that a lack of abstinence and a preference for sexual deviation were consequences of the urban environment, which could only be absolved through force of law. Although the campaigns clearly had their origins in the reforming climate of the 19th century and were formed by the prevailing mood of the Progressive era, they were also part of the same reforming zeal premised on extending the degree of social control already in place.

Ernst Roeber and his saloon. (Library of Congress)

As such, the ASL campaign focused on the saloon, rather than just alcohol itself. Time and again, readers of the ASL *Yearbook* were reminded of how "dry" the rural areas were and that more than half of America's saloons were located in the six largest cities. At the heart of "urban immorality and social disorder" (Boyer, 1978, 208) lay the saloon and the brothel. If they could be eradicated and prohibition enacted, reformers argued, most of the social, political, and moral ills identified with the city would at once be removed. As Boyer shows, ASL literature and vice commission reports demonstrated—with some justification because owners of smaller saloons, under increasing pressure from larger, franchise-operated saloons, tolerated, or even encouraged, the presence of prostitutes—an explicit connection between saloons and illicit sex, with one being a front for the other, so that prohibition thus would eradicate prostitution.

Reformers grew increasingly strident in their demands and claims throughout the decade, moving from the moderate position of earlier urban social-control advocates—whose views were tempered by a degree of reality in the form of real life urban dwellers—to a position where the saloon and the brothel were mere ciphers for a much more profound malaise: urban social change. Campaigners' invective grew increasingly truculent, so "anything less than an all-out war on vice, declared the Minneapolis Vice Commission in 1911, was foreign to the sentiment and feeling of the American people, and repugnant to their high moral sense." (Boyer, 1978, 211) Theodore Roosevelt advocated the public whipping of those who recruited women into prostitution. In Seattle, a Presbyterian minister described the saloon as "the most fiendish, corrupt, and hell-soaked institution that ever crawled out of the slime of the eternal pit." (Ibid.)

Support for the reforms in some areas ranged from lukewarm to outright opposition. Even though businessmen paid lip service to a more moral urban climate in some cases, not all were inclined to a coercive approach. Some were uncomfortable with the rhetorical and propagandistic extravagances, whereas others had significant real estate and financial interests in red light districts and brewing concerns. Others still were reluctant to combine their efforts with evangelical proselytizers for reform. Those who did allow that coercive measures were not always appropriate solutions occasionally adopted positive environmental tactics and argued that, instead of coercion, reformers should investigate the social needs provided by saloons and create alternatives that avoided the more debilitating consequences. Raymond Calkins's "temperance saloons," which provided nonalcoholic drinks and camaraderie as a substitute for liquor, were among those alternatives.

Even during this decade, some Progressive era reformers acknowledged that the reforms were "fundamentally misconceived" (Boyer, 1978, 218), and that once all available coercive strategies had been tried, they further allowed that legislative repression was not the solution. Efforts during the next decade to enforce the Eighteenth Amendment would demonstrate that quite clearly.

Values: Rural versus Urban

Urban America offered the prospect of wealth to the many masses who headed for the city in the early century, but it also provided autonomy, anonymity, and liberation from the stifling conformity of the countryside and the small town. They frequently brought rural attitudes with them, however, and it is evident from the debates and rhetoric of the period that urban and rural values differed widely during the Progressive era. Some, like Richard Hofstadter, argue that advocacy for Prohibition was greatest among "rural and small-town Americans, the more sophisticated urban Progressives" generally derided it. (Hofstadter, 1960, 288) Others believe that the crusades were effectively "an uprising of the hinterlands against the cities" (Boyer, 1978, 212), although H. L. Mencken, writing in 1913, directed his vitriol at both the "fanatical Puritanism" of rural America as well as at a state of mind that was equally evident in the city. Los Angeles political leaders, he believed, had carried to the city "a complete stock of rural beliefs, pieties, superstitions and habits" and thus administered the city "as they would a village." (Boyer, 1978, n. 348) The Eighteenth Amendment showed that "rural Protestant America" had "at last subdued the urban menace to its traditional morals and culture." (Hays, 1957, 115)

To succeed in these reforms, gaining rural support was to be a crucial weapon in the reformers' arsenal. Moralist propaganda frequently relied on a rather over-simplified rural–urban moral polarization to get the message across; George Kibbe Turner described the ASL as "a great semi-religious revival of rural feeling" (Boyer, 1978, 212) against the urban saloon. In 1915, the League itself argued that "the only way to save America was for the pure stream of country sentiment and township morals to flush out the cesspools of cities." (Ibid.) Anti-vice campaigners frequently urged rural parents to preserve their daughters' virtue by keeping them away from the city. In 1912, the historian Charles Beard (in ibid.) concluded that these efforts were most properly understood as attempts by rural communities to compel unwilling cities to accept rural moral standards.

Despite this, there was much urban support for prohibition and antiprostitution legislation; and such vice initiatives as the Committee of Fifteen and the American Social Hygiene Association were urban rather than rural phenomena. Indeed, many cities went dry before the amendment, and the ASL recorded 52 cities in which the saloon had been abolished by 1911. Businessmen were often ambivalent in their support for social-control reforms, and the poorer immigrant districts were frequently vehemently against prohibition reform, so the ASL gathered much of its support from native-born middle- and lower-middle-class residents mobilized by evangelical churches.

A significant proportion of supporters—largely Protestant and typically from rural and small town areas—wholeheartedly advocated coercive moral reforms. In marked contrast to the intellectual and economic elite, which was rather more sanguine in its reasoning, and the masses of urban poor that opposed the reforms, the classes that supplied the ASL with the bulk of its support—rural or urban—appreciated the reduction of a complex social world to simplistic dogma.

The Battle of the Church: Immigrant versus Native

The massive influx of immigrants brought cultural and religious orders into America that, as Seager observes, "were distinct from, if not alien to, the established pattern of American civilization." (1986, 107) Cultural and religious values long established in the countries of origin were thus transplanted, amended, and, to varying extents, transformed into the American way of life.

The relationship between the Protestant churches, "the dominant religious influence shaping the ideals of American culture" (Seager, 1986, 108), appeared to be a conflict between the interests of specific religious customs and an extremely generalized theology associated with the American nation, which also characterizes the relationship between immigration and the church. Along with the problem of how immigrant communities would adjust to America while simultaneously preserving their group identity was how they would also maintain their religious identity. As immigrants encountered American values, the dominant power lay with a template of cultural organization, beliefs, and ideals given an unequivocally religious value by native Protestantism. Many immigrants, however, were either Catholic or Jewish—or some other denomination—so the church was presented with a serious problem.

The importance and influence of a second area of authority (the religious traditions of immigrants themselves), however, meant that the two authorities were in almost constant conflict throughout the era. Whereas the religions of the immigrants had the authority of custom, the Protestant American tradition was the determining factor in deciding the rules whereby immigrants would be successfully assimilated into the American way of life.

Some Protestant voluntary organizations were transformed into agencies of the nascent welfare state, and there were many religiously inspired attempts at social reform. Although it is true that after 1876, when Protestantism was resolute in its defense of the religious and social status quo, there had been an ideological shift that by 1910 allowed for social criticism and a more liberal philosophy. Toward the end of the decade, however, liberal religion became more complacent and, to a certain extent, illiberal, in line with a more widespread illiberal climate characterized by immigration restrictions, 100 percent Americanism, and the Red Scare. There were some who were disappointed that "in the heat of the struggle the judgment of many a minister did not rise above that of the average citizen." (Beumler, 1986 146)

SETTLEMENTS

Settlements versus Charity

Settlement houses and the reforms they brought in their wake were central to the Progressive era. Although settlements predated the 1910s, and certainly outlasted the decade, the period 1910 to 1919 is, perhaps, the summit of the settlement movement. Settlement workers were active locally in the 1890s, and even though their work continued during the 1920s, World War I marked the end of an era.

Poverty among immigrants was at the root of the movement's foundation, and although there were charitable impulses behind settlement houses, there are important differences in approach between charitable organizations and the settlement movement. Charitable workers tended to highlight the individual grounds for poverty, whereas settlement workers believed that social and economic conditions were of greater relevance. Charity workers also attempted to aid the poor, whereas settlement workers were more concerned with those above the poverty line (the working class). Settlements were less concerned with "the poverty of clothes as with the poverty of opportunity." (Davis, 1967, 18)

Immigrant mothers and babies at University Settlement in New York, 1913. (Library of Congress)

After the depression of 1893 into the 1910s, America experienced significant divisions separating rich and poor. These chasms were so socially distancing that the nation at times seemed to have become a plutocracy on top of a sea of laborers; reconciling democratic impulses with industrial capitalism was an enduring problem throughout the era. The underlying social and economic conditions resulted, in part, from the economic depression of 1893, which was a depression so profound that critics attribute a rethinking of the causes of poverty to it. Settlements were part of a wider reform impulse that permeated the Progressive era. At their best, they were places where the urban poor could get genuine help, without the religious overtones that frequently accompanied charitable aid. At their worst, they were moralistic, social-control institutions; however, most fell somewhere in the middle, providing important services to deal with problems in education, public health, medical care, and what would now be called social services. Immigrants used the settlements to learn English, find employment, and gain protection from abusive systems, whereas settlements used immigrants to establish a foothold in the emerging welfare state.

Settlement workers themselves played an important part in publicizing the pressing need for reform, but they were also instrumental in getting the actual bills passed that would lead to reform. Davis describes the workers as "practical idealists" (1967, xiii) who nevertheless believed that if they collected enough material on the social ills, then reform would automatically follow. Despite this tendency, many workers became adept both at gathering statistics as well as at employing them to prevail upon both public and official opinion. Unlike those

Jane Addams and Hull House

In some ways, the name of Jane Addams is inseparable from Hull House, the most famous of all the settlement houses. Her visit to Toynbee Hall, a settlement house in the East End of London, was an early inspiration. Along with Ellen Gates Starr, Addams founded Hull House in 1889 in a former mansion in what had been a fashionable Chicago area. Like other college-educated women whose options were mainly limited to marriage and motherhood, Addams found a socially acceptable outlet for her experience and education in "good works." Hull House itself had been granted to real-estate developer and philanthropist Helen Culver, who subsequently granted it to Addams on a rent-free, twenty-five-year lease.

The mission of Hull House was to provide social and educational opportunities for the working class, many of whom were recent immigrants, at a time of massive social and industrial change and when immigration was at an unprecedented level. Hull House grew rapidly, and there were 13 buildings providing vocational and liberal arts classes by the early 20th century, as well as a kindergarten and a wide variety of supportive facilities for those it assisted. Its role, however, transcended the merely practical, and the settlement branched out into advocacy for reform at municipal, state, and federal levels. It also functioned as a women's sociological institution and was associated with the Chicago School of Sociology.

Although contemporary sociologists defined her activities as social work, Addams did not consider herself a social worker. Although she clearly adopted a hands-on approach to the settlement movement, to the extent of becoming personally involved in neighborhood garbage collection, she was an eminent and influential social reformer, influencing the ideologies of the Chicago School of Sociology and advocating for legislative reform on such issues as immigration, child labor, and women's rights.

whose commitment was tenuous at best, many settlement workers went as far as living in the slums. Many understood the workings of government and, whereas most were politically aware and a few joined the Socialist Party, most believed in the American structure of government while still working to improve it. Workers also embraced ideological and practical commitment to organized labor and genuine empathy with immigrants and African Americans.

Settlements also satisfied a personal need for those who created and worked in them. The settlements were dominated by women and provided an outlet for those who were denied rewarding and fulfilling employment and had few opportunities outside of marriage and motherhood. This was especially true of college-educated women who, liberated by their experience there, found an acceptable and meaningful vocation in the settlements. Many women therefore gravitated toward this field, precisely because it was one of only a limited number of professions available.

Although the beliefs that underpinned the movement were frequently highly contradictory and ambiguous, the movement became a paradigm for Progressive era reform, poised as it was between rich and poor, immigrant and native-born, and male and female worlds. The settlements transcended social space, fostering a wide diversity of social and economic reforms.

Origins of Settlement Houses

Three ideologies characterize the Progressive era: an effort to make urban life fairer and more moral; efforts by professions to employ their training and apply their knowledge to social problems; and the desire by native-born Americans to Americanize what they perceived as disorderly immigrants and other urban newcomers. These efforts were combined in urban settlement houses.

Inspired by Reverend Samuel Barnett's Toynbee Hall, the English settlement founded in 1884 to span the chasm industrialization had created between rich and poor and to provide something more than charity for the urban disadvantaged, and Walter Besant's People's Palace, the settlement idea found many advocates among Americans, among them Stanton Coit. With a collection of ministers, reformers, and labor leaders, Coit established the Neighborhood Guild on New York's Lower East Side—the most densely populated neighborhood in the country—in 1887. Although the settlement collapsed that same year, it was instrumental in establishing a belief that practical assistance and reform were achievable.

The initiative was followed by that of a group of recent women's college graduates who founded the College Settlement in 1889, again in New York. Others joined them, including Lillian Wald, who would later go on to the Henry Street Settlement. Other initiatives quickly sprang up in other urban areas of the country. The two women most closely associated with settlements, Jane Addams and Ellen Gates Starr, were similarly inspired by Toynbee Hall and began Hull House on South Holstead Street in Chicago.

Although Addams and Starr were resolute in their desire to provide an institution in Hull House that would be an agent for "social, educational, humanitarian, and civic reform" (Davis, 1967, 12), they were unsure how to achieve their aims. In this respect, they were little different from other settlement pioneers, but settlements grew from six in 1891 to around 400 by 1910. Central to the movement were efforts to remake America, improve working conditions, and Americanize immigrants. Whatever their origins, the majority were located in large urban areas, largely in the great cities of the Northeast and Midwest. Those in that area, particularly in New York, Chicago, and Boston, developed most rapidly, perhaps because they were close together and could cooperate in reform initiatives.

Attempting to combine a celebration of ethnic heritage and American values, workers provided urban slum dwellers with social and educational activities (e.g., classes in home economics such as sewing, cooking, and homemaking) while establishing nurseries and early kindergartens, employment agencies, playgrounds, and clubs and social events for every ethnicity. Living and working in the slums, workers began concerted efforts to lobby municipal officials for such services as garbage collection, clean water, increases in educational budgets, and healthcare. Acting as emissaries between immigrants and officials, settlement house workers slowly usurped the authority of urban political machines. Whether consciously or not, settlement houses helped to usher in a whole range of social welfare policies that eventually formed part of what became the American welfare state.

Reform workers were frequently those who attempted in their brief stays both to improve themselves and the world of the urban slums. Some had postponed careers, whereas others were gathering material for their writing or journalism. Although most workers' involvement in the settlements was relatively brief, some made a career in the movement (e.g., Jane Addams and Lillian Wald stayed their entire lives). In their early years, settlements had relatively little influence in their neighborhoods and cities, whereas those that were successful frequently had a dynamic head resident and a large group of male residents.

The majority of workers were women, attracted to the wider reform movement (e.g., abolitionism and temperance), partly because it provided them with a socially acceptable alternative to the conventional path to marriage and motherhood and also because reform of one kind or another appeared to protect the home from external immorality. Liberated by women's colleges, settlement work allowed middle-class, college-educated women to apply their educational experience to the real world. In a male-dominated environment where most professions were closed to women, settlement houses were one of the few opportunities available to educated, professionally trained women who could work there without the constraints placed on them by family and society. Effective as they were, even the founders of Hull House were often dependent on male residents to undertake the practical tasks associated with reform.

College-educated settlement workers appeared to have an almost obsessive interest in gathering facts, and even though some might have ingenuously believed that facts and statistics alone could bring about reform, it is evident that this material did shed some light on America's dark places. Hull House residents had earlier collected material on the ethnic origins of the South Side of Chicago, published in 1895 as *Hull House Maps and Papers,* and many workers "graduating" from the settlements and moving on to other organizations took this interest and knowledge with them. Perhaps the most ambitious effort to gather data on urban conditions was the Pittsburgh Survey, funded by the Russell Sage Foundation and undertaken by the Charity Organization Society. Published in multiple volumes between 1909 and 1914, the survey depicted the appalling conditions in the factories, shops, and tenements of Pittsburgh. The impetus behind the settlement house workers' fact collection was the conviction that poverty was caused by social and environmental conditions and provided evidence for demands to reform state and national legislation in labor, industry, public health, housing, education, child welfare, and immigration.

As the numbers of settlements began to increase and the movement developed, workers began to realize they were part of a wider reform movement. The movement began to hold conferences, publish reports and journals, and organize federations, including the National Federation of Settlements in 1911. Settlements were by no means alone in their social reform efforts in the Progressive era, and other organizations frequently called on settlement workers' experience. Because of their involvement in working class neighborhoods and their practical experience in the slums, settlement workers often gained a fresh perspective on the conditions there and frequently became instigators and organizers of reform. Although not all important social reforms sprang from the settlements, the movement was instrumental in initiating lasting reform, and although many settlements continued as adapted missions or more extensive boys' clubs, others like Hull House, South End House, and University Settlement became what Davis calls "spearheads for reform" in the Progressive era. (1967, 25)

Helping the Immigrants: Settlement House Programs

Although settlement houses were clearly concerned with immigrants, their main focus was on Americanization. Lissak observes that Hull House, for example, "was not an immigrant institution in the sense that it represented a pluralist cultural view of society. It was rather, an American institute that sought to integrate individual newcomers of different backgrounds into a cosmopolitan, American-oriented society by breaking down barriers and ending segregation." (1989, 47) Workers living in settlements and committed to creating or restoring the neighborhood soon found that many of the houses were surrounded by immigrants living in established communities and were themselves isolated from the rest of American society.

As one of the few groups to have close daily contact with immigrants, workers developed some considerable empathy with and understanding of the needs of immigrants, but not all were exempt from the widespread racism and bigotry that so characterized the Progressive era. Nevertheless, most initially attempted to understand immigrants' customs and ethnic traits and then sought to identify as much social and economic opportunity for them as possible. A number of important studies of immigration and immigrant communities came out of this period, among them Grace Abbott's 1917 publication, *The Immigrant and the Community*. It was also common for many workers either to write articles on

Immigrant girls learn to knit at the Henry Street Settlement in New York, 1910. Photo attributed to Lewis Hine. (Library of Congress)

immigrants or to give talks in local clubs or churches. It is evident now that more than a few combined compassion with an overly sentimental approach, whereas some combined both pity and contempt for the immigrants' plight in their racially stereotyped accounts.

Despite most workers' obvious sympathy and their efforts to improve immigrants' lives, they were regarded with suspicion by many newcomers and often remained outsiders in the ethnic communities. Most workers—who were largely unmarried—had their own lives and their own friends in the settlements; therefore, they had little in common with immigrant families. Moreover, few workers spoke anything but English, which isolated them still further from the immigrant community. Many immigrants were at a loss to understand the workers' concerns for reform, preferring instead to place their trust in political bosses, figures considered corrupt by settlement workers. More serious still was the apparent inability of settlements to interest neighborhood men, and because families were organized on a rigidly patriarchal basis, attracting women and children was only partially successful in establishing relationships with immigrant communities. Nevertheless, many settlements did become important agents in helping immigrants to understand America and also in helping America to understand immigrants.

Workers had more success with younger, more ambitious immigrants who had intellectual interests than they did with the majority, who sometimes appeared willing to endure rather than to make the most of the new environment. They organized clubs and classes to teach English and American history, but more importantly, perhaps, they encouraged immigrants to protect the practices and heritage of their countries of origin, instilling the belief that becoming American did not necessarily mean abandoning their heritage. In some ways, the initiatives at Hull House typified educational programs in many settlement houses, but the reading classes and art appreciation sessions were also part of Addams's and other workers' belief that immigrants would be improved by a diet of beauty and art, and they encouraged slum dwellers to borrow well-known prints from their lending libraries to hang in their tenement homes. Many of the programs, which were centered on lectures, exhibitions, and workshops, had a decidedly collegiate atmosphere. Nearby college professors and the clergy were regular speakers at Hull House's public events, all part of the settlements' efforts at cultural enrichment that were designed both to expose immigrants to Western culture and as part of a broader Americanization initiative.

Settlements and Immigration Restrictions

Encouraging immigrants to preserve their heritage both helped newcomers to overcome the huge psychological and physical barriers involved in uprooting to a new land, and was also a way of showing Americans what ethnic groups could contribute to American culture. In the often hysterical climate of calls for restrictions on immigration, this emphasis was a bulwark against the nativists' arguments. There was little consensus among settlement workers, however, regarding immigration policy. Walter Weyl, a resident of University Settlement in New York, summarized the ambiguity implicit in the views of one group who advocated restrictions when he wrote in 1912 that "many of the people who are opposed to a practically unregulated immigration are the very ones who are seeking to promote the welfare of those immigrants who are already in." (Davis, 1967, 90) When identifying the workers' dilemma, though, Lillian Wald argued in 1915 that "few, if any, of the men and women who have had extended opportunity for social contact with the foreigner favor a further restriction on immigration." (Ibid.)

Because settlement workers understood that immigration was part of a wider debate on industry and organized labor and that unlimited immigration would provide employers with a justification for holding down wages and maintaining an unorganized labor force, most favored some sort of regulation. There were others, however, like Robert A. Woods, who, writing in *American in Process* in 1917, came closer to the extremist views of nativists when he advocated isolating the "unfit" so that reformers could concentrate on those more befitting workers' efforts. (Ibid.) The more enlightened, such as Jane Addams, recognized that until underlying industrial conditions improved, critics would continue to blame immigrants for problems that should be addressed by the community.

Most workers steered well clear of nativists, who believed that immigrants would bring about the degeneration of the Anglo-Saxon race, and because settlements were committed to a policy of teaching reading and writing skills, most were also opposed to literacy tests and restrictions. In fact, Grace Abbott was instrumental in persuading President Taft to veto the literacy bill in 1912. Nevertheless, even before the situation at the outbreak of World War I made policy makers reconsider immigrants' place in American society, Woods and others had allied themselves with racial purists and had begun to establish immigration restriction leagues.

More often, though, workers attempted to make immigrants' transition into America less fraught. Chicago's Immigrant Protective League, established by Hull House residents, organized waiting rooms at railroad stations where multilingual workers could meet recently arrived immigrants and help them to deal with landlords, banks, and employment agencies, as well as to find relatives. Both Abbott and Wald worked to ensure that local and national governments would assume such responsibilities, and even though the New York Commission on Immigration was established within a few months and a permanent state Bureau of Industries and Immigrants was also created, it was apparent to most settlement workers by 1912 that action at the state level was not enough. When the Progressive Party pressed the federal government to advocate for the assimilation, education, and advancement of immigrants, it was largely the result of efforts by settlement workers.

Creating Professions

During the Progressive era, a new generation of largely middle-class callings (engineers, lawyers, doctors, teachers, college professors, and social workers) began to press for professionalization. Their demands were focused on the notion that expertise and systematic training should bring with it autonomy, social status, and economic stability, and that their professions should be self-regulatory. Industrial growth and technological change had proved advantageous to some workers and equally detrimental to others. Ironworkers, weavers, and skilled workers generally saw their jobs eroded and their futures diminished, but social workers and teachers, for example, viewed technological advances as an important rationale for improving their status.

In many ways, the gradual professionalization of social work is emblematic of similar initiatives that occurred in other professions, as well as of the modern professional in the Progressive era. Before then, social work as a profession did not exist and religion dealt with such matters as poverty and personal need. The poor were classified as either deserving or undeserving, and their failures were moral in nature and the solution was religious (i.e., a recommitment of faith). Social workers based their professional status on scientific authority and education, not on moral authority. The roots of social work lie in the earlier charity organizations of the late nineteenth century. Here, friendly visitors—usually upper- or middle-class women—visited the needy to determine whether they were genuinely poor and if charity would help or harm their situation. At the time, it was firmly believed that giving charity to the undeserving would destroy their work ethic, so reformers made recommendations to centralized organizations that distributed aid to the needy.

Salaried caseworkers soon replaced the visitors and casework itself was borne out of the settlement movement. Even though charity workers derided caseworkers, caseworkers believed that charities failed to recognize that social conditions rather than moral failure were the true cause of poverty. In 1917, following many years of conflict, the two groups merged into the National Conference of Social Work. In 1910, women made up more than 50 percent of all social workers, a figure that had increased to 62 percent by 1920. Settlement houses like Henry Street Settlement in New York and Hull House in Chicago, which were controlled and led by women, were instrumental in training generations of social workers. Differences and divisions were evident within social work. Some workers believed that social workers' role was to deliver services to clients, whereas others believed that their role was as political advocates for the poor and the development of social welfare policies.

Political differences also affected the training of social workers. Hull House residents Julia Lathrop, Sophonisba Breckinridge, and Edith Abbott gained control of the Chicago Social Work School and in 1920 moved it to the University of Chicago, turning it from a vocational institute into a graduate-level program that focused on social policy and administration. Social workers distinguished themselves from friendly visitors through their application of scientific methodology to casework. With an understanding of the environmental, rather than the moral nature of social problems, caseworkers collected and classified data on individual clients. Advanced training was required because the technique required an understanding of sociology, medicine, public health, and psychology. It is clear, then, that the advancement and perfection of the casework method conformed to one of the most significant social needs acknowledged by progressives, while simultaneously legitimizing the social workers' status as professionals.

Immigrant Assimilation and Language Classes

A major concern for reformers was that the millions of newly arrived immigrants were so different from native-born Americans that they might never fully assimilate. It only served to exaggerate reformers' fears that most lived in ethnic enclaves and tended to be clannish. Because assimilation was the cornerstone for their concepts of social and political democracy, settlement workers, particularly those at Hull House, attempted to find ways to loosen ethnic bonds and to assimilate immigrants into American culture. Jane Addams believed that democracy depended on the elimination of barriers between people. Her injunction included ethnic barriers, even those created as a defense mechanism to preserve ethnic identities in a new and sometimes hostile land. This would benefit immigrants and the nation, and, Addams believed, it was additionally what immigrants themselves most wanted.

Even though Addams contended that the decision to uproot and come to America reflected a conscious rejection of the old world, many immigrants held on to old customs and traditions. Settlement house workers like Breckenridge argued that ethnicity, language, and culture should be preserved in the privacy of immigrants' own homes and that immigrants needed to engage fully with American culture in the public realm. They therefore thought of ethnic solidarity as temporary, a product of the traumatic migration process. For these reformers, assimilation was a gradual process that could take more than a generation. What effectively distinguished settlement workers from others was their understanding and appreciation of immigrant culture. Although they might have believed American culture to be superior, they nevertheless realized they could not simply force America onto immigrants. Instead, they had to discover ways of bringing immigrants into America. This they did by emphasizing America's universalism: democracy, liberty, and equality.

It quickly became clear to settlement workers that the multiplicity of languages spoken by immigrants would prove a major barrier in their attempts at assimilation, and whereas the settlement houses provided interpreters at railroad stations under the Immigrant Protective League scheme, this was at best only a temporary solution. Public schools were of little help in teaching English, and even though a few undertook evening classes, immigrant adults were frequently dealt with by regarding them as American child learners. Progressive reformers felt that English primers aimed at immigrants should focus on words that would be useful and meaningful to newcomers, rather than those such as *rat* or *mat* that were conventionally found in reading primers. The settlements often attempted to combine citizenship studies with English, and because they understood at least some of the immigrants' needs, they attempted to ensure that teaching English had some connection with immigrants' actual day-to-day experiences and, moreover, treated them as adults. Table 1.2 illustrates the mother tongue of the foreign-born population in the decade.

Table 1.2. Mother Tongue of the Foreign-Born Population [1]

Language	1920	1910
Total	13,712,754	13,345,545
Mother tongue data available	13,705,588	13,229,272
Indo-European languages	13,216,190	12,841,870
English and Celtic	3,007,932	3,363,792
Germanic languages	3,541, 184	3,962,624
German	2,267, 128	2,759,032
Yiddish [2]	1,091,820	1,051,767
Dutch	136,540	126,045
Flemish	45,696	25,780
Scandinavian languages	1,194,933	1,272,150
Swedish	643,203	683,218
Danish	187,162	183,844
Norwegian	362,199	402,587
Romance languages	2,816,296	2,267,009
Italian	1,624,998	1,365,110
French	466,956	528,842
Spanish	556,111	258,131
Portuguese	105,895	72,649
Romanian	62,336	42,277
Greek	174,658	118,379
Albanian	5,515	2,312
Slavic languages	2,255,798	1,690,703
Russian [3]	392,049	57,926
Ukrainian	55,672	25,131
Czech	234,564	228,738
Polish	1,077,392	943,781
Slovak	274,948	166,474
Bulgarian	12,853	18,341
Serbo-Croatian	125,844	105,669
Slovene	80,437	123,631
Baltic languages	182,227	140,953
Lithuanian [4]	N/A	N/A
Lettish [4]	N/A	N/A
Armenian	37,647	23,938
Asian and Pacific island languages [5]	6,627	4,709
Turkish	6,627	4,709
Other languages	481,543	382,048
Uralic languages	423,986	349,180
Finnish	132,543	119,948
Hungarian	290,419	229,094
Semitic languages [6]	57,557	32,868
Arabic	57,557	32,868
Mother tongue, n.e.c.	1,228	646
Mother tongue data not available	7,166	116,272

[1] All races were not included in census data until 1960; languages omitted include Lithuanian; Lettish; Iranian, including Persian; Hindi; Chinese; Thai; Japanese; Korean; Indonesian; Philippine and Tagalog languages; Polynesian; Basque; Hebrew; African; and Native American. [2] For 1910–1940, Hebrew included with Yiddish. [3] For 1920, probably includes a "considerable proportion" of individuals with Yiddish tongue erroneously reported as of Russian mother tongue. [4] Lithuanian and Lettish were not included until 1930. [5] The majority of Asian and Pacific island languages were not included until 1960 [6] See [2]

Source: Adapted from U.S. Bureau of the Census, Population Division, www.census.gov/population/www/documentation/twps0029/tab06.html

HOUSING REFORM

Improving Living Conditions

Urban life at the beginning of the century was dark, cramped, and unhealthy, at least for the poorest city dwellers. Years of inward urban migration from both native-born Americans and immigrants meant that conditions in the poorest areas of America's cities were appalling by the second decade. Influenced by Darwinian thinking, urban reformers believed that the environment shaped behavior; poor conditions fostered poor character and poor character resulted in a socially destructive society. It was essential that the urban environment be improved to ensure both moral and political order. Although earlier generations had believed that poverty and slum conditions affected only the slum dwellers, during the Progressive era, reformers realized that urban poverty had more widespread consequences. This was most apparent in the efforts to improve housing.

Because there was little planning, urban housing was chaotic and haphazard. Already crowded, existing buildings were subdivided to house still more people, and new buildings were hastily thrown up to house as many residents as cheaply as possible. There were thus whole sections of cities where poverty, dirt, disease, and crowds were the norm. More than unpleasant, urban slums were unsafe, and personal injuries and disease were common. Crowded conditions encouraged the spread of major diseases, and life expectancy for slum dwellers was well below the national average. Reformers' belief that improvements in housing would lead to improvements in society inspired many to investigate the slums. Their priority was to expose the real conditions, and the resulting outcry and demands for reform would be so great that conditions would improve.

The scores of reformers who went into the slums wrote reports, held public hearings, and published articles in journals, magazines, and newspapers. As the public became aware of the conditions, demands for legislation grew, but reformers quickly realized that landlords were unlikely to change their practices without such legislation, so they looked to the state for assistance. Beginning at the municipal level, reformers demanded that city councils and mayors instigate reform, create inspection systems, and hold wrongdoers to account. Corruption and inefficiencies apparent in local politics forced reformers to look to the state capitol. As a result, a number of states enacted zoning laws that regulated land use, air space, occupancy, and the structural integrity of housing.

Reformers also discovered a disturbing mix of manufacturing and housing, so efforts to differentiate housing from commercial property became central to reforms. The greatest concern for the reformers was the sweatshop, thousands of which existed side by side with residential accommodations in the slums, thus compounding economic and physical problems in the neighborhood. Overall, reformers believed that by improving living conditions for the masses by providing sunlight, clean(er) air and water, indoor plumbing, and by decreasing density, improvements to the masses themselves and to the nation would in-evitably follow.

Housing Reform: Planning

The conviction gradually grew that a close connection existed between a city's physical and moral character and that, moreover, America's cities were regret-tably lacking in this respect. This belief was central to the "city beautiful" move-ment, an umbrella term for the burgeoning interest in civic improvement and beautification that reached its peak in the early 1900s. The thousands of "im-provement societies" that sprang up during this period were clearly concerned with providing cities with fountains, flowerbeds, statuary, and the elimination of the more unsightly aspects of America's cities. As the movement's agenda shifted towards more ambitious schemes and an all-embracing planning program, some organizations began to advocate for larger buildings (e.g., civic centers). Over-all, the ultimate aim of the advocates was the complete physical transfiguration of the city to reverse the decline of social and moral unity that seemed to be an inevitable consequence of the growth of cities.

It was evident to some, however, that the "sticking plaster" solutions of the city beautiful movement would not heal the serious environmental shortcomings of cities. A speaker at the 1912 convention of the American Civic Association castigated the city beautifiers for their emphasis on "frills and furbelows while the hideous slum, reeking with filth and disease, rotten with crime, is sapping the very life-blood of the city." (Boyer, 1978, 266) Partial and largely superficial solutions began to give way to a more all-embracing, unified approach focused on city planning, which, like the city beautiful movement, was premised on the belief that moral and social transformation would only be achieved by environ-mental initiatives. Throughout the Progressive era—and before, too—reformers had believed that they were the pivotal agents in the control and moral and so-cial advancement of the urban masses. By the early 20th century, as cities swelled with immigrants and living conditions were still little better than they were 50 years earlier, city planners translated conventional social-control ambi-tions into the language of environmental improvement.

Tenements: How the Other Half Really Lived on New York's Lower East Side

Ethnic Composition

By 1910, the Lower East Side of New York had become a cosmopolitan and highly congested immigrant Jewish district. That was also the year that the Lower East Side achieved its highest population density. Where it had once been the primary area of Jewish settlement—75 percent in 1892 and 50 percent in 1903—only 23 percent of the city's Jews lived there by 1916. There were relatively few Jews in New York before 1880. Estimates in 1870 put the percentage at around 9 percent, or 80,000, of the city's total population. That figure had risen to 1.4 million by 1915, or nearly 28 percent, a figure greater than the city's total population in 1870. (Rischin in Callow, 1973, 336)

The mass of largely poverty-stricken Jewish immigrants arriving after 1870 made their way to the Lower East Side either because friends or relatives had already settled there, or because they were directed there by the representatives of immigrant aid societies. By the second decade, the area from the Bow-

"How the other half lives" in a crowded eastern European Jewish district, Lower East Side, New York City. (Library of Congress)

ery to close by the East River and from Market Street to 14th Street had become the most densely populated quarter of the city. By 1914, therefore, close to 17 percent of the city's population lived below 14th Street on just more than 1 percent of the city's land area. In addition, the majority of the city's office buildings and factories—where more than 50 percent of New York's industrial workers were employed—were located in this district.

Few of these immigrants spoke English, and with limited resources, they were dependent on the long hours, meager wages, and seasonal employment in the factories and sweatshops of the district. Jewish immigrants were also tied to the Lower East Side by their religious and social requirements. Immigrants also endured the hardships and living conditions because even with the low wages that the majority earned, they were able to put a little aside to purchase the passage for relatives still in Europe or to support dependents back home.

Physical Composition

Restrictions imposed on expansion in Manhattan by its geography meant that there had been serious housing problems in New York since the 1830s, so any refinements in the maximization of land use were the result of necessity, rather than concern for the residents who lived in the overcrowded districts. Given the division of city lots into 25 feet wide by 100 feet deep rectangles, a decent standard of living was impossible. Developers relied on the tenement block to maximize the limited space available. Front and rear tenements, followed by the dumbbell-style tenement that became the norm in the Lower East Side after 1879, supplemented early examples, which were usually the result of adapting existing private dwellings.

These new dumbbell (so-called because of their characteristic shape) tenements were typically of six to seven stories with four apartments per floor. Direct light and air only reached one room in each apartment, and the narrow hallways had a common water closet. Despite legislation, fire escapes were not always provided, and when they were, they were frequently used to store surplus furniture and boxes. The summer heat proved intolerable, especially for immigrants from more temperate areas of Europe, and conditions were worsened by heat from coal stoves and boilers. Given that few families could afford a three- or four-room apartment without the assistance of a lodger, and that they often had families of five or more children, overcrowding was inevitable in small tenements.

Although legislation prohibited the construction of dumbbell tenements after 1901 and provided for minimum standards in new buildings, many were still in evidence by the second decade. Despite such legislation as the Tenement House Law, which stipulated modern water closets to replace outside privies in existing buildings, legislation on this issue was never adequately enforced and landlords continued to exploit tenants with exorbitant rents and low upkeep.

Public Health and Public Housing

Outhouses and Indoor Plumbing

By the second decade, indoor plumbing could not be taken for granted in either rural or urban housing. Most city families made do with outhouses and water pumped from an outdoor source or, in rural areas, a well. The lack of adequate sanitation was more than an inconvenience; it was also a serious public health issue. A typical outhouse in a crowded tenement building in a major conurbation like Chicago or Boston could service in excess of 10 families. Once children were factored in, that figure could increase to 50. Some outhouses were connected to sewer systems, but many lacked this facility. The situation was made worse by the absence of public toilet facilities in crowded districts, and because waste was not always emptied frequently enough, contemporary accounts remark on the level of filth and stench. Few apartments had baths, and those that did were often without hot water. As a result, the Lower East Side had a great many privately owned bathhouses, attributable mainly to the Jewish tenement population.

Public Health

Although the Progressive era is remarkable for discoveries and developments—generally in medicine—the changes were felt more in the field of public health than anywhere else. The "White Plague," tuberculosis, killed thousands of Amer-

Piles of garbage on the street outside a market during a garbage collectors' strike in New York City, 1911. (Library of Congress)

icans in overcrowded slums and was so deadly that sufferers hid for fear of being socially ostracized. Because of their association with prostitution and the resulting stigma, many cases of sexually transmitted diseases (STDs) went undetected until treatment was too late. Infections were passed on to unsuspecting wives, who in turn infected unborn children. Although tuberculosis and a great many STDs were treatable, the public needed to be convinced that they should come forward for treatment and that they should encourage others to do likewise. In matters of sexual health, public health officials first had to break the public's silence. The resulting publicity campaigns—like much of public health—were part medical and part educational.

Sanitation

Crowding, shared facilities, a lack of general hygiene, and unsanitary conditions meant that all communicable diseases—especially typhus, tuberculosis, and cholera—were potentially contagious. Although reformers and public health officials were at the forefront of reform initiatives, the sanitary engineers who superseded health officers as the spearhead of waste reform were perhaps more important. Once professionals realized that improvements in environmental sanitation were more significant in eradicating the spread of disease than inoculation and immunization, engineers became answerable for sanitation problems.

By 1910, engineering had become the second-largest profession, behind only teaching. The growth in the numbers of engineers, and the diverse range of engineering occupations, can be partly attributed to the impact of technology. As cities expanded, engineers inevitably gravitated there and their training frequently made them the natural choice to address the problems that resulted from largely unchecked urban expansion. As Melosi observes, "the need for safe water supplies, adequate sewerage, well-ventilated housing, and efficient refuse collection and disposal required the engineer's technical expertise and the public health officer's knowledge of sanitation." (in Chudacoff, 1994, 242) In this way, a composite of the two—the sanitary engineer—emerged to respond to the environmental problems of providing sources of water and constructing sewers in the expanding cities.

Refuse Collection and Disposal

Because sanitary engineers had accomplished much in the fields of water supply and liquid waste disposal, municipal officials entrusted responsibility for refuse collection and disposal to them, too. Perhaps because refuse had always embodied serious health, as well as engineering, implications, however, advances proved far slower than those achieved in water supply and effluent disposal. Once sanitary engineers had collected data on the issues, they concluded that refuse collection should be under municipal control rather than the contract system more common in the mid- to late nineteenth century. Between the 1890s and the outbreak of World War I, there was a significant shift away from the contract system toward increased community responsibility for street cleaning and garbage collection and disposal. A 1914 survey of 150 cities showed that street cleaning was municipally controlled in around 90 percent of cities, whereas collection and disposal was municipally controlled in at least 50 percent of cities, against only 24 percent in 1880. (Melosi, 1994, 245)

As cities expanded and became less manageable, experts, professionals, and managers of all kinds became indispensable to prevent chaos from ensuing. Melosi believes that "the progressive era gave rise to an efficiency craze—a secular Great Awakening, an outpouring of ideas and emotions in which a gospel of efficiency was preached without embarrassment to businessmen, workers, doctors, housewives, and teachers." (in Chudakoff, 1994, 246)

Model Tenements and Tenant Activism

Model Tenements

Although the origins of model tenements lie in the 1870s, they were still in existence in the 1910s, and many outlasted the decade. Even before the Progressive era, reformers were acutely aware of the environmental problems in rapidly growing urban areas where substandard and overcrowded housing was already clearly evident. Private landlords and landowners had little incentive to improve existing housing or to build better-quality accommodations. Because persuading the government to act to improve conditions proved difficult, many reformers believed that a way of demonstrating to private developers that building decent yet profitable tenements should be found.

Inspired by experimental European examples, model tenements appeared as one solution that would provide working-class tenants with decent apartments that were light, had adequate air circulation and running water, and, moreover, would be profitable for landlords. An important difference between a typical speculative tenement and the model tenement was that in the latter, owners agreed to limit the return on their investment, usually to around 7 percent, against the 15 percent to 20 percent annual return common in speculative developments. Among the first examples are Home and Tower Buildings in Brooklyn. Built by Alfred Tredway White, a wealthy, philanthropic businessman and member of the Unitarian Church, they provided decent accommodation for the "deserving" poor. Tenancy was generally limited to two-parent families who were carefully screened to exclude the "undeserving" and the undesirable.

Apartments were small and great care was taken to ensure that the buildings were fireproof. Since entry was from a balcony, exit in the event of a fire was also by way of the balcony and thence down an open staircase, thus avoiding the problem of a smoke-filled, closed stairwell. Each apartment had running water and windows with either a street or a rear courtyard aspect. Each block was also provided with a bath in the basement, a dramatic improvement for tenants who usually had no access to bathing facilities. The large courtyards had a double function: they provided greatly improved light and air for the apartments, and at a time when reformers believed that playing in the streets would have an adverse influence, children could play there, watched over by their parents above. Later examples also had playgrounds.

Although relatively few were built, those that were proved to be popular with tenants and were economically viable alternatives that demonstrated that what is now called low-income housing and profitability were not necessarily mutually exclusive. White, who operated some himself until his death in 1921, published in 1912 the book that became a staple of the movement, *Sun-Lighted Tenements: Thirty-Five Years' Experience as an Owner*.

Tenant Activism

Despite reform initiatives designed to improve life in the tenements of the great cities, improvements were often slow to materialize, sometimes as a result of inertia on the part of landlords reluctant to renovate run-down buildings and to risk losing a lucrative income. Although most tenants had little choice other than to accept the overcrowding, high rents, and poor conditions, there were others who, encouraged by a shift toward a more democratic governance and awareness of citizens' rights, began to mobilize for better accommodation. Unlike earlier activists, their demands for lower rents and improved housing conditions were grounded in a new belief that the state should be the arbiter of tenants' rights and individual welfare. They were helped in their initiatives by a growing awareness that the authority of government officials depended on popular support. This new development was thus characterized by cooperation and negotiation between tenants, political groups, landlords, and the press. As Woods and Baer argue, "tenants organized and forced an unprecedented series of negotiations not just with property owners but also with key political elites who responded with a series of progressive social reforms." (2006, 865)

Following laws that prohibited dumbbell tenements and legislation stipulating improvements to existing tenements, conditions did improve; however, newer and renovated buildings attracted higher rents, which also rose as demand and speculation increased. Many of the city's poorer inhabitants were unable to afford the higher rents, and some turned to the tactics of labor organizations, organizing picketing, demonstrations, and rent boycotts. Tenement residents also exploited neighborhood support and community groups and established social networks. Because women were often the first to be affected by housing concerns, they were particularly active in demonstrations and marches. They also organized groups that would arrange temporary accommodation and obstructed evictions, sharing information through such community newspapers as the *Jewish Daily Forward*. Groups also solicited support from municipal officials, who often sympathized with tenants.

Although tenant activism was only marginally effective in lowering rents, it did result in certain advances that foreshadowed more explicit state intervention in later years. Toward the end of the war, however, the situation grew worse when demand for housing increased. In May 1918, tenants concerned about the deteriorating situation formed the Greater New York Tenants League (GNYTL). Demands by the League for limits on rent increases and greater legal protection were largely ignored, and in the rapidly escalating postwar hysteria, some claimed that tenements had been commandeered by "renter soviets" and the GNYTL began to lose much of its support. Nevertheless, tenant activism had demonstrated that protest in various forms could provide an alternative to the orthodoxy that only market forces could resolve housing problems and initiate reform.

Intellectual Life

American intellectuals underwent a social transformation during the decade. The spirit of reform of practical concerns and real life problems that infused the Progressive era occupied writers, artists, and academics, too. As writers attempted to wrestle with the complexities of industrial capitalism, mass society, technological change, and the life of the mind, literary realism became the dominant theme for the period. The writers of this school rejected the saccharine moralism of an older generation and instead documented the realities of a turbulent decade and a population at the mercy of forces largely outside their control.

Among others, Theodore Dreiser and Jack London represented the realist tendency in literature. Born in poverty, Dreiser was the 12th of 13 children, and his upbringing in Chicago gave him first-hand experience of the era's social inequalities that were to become a feature of his writing. By the 1910s, he had already published *Sister Carrie,* a novel recounting the decline into a life of sin of a woman who leaves the country for life in Chicago. During the 1910s, Dreiser published *Jennie Gerhardt* (1911) and the first two books of the Trilogy of Desire, *The Financier* (1912) and *The Titan* (1914), a fictionalized account of the railroad tycoon Charles Yerkes. A committed socialist, Dreiser became involved in several political campaigns against social injustice, including the lynching of the unionist Frank Little in 1917, the Sacco and Vanzetti case (1920), the deportation to Russia of Emma Goldman following the Palmer Raids in 1919, and the trial of Tom Goldman, convicted after the 1916 Preparedness Day bombing in San Francisco. Dreiser's view was that "all of us are more or less pawns. We're moved about like chess pieces

Best remembered for her tragic novel Ethan Frome *and for her lighter satires of life amid the American upper class, Edith Wharton probed the personal conflicts faced by individuals who understand the limitations of social and moral conventions. (National Archives)*

by circumstances over which we have no control" (Walcutt, 1940, 266). This encapsulates the flux and chaos of the period.

An active socialist who drew on his real world experiences, London's politics are evident throughout his writing, most notably in *The Iron Heel* and his essays, *The War of the Classes* and *Revolution, and Other Essays.* Like the Ashcan painters, realist novelists attempted to connect art with urban poverty, class politics, and the widening gulf between rich and poor. Ambrose Bierce's much-quoted and much-imitated *The Devil's Dictionary,* a satirical reimagining of the English language, was published in 1911, although its origins lie in Bierce's newspaper columns and in the 1906 work *The Cynic's Word Book.*

Although Edith Wharton lived in France after 1907, her novels of this decade and the 1920s, such as *Ethan Frome* (1912) and *The Age of Innocence* (1920), are incisive dissections of New York's upper class. *The Custom of the Country* (1913) focuses on another issue of great concern during the decade: corruption involving the financial activities of large industrial enterprises. The anthology *The Book of the Homeless,* which Wharton edited in 1916, brings together contributions from many leading writers, musicians, and artists of the time, including Henry James, W. B. Yeats, and Joseph Conrad. Revenue from this collection went toward the charities that Wharton established (The Children of Flanders Relief Committee and the American Hostels for Refugees). The author and immigration rights activist Mary Antin's autobiography, *The Promised Land,* records her assimilation as a Belarus Jewish immigrant into American life. She subsequently lectured to audiences on the experience and became an advocate for Theodore Roosevelt's Progressive Party.

Not every writer dealt with urban matters. Willa Cather's 1913 *O Pioneers!*—the first book of the Prairie Trilogy, which documents another concern of the decade—portrays an immigrant family struggling to make a living on a farm when many others were giving up.

Among the decade's paintings depicting the increasingly chaotic and crowded urban environment, John Sloan's *Six O'Clock, Winter* is typical of the genre. The painting shows one of New York's many elevated trains—or Els—that ran throughout Manhattan and whose development extended the city's boundaries and changed the way that people traveled to and from work. The 1912 painting portrays the dynamism of the city at dusk when crowds of commuters, their forms lit up by the electric lights on the train and those of the shops at ground level, are dwarfed by this manifestation of new technology. Among other works, Sloan's 1918 *Bleecker Street, Saturday Night* shows the small shops and sidewalk merchants and a building truncated by the new Seventh Avenue downtown. William Glackens's *29 Washington Square,* 1911–1912, shows children playing in the small park in front of the once-stately homes opposite the southside tenements now teeming with immigrants.

As a more realistic and pragmatic mood developed in America, artists of all kinds responded to the profound social, economic, and technological changes of the decade by producing work that reflected both the mood and their changed environment and circumstances.

FACTORY REFORM

Improving Working Conditions

In the early years of the century, America was transformed from a relatively minor industrial power to the leading industrial producer in the world. The development of the railroads and the growth of national markets, increasing exploitation of such natural resources as coal and iron, and the rapid growth of a largely unskilled labor force as immigration swelled the industrial northeast all contributed to a massive expansion of industrial capacity and to dramatic changes in working conditions; however, as industry expanded, working conditions deteriorated. As Rosner and Markowitz demonstrate, "speed-ups, monotonous tasks, and exposure to chemical toxins, metallic and organic dusts, and unprotected machinery made the American workplace the most dangerous in the world." (1987, xi)

Before 1900, workers were scarcely safeguarded by partial state and federal legislation centered around a number of quite distinct workplace conditions. During the Progressive era, however, there were calls for a more methodical, more unified approach. Thus, an all-embracing alliance of radicals, progressives, labor leaders, businessmen, and reformers emerged within a much wider social context—including reforms to workers' housing conditions, sanitation, and living conditions generally—to address occupational health and safety conditions. Union demands to improve workplace sanitary conditions were connected to other public health concerns—notably, the crusades against infectious disease—whereas improving workers' health and standards of workplace cleanliness were viewed as beneficial to both worker and public.

To some extent, middle-class consumer groups' concerns regarding contagious diseases reflected their anxieties that any potential contamination from goods (e.g., garments produced in tenement slums) touched by sick workers would not be passed on to the middle-class consumer. It was in part these concerns that inspired the National Consumers League to participate in tenement reform and antituberculosis crusades. The League's label, and those of the International Ladies' Garment Workers' Union, became the signifier that the garment had been made under hygienic conditions. During the era, the League became active in a diverse range of such labor-related concerns as fire regulations and safety, workers' compensation, and legislation on workplace diseases.

As occupational health and safety became part of a much broader reform movement, it reflected many of the apparently incongruous alliances between reformers from the larger reform constituency. Such radicals as Crystal Eastman represented one side of the political spectrum, whereas allegedly humanitarian business owners from International Harvester, for example, who conspired to divert the lobby toward voluntary welfare and safety measures, represented the opposite faction. There were many conspicuous legislative successes during the decade, however, such as those initiated by academics and politicians under the Wisconsin Idea. Among other pieces of legislation, these included workers' compensation and increasingly regulated and improved working conditions.

There was a marked shift in both the philosophy and the agenda of health and safety reformers toward the end of the Progressive era. As the larger movement tapered off, health and safety was demoted to the private sector. Corporations, aware that health and safety measures could reduce costs like insurance premiums, were nevertheless conscious that public concerns might lead to more stringent legislation and thus attempted to identify ways in which the reform movement could be more effectively controlled. Their efforts therefore became

Florence Kelley

As a social reformer and political activist, Florence Kelley was a passionate advocate for government regulation to protect working women and children. Following her graduation and a spell at the University of Zurich, Kelley returned to America where she joined Jane Addams and other reformers at Hull House. Her early career included time at the Illinois Bureau of Labor Statistics, where she was hired to investigate sweated labor in the garment industry, and an appointment as Illinois chief factory inspector. There, she was frequently frustrated by public indifference to the law and increasingly caught between employers who opposed her activities and reformers who advocated stricter measures. In 1899, Kelley was appointed head of the recently established National Consumers' League (NCL), a position she held for 30 years and where she pioneered the use of consumer boycotts and clothing labels to certify that garments had been produced without child labor and within the framework of legislation regulating factory work.

Kelley lobbied in this role for improved working conditions, a minimum wage, and shorter working hours legislation. Her work on the minimum wage campaign ultimately led to the passage of fourteen state laws for women, legislation later extended to male workers. Kelley supported Lillian Wald—who, along with Kelley, lived at the Henry Street Settlement in New York—in her advocacy for a federal bureau to study and attempt to improve conditions for children. She was a founder of the National Child Labor Committee and her efforts there also contributed to the foundation in 1912 of the United States Children's Bureau, which at the time was the only government agency run by women.

focused around the National Safety Council. Business began to stress that workers themselves were responsible for their safety, a policy that applied particularly to immigrants, whose habits some commentators condemned as the source of high accident and disease rates. They also prioritized health concerns over safety and emphasized the importance of professionals in instigating change, thus removing health and safety from the public domain.

The Wisconsin Idea

After 1900, the progressive Republican faction in Wisconsin, led by Governor Robert La Follette, sponsored and passed legislation of massive social and economic significance. In these reforms, the state led where others would follow and the progressive and essentially experimental reforms instigated in Wisconsin were ultimately accepted and passed by the national administration.

Several progressive academics at the University of Wisconsin who contributed to the establishment of the Wisconsin Idea were opposed to the inequities of

John R. Commons

As an eminent institutional economist, progressive social scientist, and labor historian, Commons influenced a broad range of labor legislation in the early 20th century. He is perhaps best known for founding an evaluation of cooperative action by the state and other institutions—continuing the tradition established by economist and social theorist Thorstein Veblen—that he saw as indispensable to comprehending economics. Commons—either himself, or through the work of his students and colleagues at the University of Wisconsin—influenced such disparate aspects of American labor as apprenticeships, vocational training, workers' injury and unemployment compensation, workplace safety and inspection, social security, labor organization, collective bargaining, and the administration of labor law.

He also has a claim to being the first American social scientist to yoke science to improving labor conditions. At Wisconsin, Commons collaborated with state governor Robert La Follette, Sr., in what became known as the Wisconsin Idea, a partnership in research and economics between the state government and the university. Commons's radical policies were achieved incrementally through conservative means. He believed that when appropriately employed, government could perform an active and positive part in alleviating workplace injustice—an enterprise he felt could not be left to the market—but that such reforms had to be achieved within an improved capitalist system. To eliminate corruption, patronage, and special interests from bill drafting, Commons used a strategy common to other Progressive era reforms: using trained professionals who would, "apply to labor legislation the same study of causes, of processes and of effects that lie at the basis of our modern science." (Barbash, 1989, 44)

Employers could be given incentives to comply with labor legislation, he believed, by using the profit motive, which would benefit the entire community. Commons accomplished two important examinations of the history of labor unions. As editor of the first, *A Documentary History of American Industrial Society*—a 10-volume set begun in 1910—he helped preserve many original source texts of the labor movement. The second, *History of Labor in the United States* (1918), is a narrative work that continues the themes begun in the earlier work.

the era (the emergence of big business and the accumulation of wealth and economic power in the hands of fewer individuals and smaller groups and political machinery that did little for the average citizen). Such academics as John R. Commons, Richard T. Ely, and Paul Reinsch collaborated with the state administration under the maxim that "the boundaries of the university should be the boundaries of the state," and that research undertaken at the university should be applied to improve health, the quality of life, and the environment for all citizens. This interchange between the university and the state was at the heart of the Wisconsin Idea, a joint effort between the academic and the politician to benefit the shared interests of all people, rather than the special interest of specific groups ("democratic liberalism in practice"). (Doan, 1947, 15)

It is likely that without the dynamism of La Follette and the dedication and pragmatism of the political and academic radicals who followed him, the reform of public utilities, the railroads, and the inequitable taxation system would not have been possible. By 1914, among the many reforms the Republican platform could boast were: a rigorous corrupt practices act; a railroad commission with lower fares and shorter hours for employees; dairy and food laws that protected both producer and consumer; legislation on health, sanitation, and child labor; mandatory minimum education for minors undertaking manual labor; public utility legislation; workers' compensation that established fixed payments, rather than compelling workers to go to law against employers; and an industrial commission to enforce its provision. Alongside these reforms were others that stipulated primary elections whereby the rank and file, rather than caucuses frequently dominated by political bosses, could choose nominees; and progressive taxation, imposing a higher rate on the better off than the less affluent.

At the time, the reforms and their enduring results were considered daring advances and nearly all were challenged in the courts, although no measure was ever declared unconstitutional. Together with a cooperative electorate, La Follette and those he inspired reinvigorated the state government and made "all people equal in law" (Doan, 1947, 42) in practice as well as in theory.

Workers' Health: The Dangerous Trades

In the early 1900s, workplaces were highly dangerous places. Mechanical accidents were frequent and workers were often exposed to toxic substances and chemicals. In certain occupations—the dangerous trades—workers' clothing was encrusted with poisons, they breathed toxic dust and fumes, and they ate with poison-coated hands. Industrial hygiene was so lax that employers believed that they had acquitted their responsibility if they advised workers to scrub their fingernails. Illnesses and conditions resulting from industrial poisoning were frequently serious, and often fatal. Workers in the felt hat trade, for example, who were poisoned by mercury, developed uncontrollable jerking of the limbs and mental illness—hence, the expression "mad as a hatter." Andrea Shen demonstrates how, in the many industries that used lead, workers there suffered from "colic attacks, convulsions, partial paralysis, and premature senility." (www.hno .harvard.edu/gazette/1997/10.23/PublicHealthPio.html1)

As part of the broader reform climate, public and professional concerns regarding the unacceptable health risks facing workers began to lead to more positive initiatives to improve conditions in these industries. Support generally came from groups conventionally associated with this role: the Consumers Leagues and the organization that perhaps played a more decisive part than any other,

Women work in an ordnance shop of Midvale Steel and Ordnance Company in Pennsylvania, 1918. During World War I, the Bureau of Labor investigated munitions and airplane manufacturing. (National Archives)

the American Association for Labor Legislation. Early successes were in part the result of efforts by Charles P. Neill, U.S. Commissioner of Labor, who had been responsible for the increase in interest in industrial poisons, and Dr Alice Hamilton, a former Hull House resident and pioneer in industrial toxicology. An early achievement occurred in 1910, when legislation banning phosphorus matches from interstate commerce resulted from a collaboration between the Bureau of Labor and the American Association for Labor. Shortly thereafter, at Neill's invitation, Hamilton began investigations for the Bureau, initiating a decade of cooperation in which she studied diseases and risks associated with the lead, explosives, pottery, and dye industries.

Hamilton discovered that there was little published medical material on the dangerous trades and that many companies simply relied on a large pool of labor and high turnover rate to reduce exposure to hazardous materials. As special investigator for industrial diseases, Hamilton first examined the white lead industry before moving on to problems of lead poisoning in potteries and allied trades, where her efforts resulted in the elimination of some of the most dangerous processes. Her work continued in the rubber industry, the printing trades, explosives, and the manufacture of aniline dyes.

Through a process of what has been termed "shoe leather epidemiology"—talking to doctors, labor organizers, and sick workers in their homes, reading hospital records, and inspecting factories—Hamilton began to correlate certain illnesses with specific industrial processes. During World War I, the Bureau investigated munitions and airplane manufacturing, and, since American manufacturers were forced to replace material previously imported from Germany, the use of aniline and other coal tar dyes. Writing in the journal *The Survey* in 1917 (cited in Moye, 1986, 26), Hamilton noted a new form of industrial poisoning resulting from the use of "dope" on aircraft wings, but she was subsequently convinced that American manufacturers had improved. Nevertheless, wartime restrictions on information frequently meant that the Bureau had to discover the location of munitions factories for themselves. When investigating the manufacture of picric acid—an explosive, the nitrous fumes from which often caused fatal burning of the lungs—Hamilton followed the chemical's characteristic fumes to their source, or she merely spotted the orange- and yellow-stained workers—"canaries"—who would then lead her to the location. In visits to 41 plants, at least thirty poisonous substances were subsequently identified.

Despite opposition from some employers, who frequently attempted to cover up poor conditions, and antipathy from some colleagues, Hamilton, and the Bureau itself, continued their efforts. The Bureau participated in collaborative projects with agencies in the War Labor Administration of the Department of Labor and with the Woman in Industry Service, linking with the Public Health Service. For the Working Conditions Service, Hamilton chaired a committee of experts investigating health issues that resulted from industrial poisons. Appalled by "the sight of men sickening and dying in the effort to produce something that would wound or kill other men like themselves" (Moye, 1986, 26), she nevertheless opted not to oppose the war too conspicuously so that she could continue to work for the Bureau and expose hazards and establish protective standards.

THE IMPACT OF SOCIAL REFORMS IN THE 1910s

Although there is some debate about when the Progressive era finished, it was largely over by 1915, although progressive measures were still passed in the next decade. "Participation in the war put an end to the Progressive movement," Hofstadter believes (1955, 275); it was both the epitome and the annihilation of the Progressive spirit. As the reform climate gradually declined, there was a reaction against both the war itself and the Progressive movement. It is possible that people felt that they had responded too eagerly to the Progressive calls for self-sacrifice and altruism, whereas America's international moral crusade (its participation in the war) had been so closely yoked to its national moral crusade and the values pervading the era that there was almost bound to be a negative reaction. The reaction went beyond rejecting Wilson and all he stood for, "it destroyed the popular impulse that had sustained Progressive politics for well over a decade before 1914." (Hofstadter, 1955, 282)

Conservatism returned, even before the reversals of Progressive policies that occurred in the next decade. Radicals, muckrakers, and intellectuals all retreated from politics and the public sphere toward the private and the personal. For some, the war destroyed their trust in humankind's capacity to change society for the better. For example, Lincoln Steffens expressed some affinity with the authoritarian forces surfacing in Europe, whereas Walter Lippmann articulated his skepticism regarding public opinion and his wish that more authority be conceded to experts. Former liberal progressives like Albert J. Beveridge abandoned the crusade for reform, denouncing the Adamson Act as a "surrender by government to the threat of force by special interests." (Heale, 2004, 70)

Unsettled by wartime taxes, labor unrest, and American participation in the war, public support for reform also evaporated in the last years of the decade. Once the reforming impulse was over, the most significant legacy of the Progressive Protestant crusade for morality seemed to be Prohibition, a legacy that now seems like a "meaningless nuisance, an extraneous imposition upon the main course of history . . . and a grim reminder of the moral frenzy" of the era. (Hofstadter, 1955, 289) Rather than the valid Progressive reform that some would claim it to be, Prohibition now seems like a counterfeit reform, a surrogate that had a broad populist appeal for a certain sort of crusading intellect. It symbolized parochial hostility to urban vice, pleasures, and intemperance, as well as to immigrant habits, and the amendment was carried on a wave of evangelical hysteria. Above all, it fit in well with the sense of self-denial and moral authority that characterized the era.

As urban development changed—partly as a result of the drop in immigration after 1914—to some extent, the specter of the "wicked" city began to disappear toward the end of the decade. Despite the enduring stereotype perpetuated in numberless diatribes of the city as the "cesspool of wickedness" (Boyer, 1978, 287), it became clear that the growth of the city did not necessarily prefigure an inevitable disintegration of morality and social order. Nevertheless, there were still those Americans who resented American casualties in a war not of their making and rejected the European world and its values. It was this reactionary faction that still felt threatened by the cosmopolitan nature of the cities and which insisted on dedication to the principles of 100% Americanism. The reaction was at its most fervent immediately after the war and during the short postwar depression, but its effects would be felt well into the next decade.

Historians' Debate:
Were Prohibition and Antiprostitution
Valid Progressive Reforms?

Since the Progressive era itself, historians have debated with some vigor whether Prohibition and, by inference, the crusade against prostitution should be considered valid Progressive reforms. Hofstadter thinks not, believing that Prohibition was "a ludicrous caricature of the reforming impulse," a "pinched, parochial substitute" for real reform, subjected by "spiteful rural folk upon the more tolerant and urbane cities." (1955, 289) In a similar mood, Feldman (1967, 197) characterizes the coercive features of the antiprostitution campaigns as "irrational, evangelical, uncompromising, and completely divorced from the humanitarianism of the early 20th century." Nevertheless, there are many historians (e.g., Timberlake and Hohner) who demonstrate the close connections between the moral control campaigns and other aspects of Progressive reform, arguing that the former is genuinely an expression of a wider Progressive reform impetus.

There was little consensus on this issue even during the Progressive era. Even though some acclaimed the Prohibition and antiprostitution campaigns, others disallowed that there was any link between what the reforms represented and the coercive moral campaigns. Walter Lippmann derided the "raucous purity" (1961, 118) of some moralists, whereas Herbert Croly observed that reformers who acted as "moral protestants and purifiers" were involved in an essentially "misdirected effort," asserting that all that would result from such "illiberal Puritanism" was "personal self-stultification." (1965, 150)

How Progressivism is defined is central to this question, and as Boyer demonstrates, a characteristic that was common to most reformers of the era—and one that, in part, formed a connection between coercive reformers and other Progressives—"was an infinite capacity for moral indignation." (1978, 196) For all Progressives, many of the perceived ills of the period (e.g., social inequities, corporate misdemeanors, corruption in government, and personal moral issues) were inseparably connected. Nearly every Progressive campaign had a moral significance, and those that were seen as ripe for reform were viewed as a contributory factor in the enervating social climate. Whether the cause was child labor or the long hours worked by women, government corruption, or prostitution, they all harmed victims' moral development and demeaned the moral climate of the city, and for some, at least, it is this aspect that makes the coercive moral crusades authentically Progressive reforms.

BIOGRAPHIES

Sophonisba Preston Breckinridge, 1866–1948

Reformer

Sophonisba Breckinridge was a pioneer in social work, a social scientist, and an advocate for social reform. She was a part-time resident at the Hull House Settlement in Chicago, living there intermittently for almost 15 years until 1921. As part of a group of much better known residents, which included Jane Addams, she took part in many of the same reform initiatives.

Breckinridge was born into a prominent Kentucky family with a long history of political activism. She studied law after graduating from Wellesley College, becoming the first woman to be admitted to the bar in Kentucky. She moved to Chicago after a political scandal involving her father and a subsequent surge of anti-Breckinridge sentiment. There she entered graduate school at the University of Chicago, where she gained her doctoral and law degrees. A part-time professorial appointment allowed her to stay in Chicago, but it also meant that she had to look for other work to supplement her academic income.

Breckinridge was active in many organizations throughout the decade, including the Progressive Party, the Women's Peace Party, the International Congress of Women, and the Chicago National Association for the Advancement of Colored People. She participated in a committee established in 1911 to investigate the garment workers' strike. Breckinridge also took part in several important reform initiatives, assisting in the drafting of legislation regulating women's pay and hours, while also authoring several legislative bills. She was also instrumental in the establishment of social work as a professional academic discipline. Her role in the merger of the Chicago School of Civics and Philanthropy with the University of Chicago was pivotal. Accomplished in 1920, the school became the first graduate school of social work affiliated with a major research university.

Breckinridge also wrote numerous important and influential texts, some with the reformer and Breckinridge's long-term intellectual collaborator Edith Abbott. Major works in this decade include *The Delinquent Child and the Home* (1912) and *Truancy and Non-Attendance in the Chicago Public Schools*

Social reformer Sophonisba Preston Breckinridge (1866–1948). (Library of Congress)

(1917). Breckinridge and Abbott also co-authored several pioneering studies on the effects of industrialization and urbanization in Chicago, which focused on housing conditions and women in industry. As an eminent scholar and academic, Breckinridge was dedicated to the belief that social research could be a significant factor in the alleviation of social problems as well as a valuable tool in pressing for reform. She left an important documentary legacy on the social consequences of industrialization, immigration, and urbanization in the early 20th century.

Crystal Eastman, 1881–1928

Lawyer

A lawyer, opponent of militarism, early feminist, socialist, and journalist, Crystal Eastman graduated from Vassar in 1903, after which she investigated labor conditions for the Pittsburgh Society. The resulting report, *Work Accidents and the Law,* was instrumental in the establishment of early workers' compensation legislation. While living in Milwaukee, she participated in the 1912 Wisconsin suffrage campaign. Returning east in 1913, Eastman worked as an investigating attorney for the U.S. Commission on Industrial Relations. She joined other feminists, including Alice Paul and Lucy Burns, in founding the militant Congressional Union for Woman Suffrage (later the National Women's Party), a campaigning organization for a constitutional amendment guaranteeing woman's suffrage.

During the war, Eastman established the Woman's Peace Party, becoming president of the New York branch, and acted as executive director of the American Union Against Militarism. The Union lobbied against American involvement in the war and, with greater success, against war with Mexico in 1916. Following America's entry into the war in 1917, Eastman, along with Roger Baldwin, became a founding member of the National Civil Liberties Bureau (later the American Civil Liberties Union), part of whose remit was the defense of conscientious objectors.

Crystal Eastman was an American feminist who fought for a wide variety of causes during the early 20th century, including women's suffrage, socialism, and new relationships between men and women outside of marriage. (Library of Congress)

After the war, Eastman organized the First Feminist Congress in 1919 and with her brother, Max, co-founded and co-owned the radical journal, *The Liberator,* which contained trenchant coverage of politics, art, and literature, as well as some biting political cartoons. She was blacklisted during the Red Scares of 1919–1921 and, unable to find work elsewhere, worked as a columnist for feminist journals.

Josephine Clara Goldmark, 1877–1950

Reformer

A researcher and dynamic investigator, prolific author, and expert on legislation, Josephine Goldmark made a significant contribution to the reform movements involved in improving workers' conditions. After an education at Bryn Mawr College, Goldmark chaired the committee on labor laws for the National Consumers League (NCL) and was subsequently that organization's publications secretary. In 1907, along with Florence Kelly, head of the NCL, she persuaded the lawyer Louis Brandeis to defend the maximum-hour law for women in Oregon in *Muller v. Oregon,* assisting Brandeis in researching and writing the "Brandeis Brief," *Women in Industry.*

As an expert on labor conditions, Goldmark was invited to serve on a diverse range of non-NCL labor investigations, including the committee investigating the Triangle Shirtwaist Company Fire in New York in 1911. The Russell Sage Foundation published *Fatigue and Efficiency,* one of her most influential books, in 1912. In this, Goldmark demonstrated workers were both physically harmed by excessive working hours and that productivity was also reduced. In 1919, she was named secretary of the Rockefeller Foundation's Committee for the Study of Nursing Education. She was also assistant director of social research for the Russell Sage Foundation and executive secretary of the Committee on Women in Industry during World War I. Between 1918 and 1920, she served as manager of the Women's Service Section of the U.S. Railroad Administration, in which capacity she investigated women and children's working conditions across the nation. From 1919, she also acted as an expert on women's health issues in the research department at American Telephone and Telegraph and served as vice-chair of the New York City Child Labor Commission.

Robert M. La Follette, Sr., 1855–1925

Politician

Robert Marion La Follette, Sr., served as a United States congressman, 20th governor of Wisconsin from 1901 to 1906, and senator for that state from 1905 to 1925. As a highly vocal reformer, life-long Republican, and leader of the Progressive faction within the party, his frequent skirmishes with party leaders won him the nickname "Fighting Bob." A tireless campaigner against political corruption, La Follette campaigned for electoral reform, supported resolutions to increase railroad taxes, advocated the eradication of monopolies and the protection of workers' rights—including the first workers' compensation system—and defended small farmers. He established close links between the state government and the University of Wisconsin in the cultivation of progressive policies, which principle became known as the Wisconsin Idea.

As senator, La Follette pursued a similar reform agenda in Washington. His campaigns included woman's suffrage, child labor legislation, and social security. His belief that America's economy was in the hands of a small number of corporate leaders encouraged him to advocate for the development of labor organizations to act as a buffer against the power of large corporations. His campaign in 1911 to mobilize support for his presidential bid was unsuccessful, and he subsequently opposed both Roosevelt and Taft in the election the following year, supporting Woodrow Wilson instead. Despite his advocacy for Wilson, he strenuously opposed U.S. entry into the war—making many enemies in the process—contending that American involvement would curtail domestic democratic reforms. La Follette also opposed the prosecution of the labor leader Eugene Debs and other opponents of the war. Accusations that he was unpatriotic did not appear to harm his support and he was re-elected to the Senate in 1922.

Walter Lippmann, 1889–1974

Journalist

Walter Lippmann was a noted liberal writer, journalist, and political commentator whose influence spread beyond the Progressive era. Born in New York City to German Jewish parents, Lippmann studied philosophy and languages at Harvard, where his early exposure to socialism led to his involvement in the founding of the Harvard Socialist Club. He returned to New York in 1910 to work for the campaigning journalist Lincoln Steffens on the editorial staff of *Everybody's*. In 1911, both supported Theodore Roosevelt's Progressive Party in the 1912 presidential election, but although participation in active politics became one of Lippmann's ambitions, he became convinced during a short spell in the socialist municipal government in Schenectady in 1912 that he could be more influential as a thinker and political essayist than as an active political participant. Over the next two years, he renounced socialism and in 1913 published *A Preface to Politics*. In 1914, with Herbert Croly, he co-founded the liberal and progressive magazine of political criticism *The New Republic*. The magazine was intended as both a response to the changes brought about by industrialization and mass production and as an antidote to what he regarded as the muckraking tendency of contemporary political journalism.

His next book, *Drift and Mastery,* is widely regarded as an indispensable text for understanding political thought in early 20th-century America and is considered to be one of the most important and influential documents of the Progressive Movement. In this book, published at the height of progressivism, Lippmann argued for a national disengagement from the political and intellectual dogmas of both past and present, including some of the formulas of progressivism itself. Although he criticized Woodrow Wilson and the New Freedom Democrats for their allegedly obsolete and exhausted assault on the organizational currents in business and industry, he nevertheless became an advisor to Wilson during the war and assisted in the drafting of the Fourteen Points.

H. L. Mencken, 1880–1956

Journalist

Controversial journalist, contrarian, editor, social critic, and satirist Henry Louis Mencken is often perceived as one of the more influential, if simultaneously, one of the more cynical, writers of the early 20th century. He was born to parents of German descent in Baltimore, Maryland. At age three, the family moved to the house where Mencken would live for the rest of his life, apart from five years of married life. After a spell reporting for the *Baltimore Morning Herald,* he then wrote for the *Baltimore Sun* while also writing short stories, poetry, and a novel. Work as a literary critic, and later as editor on the magazine *The Smart Set,* began in 1908.

Mencken's early influences included Rudyard Kipling, Ambrose Bierce, Jonathan Swift, and Mark Twain, who taught him that the lampoon was more powerful than the lament, and he counted Theodore Dreiser, F. Scott Fitzgerald, and the publisher Alfred Knopf among his close friends. A tireless critic of what he perceived as "quackery," his targets were wide-ranging and included social reformers, hygienists, politicians, religious leaders, and what he called the "booboisie," the ignorant, reactionary mass of middle-class Americans.

H. L. Mencken, as editor, newspaperman, iconoclastic critic, and literary stylist, was a liberalizing influence on American literature and social thought through the years before and after World War I. (Bettmann/Corbis)

His publications during the decade include *A Book of Burlesques* (1916), *A Book of Prefaces* (1917), and *In Defense of Women* (1917). His influential multi-volume defense of American grammar, *The American Language,* documenting the changes Americans made to the English language—and the ways in which English was actually spoken by the masses, instead of the often prescriptive grammar of text books and schoolmarms—was first published in 1919.

Mencken's later career is marred by his views on race, although there are some who contend that he assumed positions on many issues merely to be controversial. He is also remembered for his acerbic reporting of the Scopes trial in the following decade, his campaigns against the Puritan strain in American literature, and his support of writers like Sinclair Lewis and Eugene O'Neill.

Walter Rauschenbusch, 1861–1918

Baptist Minister

Born in Rochester, New York, of German Lutheran and Baptist ancestry, Walter Rauschenbusch was a Christian theologian, Baptist minister, and a leading figure in the Social Gospel movement. His spell at Rochester Theological Seminary taught him to challenge conventional ideologies, whereas his beliefs were further challenged by the intolerable conditions of his first parishioners near Hell's Kitchen, New York City.

Meetings with Edward Bellamy, author of *Looking Backward, 2000–1887,* and Henry George, writer of the influential *Progress and Poverty,* convinced Rauschenbusch to work in the interests of the underprivileged of New York City and led to the foundation of the Brotherhood of the Kingdom. His first book, *Christianity and the Social Crisis,* was based on the notion that social, rather than individual responsibility was of more significance. It was an immediate success and established him—by then, a Rochester professor—as a leading figure in the increasingly visible Social Gospel movement. His 1912 *Christianizing the Social Order* was an exhaustive socialist evaluation of capitalism in which he described how a Christian social order must be founded on social justice and economic democracy. *The Social Teachings of Jesus,* published during the war, was widely circulated and became a text for YMCA service associations in the armed forces.

Politically more uncompromising than most Social Gospelers, Rauschenbusch belonged to a more radical faction whose ideology occasionally approached Christian Democratic Socialism. He believed that the capitalist ethos was anti-Christian, yet opposed the anticlericalism of Marxian socialism. His last book, *A Theology for the Social Gospel* in 1917, was an attempt to remodel orthodox Christianity to fit the Social Gospel representation. Believing that modern humankind should be able to find a solution to the most complex problems without resort to barbarism, Rauschenbusch was vigorously opposed to World War I, but in this, his views were antithetical to most Social Gospelers. His critics asserted that in his enthusiasm to reform society, he disregarded individual needs, arguing that his social liberalism excluded an appropriate role for women and that he exhibited a limited humanity for the adversity of African Americans.

REFERENCES AND FURTHER READINGS

Ahlstrom, Sydney E. 1972. *A Religious History of the American People*. New Haven: Yale University Press.

Barbash, Jack. 1989. "John R. Commons: Pioneer of Labor Economics." *Monthly Labor Review* 112, no. 5 (May).

Bernstein, Barton J., and Allen J Matusow, eds. 1972. *Twentieth Century America: Recent Interpretations*. San Diego: Harcourt Brace Jovanovich.

Beumler, James D. 1986. "Church and State at the Turn of the Century: Missions and Imperialism, Bureaucratization, and War, 1898–1920." In John F. Wilson, *Church and State in America: A Bibliographical Guide, The Civil War to the Present Day*. Oxford: Greenwood Press.

Boyer, Paul. 1978. *Urban Masses and Moral Order in America, 1820–1920*. Cambridge, MA: Harvard University Press.

Callow, Jr., Alexander B., ed. 1973. *American Urban History: An Interpretive Reader with Commentaries*. New York: Oxford University Press.

Croly, Herbert. 1965. *The Promise of American Life*. Indianapolis: Bobbs Merill.

Davis, Allen F. 1973. *American Heroine: The Life and Legend of Jane Addams*. New York: Oxford University Press.

Davis, Allen F. 1967. *Spearheads for Reform: The Social Settlements and the Progressive Movement 1890–1914*. New York: Oxford University Press.

Doan, Edward N. 1947. *The La Folettes and the Wisconsin Idea*. New York: Rinehart and Company.

Feldman, Egal. 1967. "Prostitution, the Alien Woman and the Progressive Imagination, 1910–1915." *American Quarterly* 19 (Summer).

Gardner, Todd K. 2007. "Population and Population Growth." In David Goldfield, *Encyclopedia of American Urban History*. Thousand Oaks, CA: Sage Publications.

Gould, Lewis L., ed. 1974. *The Progressive Era*. New York: Syracuse University Press.

Harvard University *Gazette*. 1997. "Public Health Pioneer." www.hno.harvard.edu/gazette/1997/10.23/PublicHealthPio.html1.

Hays, Samuel P. 1957. *The Response to Industrialism, 1855–1914*. Chicago: University of Chicago Press.

Heale, M. J. 2004. *Twentieth-Century America: Politics and Power in the United States 1900–2000*. London: Arnold.

Hofstadter, Richard. 1960. *The Age of Reform: From Bryan to FDR*. New York: Alfred A. Knopf.

Link, Arthur S. 1966. *American Epoch: A History of the United States since the 1890s*. New York: Alfred A. Knopf.

Lippmann, Walter. 1961. *Drift and Mastery, 1961*. Englewood Cliffs: Prentice-Hall.

Lissak, Rivka Shpak. 1989. *Pluralism and Progressives: Hull House and the New Immigrants 1890–1919*. Chicago: University of Chicago Press.

McLoughlin, William G. 1978. *Revivals, Awakenings, and Reform: An Essay on Religion and Social Change in America, 1607–1977*. Chicago: University of Chicago Press.

Melosi, Martin V. 1994. "Refuse as an Engineering Problem: Sanitary Engineers and Municipal Reform." In Howard P. Chudakoff, ed., *Major Problems in American Urban History: Documents and Essays*. Lexington: D. C. Heath.

Moye, William T. 1986. "BLS and Alice Hamilton: Pioneers in Industrial Health." *Monthly Labor Review* 109, no. 6 (June).

Nelson, Daniel. 1995. *Managers and Workers: Origins of the Twentieth-Century Factory System in the United States 1880–1920*. Madison: University of Wisconsin Press.

Pease, Otis, ed. 1962. *The Progressive Years*. New York: George Braziller.

Philpott, Thomas Lee. 1978. *The Slum and the Ghetto: Neighborhood Deterioration and Middle-Class Reform, Chicago, 1880–1930*. New York: Oxford University Press.

Riis, Jacob A. 1971. *How the Other Half Lives: Studies Among the Tenements of New York*. New York: Dover Publications.

Rosner, David, and Gerald Markowitz. 1987. *Dying for Work: Workers' Safety and Health in Twentieth-Century America*. Bloomington: Indiana University Press.

Seager, Richard Hughes. 1986. "Immigration and Urbanization: Changing Patterns of Religious and Cultural Authority." In John F. Wilson, *Church and State in America: A Bibliographical Guide, the Civil War to the Present Day*. Oxford: Greenwood Press.

University of Illinois at Chicago. No date. "Urban Experience in Chicago: Hull-House and Its Neighbors, 1889–1963." www.uic.edu/jaddams/hull/urbanexp/.

U.S. Bureau of the Census. No date. "Mother Tongue of the Foreign-Born Population: 1910–1940, 1960, and 1970." www.census.gov/population/www/documentation/twps0029/tab06.html.

Walcutt, Charles Child. 1940. "The Three Stages of Theodore Dreiser's Naturalism." *Transactions and Proceedings of the Modern Language Association of America* 55, no. 1 (March): 266–289.

Ward, Colin. 1978. *The Child in the City*. London: The Architectural Press.

White, Ronald C., and C. Howard Hopkins. 1976. *The Social Gospel: Religion and Reform in Changing America*. Philadelphia: Temple University Press.

Wiebe, Robert H. 1967. *The Search for Order, 1877–1920*. London: Macmillan.

Wood, Andrew and James A. Baer. 2006. "Strength in Numbers: Urban Rent Strikes and Political Transformation in the Americas, 1904–1925." *Journal of Urban History* 32: 862–885.

Industrialization and Labor Discontent

OVERVIEW

The decade of the 1910s was characterized by labor unrest. The decade opened with massive strikes in New York and other cities by garment workers fighting sweatshop conditions and ended with the great steel strike of 1919. The reason this ten-year period was so defined by labor unrest is in part explained by the far-reaching transformations experienced in America during this decade. America entered the 20th century not fully industrialized. By 1919, the nation had transformed into a major industrial world power. This economic revolution changed the way Americans did business, how they lived, and how they saw themselves. It created enormous wealth and great pockets of poverty.

The Ford Motor Company was at the forefront of technical and social changes that characterized industry in the decade, creating a prototype for technical innovation in mass production industries; however, the social consequences of those increases in efficiency, the reductions in cost and price, mechanization, and Ford's antiunionism would have implications far beyond the decade.

TIMELINE

1910   Continuation of the shirtwaist makers' strike begun in 1909—the uprising of 20,000—in New York and Philadelphia.

20 die and 17 injured when John J. and James McNamara blow up the *Los Angeles Times* building in an open shop dispute.

Ford opens Highland Park, Detroit, plant.

"The Great Revolt," the strike by 60,000 cloakmakers belonging to the International Ladies' Garment Workers' Union (ILGWU), involved months of picketing and, after mediation by prominent members of the Jewish community between the ILGWU and the Manufacturers' Association, resulted in the Protocols of Peace agreement, which won union recognition and higher wages, as well as a basic health benefits program.

1911   Triangle Shirtwaist Factory fire, New York, in which 146 young, mostly immigrant garment workers die leads to creation of New York Factory Investigating Committee, but for others it resulted in further radicalization.

Publication of *Principles of Scientific Management* by Frederick Winslow Taylor.

1912   U.S. Commission on Industrial Relations established.

Textile strike, Lawrence, Massachusetts, sometimes known as the Bread and Roses Strike and led by Industrial Workers of the World (IWW), wins wage increases.

1913   In one of his last acts as president, Taft establishes the U.S. Department of Labor "to foster, promote and develop the welfare of working people, to improve their working conditions, and to advance their opportunities for profitable employment."

First Model T rolls off Ford assembly line.

1914   Ludlow massacre, Colorado. Conflict resulting from the coal miners' strike escalates into tragedy when National Guardsmen open fire on striking miners and their families. At least five die in conflict and subsequent fire.

Ford Motor Company raises basic wage from $2.40 for a nine-hour day to $5.00 for an eight-hour day.

Clayton Act limits use of injunctions in labor disputes.

1915   La Follette's Seaman's Act systematizes conditions for seamen.

Labor leader and activist Joe Hill arrested on charges of murder in Salt Lake City.

"Yellow dog" contracts, agreements between employers and employees that the employee renounces the right to join a labor union, upheld by Supreme Court.

1916   In June, the Seattle Longshoreman's strike spreads to many ports on the West Coast. Although a relatively early settlement was reached, the strike flared up again after the murders of two strikers and is finally settled in October, but with few, if any, concessions to the strikers.

Everett Mills strike, Everett, Washington.

Federal Child Labor Law passed.

Federal employees win the right to Workers' Compensation insurance.

The first federal law regulating the hours of workers in private companies, the Adamson Act, enacted to forestall a railroad strike.

Samuel Gompers nominated to advise Council of National Defense.

1917   United States entry into World War I.

IWW organizer Frank Little lynched in Butte, Montana.

Federal agents raid IWW offices in 48 cities.

1918   Federal Child Labor Law, which had been enacted two years previously, declared unconstitutional.

National War Labor Board established.

1919   General strike in Seattle begins in February after workers attempt to achieve higher wages after two years of wage constraints. Although the general stoppage ended after a week, the initial shipyard strike continued.

The steel strike, an attempt by the Amalgamated Association of Iron, Steel, and Tin Workers to organize the industry in the aftermath of World War I, begins in September, but collapses after three and a half months.

Following the steel strike, 250 "labor agitators," "communists," and "anarchists" are deported to Russia, signaling the beginning of the Red Scare.

FORDISM AND THE AMERICAN FACTORY SYSTEM

Background

Histories of industrial technology frequently emphasize the achievements of the innovators and entrepreneurs and on the technical and methodological advances, but neglect the effects of industrial technology on workers. The Ford Motor Company in the decade 1910 to 1919 therefore constitutes an opportunity to integrate technological and social history. Production technology at Ford established the prototype for technical development in mass production industries. In the space of a few years, the evolution from traditional craft processes to modern industrial ones was managed and exemplified by one company. The developments instigated at the Ford factory in 1913 and 1914 were significant both for automobile manufacture and, as Hounshell (1984, 218) acknowledges, Fordism, the term that defines both the production system and its complementary labor system—it changed the world, too. The growth of the Ford Motor Company in the 1910s was premised on the simultaneous development of mass production. As Hounshell (1984, 9) notes, as well as being almost wholly responsible for the coupling of "mass" to production, the rise of Ford also denotes a new era in the production of consumer durables in America. Before Ford made the Model T, "mass" or "masses" was generally used in a pejorative sense. Ford's goal was to make an automobile for the masses, "a seemingly unlimited market for the most sophisticated consumer durable of the early twentieth century." (Hounshell, 1984, 10) The products of his predecessors—Singer sewing machines, McCormick reapers, and Pope bicycles—were all the most expensive in their respective industries, yet their manufacturers dominated their fields. Unlike them, Ford wanted to make an automobile that cost less than all its rivals and to increase demand by continually reducing the price. For the first time, Ford was able to maximize profit by maximizing production and minimizing cost. Developments in production technology, particularly, the moving assembly line, were central to Ford's success.

Technical innovation meant unprecedented increases in efficiency and remarkable reductions in costs, but it also led to worker disaffection; notwithstanding the much-discussed $5 day (a dubious benefit at best), the monotony of the assembly line and Ford's intrusion into workers' personal lives were responsible for much labor unrest, and the later years of the decade at Ford were characterized by the displacement of a broadly paternalistic climate by a harsher regime altogether.

Ford and Mass Production

"Mass production is not merely quantity production, for this may be had with none of the requisites of mass production. Nor is it merely machine production, which may also exist without any resemblance to mass production. Mass production is

The Moving Production Line

The moving assembly line was the final piece in the jigsaw that revolutionized automobile production. Before that, Ford's engineers managed to combine the two different and prevailing production methods of the bicycle era before applying them to the manufacture of the Model T on a moving assembly line in 1913: sheet metal stamping and the technique developed in the small arms industry of standardized, interchangeable parts. Together, they provided Ford with the means to produce almost unlimited numbers of components. The remaining obstacle—how to assemble the parts—was solved by "flow production," the moving assembly line. This technique was adopted in nearly all subassemblies as well as the final chassis itself within 18 months. In terms of productivity gains (as much as 10 times the yield of static methods), the assembly line revolutionized production. Inspiration for the technique came from at least two sources: the "disassembly lines" of Chicago and Cincinnati meatpackers and flour-milling technology. In addition, it is possible that Ford's engineers had seen food-canning machinery and this might also have been influential.

In moving the work to the workers—the indispensable principle behind the assembly line—Ford discovered a way of speeding up the slower operatives and slowing down the fast men. With the establishment of the line and the spread of its principles within a year of its initial trials to all stages of operations—every *thing* moved and every *worker* remained static—genuine mass production was brought about.

The parentage of the moving assembly line and the technical innovations that it reflected are, perhaps, less significant than its effects. Although the moving line unquestionably solved the problems of assembling a great many components on to the number of units that would bring about the economies of scale required for profitable operation, it also generated severe labor problems. The moving line suggested that workers as well as machines could be mechanized. Within a year, Ford's annual labor turnover reached unprecedented levels. The changes that Ford instigated (e.g., the $5 day) were intended to address these problems. Production of the Model T increased from less than 190,000 to more than 585,000 between 1913 and 1916, and would reach more than 2 million by 1923. Alongside mechanized production, a wage level higher than any other automobile manufacturer, and low prices, the moving assembly line brought about what would become known as "Fordism."

the focusing upon a manufacturing project of the principles of power, accuracy, economy, system, continuity, and speed." (Henry Ford, "Mass Production," cited in Hounshell, 1984, 217)

Like many developments in industrial technology, shortages in skilled labor were largely responsible for the rapid technical and organizational changes that

Rows of completed Model T's roll off the Ford Motor Company assembly line in the United States, ca. 1917. (Library of Congress)

were initiated at Ford. The remarkable increase in the volume of Model T production and the simultaneous increase in the workforce (from an estimated 450 in 1908 to some 14,000 in 1913) forced Ford to investigate new methods of production. Huge numbers of semi-skilled and unskilled workers were hired because of the drastic shortages of skilled mechanics able to machine and put together components. Unlike the early workforce, who were mainly skilled Americans and Germans, the majority of those taken on to meet demand were immigrants, lacking any traditional industrial skills. By 1914, three-quarters of the labor force was foreign-born, with more than half originating in southern and eastern Europe. Technical and organizational changes initiated by Ford engineers thus allowed the production of high-quality, high-volume work by unskilled labor.

As Giedion observes, "Ford had the advantage of coming not at the start, but at the end of the mechanistic phase." (1948, 117) He recognized the significance of interchangeable components, continuous flow, and the rise of a work efficiency movement. He also identified the relationship between design and production processes: "The way to make automobiles is to make one automobile just like

Two men work to repair a tire during a joy ride in a 1913 Ford Model T touring automobile. The surge in popularity of the "horseless carriage" led to widespread improvements in road quality. (Fred Hultstrand History in Pictures Collection, NDIRS-NDSU, Fargo)

another automobile, to make them all alike, to make them come through the factory alike." (Meyer, 1991, 337) Deciding that what the market needed was a light, low-priced, simply designed car that was sufficiently powerful and easy to repair, Henry Ford proposed that the Model T should replace the Model N. The model T was cheap to run and required no mechanical aptitude from the operator. It was also within the price range of millions who could not hitherto have afforded an automobile (i.e., it was less a luxury item for the wealthy than an everyday commodity). Financial autonomy allowed Ford to experiment and substantial profits enabled the company to invest heavily in an apparently ad hoc research and development program of constant refinement of production processes.

In addition to the technical innovations, the group of talented individuals employed at Ford during the decade also played a decisive part in the success of the car. Among these was Walter Flanders, who had experienced quantity manufacture at Singer and whose role in developing the company for mass manufacture was extremely significant. Although he subsequently left Ford, Flanders observed later that it was essential to make automobiles equal in quality to those priced at $700 to $900, making them in sufficient quantities and building and

Table 2.1. Manufacturing and Marketing of Model T Fords, 1908–1916

Year	Retail Price (Touring Car)	Total Model T Production	Total Model T Sales
1908	$850	NA	5,986
1909	$950	13,840	12,292
1910	$780	20,727	19,293
1911	$690	53,488	40,402
1912	$600	82,388	78,611
1913	$600	189,088	182,809
1914	$550	230,788	260,720
1915	$490	394,788	355,276
1916	$360	585,388	577,036

Source: Adapted from Hounshell, 1984, 224.

equipping factories where every part could be economically made. Approval to develop 60 acres at Highland Park was thus obtained and the factory opened early in 1910, although construction there continued for the next 6 years.

Once the plans had been drawn up for a smooth transition into the new facility, production then, and subsequently, was made more straightforward when Henry Ford decided to make only the Model T and that all variants would have an identical chassis. This decision allowed the engineers and planners to instigate the design, manufacture, or acquisition of large numbers of special- or single-purpose machine tools, which, as Hounshell notes, is "what the American system of manufactures is all about." (1984, 227)

By 1913, Ford's figures accounted for more than half the entire automobile production of the United States. A complete Model T came off the production line every 40 seconds. Five daily trains carrying 40 finished cars each left the factory. Annual production had increased from about 6,000 Model T cars to some 200,000 at significantly lower costs in just five years. Table 2.1 shows how the retail price declined as sales rose. It is difficult to imagine how this could have been achieved without the technical innovations and initiatives such as the $5 day.

Frederick W. Taylor and Social Efficiency

The coordination of the assembly process was central to manufacturing efficiency and had required (perhaps rudimentary) time-and-motion studies to avoid chaos. Because Ford grew at a time when scientific management was highly influential, it is widely assumed that some contemporary form of systematic management determined or influenced developments at Highland Park. The extent, however, is debatable. Although the widely publicized *Eastern Rate* case (whereby railroad operators attempted to pass on a pay increase to customers only to be challenged by a group of eastern trade associations who argued successfully that railroads should increase their efficiency rather than their income) and the publication of Frederick Winslow Taylor's *Principles of Scientific Management* just predated the innovations at the plant, contemporary sources regarding its significance are inconclusive.

Taylorism refers to the principles of rationalization by analyzing work (i.e., eliminating wasteful movements through time-and-motion studies and the assignment of operatives to designated tasks by "scientific" methods). Later analyses of Ford's working practices conclude that the factory was "Taylorized," but they stop short of saying that engineers followed a specific program, but rather that they followed general principles of scientific or systematic management. It is certainly true that work routines were standardized after jobs and workflow patterns were evaluated, and as special-purpose machine tools were more widely used, semi-skilled and unskilled operatives were employed (scientifically selected, in Taylor's words). The Ford factory had a time study or work standards department as early as 1912 or 1913, and the notion that setting down work standards (i.e., the amount a manufacturer can expect from a given tool or process by labor) is fundamental to both Taylorism and to scientific management. Moreover, in line with Taylorist principles, there was a clear demarcation between management and workers at Ford.

Because Ford himself denied that the company had used Taylorism or any other system, however, there is reason to question whether it made any significant contribution to assembly at Highland Park. Although Taylor stated that Detroit manufacturers had met with some success in introducing the principles, others who heard him speak claimed that his ideas had already been employed by several manufacturers. Hounshell argues that Ford "could have been Taylorized without Taylor." (1984, 251)

Moreover, there is a significant difference between Fordism and Taylorism. Whereas advocates of scientific management typically evaluated a production process and boosted the efficiency of workers through time, motion, and pay incentives, Ford's thinking more often centered on replacing labor with machinery. Because Taylorist philosophy centered on the fixed nature of production hardware, advocates attempted to modify labor processes and the structuring of work, whereas Ford engineers applied mechanical solutions to work processes, finding operatives to attend machines. Once the process had been analyzed, the machine, rather than a piece rate, established the pace.

Given that assembly of multicomponent products was highly labor-intensive, mechanization—and the consequent reduction of labor costs—was a key factor in Ford's policy of continual price reduction. The mechanization was so complete that by 1914, Highland Park had more than 15,000 machines and fewer than 13,000 workers. Reductions were achieved by assembly lines, fed by various conveyors and slides, along with complete interchangeability and the system of machining developed by Ford, which had eliminated almost all skill requirements from the process. Indeed, as Meyer observes, experienced Ford staff referred to some mechanical devices as "'farmer's tools' because they allowed green farm hands to produce large amounts of high quality work." (1991, 341) The radical changes and subsequent gains in efficiency and cost reductions, however, brought with them serious labor problems. The $5 day was Ford's attempt to find a solution.

The $5 Day

The rationale behind the $5 day was a mixture of industrial philanthropy and hardheaded pragmatism. By 1913, labor turnover had risen to an unprecedented 380 percent. Mechanization was so unpopular with workers that Ford had to employ close to 1,000 operatives to add 100 men to the labor force. Although this led to significant administrative problems, it also disrupted production. Several factors thus combined that forced Ford to undertake a policy of labor reforms in 1913: high turnover and the obvious unpopularity of mechanization, strikes at other Detroit automobile manufacturers, and increasing signs of unionization.

Jobs throughout the plant were re-evaluated and some sense of parity between them was attempted. Efficient employees were rewarded with pay raises, whereas a factorywide 13 percent average pay increase was brought in with a minimum daily wage of $2.34. These reforms, however, did little to halt labor problems and unrest. Increasing mechanization and efficiency seemed to exacerbate labor turnover and unrest throughout the rest of 1913. The extent of high labor turnover is demonstrated by the fact that the 10 percent bonus for employees of three years or more only applied to 640 out of some 15,000 workers. Among these other factors, concern regarding the disparity between the wages of most operatives and the salaries and profits of directors and production experts led Henry Ford to a decision to adopt the $5 day. Philanthropic though this unprecedented rate of pay seemed, it allowed Ford to demand that "acceptable" workers spend eight hours a day as part of a highly efficient production machine. "Bonding" workers to the company by a strategy of high wages proved to be highly effective almost immediately, but although the much-discussed $5 day appeared to be a significant increase in wage levels, it was not a wage system. The $5 was divided between 50 percent wages and 50 percent profit sharing. Once workers received the initial half (the wage), they would have to meet various social, cultural, and production standards to get the other half. Ford's plan was to transform workers, to reshape their social world, and thereby create more efficient workers. Operatives would receive the $5 only when they achieved the new efficiency standards at work and the new social standards at home. Ford realized that even though many workers might achieve the maximum, most would attempt to reach it, thus increasing efficiency and, hence, profitability.

*Immigrants attend an English class given by the Department of Labor in the Ford
Motor Company factory in Detroit in the early 20th century. (Library of Congress)*

As part of this essentially paternalistic strategy, a new division was created
within the employment department: the Ford Sociological Department. Teams
of what were effectively social workers were employed to examine workers'
private lives. The investigators advised employees how to live—and thus become eligible for profit sharing—and also evaluated their domestic life and measured their leisure time and family for the company's benefit. The department
adhered to the belief—and emphasized it, too—that "American" workers with
"American standards of living" made the best workers. To assist in the assimilation and Americanization of the workforce, which included a high proportion
of immigrant labor, Ford encouraged workers to learn English and established
an English school for this purpose. Employees were also expected to adopt
American values and relinquish old world customs. Workers who were "too foreign" or "too immigrant" were not deemed to be good Ford material and were
not permitted to participate in the program.

Investigators' duties included visiting workers' homes and interviewing teachers, neighbors, and religious leaders. They checked homes for standards of cleanliness, ensured that families adopted an American diet, and assessed taste and
decor. The policy, which was intended to motivate workers, was also a method
of control. Control was further emphasized by Ford's policy of including with
each worker's pay stub the "withheld profits," a listing of those profits workers
had not received because their home or social life did not meet Ford standards.
If workers rectified any perceived misdemeanor, they might be reimbursed those
withheld profits. By controlling workers' pay in this way, Ford gained enormous
power and leverage over workers' lives, extending beyond the factory floor and

into the domestic and moral environment of their employees. In attempting to instill middle-class values, the Department emphasized values of home ownership, thrift, religious convictions, morals, and manners. The program continued until World War I, when it was ended by inflation, rising wages elsewhere, and a tight labor market. The program was ultimately relatively unsuccessful because it was impossible to control workers in the way that Ford imagined was achievable. The paternalistic system was replaced by one of fierce antiunionism, industrial espionage, and attempts to extract still more productivity gains from the workforce by speeding up production.

Unionization

Henry Ford believed that any kind of unionism threatened to undermine the much-vaunted efficiency of the Ford factory. His resolution was tested during this decade by a tripartite challenge from three militant unions. Automobile workers were the targets for an aggressive campaign to organize workers into their "One Big Union" by the Industrial Workers of the World (IWW). The second confrontation emerged from the first meaningful attempts by the Carriage, Wagon, and Automobile Workers' Union (CWAWU) to organize automobile workers. Last, the skilled metal trades in the American Federation of Labor (AFL) attempted to enlist workers engaged in their trades. Early 20th-century Detroit was resolutely nonunion and Ford was by no means alone in adopting a policy of complete nonrecognition of organized labor. The various unions in the metal trades, although traditionally strong, were nevertheless defeated by a robust fight waged by the Detroit Employers' Association. Metal trade workers were unrepresented in factories and shops associated with the automobile industry until well into the second decade. The Association maintained its stance toward organized labor until at least 1912, and there were few successful strikes in Detroit's automobile shops and factories.

Ford's opposition was based on a belief that labor organization was essentially antithetical to efficient production. Unions either provoked strikes, or they encouraged restrictive practices. Like many supporters of the "open shop" (i.e., the nonrecognition of organized labor), Ford was not publicly opposed to unions, claiming that he was not against any organization that makes for progress, only against organization that limited production. Whether or not his employees belonged to unions was irrelevant to Ford—he would not negotiate with those unions.

His attitude was exemplified in late 1912 when a strike at the recently purchased component supplier Keim Mills closed the factory. Ford's response was not to negotiate with the strikers, but rather to move the presses and machinery to Highland Park, allowing those who wanted to work to follow the machinery there. In early 1913, following a series of dramatic strikes in Lawrence and Paterson, the IWW attempted to organize unskilled workers in the automobile and allied industries in the Midwest. A sizeable and apparently spontaneous walkout in the rubber factories in Akron, Ohio, marked the start of the campaign, resulting in sometimes violent clashes between employers and 15,000–20,000 American and immigrant workers. Following the collapse of the strike, the IWW shifted its focus to Detroit in an attempt to unionize automobile workers there.

In Detroit, IWW efforts were concentrated on mobilizing Ford workers through a number of outdoor meetings. When 3,000 workers gathered at a rally at the factory gate, the company "summarily withdrew the workers' outdoor lunch privileges." (Meyer, 1981, 91) Workers at other automobile plants were targeted by the IWW, and in June, around 6,000 workers at Studebaker and elsewhere walked out. Despite the failure of the strike, arrests among strikers and organizers, mass protests, and police brutality heightened tension in the city. Threats by the IWW to return in 1914 to organize workers and to continue its policy of "sabotage" did little to allay management fears. Although the IWW were fundamentally opposed to capitalism, "sabotage" in this context should be taken to mean a challenge to scientific management by restricting output (i.e., the deliberate elimination of efficiency) rather than a policy of outright violence. As a working-class response to capitalist exploitation, this strategy had some attraction for workers, but to management it was an explicit and devious threat to productivity.

While Ford was occupied with potential disruption by workers mobilized by the IWW, the relatively new craft union, the CWAWU, challenged Ford and other automobile makers on other issues. Before 1910, the Detroit branch had grown into a small, but prospering industrial union. From 1910 until 1912, union involvement in a number of strikes in smaller shops resulted in superficial benefits for automobile workers. A 13-week strike involving more than 1,000 workers occurred in 1912. The CWAWU was also involved with the IWW strike in 1913. Although such Ford labor policies as the high pay and welfare programs temporarily halted attempts at unionization, the wartime situation (a decline in real wages as a result of wartime inflation, the dilution of skills, the pace of work accelerated to cope with increased war production) led to growing industrial unrest, and unions became increasingly militant in their challenges to managerial attempts at control and domination. Although the War Labor Board often attempted to ensure worker cooperation by acknowledging demands for wage increases, improved conditions, reductions in hours, and collective bargaining, the rapid escalation of federal power meant that labor—and, especially, allegedly subversive organizations like the IWW—was constrained by an increasingly repressive climate.

As in other industries, labor unrest among automobile workers escalated after the war. The independent United Automobile, Aircraft, and Vehicle Workers' Union—created by socialist CWAWU leaders in 1918—grew rapidly to become the largest in Detroit with 40,000 members by 1919. Although not strong enough to challenge Ford directly, this Auto Workers' Union (AWU) addressed its efforts at the Wadsworth Manufacturing Company, a leading supplier of Ford bodies, where 1,500 workers walked out on strike. The stoppage had a significant impact on production at Ford and the company moved swiftly to curtail any losses by sending Ford strikebreakers to Wadsworth. Once there, Ford workers refused to break the strike and Ford's activities increased unrest among workers elsewhere, including at Ford itself, where traditionally passive workers joined the AWU.

Confronted with this militancy, Ford resumed its wartime policy of industrial espionage, using workers as spies and informants to report on the activities of their workmates. Underhanded employer tactics and other factors meant that organization in the automobile industry stood little chance of success. There were numerous other strikes in the industry during 1919, but the will of the unionists was ultimately sapped by employer activities. In 1919, the River Rouge plant was adapted to make Model T bodies, thus undermining the strike at Wadsworth. Henry Ford got his own way by publicly avoiding any support for an open shop policy and quietly embracing his own way of resolving labor disputes. In any case, labor relations in postwar America were part of a harsher climate, brought about, in part, by the Red Scare and a more generalized and rabid fear of immigrant radicalism. As Ford policy shifted from welfare capitalism to his own interpretation of the American plan, paternalism disappeared to be replaced by strident antiunionism.

THE TRIANGLE FIRE

Background

The fire on March 25, 1911, at the Triangle Shirtwaist Factory, Greenwich Village, New York, was a tragedy compounded by the conclusion that it was both predictable and avoidable. A combination of factors meant that any fire that did break out would probably result in serious loss of life. In the event, 146 mostly immigrant young women died, either in the fire itself or by jumping to their deaths. Most were Italian and Jewish immigrants. Pictures and reports of the tragedy horrified the public, but also galvanized and united workers and unions, and created a coalition of reformers across social and class boundaries who joined with politicians and workers to create a new reform impulse with lasting consequences for the city, state, and nation.

The fire was preceded by the notorious Uprising of 20,000, the settlement of which in 1910 did little to resolve the underlying causes: sweated labor, reduced piece rates, and poor and unsafe working conditions. The solution appeared to be the pioneering and egalitarian labor agreements of the Protocols of Peace, which provided temporary improvements in working conditions and safety measures. Once undermined, however, stoppages again became common. Despite amendments, unrest continued to escalate, and it was abandoned in 1916 after a 14-week strike. Even though it was temporary, however, there was

The Funeral March

The funeral became a catalyst for protest. A week after the fire, the majority of bodies had been identified and buried, but seven remained unidentified. The public funeral became a political issue as the City of New York, alarmed that a large funeral might lead to unrest, refused to release the bodies, preferring instead to bury the dead in a private, separate ceremony. The Joint Committee of the Women's Trade Union League (WTUL) and the ILGWU decided that without bodies, they would still march and follow empty coffins in a demonstration of labor solidarity that became one of the largest symbolic gestures of working-class unity in New York. Despite disagreements between mainly Jewish middle-class reformers and working-class socialist eastern European Jews about whether a funeral was the appropriate occasion for protest, a call for a general strike to accompany the march was issued.

On April 5, 30,000 marchers followed empty hearses past Washington Square Arch, Greenwich Village—two blocks from the Triangle. They passed along a route lined with hundreds of thousands of workers toward the 23d Street Pier and the ferries that would take them to the Brooklyn cemetery. There, with activist Rose Schneiderman leading the workers' procession, they were met by a crowd of nearly 10,000. As ferries left, crowds massed in Manhattan for a memorial service at the Metropolitan Opera House. The union had announced that, apart from black flags, only ILGWU banners would be used. Only one was carried. It read: "We Demand Fire Protection."

Trade union procession for Triangle Shirtwaist Company fire victims, 1911. Firemen on horseback in foreground. (Library of Congress)

a relatively brief and more productive period of optimism and change in the garment industry.

The Women's Trade Union League

The priority for organized labor in the early 1900s was for men to earn a "family wage," one that would sustain a family without the assistance of a working wife. Labor leaders also believed that the growing number of working women would drive down men's wage levels and were therefore reluctant to allow the organization of women.

The National Women's Trade Union League of America (NWTUL)—a coalition of working-class women, professional reformers, and women from affluent and eminent families—was intended to "assist in the organization of women wage workers into trade unions and thereby to help them secure conditions necessary for healthful and efficient work and to obtain a just reward for such work." (ocp.hul.harvard.edu/ww/events_league.html) Modeled on the identically named British organization and the settlement house movement, increased unionization in such industries as garments and textiles, where women formed the majority of the workforce, was also a factor in the decision to establish the League. Although founded to support women as oppressed workers, it also acknowledged that all women, irrespective of class, were joined together by the "bonds of womanhood," and thus welcomed middle- and upper-class members —the "mink brigade"—who could fund the cause, act as spokespeople, and organize legal representation, but who were quite prepared to do manual work and picket employers, risking arrest alongside the strikers.

The League was instrumental in organizing women workers and supported a number of strikes like the Uprising of 20,000 and the New York City and Philadelphia shirtwaist workers' strike. Despite the collapse of the strike, workers achieved some limited gains, and the stoppage provided both the NWTUL and women workers with practical organizing experience. The organization was active in such later strikes as the cloakmakers in New York City, male clothing workers in Chicago in 1910, the 1911 Cleveland garment workers' dispute, as well as others across the country. The League, which was increasingly critical of the largely male leadership of the ILGWU, believing it did not fairly reflect the proportion or concerns of women workers, began to dissociate itself from the labor movement in 1912, only supporting strikes when they subscribed to the leadership's strategy. In that year, the NWTUL also came into conflict with the AFL when an affiliate demanded that the League halt relief for the Lawrence woolen mills strikers, a dispute that also led to considerable tension within the organization itself.

Since the AFL was often highly reactionary in its attitude toward women and foreign-born workers, the League formed closer ties with the more tolerant and radically minded locals of the Amalgamated Clothing Workers of America, which comprised mainly immigrant workers and was outside the AFL. The NWTUL was central in organizing New York Italian garment workers, and at its Chicago institution, established in 1914, it also schooled women as labor leaders and organizers.

Along with material and practical support, the League campaigned for a number of legislative reforms, especially the eight-hour day and the minimum wage. Given the Supreme Court's antipathy toward economic reform during the decade, few such reforms were ratified, and only special protections for women and children remained unchallenged by the Court. Because the AFL believed that such reform inhibited collective bargaining by supplanting the role of the unions and setting a precedent for still more government intervention, they, too, regarded the legislation with hostility. Even before the Triangle fire, the NWTUL had campaigned vigorously for safer working conditions, but as well as animating public opinion, the tragedy also helped to expose fractures between the League's affluent supporters and its working-class militants, already evident during the Lawrence strike.

Along with other organizations, the NWTUL began to press for women's suffrage before the 1919 Nineteenth Constitutional Amendment, believing that the reform would also achieve improved protective legislation for women. In marked contrast to the National Woman's Party (NWP), which had adopted an equal rights approach to suffrage, the NWTUL preferred a wider reform program better suited to contemporary labor and progressive movements. The NWP-drafted Equal Rights Amendment was strongly opposed by the League, believing it would have obliterated much of the protective legislation for which NWTUL activists had campaigned. The end of the decade saw the League's focus shift from organization and support toward legislative reform.

The Protocols of Peace

Although the issues that caused garment workers to strike were partially resolved by the 1910 settlement, it did little to solve the underlying instability that had long racked the industry. Agreements between employers and workers were frequently breached, and reformers questioned whether an overarching strategy could be implemented that allowed workers to retain their benefits and thus avoid costly strikes and continually interrupted production. The solution appeared to be the Protocols of Peace, a set of innovative and democratic labor agreements in the women's garment industry.

Although labor disputes were essentially a matter between employers and labor, Lincoln Filene, of Filene's department store, realized that the public also had a stake because strikes deprived consumers and inefficient production drove prices up. Mediation and conciliation, he believed, would assist both. So he brought in the corporate lawyer and future Supreme Court justice Louis Brandeis to broker the deal. The industrywide policy would avoid the need for stoppages through a system of appeals to clerks and Boards of Arbitration and Grievances. The Protocol also established a Joint Board of Sanitary Control whereby employers and unionists cooperated to investigate and improve health and safety conditions.

In return for cooperation, the promise of fewer strikes, standardization of labor costs, and the abolition of unjust competition by exploitative sweatshops, workers had to relinquish violence and demands for a closed shop. Despite some reservations, workers who were tired of often-fruitless struggle went along with the Protocol. Between April 1911 and October 1913, the results were impressive. Out of more than 7,500 complaints, there was sufficient cause in only 20 cases for Board of Arbitration intervention. Moreover, under the Board of Sanitary Control, hundreds of shops were cleaned up, electric power was introduced, stricter safety measures were enforced, wages rose, subcontracting was reduced, and employers' profit increased. The Protocol was widely praised by the press, with a writer in *Munsey's* celebrating it as a "whole new economic order" and the realization of a "cherished dream of industrial democracy." (Adams, 1966, 121)

Praise from outside, however, could not disguise the reality that there was considerable resentment within the industry. Unionists contended that workers could be sacked arbitrarily, and because the burden of proof lay with the worker, the Board of Grievances frequently found in the employers' favor. The Protocol began to be undermined by frequently unfair discrepancies between piece rates among different firms and by some employers who sidestepped the agreement by shipping work to out-of-town shops that had cheaper labor. Although the Board of Arbitration ruled that firms reaching agreements with Protocol companies fell under Protocol regulations, some avoided this ruling by submanufacturing (selling raw materials to outsiders and subsequently buying back finished goods). By 1912, several hundred such companies traded with Protocol members.

Stoppages also began to affect companies, an irritation particularly annoying to those who believed that agreement would relieve them of strikes. Internal dissent simultaneously threatened to fracture the formerly solid union ranks. A hearing by the Commission on Industrial Relations concluded that the Protocol should be retained. Over the following three years, various amendments were instigated, but the underlying reasons for the unrest remained intact. In July 1915, a general strike was narrowly avoided, but the following May, after 14 weeks of one of the most acrimonious strikes in ILGWU history, the Protocol was abandoned for an agreement preserving many of its aspects.

Although some believed that the Protocol was—albeit temporarily—a pragmatic solution replacing discord with cooperation and rationality, others felt it was inherently contradictory; cooperation between labor and capital was inimical to labor relations. The fragile "ceasefire" ultimately failed, and in common with almost all of industry, labor relations in the garment trade were overshadowed by the inadequate civil jurisdiction, antagonism, and brutality that would rack the country for many more years.

The Fire

The Triangle Fire of March 25, 1911, is one of the most memorable and most notorious events in American labor history. It galvanized workers politically, unified unions, and created a cross-class coalition of reformers, politicians, and workers that created a new reform impulse that had lasting consequences for the city, state, and nation.

At the time, industrial fires were not uncommon in New York, and the Triangle Factory already had a history of suspicious fires. Owned by Max Blanck and Isaac Harris, the factory, which employed more than 500 workers, occupied the top three floors of the ten-story Asch building, east of Washington Square. The factory was unusual in that even though the majority of garment making took place in small, cramped premises, the Triangle was relatively large, operating several shops. Workers making shirtwaists (women's blouses) worked 14-hour shifts over a 60- to 72-hour week for wages as low as $1.50 per week.

Triangle's reputation had already transcended the garment trade during the 1909 Uprising of 20,000. Following the four-month strike, the ILGWU had negotiated a collective-bargaining agreement applying to most workers, but the Triangle Shirtwaist declined to sign.

The Asch was a new, relatively modern building, advertised, ironically, as fireproof and by no means typical of the city's sweatshops. Whereas most of the garment trade was situated on the Lower East Side—effectively, an immigrant ghetto—the Triangle was in the heart of fashionable Greenwich Village, better known for stylish townhouses and artists' studios than for garment factories crammed with immigrant workers.

Conditions in the factory were typical of many in the district: piles of flammable textiles and tissue paper, smoking among many workers, open gas lighting, and no fire extinguishers. Because the owners used every available space for production, conditions were extremely cramped and workers complained they were forced to work elbow to elbow. In an attempt to control workers and prevent theft, exits were locked with chains. Oil cans stored on stairways provided a further fire hazard.

Workers were required to work a half-day on Saturday, and when they finished, it was not unusual for those anxious to make the most of what weekend remained to leave as quickly as possible. Although unproven, a cigarette butt carelessly thrown onto scrap cloth may have caused the fire, which was first

Damaged fire escape at the Triangle Shirtwaist Company building after the 1911 fire, New York City. (Library of Congress)

noticed by a cutter in a scrap bin on the eighth floor. Like many others, the bin contained a large quantity of scrap cloth, and although attempts were made to extinguish the fire, it spread quickly to the tons of cotton and tissue paper in the shop. The main floor was separated from the dressing rooms by a thin wood partition that allowed only one worker through at a time so they could be searched as they left, which caused a bottleneck that worsened matters as workers panicked and the floor rapidly became chaotic.

Tenth-floor executives and staff were eventually alerted and most there, as well as some from below who had reached the tenth, managed to escape on ladders to the adjoining building. Although the ninth floor had two exit doors, one had been locked, apparently to prevent pilfering or unauthorized breaks and to keep union officials out. Workers on the ninth were unaware of the fire until smoke and flames had engulfed the stairwell. The single external fire escape soon collapsed under the weight of those attempting to escape and the elevator also stopped working, so the workers were effectively trapped.

Firefighters had arrived at the factory within minutes of the outbreak, but even though the neighborhood was part of a recently constructed high water pressure district, they discovered that the pressure was insufficient to reach the ninth floor. As the ladders would not reach beyond the sixth, trapped workers were faced with either burning to death or jumping from windows. Some jumped, hoping that safety nets would save them, but the majority were killed as nets gave way on impact. Others jumped to their deaths rather than stay to perish in the flames, while others fell to their deaths in the shaft after forcing open the elevator doors. Very few workers survived the falls.

The Aftermath

After the fire, the response crossed both class and neighborhood boundaries. Eyewitnesses recounted horrific stories of young women jumping from windows and images of scenes from the fire and the grim aftermath as relatives attempted to identify bodies resonated throughout New York. Protests grew and demands were published from the conservative, progressive, and union press for safer working conditions and for the owners to be brought to trial. The Executive Board of the Ladies' Waist and Dress Makers' Union, Local No. 25 of the ILGWU, to which some of the workers belonged, planned relief work for the survivors and the victims' families. Several organizations, including the WTUL, the Jewish Daily Forward, and the United Hebrew Trades established the Joint Relief Committee and provided lump sums, many of which were sent abroad. Weekly pensions were distributed and young workers and children cared for in institutions whereas work and decent accommodation was arranged after workers recovered from their injuries.

Other initiatives included a WTUL campaign for an investigation of conditions among Triangle workers. Within a month, the Factory Investigating Commission was appointed and for five years ran statewide hearings resulting in the passage of important safety legislation. The ILGWU, along with others in the labor movement and progressive organizations and reformers, worked with Tammany Hall officials and, in initiatives that would continue for decades, pressed for wide-ranging safety and compensation measures. The fire epitomized the many grave problems facing workers, and the responses to it prepared the ground for attempts at remedies through protective legislation.

The factory's owners survived by escaping to the roof soon after the fire started. At their subsequent trial, defense counsel successfully undermined the testimony of a survivor, Kate Alterman, by claiming that her repeated—and identical—statements had probably been memorized and that she, as well as other witnesses, may have been coached by the prosecution. Defense also argued that the prosecution failed to prove that the owners knew of the locked doors. Blanck and Harris were acquitted, but 23 civil actions were subsequently brought against the owners. In 1913, they settled in the sum of $75 for each life lost.

Table 2.2. Industrial Conflict, 1914–1918

Year	No. strikes	No. persons involved
1914	1,204	no data
1915	1,593	no data
1916	3,789	2,275,000
1917	4,450	2,349,000
1918	3,353	1,931,000

Source: Hacker and Zahler, 1952, 195.

STRIKES AND SABOTAGE

Economic Revolution

The reason the 1910s are so characterized by labor discontent can in part be explained by the massive and far-reaching developments in industry and the resulting social changes that occurred, and in part by the decline in purchasing power, particularly during the period between July 1914 and July 1917. In these three years, the index of the purchasing power of the consumer's dollar dropped from 136.6 to 107.4 (1939 = 100) to an average of 92.5 by 1918, which in percentage terms represents a fall of 37.6 percent between the outbreak of World War I and the armistice. (Hacker and Zahler, 1952, 195) Disaffection, which at times broke out into acrimonious and often brutally suppressed strikes, was fostered by a climate of exploitation and greed; an economic revolution created enormous wealth for some and great pockets of poverty for many others and changed forever the way Americans did business, how they lived, and how they saw themselves. America entered the 20th century not yet fully industrialized. By 1919, however, the nation had been transformed into a major industrial world power.

The Lawrence Textile Strike

The stoppage by textile workers in Lawrence, Massachusetts, in 1912, which is sometimes known as the "Bread and Roses" strike, was inspired by a wage cut. Although on the surface, the textile industry in Lawrence was prosperous, that prosperity was founded on increasing mechanization, speeding up of production, and deskilling of labor and the use of large numbers of unskilled immigrants, many of them young women and children. Working conditions were dangerous and the majority of workers lived in overcrowded, shared apartment buildings. The mortality rate for children was 50 percent by age six and few workers of both sexes survived beyond age 25.

Divided along ethnic lines, skilled jobs were largely undertaken by native-born workers of English, German, and Irish descent, whereas unskilled workers were

Strikers in Lawrence, Massachusetts, during the mill workers' strike of 1912. (Library of Congress)

from central, southern, and eastern Europe. Many skilled workers, at least notionally, belonged to the AFL-affiliated United Textile Workers, but few paid dues, and although the IWW had been organizing there for some time, they had few members. In response to reports of the appalling conditions, the state legislature voted to reduce the working week from 56 to 54 hours on January 1, 1912, but inevitably, along with the cut in hours, employers cut wages, too. The cut led to a spontaneous walkout by the majority of workers. Because AFL membership comprised largely white, English-speaking skilled workers, they had little interest in the grievances of immigrant, unskilled workers.

Following the arrest of the original IWW organizers, Joseph Ettor and Arturo Giovannitti, on a murder charge on which they were later acquitted, IWW activists Bill Haywood and Elizabeth Gurley Flynn and other organizers were sent to Lawrence. There, they organized relief committees to provide food, medical care, and clothing, and the ethnically diverse strikers became more unified. Once it was evident that there was considerable solidarity, the employers responded forcefully, dispatching state militia to disperse strikers and break up meetings and marches. Flynn arranged for strikers' children to live with sympathizers outside Lawrence. Despite the authorities' refusal to allow this, in late February a group of women accompanied children to the railroad station where they were surrounded by police who used clubs on both women and children. Subsequent newspaper coverage inflamed the public and led to a congressional investigation. As witnesses testified to the deplorable standards in Lawrence, President Taft ordered an investigation into conditions there and across the nation.

The Paterson Silk Strike

The five-month strike that began in the silk mills in Paterson, New Jersey, in February 1913 was one of a series of industrial conflicts in the eastern states between 1909 and 1913. Unlike the majority of textile strikes, including the strike in Lawrence, Massachusetts, the previous year, the 25,000 striking workers in some 300 silk mills and dye houses did not stop work to prevent a cut in wages. The broad-silk weavers, who were quickly joined by ribbon weavers and unskilled dyers' helpers to make this the biggest strike in Paterson's history, walked out to thwart an increase in loom assignments from two to four.

The silk industry in Paterson depended to a large extent on highly skilled immigrants who knew that despite the shift from hand to power looms, the only way they could protect their skills was to continue the tradition of militancy and radicalism that had characterized Paterson for several decades. The strike in 1913 cut across boundaries of ethnicity, gender, and craft, and the unity between disparate nationalities and between crafts was central to the sense of solidarity in Paterson. Unity between workers was reinforced by the call for an eight-hour day, which, unlike the four-loom dispute that affected only the broad-silk weavers, involved all workers.

Because of their widely publicized success in organizing immigrants in Lawrence, strikers invited the Industrial Workers of the World (IWW)—Elizabeth Gurley Flynn and Bill Haywood among them—to Paterson. They were also joined by Greenwich Village intellectuals. By April, the strike had spread to mills in New Jersey, Pennsylvania, New York, and Connecticut, but after three months workers were experiencing real financial difficulties. Despite efforts at fund raising (e.g., the Paterson Pageant organized by Village intellectuals and Flynn's decision to send some 600 workers' children out of the city), the strike began to crumble seven weeks after the pageant.

Although strikers had succeeded in closing down Paterson, resisted an attempt by the AFL to undercut the strike, and defeated a police assault without resorting to violence, they ultimately could not hold out against the employers. The manufacturers' ability to outlast the strikers proved crucial. With large surpluses in warehouses and cheap labor in eastern Pennsylvania mills expanded by employers explicitly to frustrate the militancy of Paterson silk workers, manufacturers could fulfill orders from either. Although the dyers went back without achieving any concessions, ribbon weavers settled on a nine-hour day on a shop-by-shop basis, whereas broad-silk weavers received pledges regarding the four-loom system. By the end of the decade, four looms was the norm in the industry, but in Paterson, where employers were reluctant to confront workers, weavers still worked two looms. The structure of the silk industry in Paterson was further transformed by the exodus of large manufacturers, and within a decade of the strike, Paterson was dominated by the small shop. Militancy continued there, and in 1919, after a series of shop strikes, the broad-silk and ribbon weavers achieved the eight-hour day.

Stung by the negative publicity, the American Woolen Company capitulated, and they and other employers eventually agreed to the strikers' demands for a 15 percent pay increase, double time for overtime, and an amnesty for strikers. Over the next few years, however, workers in Lawrence were to lose the gains achieved in 1912 as employers gradually cut back on improved wages and conditions and sacked union activists. Despite this, the strike demonstrated that, contrary to AFL expectations, immigrant, mainly female, ethnically diverse workers could be organized.

The Seattle General Strike

Although the strike lasted less than a week, the stoppage had implications that outlasted both its duration and the decade itself. The strike—the first large-scale general walkout in the United States—was notionally about wage grievances, but it rapidly escalated into a wider dispute between the AFL and Seattle's politicians, businesses, and federal war agencies, who all believed that the dispute was central in determining the power of unions in the aftermath of World War I.

In a climate of growing labor organization throughout America, workers in the Pacific Northwest were among the most organized and radical in the country. In Seattle itself, union membership had grown from 15,000 to 60,000 in just three years, fueled by the boom in shipbuilding during the war. Despite their affiliation with the largely craft-based AFL, most locals maintained industrial links with Metal and Building and through the Seattle Central Labor Council (CLC), as well as organizing in unskilled areas, which were shunned by the AFL. Many unionists—Wobblies and Socialists among them—in the port were politically significantly to the left of the AFL. Growth in wartime shipbuilding was largely the result of orders placed by the government-created Emergency Fleet Corporation (EFC). In Seattle, the almost immediate requirement for some 35,000 extra workers created a fertile ground for labor organization, and locals achieved a significant victory in the closed shop.

An economy founded on wartime prosperity, however, was unlikely to be maintained after the 1918 armistice. Following a number of disputes and short strikes, there was a sharp downturn in orders once peace was declared. A demand by the Metal Trades Council for increased wages across the board produced an offer of a small increase for skilled workers but, perhaps in an attempt to divide the ranks, refused to discuss raises for underpaid lower-skilled workers. When the union discovered that both the government and employers were attempting to revoke wartime labor gains, the Seattle workers walked out on January 21, 1919. Some 110 locals supported calls by shipyard workers for a general strike, which began on February 6.

In addition to bringing Seattle to a halt, the strike had other, perhaps unintended, consequences in that alternative public provisions (e.g., food and milk distribution, garbage collection, and a peacekeeping force) were quickly established; however, the strikers ran into trouble in attempting to reduce the electricity supply. Under considerable pressure from business leaders, Mayor Ole Hanson declared that the strike was a Bolshevik action and announced that unless City Light was operated normally, the National Guard would run it. The AFL, concerned that the Seattle strike would hamper organizing efforts in the East, stated that the strike was unauthorized, withheld support funds, and warned that locals' charters would be revoked. As extra police and special deputies augmented federal troops, fears grew among the unions that they would be subjected to the kind of violent repression already seen elsewhere. A small number of workers began to return to work, and the general strike was over by February 11.

The wage bid was lost, and many of the gains achieved by the union (e.g., the closed shop) were also relinquished. Foreshadowing the Palmer Raids, local IWW members and editors of the left wing *Union Record* were arrested on charges of sedition. Nevertheless, from a labor perspective, it demonstrated that workers could cooperate in alternative forms of production and distribution, initiatives that grew in the months after the strike.

The Bombing of the *Los Angeles Times*

Under its flamboyant editor, Harrison Gray Otis, the *Los Angeles Times* became a powerful and influential instrument in early 20th-century California, promoting regional growth and local business. Both Otis and the paper were staunchly Republican and Otis pursued a vigorous antiunion editorial policy through the *Times*. Condemned by the AFL as "the most unfair, unscrupulous, and malignant enemy of organized labor in America" (Adams, 1966, 3), the newspaper's front page advocated "True Industrial Freedom," while both editorials and news features mirrored Otis's intransigent hostility to the union shop.

At the beginning of October 1910, during a strike that had been called to unionize the city's metal trades, the *Times* building was dynamited. Damage from the explosion and the subsequent fire led to 21 deaths and many more injuries among workers trapped in the building. A second bomb exploded at Otis's home, and a third was found at the home of the secretary of the Merchants and Manufacturers Association. In an unusual move, the mayor called in the famous private investigator William J. Burns, who was able to implicate several men in the bombing, including brothers John McNamara of the Typographical Union and James McNamara and Ortie McManigal. It was discovered that before the incident, John McNamara, at the time secretary-treasurer of the International Association of Bridge and Structural Iron Workers Union in Indianapolis, had sent his brother to Los Angeles to protest antiunion ordinances.

Despite the evidence, including bomb-making equipment discovered in John McNamara's office, some union supporters believed that the brothers had been falsely implicated in the incident in an attempt to discredit the labor movement. Because workers in Los Angeles had agitated relentlessly and had made significant gains in the two decades before the incident, evidence of labor responsi-

Los Angeles Times *building in ruins after it was dynamited during a strike to unionize the city's metal trades, on October 1, 1910. James Burns, a private investigator, implicated John and James McNamara, brothers with ties to a metal trades union, in the bombing. (Bettmann/Corbis)*

bility for the explosion would wipe out all those gains. Once McManigal was confronted with the evidence, he offered to testify in exchange for immunity. The eminent union lawyer Clarence Darrow was hired by the AFL to defend the brothers, but once he realized that their protestations of innocence were untrue, Darrow persuaded the judge to allow the brothers to withdraw their not guilty pleas. Instead of almost certain execution, John and James—who had planted the bomb—were sentenced to fifteen years and life, respectively. The McNamara case effectively signaled the end to any hopes for fairer treatment in the struggles between the Los Angeles labor movement and the employers.

The National Civic Federation
Founded in 1900 by well-known figures from business, labor, and government, the National Civic Federation (NCF) quickly became a leading agency for the arbitration of industrial disputes. Sponsors included the federation's first president, Republican senator Mark Hanna, Grover Cleveland, Samuel Gompers, who

became its first vice president, and John Mitchell. Although the NCF was a private institution, it nevertheless cooperated with federal and state agencies, usually offering its services during any major dispute between labor and employers. Hanna envisaged NCF as an alliance that would unify capital and labor against socialism, and its advocates favored moderate reform rather than radical change. At its high point, the NCF participated in the satisfactory outcomes of some of the nation's most significant strikes. Despite misgivings by the federation's full-time chairman of the executive committee, Ralph Easley, the NCF enlisted in the initiative proposed by President Taft in 1912, the Commission on Industrial Relations, established to replace outdated and ineffective mediation mechanisms and act as arbitrator in the wave of increasingly violent and insoluble labor disputes across America.

Easley was a conservative Republican who castigated the founders of the Commission on Industrial Relations as "radical preachers and charity workers" intent on promoting "a political Socialistic inquiry." (Adams, 1966, 35) By then, Easley had arrived at his own solution that would avoid any perceived left-wing bias. His program was for an appraisal of industrial relations in which he set out to justify his belief that, notwithstanding socialist orthodoxy, capitalism had favored American workers with increasing affluence. By 1914, the ambitious research enterprise comprised 25 subdivisions and employed 400 staff, working diligently, as Adams (1966, 35) notes, "to verify a preconceived conclusion."

Despite Easley's confidence, the Federation encountered significant problems that effectively halted the publication of his "evidence" of the generous consequences of capitalism until the middle of the next decade. First, labor's involvement led to internal rifts within the AFL, as socialists believed that the only way to aid workers lay in the destruction of capitalism itself. Moreover, the conclusions of the Commission's report challenged Easley's own. Because both Taft and Gompers were members of the NCF's executive council, Easley was reluctant to challenge the legislation, so Easley did not intervene when the Federation unanimously ratified Taft's proposal. Nevertheless, Easley's distrust of the whole concept of a federal commission did not prevent him from attempting to ensure that the commission's membership met with his approval.

LUDLOW

Labor Relations Explode

"Worse than the order that sent the Light Brigade into the jaws of death, worse in its effect than the Black Hole of Calcutta." Thus was the "Ludlow Camp Horror" reported in the usually moderate *New York Times*. (Adams, 1966, 146) A camp of coal miners' tents housing hundreds of women and children had been machine-gunned by state troops in Colorado. The fire that burned afterwards for

The Robber Baron of the American Imagination

The term *robber baron* is derived from 12th- and 13th-century Germany, where it was used to describe feudal lords who exacted unauthorized and exorbitant tolls from shipping. Its (pejorative) use in 19th-century America follows its application to businessmen using allegedly anticompetitive activities to accrue vast personal wealth and power. First believed to have been applied to railroad magnates in Kansas in the 1880s, the phrase has subsequently achieved some popular currency in the American imagination because of its association with the charismatic and fantastically wealthy industrial demagogues of the late 19th and early 20th centuries (e.g., John D. Rockefeller, Andrew Carnegie, Henry Ford, and J. P. Morgan).

Much controversy has been attached to the business and subsequent philanthropic activities of these men. Among numerous other discourses, a belief that their wealth and power amounted to a serious misallocation of resources prompted Thorstein Veblen's *The Theory of the Leisure Class;* however, other writers argued that such industrialists were great benefactors and humanitarians and believed that the United States would not have developed into a world power without their substantial contributions to industry, commerce, infrastructure, and trusts benefiting education and humanitarian interests. Economist Thomas J. DiLorenzo contends that such entrepreneurs as Rockefeller obtained their wealth legitimately. The true robber barons were those who manipulated politics (e.g., through government-sanctioned cartels, protective tariffs, and subsidies) for their own gain.

Nevertheless, in 1911, the Supreme Court decreed that Rockefeller's Standard Oil, which still enjoyed a 64 percent market share, originated in illegal monopoly practices and ordered it to be broken up into 34 new companies. After a scandal involving bribes to congressmen, his son, John D. Rockefeller, Jr., resigned his company directorships in an attempt to distance his philanthropic activities from commerce and finance; however, he was implicated in the furor surrounding the Ludlow Massacre, when it was discovered he had condoned and even encouraged the coercion of the state governor.

The contradictory nature of the American imagination regarding robber barons perhaps extends the imaginings into the "rags-to-riches" aspect of the American Dream. As far back as 1870, however, a survey (Zinn, 2003, 248) of more than 300 wealthy industrialists concluded that 90 percent of them had their roots in the middle and upper classes.

15 hours engulfed the whole community and provided the climax to a labor struggle that had threatened to escalate into civil war throughout the state.

After demands to the Commission on Industrial Relations for an investigation, the catastrophe was covered by the journalist George Creel. Appalled by the atrocities he discovered, Creel called a mass meeting where in front of a crowd of 10,000, he castigated the governor. He saved his most vitriolic comments for those "traitors to the people, accessories to the murder of babes" (Adams, 1966, 146): the Rockefellers, whose family controlled 40 percent of the state's largest mining company, the Colorado Fuel and Iron Company. Material gathered by Creel was then presented to the Commission, which held a short session on the disaster after further entreaties by the humanitarian Jane Addams. Although the Commission concluded that Rockefeller had been complicit in resisting unionization, and in various corrupt practices, his contrite attitude afterward and the project he established to improve conditions and benefit workers—despite having no provisions for union recognition or collective bargaining—appeared to deflect criticism. The strike dragged on as scabs were brought in to maintain production. It ended in defeat for the union after fifteen months of hardship.

The Background to the Strike

The events leading up to the massacre began with a strike at the Colorado Fuel and Iron Company (CFI), owners of a large tract of mineral-bearing land in the southern part of the state. Controlled by the vast financial Rockefeller dynasty, and dominating its smaller competitors, the CFI was sufficiently remote geographically to have imposed a modern sort of medieval feudalism on its 30,000 employees, the majority of whom lived in camps far away from major towns. Miners were compelled to rent shacks that were often no better than hovels because the company, which owned both dwellings and land, frustrated any attempt at home ownership. The unsanitary conditions in the settlements and the absence of freshwater (mains water was considered too expensive by the company) meant that disease was rife. Workers were reluctant to speak out because they risked losing both job and home.

Until the custom was made illegal, workers were paid in scrip redeemable only in company stores, which could charge extortionate prices because they had a monopoly. In addition to these tyrannies, the CFI dictated policy on education (in selecting and dismissing teachers) and religion (in firing ministers it considered "unsuitable") and exercised a policy of censoring movies and reading material it considered seditious, including Darwin's *Origin of the Species*. The company wielded enormous political power and reports of corrupt practices surfaced regularly. Although the company claimed to have cut back on its political activities, the Commission discovered that attempts had been made during the 1914 gubernatorial campaign to influence a Prohibition amendment so that a law-and-order platform would be accepted more readily, thus assisting the prosecution of strikers and unionists. In the same year, following the discovery of a great many illegal and fraudulent practices, Colorado's Supreme Court excluded all returns from the CFI precincts from the count.

Other corrupt practices uncovered by the Commission included coercing prostitutes to contribute money to the party to carry on their trade and influencing the election of judges and sheriffs and the selection of jurors. Colorado also had a mine death rate that was double that of any other state, yet for ten years before the Commission, coroner's juries blamed workers for 89 out of 90 accidents and seldom heard the testimonies of miners or their families.

Although the United Mine Workers had attempted to organize the mines since 1900, they were continually thwarted in their efforts by management. In 1913, however, the union began a concerted campaign, which resulted in mass enrollments from miners who threatened an immediate walkout. First, though, officials attempted to negotiate a settlement, listing a raft of demands that included an eight-hour day, compulsory imposition of safety regulations, withdrawal of armed guards, elimination of company wages scrip, union recognition, and numerous other benefits. The company, whose lead was followed by smaller employers, categorically refused to discuss the demands, believing that negotiation would lead to the infiltration of the company by "disreputable agitators, socialists, and anarchists." (Adams, 1966, 152)

The Strike

In September, faced with little alternative, between 40 percent and 100 percent of miners in each mine—around 10,000 in all—walked out. Families left behind them their company-owned houses, loading their belongings onto carts and headed for union camps, where they lived in canvas-covered pits—determination regarded by the Commission as evidence of the depth of discontent felt by workers. The strike rapidly escalated as armed guards from outside the state were recruited and "troops" hired by CFI were positioned in trenches and equipped with searchlights and machine guns. For their part, workers had already armed themselves surreptitiously, but now the union bought weapons openly, storing them where strikebreakers were known to pass.

As tensions rose, outbreaks of serious violence led to deaths on both sides and Ludlow rapidly became a focus for acute disorder as attacks and counter-attacks went on through the night. Following the call-out of the National Guard and a decree by Governor Ammons that guardsmen should under no circumstances assist in the introduction of strikebreakers, an uneasy peace returned to the community. Ammons soon revoked this order, however, apparently believing that he had exceeded the law, and violence erupted once more. In an effort to restore civil liberties, the aged Mary "Mother" Jones, a UMW organizer and activist with years of experience in some of the most dangerous labor disputes and territories, attempted to visit Ludlow, but was deported on her arrival at the town of Trinidad. Two more attempts resulted in her incarceration in a hospital

Portrait of men, women, and children at the UMW camp for coal miners on strike against CFI in Ludlow, Las Animas County, Colorado, 1913–1914. (Denver Public Library/Western History Collection, Bartosch, X-60475)

for nine weeks and in a cell for 26 days, each time without warrant. Hostility among strikers was aroused still further by the tactics of the National Guard—particularly the replacements for the original contingent—as reports of lootings, robberies, and the protection of scabs circulated around the camps.

The Violence

The worst violence occurred on April 20, 1914. Ludlow was a large tented community housing many miners, their families, and strike sympathizers, and there had been numerous raids by the militia prior to the massacre. It is difficult to determine which side fired the first shots, but very soon a battle began, and it continued across the entire colony for the next 12 hours. During this, there were numerous deaths and serious injuries, both among strikers and militia, as well as among the women and children sheltering in the tents.

Fire then broke out in three of the largest tents and swept through the community with alarming speed, killing at least 2 women and 11 children. A military commission investigating the disaster heard that troops themselves had been responsible for assisting the blaze and that burning and looting had been deliberate. Although it was found that many of the militiamen were recently enlisted civilians whose records and background were less-than-thoroughly investigated, it was conceded that they should have been under tighter jurisdiction by regulars. Further cross-examination revealed that most of the troops at Ludlow were employed by CFI and even Major Boughton, their direct commander, received an annual retainer from the Colorado Mine Owners' Association.

After Ludlow, the situation degenerated still further as for 10 days, a workers' army intent on vengeance swept across the state, killing guardsmen and strikebreakers and burning CFI resources. Governor Ammons finally caved in, appealing to President Wilson for the U.S. Army to quell what had now become a civil war. On April 28, 1914, several regiments of federal troops marched in to Colorado and an investigation into the disaster began.

Investigations

After two weeks in Denver questioning participants on all sides of the disaster, the U.S. Commission on Industrial Relations moved east to New York to question CFI's representative, John D. Rockefeller, Jr. Apparently indifferent to the hostility of the mostly left-wing audience, Rockefeller denied direct responsibility for managerial policy in Colorado, claiming that his focus was the financial affairs. He also refuted charges that he influenced CFI's attitude toward labor, stating that he was not opposed to unions and was unaware of the company's refusal to recognize the UMW until after the strike had begun. Admitting that he had not visited the company for 10 years, the young Rockefeller claimed total ignorance of any of the day-to-day details or the overall policy, and he appeared genuinely contrite about the situation that occurred. Rockefeller appeared to have won over almost everyone involved in the commission, even the most hard-line activists.

He had not, however, convinced the commission chairman, Frank Walsh, whose researchers had assembled a growing file of letters from Rockefeller and company executives. The contents of the correspondence convinced Walsh that additional hearings were required. At the hearing in Washington, despite protestations from Rockefeller of his ignorance of strike issues, the Commission was told of letters from CFI executive board chairman L. M. Bowers describing the exact causes of the dispute and the company's policy on nonrecognition. Rockefeller's replies indicated that he was in complete agreement with the company and, further, that he had sanctioned CFI's coercion of Governor Ammons. Once the strike was underway, Rockefeller personally funded a propaganda campaign against the UMW, during which the country was flooded with pamphlets and newspaper advertisements. The most damning item, Walsh revealed that Rockefeller had collaborated with a public relations expert, Ivy L. Lee, in ghostwriting a letter that presented an entirely partisan view of the strike for Ammons to send to President Wilson.

Walsh was relentless in his pursuit of what he considered to be the true facts, brushing aside criticism from Commissioner Harriman, for example, that he was too severe. Newspapers across the nation carried extensive coverage of the sessions. The anti-Commission, largely conservative press condemned Walsh's methods and his perceived bias unequivocally, but radical and labor publications and the midwestern press praised Walsh, noting that he had refused to be cowed by Rockefeller's wealth and power, and that he had merely presented conclusive evidence of the millionaire's complicity in the horrific conflict. Although Rockefeller had been "turned inside out" (Adams, 1966, 171) in Walsh's own words during the hearing, he appeared afterward as contrite as he had been after the New York sessions. The events had inspired in him a new conception of "the kinship of humanity" (Adams, 1966, 172) and signified a sharp change in his attitude toward labor.

In September, he visited Colorado, inspecting the mines and talking to laborers. The apparently reformed Rockefeller announced a radical program that would benefit workers, the Colorado Industrial Plan, which promised and achieved improvements in housing, education, and recreation. The project also abolished company stores and established grievance procedures, while elected worker representatives would liaise with management to improve working conditions and safety. There was nothing in the proposal, however, regarding recognition or agreement on a policy of collective bargaining.

Responding to all this with undisguised and universal hostility, organized labor in the shape of UMW president Frank Hayes called it "pure paternalism" and "benevolent feudalism." (Adams, 1966, 172) Meanwhile, the strike continued as CFI managed to recruit enough scabs to stay in operation. UMW officials still suffered prosecution, and when management dismissed all the peace offers, the union acknowledged defeat. For 15 months, the workers had endured starvation, brutality, and death and accepted the CFI's only concession, a company union.

THE IWW AND SYNDICALISM

Unorganized Workers Unite

"The working class and the employing class have nothing in common. . . . Between these two classes a struggle must go on until the workers of the world organize as a class, take possession of the earth and the machinery of production, and abolish the wage system." (Burtt, 1980, 144–145) This was the preamble to the 1905 constitution of the IWW and characterized the growth of radicalism among unorganized workers and their fervent wish for direct action to achieve a share of prosperity in an expanding economy.

Working the Docks with the Wobblies

In the early part of the 20th century, segregation of African Americans and whites permeated every element of society. Industry was no exception and unions reflected the racial bias of industry, carrying out a policy of exclusion and discrimination. The single exception was the IWW, who, governed by their allegiance to colorblind organizing, advocated statutorily endorsed, racially assimilated unionism as a matter of fundamental conviction. Although the policy had mixed results, one territory (the Philadelphia waterfront) is an example of successful integration that, although the barricades were eventually restored, achieved the apparently impossible: whites and African Americans in one organization in which racial differences were eliminated at both the leadership and grassroots level.

Long-term employer obstinacy and antilabor shipping organizations meant that waterfront unionization was late in coming to Philadelphia, resulting in a more catholic workforce with a high proportion of ethnic diversity among its ranks. Delayed organization also meant that dockside workers were not forced to endure the discriminatory customs that resulted in more homogenous workforces in such places as Boston or New York. Without unions, and thus without a tradition of exclusion, different races and colors could compete equally for jobs.

In 1913, dockworkers demanded a standard rate of pay for all waterfront workers, reduced hours, and union recognition. They were led in this by the IWW, who acknowledged that they would have to bring African Americans around to their cause to succeed. They declared that each ethnic group should be represented on all groups responsible for making decisions, and this, combined with their commitment to racial integration and an emphasis on class solidarity rather than racial victimization, encouraged African Americans to look favorably on the IWW. Such explicit demonstrations of integration were in marked contrast to the racial status quo (the AFL had accepted fewer than 200 African Americans), and the organization consequently attracted several hundred longshoremen, white as well as African American.

The recently chartered, IWW-affiliated Local 8 then initiated a policy whereby African American and white officers alternated monthly in top positions, whereas day-to-day activities were directed by at least one African American secretary. In 1916 and 1917, strikes and violent clashes occurred as African American strikebreakers were brought in. Although this began to undermine IWW interracial solidarity, a temporary respite came with increased work from wartime shipping. After the war, however, the severe decline in work and the influx of southern African American migrants with few loyalties to, or experience of, unions swelled local membership to a worrying extent. Forced to raise initiation fees in an attempt to control the flow and shift the balance of power in a saturated market back from employer to worker, the local was twice suspended from the IWW for transgressing IWW rules on initiation fees and for loading a ship with military resources allegedly intended for White forces in Russia. In the postwar climate of increasing racial tensions, and anxious to avoid potential discrimination, African American workers began to migrate to the now all-African American Local 1116 of the International Longshoremen's Association (ILA), attracted by its ethnic solidarity. By the mid-1920s, Local 8's membership had become seriously eroded and the ILA became the port's sole negotiating body.

In a period in which the atmosphere in the country was one of optimism and self-belief, this increase in militancy may have seemed paradoxical but was, nevertheless, an accurate reflection of the extent to which the welfare of the unskilled masses was being disregarded. As increasing numbers of American and immigrant mass production workers felt that their interests were overlooked by the AFL, their frustration provided a fertile breeding ground for the creation of a new, and radical, labor movement whose most pressing aim was the dissolution of the wage system and the defeat of capitalism. The constituency for the new organization included socialists from the unorganized industrial workers in the East joined by a disparate group of migratory workers—loggers, miners, and harvest hands—in the West.

Emerging from a meeting in Chicago in 1905, the "Wobblies," as they came to be called, agreed on little except their mutual antagonism and disdain for the tactics of the AFL. Central to this group—which, with 27,000 members, was by far the largest union was the Western Federation of Miners (W.F.M.), whose leaders turned to militant socialism, partly the result of a long period of violent strikes characterized by extremely aggressive retaliatory action by employers. Socialists like Eugene V. Debs and Daniel de Leon represented the other main group. The IWW was, in the main, established by individuals, rather than organizations, and largely by characters who had courted controversy throughout their careers. These included William D. ("Big Bill") Haywood, who represented the W.F.M.; William E. Trautmann, a militant leader of the United Brewery Workers and editor of its German-language journal; and "Mother" Jones, a spirited and doughty 75-year-old dissident.

The organization was founded on the doctrine of inclusiveness: "One Big Union" encompassing workers without regard for trade, skill, race, or ethnicity. In contrast to the high union dues levied by the AFL, fees were kept low so that no one would be barred on account of poverty. From the start, the Wobblies attracted the derision of Samuel L. Gompers, president of the AFL, whose view that incompatibility among the leaders would soon lead to the downfall of the organization appeared to be borne out by factional disputes over whether action should be political or economic. Following the withdrawal of the W.F.M in 1907, the remaining members supported the overthrow of capitalism by direct economic action and, over time, embraced increasingly revolutionary doctrines. "One Big Union," they believed, was the only effective weapon in the class struggle. Day-to-day assaults on poor conditions and wages were merely preliminary tactics in the overall battle that would lead to a general strike and the downfall of capitalism.

Because temporary, unskilled, migratory workers were generally uninterested in political action—and in any case, seldom had the vote—these were the workers for whom the IWW had the greatest appeal. Often single and rootless, and usually poorly paid, they believed themselves casualties of a deliberately exploitative economy. In the East, the IWW performed an English-speaking role

Industrial Workers of the World (IWW) demonstrate in New York City, April 1914. The IWW is known as one of the most radical unions in U.S. history. (Library of Congress)

for immigrant workers, particularly those in textile factories neglected by the small and moderate United Textile Workers union.

Although IWW membership was never particularly large (around 60,000 at its height), its importance was its radical leadership. Throughout the decade, the organization became associated—usually unfairly—with violence, frequently as protagonists in the many strikes of the period. Leaders, including Haywood, who had remained with the IWW after the withdrawal of the W.F.M., were prepared to support unorganized workers, and "free-speech" fights and strikes broke out across the country, including perhaps the IWW's most significant victory, for textile workers in Lawrence, Massachusetts, in 1912.

Although the victory and the potential for still more aggressive tactics and sabotage caused alarm among employers and the AFL alike, these anxieties proved baseless. Rather than a portent of a workers' revolution, Lawrence, and the next strike in which the IWW took part, in Paterson, New Jersey, proved to be signals of the organization's decline. The aftermath also demonstrated how much more dominant—and probably aggressive and underhanded—the employers were. In the remaining years of the decade, the Wobblies participated in a great many minor strikes, many of which were brutally put down, including one in Everett that resulted in seven deaths.

When war broke out in Europe, the IWW proclaimed that they would refuse to fight for anything other than industrial freedom. Following America's entry in 1917, this position was played down, but the organization refused to end its commitment to strike, even temporarily. Public reaction was predictably hostile, and the IWW was damned as "unpatriotic, pro-German, and treasonable." (Dulles and Dubofsky, 1993, 212) Public, employer, and press criticism was expressed in the Espionage Act of 1917, and in September, raids of IWW headquarters began across the country, in which federal agents arrested leaders and confiscated goods. In subsequent mass trials, many Wobblies—including Haywood—were convicted of sedition and conspiracy and received sentences of up to 20 years, often on shaky and contradictory evidence. Few explicit criminal acts were proven, but in the hysterical climate, jingoistic courts were little interested in definitive proof of guilt.

In the absence of any action by the authorities, vigilante groups meted out summary justice in the form of whippings, tar-and-featherings, and, in at least two cases, lynchings. Strikers, who often had only tenuous links with the IWW, were everywhere subjected to brutality and unfair treatment. As the organization gradually unraveled, many of its leaders left, including Haywood, who jumped bail and went to Soviet Russia. With increasing mechanization of agriculture and changing economic conditions, the numbers of migratory workers at the core of the organization gradually declined, while the Communist Party of America attracted many of the radical socialists as IWW policy began to shift toward less revolutionary strategies. After 10 years, the membership stood at around 15,000 (less than 1 percent of that of the AFL).

Despite its relatively low—and constantly fluctuating—membership and its inconsistent strike activity, the IWW was both important and influential. Working conditions in industries comprised of large numbers of migratory workers did improve as a result of IWW activity, and the organization managed to focus the nation's attention on the privations of huge numbers of unskilled workers, stimulating industrial unionism in the process. Class struggle failed to eliminate the wage system and bring down capitalism, but it did, for a time, shake reactionary labor leaders out of their self-satisfied attitude and the notion of direct action was influential elsewhere in the labor movement. The Wobblies achieved a mythic reputation, too, in the organization's slogans and songs, particularly those of Joe Hill, who was executed after his conviction for murder in 1915.

Syndicalism

When William E. Trautmann, editor of the *Brauer Zeitung,* official organ of the United Brewery Workers, and the driving force behind the establishment of the IWW, stated in the Industrial Union Manifesto that "the document is based on the same principles as organized labor in Continental Europe," he meant explicitly the organization of labor under "revolutionary syndicalism." (Foner, 1965, 19) Although it is possible to dismiss Trautmann's comments as simply one individual's belief, he nevertheless played a leading role in the proceedings leading to the IWW's establishment.

Syndicalism can be defined in various ways. William Z. Foster, a committed syndicalist and union leader, defined it as "that tendency in the labor movement to confine the revolutionary class struggle of the workers in the economic field. . . . Its fighting organization is the trade union; its basic method of class warfare is the strike, with the general strike as the revolutionary weapon; and its revolutionary goal is the setting up of a trade union 'state' to conduct industry." (Foner, 1965, 20) This definition mirrors French revolutionary or anarchosyndicalism, which emerged in the 1890s when anarchists penetrated the unions and which combined trade unionism, Marxism, and anarchism.

These aims appealed particularly to discontented Marxists; by stopping production, the general strike would destroy the power of the capitalist class, thus allowing the working class to appropriate industry, and with the dissolution of the state, unions would then undertake production and economic management. Thus, the trade union, or *syndicat,* would be a weapon in the enduring war on capitalism.

Phrases like "sabotage" and "direct action" almost inevitably associated syndicalism with revolution; however, few theorists espoused violence, with most believing it to be prejudicial to working-class morality and preferring instead to use passive resistance and the ceding, rather than the seizing, of power. "Sabotage" could assume an almost infinite number of meanings, from destroying machinery to a deliberate reduction in efficiency, thus restricting output; however, most embraced the notion of "no compromise" with their traditional foe, the employer. The principles of European organized labor, an authentically militant working-class movement, and a united front were, Trautmann believed, the foundations on which American syndicalism would be based. Although European syndicalism was influential, economic and political developments in the United States (the hardships, despair, and compromises of American life) brought the organization into being. American labor's antipolitical inclination predated the IWW, and enormous numbers of disfranchised immigrants and transient workers alienated by far-reaching corruption in politics, regressive AFL policies, and socialists who increasingly felt that political reform and the franchise were ineffective in achieving immediate benefits for workers or for establishing a socialist republic were central to its emergence.

Foster believed, however, that these factors led some to conclude—wrongly—that politics could be relinquished and all efforts directed instead into a revolutionary labor union. Such advocates ingenuously believed that the workers, combined in "One Big Union," could soon strike and destroy capitalism, subsequently governing the new workers' republic solely by labor organization. For most of the decade, perceptions of, and allegations against, the IWW focused on its commitment to violent revolution. Although much of the vilification—by employers and the AFL alike—was local and used to foment hostility in a specific area, two accusations were repeatedly leveled nationally at the organization: first, that its origins were foreign, derived from syndicalism, Marxism, and anarchism, and, second, that the IWW was dedicated to violence as a means to an end.

Although several of those instrumental in shaping the early IWW were heavily influenced by French syndicalism, there are significant differences between the two. Whereas the French believed in working within a union framework, the IWW established themselves as a rival to the AFL, declining to deal with unions thus affiliated and repudiating the creed of "boring from within." When the organization rejected that concept, Foster—arguing that using existing unions was fundamental to syndicalism—founded the Syndicalist League of North America, thus distinguishing the IWW from syndicalism. In addition, even though French syndicalism assimilated craft unionism, the IWW—excluding the "mixed locals" —organized solely on an industrial union basis.

Although there were no close links between French syndicalists and the IWW after 1908, the organization's journals persisted in reporting European events, whereas several IWW leaders continued to assert that the organization was constituted along French lines and that IWW tactics went beyond those of the French. Nevertheless, most members were attracted to the IWW because it offered an apparent solution to American problems, and not because of any syndicalist doctrine. After Haywood visited the Labor and Socialist Congress of the Second International in Copenhagen in 1910, French syndicalism proved even more influential. Haywood consulted with the French there and the pamphlet *Sabotage* was distributed following his return. In 1911 and 1912, the *Industrial Worker* and *Solidarity* published articles on French syndicalism and discourses by leaders and members on direct action, sabotage, and the general strike.

On most basic issues—the overthrow of capitalism and the political state by direct, not political action by the working class and that trade unions would henceforth own and manage the means of production—there was little difference between the French and the IWW. *Solidarity,* however, continued to emphasize that the IWW was specifically a product of American circumstances. Evidence of the influence of French syndicalism was, Foner believes, evidence "only of the international solidarity of the working class." (1965, 160)

The IWW and Sabotage

In one area, the influence of French syndicalism was particularly evident. The promotion of sabotage by the IWW was perhaps the single most controversial doctrine. Following early denials of its use, by 1910 sabotage was an integral tactic in the class war waged by the IWW. The first use of the word by the IWW appears to have been in 1910 when *Solidarity* reported on a strike by Chicago clothing workers. Inspired by French railroad workers, *Industrial Worker* proclaimed that "sabotage means in a general way, going on *strike without*

Arturo Giovannitti and Joseph J. Ettor in handcuffs, accused of fomenting disorder as organizers of the Industrial Workers of the World, 1912. (Library of Congress)

striking." (Foner, 1965, 160; italics added), encouraging American workers to follow the French example. Articles promulgating the use of sabotage began to appear regularly in the Wobbly press in 1912. In both editorials and cartoons (depicting the habitual trademark Sab-Cat: the wooden shoe or *sabot,* which was erroneously thought to be the origin of sabotage, alongside the black cat), propaganda exhorted workers to sabotage the means of production as a way of taking the class war back to the capitalists.

Other pamphlets and articles followed, including, in 1913, praise from *Industrial Worker* regarding the introduction to Émile Pouget's *Sabotage,* written in prison by Arturo Giovannitti, one of the IWW leaders of the Lawrence strike. Despite the published material, the IWW itself was cautious about formal acceptance of the strategy as a legitimate weapon. Even though individual Wobblies had defended its use, no official IWW group did so until 1914, when the ninth IWW convention ratified a motion recommending that workers cut back on production by slowing down and sabotage. With this endorsement, the IWW became the first and, at that time, the only labor group in America officially to advocate sabotage.

Sabotage did not necessarily equate with violence, however, because the only form advocated by the convention was that "all rush work should be done in a wrong manner." (Foner, 1965, 161) The IWW generally claimed that sabotage meant merely the elimination of efficiency, "soldiering" (i.e., malingering or loafing) on the job, or temporarily disabling, rather than destroying, a machine. It was also explicitly targeted at property rather than persons. Official IWW advice was often contradictory, though, ranging from temporarily incapacitating machinery to violent destruction of property, whereas some individuals unreservedly advocated the more extreme forms of sabotage.

Although its exact meaning might have been vague, the IWW was unequivocal on the grounds for its use. Four main reasons were proffered to justify its use: sabotage curtailed capitalist profits and thus was an assault on the system itself; because capitalists "sabotaged" the public and the workers (e.g., by cheating on contracts or adulterating foodstuffs), they themselves were culpable; it was the only weapon available to exploited workers; and last, it was the most appropriate form of striking because walking out would jeopardize workers' pay or their jobs. Although there was much sloganeering, the amount of sabotage the Wobblies carried out is debatable. In trial after trial and in the course of much research, little evidence of actual sabotage emerged, and the reputation for sabotage seems largely to have been the result of public hysteria, which in some cases was inflamed by members themselves.

Although a great deal was written and spoken about the violence allegedly inherent in the organization, and strikes were frequently associated with violence, the IWW hoped to achieve its goals through other means, not least because they realized that violence generally led to the forces of the establishment being organized against them. Although some leaders advocated violence and others the general strike, all were agreed that the capitalist system would use force to overwhelm the workers' struggle. The predicament was how to counter capitalist violence. Whereas one faction favored passive resistance, there were others who made it explicit that in resisting violence, they meant only unprovoked violence. Capitalist-provoked violence would be countered with violence by the working class.

The IWW argued that employers actually benefited from the presence of the organization because without their leadership, workers would resort to the tactics of the mob, retaliating against the hired gunmen and thugs of the employers. Although the Wobblies appropriated some anarchist tactics, they were at pains to distance themselves from the more extreme anarchist strategies, acknowledging that the murder of capitalists and public figures would not bring about the downfall of the system. Most IWW publications distinguished between anarchism and their brand of subversion, observing that anarchism was based on the individual, whereas the IWW supported the "collective ownership of the means of production and distribution by the working class." (Foner, 1965, 166)

Even though violence was not wholly proscribed as a legitimate tactic, it was not seen as the principal method. Neither was it regarded as the tactic that would necessarily guarantee success. Instead, the defeat of capitalism would be achieved by the organization of labor strength—mass action and the withdrawal of labor power would immobilize the production of wealth and "achieve a non-violent transition to the new society." (Foner, 1965, 167) Haywood predicted that "it will be a revolution, but it will be a bloodless revolution." (Ibid.)

IWW and Immigrant Workers

As part of the IWW's inclusive policy, in 1907, the organization made a concerted attempt after its second convention to organize immigrant workers. Foreign language pamphlets were circulated, and, following the campaign, the *Industrial Union Bulletin* reported that positive results were being achieved, particularly among Polish workers. Among other initiatives, foreign-language branches were established, Jewish and Italian organizers were appointed and those who could speak foreign languages consistently pursued, and relations were established with the Roumanian (sic) Syndicalist General Commission in Bucharest so that workers intending to emigrate to the United States would be made aware of the high union dues levied by the AFL and its exclusionary policy toward foreign-born workers.

Given the hardships and injustices of life as a migratory worker, many were attracted, at least temporarily, to the revolutionary program of the IWW, which they saw as their "single hope of rehabilitation and human dignity." (Foner, 1965, 120) For much the same reason, the organization appealed to unskilled immigrant workers in the East and Midwest. The IWW referred to workers with a settled home life and a single job as the "home guard." The differences between the agitators in the West—mainly men—and the mass production workers in the East, whose numbers comprised a significant proportion of women, led some to believe that two separate organizations had resulted from these disparities. Eastern members were typically foreign-born and were less likely to have retained links to the old country, whereas those in the West were mainly native Americans. Despite their differences, both had found that the AFL were more interested in skilled craftsmen and thereby turned to the IWW, which provided a rather more dignified environment for immigrants derided by both the public and the press. Moreover, because few immigrants were naturalized, the emphasis on direct, rather than political, action lent the organization added appeal.

As the organization intensified its efforts to attract immigrant workers, *Industrial Worker* and *Solidarity* frequently published advice for organizers concerning how potential members should be approached, cautioning them not to regard immigrants as inferior because of their inability to speak English. As a result, the IWW achieved a reputation as a mouthpiece for foreign-born workers.

Although the orthodox press acknowledged that the Wobblies appealed to immigrants, they maintained that this was more a consequence of the immigrants' inferior intelligence than the result of conditions that fomented unrest and motivated workers to look for an advocate. During the decade, then, the IWW engaged mainly with those workers disdained by the AFL—the lowest paid and the most ill-used. In a decade when $800 per year was judged to be the minimum required to provide a decent standard of living for a family, around 25 percent of adult male wage earners received less than $400, whereas some 50 percent made less than $600.

The IWW maintained its policy toward immigrant workers toward those nationalities from southern, central, and eastern Europe, who had been routinely marginalized, and, unlike almost every labor organization up until then in America, also toward organizing Chinese, Japanese, and Mexican workers. IWW literature was translated into Japanese and Chinese, ridiculing the notion of a "yellow peril." They were particularly critical of Pacific Coast socialists for accepting the capitalist fabrication that the Japanese and Chinese were an inferior people whose very presence would cause a decline in American standards of living. The *Industrial Worker* scorned Californian socialists who supported Asian exclusion while espousing Marxist views. Establishing the actual number of Asian members during the decade is difficult, but between 1910 and 1913, the IWW press regularly celebrated the inclusion of Japanese, Chinese, and Filipinos in IWW locals, suggesting that the claim of inclusiveness toward all nationalities had some foundation.

Some of the most protracted and violent strikes that took place in America during the decade were in industries where unskilled immigrants comprised a high proportion of the work force. In all of these (e.g., Lawrence, Everett, and Paterson), the IWW supported workers in attempting to achieve better conditions and higher wages and, not least, to eliminate discrimination against foreign-born workers by employers and the AFL. Although conditions and wages did improve slightly, few of these strikes produced any lasting benefits. By 1920, the influence of the IWW had declined considerably as unskilled immigrant workers were gradually co-opted into the mass production and mechanized system, leaving many with little representation other than the organization that had neglected them so consummately—the AFL.

Free Speech

From its formation, the IWW engaged in free speech fights to achieve the right of labor organizers to speak without restraint to workers. Because IWW ideologies were frequently at odds with those communities that perceived the growth of unions as a threat, local ordinances and police persecution were often employed to restrict free speech. A commonly used IWW tactic in areas of free speech fights was to use large numbers of protesters, whose deliberately illegal activities would inevitably result in their arrest. Once the jails and courts

The *Little Red Songbook*

From the early beginnings of the IWW, songs played a central role in broadcasting the message—"to fan the flames of discontent"—of the One Big Union. Many of these were collected together in the *Little Red Songbook*, first published in 1909. It included songs written by several of the best-known activists in the organization. Of these, Joe Hill contributed such songs as "The Preacher and the Slave," a parody of the Salvation Army hymn, "In the Sweet Bye and Bye." The song includes the first known use of the phrase, "pie in the sky," a reference to the preaching style of the Army who, Wobblies believed, were more concerned with saving souls than filling stomachs. The lyrics and tunes for labor songs by Hill and others were frequently borrowed from other popular songs simply because they were familiar, memorable, and easy to sing along. Hill's "The Tramp," for example, took the tune from "Tramp, Tramp, Tramp, the Boys Are Marching." Others include "Rebel Girl," written for Elizabeth Gurley Flynn, the IWW organizer, "There is Power in a Union," and "Casey Jones—Union Scab." Hill also wrote "John Golden and the Lawrence Strike," which appeared in the 1912 edition of the songbook. Using a tune appropriated from a song popular in Sunday schools and skid row missions, the song pillories the activities of an AFL official who tried to gain control of the strike.

The hobo and songwriter T-Bone Slim, the pseudonym of Matti Valentine Huhta, is widely regarded as one of the organization's leading songwriters and columnists. Among his works are "The Popular Wobbly"—based on the popular song, "The Girls They Go Wild, Simply Wild Over Me"—"The Mysteries of a Hobo's Life," and "The Lumberjack's Prayer." Early editions of the songbook included many of the labor songs that have endured to the present day (e.g., "The Red Flag," "The Internationale"). Perhaps the best-known IWW song in the songbook is the union anthem, "Solidarity Forever," which began life as a poem by the labor activist Ralph Chaplin and uses the melody of "The Battle Hymn of the Republic."

World War I created an acute nationalistic frenzy and the ideology of the IWW could not withstand the hysteria of the Red Scare. The messages in the songs (e.g., collective, direct action and solidarity in the face of capitalism) were seen by many as too closely linked to Bolshevism, and for a while, the songs fell from public favor, too. Nevertheless, the *Little Red Songbook* has remained in print to the present day.

were overwhelmed with protesters—and as more activists arrived—smaller communities often had little alternative other than to quash their embargo on free speech.

The fight that took place in San Diego that began in February 1912 was typical of these conflicts, although it was more violent than most; hostility between the IWW and the authorities had gone on at least since 1910 when a number of IWW activists were arrested for taking their campaign to the streets.

The organization concentrated their efforts on the Stingaree, an ethnically diverse, working-class area of San Diego, where there was also a number of cheap hotels, saloons, and brothels, as well as a "soapbox row" where orators of all persuasions spoke. In late 1910, the police had closed Germania Hall where IWW speakers had hoped to celebrate the martyrs of the 1887 Haymarket Riot. In early 1912, after petitions and protests from property owners and preeminent citizens ostensibly concerned about public disorder and a violent incident involving an off-duty constable, the city passed an ordinance calling for the immediate suspension of the right to free speech in the center of the city.

As arrests of those detained for violating the ordinance increased, the jails rapidly filled up and police resorted to placing pro–free speech detainees in drunk tanks. In atrocious conditions, inmates were subjected to police brutality. As the conflict became increasingly violent, the IWW called for still more supporters to converge on San Diego so that the legal system would become clogged. Incited by hostile editorials, groups of vigilantes transported protesters to the county line and intercepted incoming trains to prevent activists from reaching the city. Finally, the state intervened and Colonel Weinstock, the investigating commissioner, determined that the arrests and restrictions were unlawful, but that the IWW had erred in persisting with an activist approach. Although there was a temporary lull in the conflict, the violence flared up again after the death—apparently at the hands of the police—of an IWW activist.

There was to be no satisfactory conclusion to the free speech fight: By fall, the vigilantes had subjected the majority of pro–free speech activists to terrible brutality or had chased them out of the city altogether. The IWW did not return to San Diego until 1914.

THE IMPACT OF INDUSTRIALIZATION AND LABOR DISCONTENT IN THE 1910s

The decade opened with massive strikes in New York and other cities by garment workers fighting sweatshop conditions and ended with the great steel strike of 1919. In this decade, many of the industrial innovations that were to inform production for much of the century can also be seen. Production technology at Ford created the template for technical development in mass production industries. The transformation was managed and exemplified in one company, which, in the space of a few years, masterminded the evolution from craft to mechanization. The advances at Ford in 1913 and 1914 were momentous in automobile manufacture in creating "Fordism" (the term that denotes both the production system and its associated labor system), and they transformed the world, too. The growth of Ford also represents a new era in the manufacture of consumer durables in America. The continual reduction in price meant that the Model T was affordable by millions previously unable to afford an automobile. In democratizing travel, the automobile became less a luxury than an everyday commodity.

In the constant drive for efficiency, Ford workers were as much mechanized as the processes they operated, and the inevitable consequence was a high turnover of labor. Increased mechanization and mass production inevitably led to increased labor discontent as workers responsible for perhaps a single process or component became progressively more distant from craft skills. Along with poor and often unsafe working conditions and practices and the increasing exploitation of labor, this meant that the organization of labor became a critical issue during the decade. Ford was not

Demonstrator wears an Industrial Workers of the World hat card that says "Bread or Revolution," April 13, 1914. (Library of Congress)

unusual in refusing to recognize unions, and as manufacturers prospered, workers failed to reap the benefits of economic growth. Industrial accidents increased while tragedies (e.g., the Triangle Shirtwaist Factory fire and the Ludlow massacre) may have been worse in terms of loss of life, but the strikes, unrest, and violence that accompanied them came to define the decade.

Some industrial consensus (e.g., the Protocols of Peace) did emerge during the decade, and such organizations as the WTUL, which matured during the 1910s, and the IWW gave workers a degree of autonomy and control hitherto absent in industry; however, increasing mechanization in industries typically associated with IWW membership (e.g., logging and agriculture) and the trials and deportations that resulted from the 1917 Espionage Act ultimately led to its decline. Nevertheless, the IWW was decisive and influential in helping to improve working conditions in industries with large numbers of migratory workers, and the organization concentrated the nation's attention on the hardships of huge numbers of unskilled workers, galvanizing industrial unionism in the process. IWW activism failed to abolish the wage system and bring down capitalism, but it did, for a while, jolt reactionary labor leaders out of their complacency, and their policy of direct action also inspired others in the labor movement.

Real wages, particularly for unskilled workers, did begin to rise after 1917, and apart from in 1915, union membership increased year on year. Despite these gains, where employers wielded enough power (e.g., in steel), organized labor made no progress. With the massive steel strike of 1919, the decade ended as

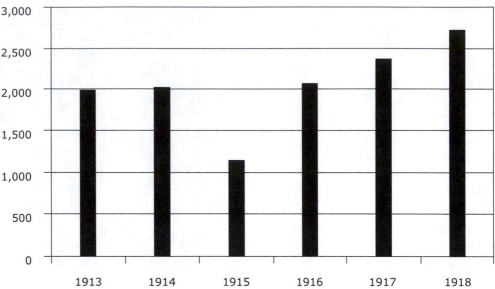

Figure 2.1 *Union Membership between 1913 and 1918 (in thousands).* Source: *Adapted from Hacker and Zahler, 1952, 197.*

Historians' Debate: Ford and Mass Production

Mass production at Ford was a phenomenon that contemporary historians, as well as those of later years, would investigate and attempt to comprehend. Once Henry Ford was certain that the technical and organizational innovations were providing a route to efficient mass production, he was cooperative and open with journalists, encouraging other industrialists wishing to follow his lead. As a result, Ford production technology was rapidly disseminated throughout American industry. Once the concept of the assembly line appeared in print, other companies (e.g., household appliance manufacturers as well as automobile makers) used the system. Nevertheless, despite the enthusiasm of manufacturers for mass production, consumers were more resistant to the standardization of their tastes in furniture, housing, and clothing. Edward A. Rumley and Harry Franklin Porter hailed Ford as "The Manufacturer of Tomorrow" (Hounshell, 1984, 261), but not everyone was so sanguine about the innovations, nor the changes that they brought about. Soon after the first trials with assembly line production, in "How Many Automobiles Can America Buy," Reginald McIntosh Cleveland observed that the industry had surrendered to "the fetish of 'The New Model.'" (Ibid.)

Although Ford emphatically resisted regular model changes, eventually—and only after 15 million Model Ts had been produced—competition forced the company to implement the practice. By then, the emphasis on specialization, which had been so successful, worked against the company as tooling up for the new

> ### *Historians' Debate: Ford and Mass Production, Continued*
>
> Model A cost the company much in lost production and sales. Solving these difficulties led Ford away from a "one size fits all" policy and into the era of flexible mass production, what Charles F. Kettering termed "the new necessity." (Ibid.)

it had begun; strikes, violence, and general unrest had characterized the decade, as they would the next, too.

BIOGRAPHIES

Roger Nash Baldwin, 1884–1981

Civil Rights Leader and Activist

Born into an affluent and progressive Boston family, Baldwin was clearly influenced by his near relatives' reforming zeal and radicalism. He directed a settlement house in St. Louis after graduating from Harvard and became the chief probation officer for the juvenile court there. In 1910, Baldwin became secretary of the urban reform agency, the St. Louis Civic League, which is where he met the anarchist Emma Goldman. Early exposure to free speech came when Baldwin spoke in support of the crusader for birth control rights Margaret Sanger.

Baldwin was attracted to the reform and labor movements, so he organized the Division on Industrial and Economic Problems in 1916 while advocating the replacement of competitive labor systems with cooperative production and distribution. America's entry into World War I inspired Baldwin to organize the American Union Against Militarism (AUAM), whose main agenda was the defense of those opposed to the draft. Following the passage of the 1917 Selective Service Act, which mandated military service and effectively expanded the scope of those eligible for the draft, Baldwin urged the AUAM to establish a legal division to guard the rights of conscientious objectors. The resulting organization, the Civil Liberties Bureau (CLB), was thus founded in July 1917 with Baldwin himself as its head. In October, the CLB split from the AUAM, subsequently becoming the National Civil Liberties Bureau (NCLB), with Baldwin as director. He received a year in jail because he was among those conscientious objectors and was vehemently opposed to any form of conscription by the state. After serving the year in jail, he worked as a laborer around the Midwest and joined the Industrial Workers of the World. In 1920, Baldwin became the first executive director of the newly renamed American Civil Liberties Union (ACLU).

Although Baldwin was most closely associated with leftist causes, the ACLU's agenda was to defend the rights of all U.S. citizens, regardless of their allegiances.

Baldwin himself acknowledged that the civil liberties of the right were as much at risk as were those of those of the left. As a result, he is difficult to locate in either liberal or conservative camps because he was a member of the National Audubon Society, the American Political Science Association, as well as other organizations at various points on the political spectrum. Baldwin himself would only recognize the term "reformer" to describe his activities.

Edward Filene, 1860–1937

Businessman, Social Reformer, and Philanthropist

As president of William Filene's Sons Department Store in Boston, Edward Albert Filene, along with younger brother Albert Lincoln, built up the family business inherited from their father in 1890. The store, which was a great retailing success, included an early example of the bargain basement, offered customers honest descriptions of goods, and operated a "money back if not satisfied" policy. As part of his policy to improve employee relations, Filene also instigated profit sharing, a minimum wage for women, a five-day 40-hour week, and paid vacations.

Described by one of his associates as the "philosopher of our machine economy," Edward Filene was the president of one of Boston's best-known department stores and a forward-looking leader in business and civic affairs. (Library of Congress)

After a trip to India in 1907, where he visited rural cooperative banks, Filene suggested to associate Franklin D. Roosevelt that a similar type of association, effectively a credit union, could assist workers who needed loans and keep them away from moneylenders. Along with other businessmen, he assisted in the foundation of the Massachusetts Credit Union Association in 1914 and established the Credit Union National Extension Bureau, to which he donated significant sums of his own money. Filene played a central role in passing the 1911 Workmen's Compensation Law, America's first, and with Lincoln formed the Filene Cooperative Association, possibly the nation's first company union, established on the basis of collective bargaining.

As a lifelong pacifist, Filene joined the League to Enforce the Peace in 1915. In 1919, he founded the Twentieth Century Fund, an organization whose aims included investigating and solving social and economic problems. As a social reformer who believed that capitalism needed a more humane face and that it should benefit the individual as well as the employer, Filene was an advocate of self-help rather than charity. He rejected materialism and lived modestly without such possessions as an automobile, which had become commonplace by the 1910s. Believing that he was a caretaker for money that could be turned toward the common good, he was extremely careful about small personal expenditures.

Henry Ford, 1864–1947

Industrialist

Henry Ford was the founder of the Ford Motor Company and was hailed as "The Manufacturer of Tomorrow." His dogged determination and insistence on standardization, as well as such innovations as the moving assembly line and, with the introduction of the Ford Model T, the democratization of travel, make him one of the most important industrialists of the 20th century. Linked irrevocably with the term "Fordism," Ford became one of the world's wealthiest men.

Poorly educated and reluctant to work on the family farm, Ford first became an apprentice machinist and only later returned to the farm, where he exhibited his enduring passion for machinery. After a spell as an engineer with the Edison Illuminating Company, he experimented with gasoline engines, later forming the unsuccessful Detroit Automobile Company. With 11 other investors, Ford established the Ford Motor Company in 1903. The decade 1910 to 1920 was perhaps the most significant for the company. Henry Ford had already decided on the Model T as the successor to the Model N. Its replacement had to be affordable for the masses, who had been excluded from the revolution in personal transport up until then. It also had to be simple in design, easy to repair and drive, and cheap to run.

Emphasizing the interchangeability of parts—"The way to make automobiles is to make one automobile just like another automobile, to make them all alike, to make them come through the factory alike," he said—Ford initiated a program of radical innovations in production and organizational technology, culminating in the introduction of the moving assembly line and the $5 day for factory workers at the new factory at Highland Park, Detroit. Efficiency and cost reduction resulted in continual reductions in price and, therefore, massively increased sales so that half of all the cars in America by 1918 were Fords. He was always enthusiastic about selling to farmers, who, rightly, saw a commercial implement that would aid their business in the Model T.

In 1918, Ford was asked by President Woodrow Wilson to stand as a Democrat for the Senate for Michigan. Although America was still at war, Ford stood as a peace candidate and a firm advocate of the proposed League of Nations. In December of that year, Henry Ford relinquished the presidency of the company in favor of his son, Edsel, nevertheless retaining final authority on decisions. A decision that he and Edsel should buy all residual stock from other investors gave the family exclusive ownership of the company.

Although Ford was widely praised as a pioneer of "welfare capitalism" after the introduction of the $5 day, the much publicized "wage" was part salary and part profit sharing, and the latter was dependent upon workers' "acceptability" to the teams of investigators from Ford's Sociological Department. Ford was a curious mixture of philanthropy and stereotypical capitalism and reactionary politics. He was stridently antiunion, but he nevertheless funded a trip to Europe on a "Peace Ship" in 1915 for himself and 170 other notable peace leaders. Lacking government support, the ship docked in neutral Sweden, where Ford left the ship, having become the subject of much derision. Although he argued that the financiers of war had deliberately planned the sinking of the *Lusitania* to bring America into the war, he nonetheless made considerable profits from the conflict. Further controversy followed when, in 1918, Ford bought the weekly newspaper the *Dearborn Independent* as a vehicle for his virulently anti-Semitic opinions.

Henry Ford transformed the way America worked, played, and lived. He was credited with some 160 patents and for coining various famous phrases (e.g., "you can paint it any color you like, so long as it's black" and "history is more or less bunk"); he is nevertheless a controversial and paradoxical figure in the social and industrial history of 20th-century America.

William Z. Foster, 1881–1961

Union Leader

William Zebulon Foster was a trade union leader, a member of the Socialist Party of America and the IWW, and, later, the general secretary of the Communist Party of the United States of America (CPUSA).

He was born in Taunton, Massachusetts, and worked in a number of laboring and construction jobs after leaving school at age 10. He had joined the Socialist Party in 1901, but was expelled in 1909 for his activities in a left-wing faction of the party. He was arrested while reporting for *The Workingman's Paper* during the free-speech fight in Spokane, Washington, and sentenced to 30 days hard labor. Disgust at the petty-bourgeois leadership and policies of the Socialist Party prompted Foster to join the IWW, and he quickly became a notable figure in the organization. Touring Europe during 1910 and 1911 brought him into contact with syndicalism, and he rapidly became a committed advocate for its principles and a leading authority on the movement. He represented the IWW at the Trade Union Secretariat in Budapest in 1911. Inspired by the French revolutionary syndicalists, who had gained control of the trade unions, Foster became committed to the tactic of "boring from within," the policy of penetrating moderate unions to achieve the creation of a trade union "state" to run industry. He returned to the United States in September 1911, convinced that this tactic could be applied there. Although Foster attempted to have the policy adopted by the IWW, his efforts had little effect, particularly after the Lawrence strike, when the organization had gained many new members and appeared to have reached a peak in terms of influence and power. Now fundamentally opposed to the "dual unionism" policy of the IWW, whereby it was both a labor *and* a propagandist organization, undermining the principles of true syndicalism, Foster helped establish an IWW Syndicalist Minority League in early 1912 with Foster himself as secretary.

William Zebulon Foster was a leading figure in the effort to unionize the American meatpacking industry. (Library of Congress)

Although he toured the country attempting to recruit members and advance the cause, his efforts were largely in vain. In February, following his policy of boring from within, Foster joined the AFL union of his craft, the Brotherhood of Railway Carmen (BRC). Foster's campaign to encourage IWW members to establish Syndicalist Leagues and join the AFL unions was relatively successful; therefore, he announced the formation of a national organization, the Syndicalist League of North America (SNLA), and was duly elected national secretary. The League was relatively ineffectual, however, and it disbanded in 1914, after which Foster became a business agent for a local of the BRC. Continuing his syndicalist campaign through the international Trade Union Education League, he also became a general organizer for the AFL in 1915. Unlike other radicals, such as Eugene V. Debs, Foster did not publicly oppose America's entry into the war, helping to sell war bonds in 1918 and remaining silent, at least publicly, during the arrest of IWW activists.

High wartime demand for meat and labor shortages convinced Foster that the time was right to organize workers in the meatpacking industry, so he became secretary of the relatively short-lived Stockyards Labor Council in 1917. Even though this campaign was still active, Foster also joined initiatives to organize steel workers and was a member of the National Committee for Organizing Iron and Steel Workers. The subsequent strike, in September 1919, was eventually defeated, and in the ensuing violent backlash, vigilantes in Johnstown,

Pennsylvania, expelled Foster at gunpoint. He resigned from the Committee in 1920 while the subject of a congressional inquiry. Although the Communist Party had denounced Foster as an opportunist and class collaborator for his perceived compromises with the leadership of the AFL, he was subsequently brought into the party's sphere in 1921 and joined in 1923.

A. J. Muste, 1885–1967

Minister and Activist

Abraham Johannes Muste was a highly active socialist and pacifist who became associated with the labor movement and, later, the U.S. civil rights movement. Ordained a minister in the Dutch Reformed Church in 1909, Muste was installed in New York City, where his exposure to the inequities and ill effects associated with industrialization and urbanization led him to reconsider his role as a minister. His decision to vote for Eugene Debs, the radical labor and political leader, in the presidential election of 1912 opened the way to a life of radical activism. Muste grew increasingly dissatisfied with the Reformed Church, and in 1914, he became pastor of the Central Congregational Church in Newtonville, Massachusetts. Inspired by the religious ideology of the Quakers and dismayed by the outbreak of war in Europe, Muste turned to pacifism, joining the Fellowship of Reconciliation, and the denunciation of war from the pulpit. Muste was dismissed from his church for his outspoken attitude in 1917, after which he grew closer to Quakerism, eventually becoming a Friend in 1918. He also worked with the emergent American Civil Liberties Union in Boston.

Following the lead of the Quaker scholar and activist Rufus Jones, Muste began to apply his faith to action, counseling conscientious objectors at Ft. Devens, Massachusetts, and defending opponents of war charged under the Sedition Act. In 1918, he traveled throughout New England, speaking on war and social injustice. Following the Armistice, his growing commitment to labor activism resulted in his role in leading striking mill workers in the bitter dispute in Lawrence, Massachusetts, in 1919. That same year, he became the general secretary of the Amalgamated Textiles Workers of America.

John Reed, 1887–1920

Activist and Journalist

John "Jack" Reed achieved fame and a certain degree of notoriety through his reporting of labor issues, worker rights, strikes, and the Mexican Revolution. After graduating from Harvard in 1910, Reed wrote for the *American Magazine* and for the radical journals *The New Review* and *The Masses*. He reported on the strike in Paterson, New Jersey, after which he organized the Paterson Pageant at Madison Square Garden to raise money for the strikers. After reporting on the

Mexican Revolution for *Metropolitan Magazine* in 1914—later, the subject of *Insurgent Mexico*—Reed covered the strike of coal miners in Ludlow, Colorado. His travels brought him into contact with the wealthy and the bohemian, including socialite Mabel Dodge, with whom Reed had an on–off affair, and journalist Louise Bryant, who Reed married. He was a war correspondent for *Metropolitan Magazine* during World War I, and his reports on the fighting in Europe were later published as *The War in Eastern Europe.*

He returned to the United States, after which Reed and Bryant traveled to Russia to cover the October Revolution for *The Masses*. His pro-Communist articles were, in part, responsible for the journal's indictment on charges of sedition. In 1919, Reed became involved with the emerging Communist movement and the IWW, and with the foundation of the Communist Labor Party, which at that time was vying for support from the newly established Communist International (Comintern). Indicted for sedition for articles in the *Voice of Labor,* Reed returned to Russia, but was held in Finland by anti-Bolsheviks. After his release, Reed returned to Russia, where he succumbed to an early death from typhus in 1920. He is buried in the walls of the Kremlin. Although widely praised and influential, his account of the Revolution, *Ten Days that Shook the World* (1919), is felt by some to be inconsistent and more literary than historical.

Rose Schneiderman, 1882–1972

Union Leader

Rose Schneiderman was a renowned labor union leader and socialist in the first years of the 20th century. She was born in Poland, and her family emigrated to the United States in 1890, where, following the death of her father, she was placed in an orphanage for a year. Schneiderman worked for a short period in New York's Lower East Side garment industry. Her interest in radical politics and the labor movement stemmed from a brief period in Montreal in 1902, after which she returned to New York and began organizing women workers at her workplace. Schneiderman became closely involved with the New York WTUL, an organization established to support working women in their organizing activities. Elected vice president of the New York branch in 1908, she left factory work for employment with the League while a provision from a wealthy League supporter allowed her to attend school.

As part of the WTUL, Schneiderman played an active part in the New York Shirtwaist Strike of 1909. The union had already detailed unsafe working conditions (e.g., locked exits to prevent workers stealing materials and factories lacking fire escapes) in sweatshops in New York. In 1911, the death of 146 mostly immigrant garment workers in a fire at the Triangle Shirtwaist factory led to an impassioned speech by Schneiderman at the memorial service in which she criticized the public for ignoring the appalling working conditions and regular

Despite a ghetto upbringing and only a grammar school education, Rose Schneiderman became a well-known trade unionist in the United States from the Progressive Era through the 1960s. (Library of Congress)

tragedies in the industry. A largely unproductive year working at the male-dominated International Ladies' Garment Workers' Union was followed by her election as president of the New York WTUL and, subsequently, as its national president.

As a member of the National American Woman Suffrage Association, Schneiderman campaigned for women's suffrage. In 1920, she stood, unsuccessfully, for the Senate as candidate for the Farmer Labor Party. Despite her support for suffrage, she nevertheless opposed the Equal Rights Amendment to the Constitution because she believed that the Amendment would cheat women of the hard-won statutory protections for which the WTUL had campaigned.

Schneiderman is generally credited with one of the most noteworthy slogans of the women's movement, "bread and roses," which originated from her belief that "the worker must have bread, but she must have roses, too." There is some contention regarding its origin, however, because it is attributed by some to the 1911 poem of that name by James Oppenheim. Nevertheless, the slogan has become associated with the 1912 Lawrence textile strike, although its use on placards here, too, has been disputed by strike veterans.

Anna Louise Strong, 1885–1970

Journalist and Activist

After receiving a PhD from the University of Chicago in 1908, Strong became an advocate for child welfare for the U.S. Education Office, organizing an exhibit that she toured both at home and abroad. She became convinced that social inequality and capitalist exploitation were the root causes of poverty and was increasingly attracted to radicalism. From 1915, Strong lived in Seattle, where, supported by women's groups and organized labor, she ran for the school board. As the only woman board member, she argued for social service programs for underprivileged children in public schools.

In 1916, Strong was taken on as a stringer to report on the Everett strike in Colorado for the *New York Evening Post*. After observing the brutality there, she became a passionate advocate for workers' rights. Her radicalism isolated her from other members of the board, whereas her pacifism and her outspoken opposition to the draft in 1917 had her marked as unpatriotic. In 1918, Strong defended Louise Oliverau, a typist charged with sedition, which led to her recall from the board. Away from these responsibilities, Strong became more overtly associated with the radical press, notably *The Union Record,* in which she wrote strident prolabor articles and propagandized the new Soviet government. She became disillusioned with the erosion of the labor movement after the collapse of the Seattle general strike, and on hearing the prominent muckraking journalist Lincoln Steffens speak about his experiences in Russia, Strong left America for Moscow, supporting herself there as a foreign correspondent for the radical press.

REFERENCES AND FURTHER READINGS

Adams, Jr., Graham. 1966. *Age of Industrial Violence, 1910–1915: The Activities and Findings of the United States Commission on Industrial Relations*. New York: Columbia University Press.

Burtt, Everett Johnson. 1980. *Labor in the American Economy*. London: Macmillan Press.

DiLorenzo, Thomas. 2004. *How Capitalism Saved America: The Untold Story of Our Country from the Pilgrims to the Present*. New York: Crown Forum.

Dulles, Foster Rhea, and Melvyn Dubofsky. 1993. *Labor in America: A History*. Arlington Heights: Harlan Davidson.

Foner, Philip S. 1965. *History of the Labor Movement in the United States, Volume IV*. New York: International Publishers.

Giedion, Siegfried. 1948. *Mechanization Takes Command: A Contribution to Anonymous History*. New York: Oxford University Press.

Gold, Roberta. 2003. "The Seattle General Strike of 1919." In Neil Schlager, ed., *St. James Encyclopedia of Labor History Worldwide*. Farmington Hills: St. James Press.

Greenwald, Richard A. 2005. *The Triangle Fire, the Protocols of Peace, and Industrial Democracy in Progressive Era New York*. Philadelphia: Temple University Press.

Harvard University Library, Open Collections Program. "Women Working, 1800–1930." ocp.hul.harvard.edu/ww/events_league.html.

HistoryLink.org. www.historylink.org/.

Hounshell, David A. 1984. *From the American System to Mass Production 1800–1932: The Development of Manufacturing Technology in the United States.* Baltimore: Johns Hopkins University Press.

IWW Songs—to Fan the Flames of Discontent: A Reprint of the Nineteenth Edition (1923) of the Famous Little Red Song Book. 2003. Chicago: Charles H. Kerr Publishing.

Kimeldorf, Howard, and Robert Penney. 1997. "'Excluded' by Choice: Dynamics of Interracial Unionism on the Philadelphia Waterfront 1910–1930." *International Labor and Working-Class History* 51 (Spring): 50–71.

Meyer, Stephen. 1981. *The Five Dollar Day: Labor Management and Social Control in the Ford Motor Company, 1908–1921.* Albany: State University of New York Press.

Meyer, Stephen. 1991. "The Making of Ford's Assembly Line." In Eileen Boris and Nelson Lichtenstein, eds., *Major Problems in the History of American Workers.* Lexington: D.C. Heath.

Pelling, Henry. 1960. *American Labor.* Chicago: University of Chicago Press.

Zinn, Howard. 2003. *A People's History of the United States: 1492–the Present.* New York: HarperCollins.

Immigrant, Migrant, Citizen

OVERVIEW

Give me your tired, your poor,
Your huddled masses yearning to breathe free,
The wretched refuse of your teeming shore,
Send these, the nameless, tempest-tost to me,
I lift my lamp beside the golden door!
> —Emma Lazarus, "The New Colossus"

Lazarus's poem, written in 1883 to assist in the campaign to raise money for the Statue of Liberty's pedestal, evokes images of a homogenous mass of undifferentiated immigrants, driven by visions of economic security or forced by social, political, or religious pressures to get to an America that was simultaneously the land of opportunity and of exploitation. Once there, they could achieve wealth and fulfillment purely by their own efforts, provided they forsook their cultural heritage, or, alternatively, they were fleeced by ruthless profiteers, caught in an urban poverty trap, and exploited by callous employers.

These facile and inflexible stereotypes mask the reality of the widely divergent dreams and their consequences of the 6.3 million immigrants who reached America between 1910 and 1920. Members of ethnic or religious bodies shared neither identical visions nor motives; such subgroups as "the Jews" or "the Greeks" were far from uniform in principles, ideologies, or conduct, and immigrants were not the submissive figures as they were sometimes depicted. Although America became the preferred destination, eastern and southern Europeans often did have alternatives to crossing the ocean (e.g., new skills, migration within Europe, or making things better where they were).

Immigration figures between 1910 and 1920 were the second highest since records began (figures for 1900–1910 were higher) and would have been still higher had it not been for World War I. Although the social, technological, and economic causes that brought immigrants to America were largely the same as they were in earlier decades, this decade is distinguished from earlier periods by the growing hostility toward an immigrant population increasingly under siege from the cumulative effect of calls for immigration restriction; Americanization campaigns and nativism, and the transition from assimilation through education to mandatory Americanization programs; legislation to curtail the freedom of the press and the Espionage Act; anti-German hysteria; and the 100 percent American campaign.

TIMELINE

1910   Ten-yearly census. Amendments included refinements to classifications and definitions of native and foreign-born individuals, giving a clearer picture of immigration.

Following the destruction of the cotton crop, continuing poor weather, African American disenfranchisement, and Jim Crow legislation, the mass migration of agricultural workers from rural areas to southern cities, subsequently to northern industrial areas, begins.

The Dillingham Commission, set up in 1907 to investigate immigration, is published in a 41-volume report. Conclusions concentrated on the split between "old" immigrants (those from northern and western Europe) and "new" immigrants after 1880 (those whose origins lay in southern, central, and eastern Europe). The report focuses on the supposed- "inferiority" of the latter group and the economic consequences of immigration.

1913   After concerns at rising levels of Asian immigration, California passes the Webb Act, denying Japanese the right to acquire land or long leaseholds. Despite protests by Japan that this violated rights given by treaty with the national government, the federal government refuses to interfere with state laws.

1914	World War I begins in Europe. Following a sharp increase in Jewish immigrants from eastern Europe, immigration begins to decline as restrictions on travel start to have an effect.

1914

World War I begins in Europe. Following a sharp increase in Jewish immigrants from eastern Europe, immigration begins to decline as restrictions on travel start to have an effect.

1915

Following atrocities in the 1890s and 1909, the genocidal massacres of Armenians in 1915 lead to significantly increased immigration from southern Mediterranean Turkey and Russian Armenia.

1917

America enters the war.

After vetoes in 1913 and 1915, the literacy test (effectively, the first significant immigration restriction to become law and the beginnings of a quota system for immigrants) is introduced in a climate of anti-immigrant hostility following America's entry into the war. Anti-immigrant hostility intensifies with a propaganda campaign sanctioned by Woodrow Wilson.

The Jones-Shafroth Act grants U.S. citizenship to Puerto Ricans, as long as they can be recruited by the U.S. military.

The Departments of State and Labor announce a combined directive requiring passports from all aliens wishing to enter the United States and obliging that instead of prospective immigrants requesting authorization to enter the United States when arriving at the port of landing, they should be provided with visas by American consular officers in their country of origin.

1918

Congress grants the president wide-ranging powers to prohibit the entry or departure of aliens during wartime.

1919

Congress passes a law granting U.S. citizenship to honorably discharged Native Americans.

Causes

Three major factors influence migration: *push,* those environmental, economic, religious, or political pressures that motivate or compel emigration; *pull,* those magnetic forces originating in the migrant's target destination that can include assurances of political freedom, religious freedom, or both, and the possibility of a better climate and economic opportunity; and *means,* reducible to accessible, affordable transport, absence of restrictions on mobility in the immigrants' country of origin, and the lack of operative restrictions at the destination.

Emigrants on the crowded lower deck of a ship in mid-ocean. (Library of Congress)

Exact figures on immigration into the United States after 1820 are difficult to substantiate. As different agencies use different start and end years, figures can sometimes be misleading. The U.S. Immigration and Naturalization Service Annual Report (1976, 39) puts the number between 1911 and 1920 at 5.735 million, whereas the U.S. Bureau of the Census estimates the figure between 1909 and 1919 at around 6.3 million. Immigration peaked in the period 1900 to 1910, but unlike the years 1880 to 1889 when northern and western Europe (Great Britain and Ireland, France, the German Empire, and Scandinavia) contributed the majority of immigrants, the years between 1900 and 1919 were characterized by immigration from southern, eastern, and central Europe (Italy, Russia, Austria-Hungary, Poland, Greece, Spain, and Portugal, with the first three contributing the highest numbers).

America became the preferred destination because of a largely fortuitous amalgamation of economic opportunity, political liberty, and religious tolerance. Along with changes in transportation and communication, economic, environmental, and religious and political factors were the main determinants in immigrants' decisions to leave their homeland and go to another country.

Specific causes are clearly dependent on the immigrant's country of origin, but there are common factors, both social and technological, that accelerated external migration in the mid- to late 19th century. The telegraph and the growth of advertising, newspapers, and promotional material by agents and steamship companies enabled people to learn of conditions and opportunities much quicker; the railroad facilitated internal travel; the replacement of sail by steamships greatly reduced journey times and improved long ocean crossings, while competition among steamship companies reduced ticket prices. From the host country's perspective, rapid industrialization stimulated competition among nations to attract huge numbers of cheap, unskilled labor.

The impulses stimulating immigration in the late 19th and early 20th centuries were broadly similar to those that inspired the first waves: political and religious dissatisfaction and increased opportunity, as well as the expanding impact of economic reorganization. The disintegration of the old agrarian economy and the subsequent rise of the factory system alongside pressure caused by population growth had already stimulated emigration in northern and western Europe; now, the same occurred in other parts of Europe.

Several factors combined that together led to an increase in immigration from northern and western Europe in the years after 1860 (the agrarian crisis, industrial depression, increased hostility to military service in Germany, and a buoyant American economy). After 1890, immigration from all these countries decreased markedly, brought about by such circumstances as a decline in the birthrate in some countries, the absorption of available labor by rapid industrialization in Germany and Scandinavia, and government campaigns that either encouraged potential emigrants to stay in their homeland or diverted them toward their own colonies, coupled with the diminishing availability of land in the American West and the take up of unskilled labor vacancies by southern and eastern Europeans. This all meant that the balance in composition and country of origin changed in the three decades between 1890 and the beginning of restrictions in the 1920s.

Had conditions been amenable, it would have been impossible for many southern and eastern Europeans to emigrate before the late 19th century because of official hostility and prohibitive legislation. Such political changes as Italian unification, reorganization in Austria-Hungary, Slavic emancipation from Turkish rule, and the relaxation of official hostility to emigration in Russia in the early 20th century led to increased emigration from those areas dislocated by the disintegration of peasant economies. Two parts of Europe epitomize the extensive and enduring changes in agrarian communities: Austria-Hungary and southern Italy.

In Russia, the growth of Pan-Slav nationalism led to a renewal of Jewish persecution, which, added to the pogroms of the late 19th and early 20th centuries in which numberless Jews were massacred, prompted an exodus to America. Other parts of eastern Europe (e.g., Bulgaria and Romania) were affected by the progression from a peasant economy to wholesale modern agriculture, whereas in Finland, the same issues were exacerbated by the worsening relationship with Russia. The Armenian massacres led to emigration from that part of the Ottoman Empire. Not all immigration was from across the Atlantic. Although immigration from China and Japan had been halted, respectively, by the Chinese Exclusion Act in 1882 and the Gentlemen's Agreement of 1907–1908, a significant influx of Japanese women continued as the agreement allowed U.S. residents to send for their wives. Canada was another important source of immigration, particularly between 1910 and 1919 when figures increased from around 120,000 to more than 700,000. Immigration from the Maritime Provinces and Quebec had been under way since before the Civil War, whereas major changes in land use in Ontario stimulated emigration south. Immigration from Mexico, the West Indies, and Central and South America also doubled during this period.

Immigration peaked in 1906–1907, but the beginning of the industrial depression in October 1907 stemmed the flow. Concerns in Europe about the approach

Table 3.1. Decennial Immigration to the United States, 1880–1919

	1880–1889	Percentage	1890–1899	Percentage	1900–1909	Percentage	1910–1919	Percentage
Total	5,248,568		3,694,294		8,202,388		6,347,380	
Northwestern Europe								
United Kingdom[1]	810,900	15.5	328,759	8.9	469,578	5.7	371,878	5.8
Ireland	674,061	12.8	405,710	11.0	344,940	4.2	166,445	2.6
Scandinavia[2]	671,783	12.7	390,729	10.5	488,208	5.9	238,275	3.8
France	48,193	0.9	35,616	1.0	67,735	0.4	60,335	1.0
German Empire	1,445,181	27.5	579,072	15.7	328,722	4.0	174,227	2.7
Other[3]	152,604	2.9	86,011	2.3	112,433	1.4	101,478	1.6
Central Europe								
Poland	42,910	0.8	107,793	2.9	not returned separately		not returned separately	
Austria-Hungary	314,787	6.0	534,059	14.5	2,001,376	24.4	1,154,727	18.2
Other[4]	—	—	52	[6]	34,651	0.4	27,180	0.4
Eastern Europe								
Russia[5]	182,698	3.5	450,101	12.7	1,501,301	18.3	1,106,998	17.4
Romania	5,842	0.1	6,808	0.2	57,322	0.7	13,566	0.2
Turkey in Europe	1,380	[6]	3,547	0.1	61,856	0.8	71,149	1.1
Southern Europe								
Greece	1,807	[6]	12,732	0.3	145,402	1.8	198,108	3.1
Italy	267,660	5.1	603,761	16.3	1,930,475	23.5	1,229,916	19.4
Spain	3,995	0.1	9,189	0.2	24,818	0.3	53,262	0.8
Portugal	15,186	0.3	25,874	0.7	65,154	0.8	82,489	1.3
Other Europe	1,070	[6]	145	[6]	454	[6]	6,527	0.1
Asia								
Turkey in Asia	1,098	[6]	23,963	0.6	66,143	0.8	89,568	1.4
Other	68,673	1.3	33,775	0.9	171,837	2.1	109,019	1.7

America								
British North America[8]	492,865[7]	9.4	3,098	0.1	123,650	1.5	708,715	11.2
Mexico	2,405	[6]	734	[6]	31,188	0.4	185,334	2.9
West Indies[9]	27,323	0.5	31,480	0.9	100,960	1.2	120,860	1.9
Central and South America	2,233	[6]	2,038	0.1	22,011	0.3	55,630	0.9
Other Countries								
Australia[10]	7,271	0.1	3,225	0.1	11,191	0.1	11,280	0.2
Other	6,643	0.1	16,023	0.4	40,943	0.5	10,414	0.2
	100.0[11]		100.0		100.0		100.0	

[1] England, Scotland, Wales

[2] Norway, Sweden, Denmark

[3] Netherlands, Belgium, Switzerland

[4] Bulgaria, Serbia, Montenegro

[5] Includes Finland and boundaries prior to 1919

[6] Less than one-tenth of one percent

[7] Immigrants from British North America and Mexico not reported from 1886 to 1893

[8] Including Canada

[9] Including Jamaica

[10] Including Tasmania and New Zealand

[11] Totals are rounded to nearest percent as in Census report

Source: Carpenter, 1927, 324–25; cited in Kraut, 1982.

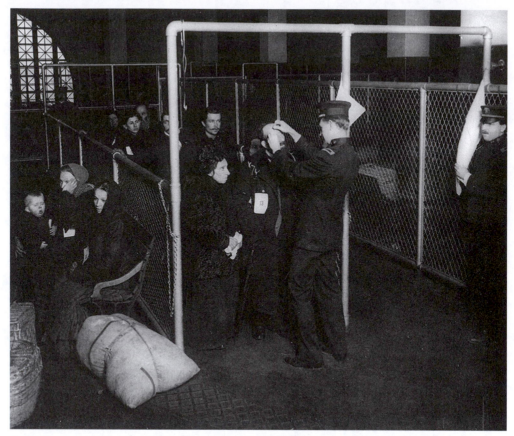

Inspectors examine the eyes of immigrants at Ellis Island, 1913. The eye disease trachoma was often a reason for the rejection of immigrants. (Library of Congress)

of World War I, however, led to an increase to 2.4 million in 1913–1914. In addition to these new immigrants were those repatriated because of fears of separation from their families. After the war, strikes and economic depression in the United States and a prevailing wariness of foreigners and reputed extremists combined to swell the number of repatriations.

Excluding eastern European Jews, the Armenians, and the Syrians, who were forced out partially by persecution, the causes that motivated other immigrants were largely economic. Between 1910 and the 1920s, when unrestricted immigration came to an end, new immigrants from southern, central, and eastern Europe arrived for broadly the same reasons that had stimulated immigration for centuries.

New Immigrants

The main finding of the Dillingham Commission, which had been set up by Congress in 1907 to investigate immigration and published a report amounting to

The Immigration Restriction League

Founded in 1894 by three Bostonians and Harvard graduates, Charles Warren, Robert DeCourcey Ward, and Prescott Farnsworth Hall, the League was active until the 1920s. Its self-proclaimed aims were "the limitation of immigration and a more careful selection, to the end that we shall receive no more aliens than can be properly assimilated." Unlike other restrictionist groups that argued for restriction on economic grounds, it emphasized the racial aspects of immigration. The League's publications promoted the distinction between "old" immigrants, antecedents of the League's own members, and "new" immigrants. As immigration mounted, League members argued that the nation was increasingly unable to assimilate recent arrivals, that these "undesirables" were intrinsically unable to assume American standards, and, moreover, that they would be more likely to become a public charge.

Among its prominent members was Massachusetts senator Henry Cabot Lodge, an exponent of statistical attempts to determine ability according to national origin, a supporter of a literacy test as a requirement for entry to the country, and a vocal opponent of new immigration. The League's national committee included the eugenicist Madison Grant, and from the early years of the 20th century, the League increasingly aligned itself with the beliefs of those who supported Social Darwinism and eugenics as a basis for the categorization and ranking of ethnic and racial groupings as strategies to discriminate against new immigrants.

The literacy test was a central plank of the League's exclusion policy. The League promoted it through lobbyists hired to pressure members of Congress to support it. Despite repeated attempts to introduce the bill, it was vetoed by successive presidents until 1917, when Congress overrode President Wilson's third veto. Notwithstanding the test, after World War I, immigration again increased, and the League's influence began to decline. Public opinion remained in favor of restriction, however, and in the 1920s, Congress passed an increasingly rigorous series of measures, limiting overall immigration and establishing quotas for specific national groups.

41 volumes in 1910 and 1911, was that a fundamental change had taken place in the constitution of immigration in the early 1880s. From a contemporary perspective, the periods before and after 1880 could be divided in to a split between "old" and "new" immigration. Old immigration could be seen as spontaneous, self-directed, almost exclusively from northern and western Europe, and characterized by families seeking a permanent home in America. New immigration was involuntary, artificially induced, temporary, and largely made up of unskilled males from southern, central, and eastern Europe. That there was a material change in immigrants' geographical origins is evident, but the distinction failed to take into account the diverse reasons for this shift.

Political cartoon by W. A. Rogers showing Uncle Sam and "Enemy Alien" sitting on a bench in "Liberty Park," 1918. (Library of Congress)

The traditional interpretation of a simplistic division between old and new fails to consider that immigrants from the two areas of Europe were not a common body, sharing mutual characteristics. Each group comprised a diverse range of distinct types. Even though it is true that old immigrants did come voluntarily, new immigrants motivated by economic opportunities, rather than those driven out by persecution, also left their homelands voluntarily. The notion that the changes were in some way artificially induced was based on the Commission's assumption that promotional methods and materials circulated by steamship companies were qualitatively and quantitatively different from those employed before 1880. This was not the case, however, because advertising that included the lure of high wages was forbidden nearly everywhere, and, in any case, inducements were unnecessary as emigrants came forward in sufficient numbers without encouragement. Immigration after 1880 did include those transients (e.g., seasonal workers and those motivated by wage differences between America and the homeland) for whom the stay in America was likely to be temporary. This was more the result, however, of the regularity of Atlantic crossings and the reduction in journey times caused by the introduction of steamships than because of any change in the countries of origin.

The Commission also failed to take into account the length of time that each immigrant group had been in the country because there was a noticeable correspondence between the percentage of males and how recently they had immigrated. For example, male percentages were much higher among Greeks, whose arrival had begun in large numbers only after 1900, than it was among Italians, whose immigration had begun a decade earlier. Thus, unaccompanied males usually constituted the early phase of immigration, but once they were established, wives and families usually followed them. The extent of male immigrants' skills is accounted for by the limited period used by the Commission. Between 1899 and 1909, the skilled percentage from northern and western Europe was twice that of those from southern and eastern Europe, but this misleading comparison failed to note that the proportion of unskilled laborers from northern and western Europe was low only because of the amount of competition from the south and the east. Transient workers who were included in immigration figures, but whose stay was necessarily temporary, were predominantly male. Once these reasons are taken into account, the main difference between new and old is that of place of origin, rather than the more loaded distinctions and comparisons that the Commission made.

The distinctions between old and new had important consequences in the years after the war when immigration increased almost to prewar levels. Those increases, along with an economic depression and resentment that so many Americans had been killed or wounded in a war caused by European incompetence, were exacerbated by the shadow of the Russian Revolution, which precipitated a Red Scare and fears concerning suspected foreign extremists and radicals. Between 1880 and 1921, new immigrants met with significant and increasing hostility, and although the pattern was already well established by midcentury during the mass influx of Irish and German immigrants, resentment was now directed at immigrants from southern and eastern Europe. Well before the Dillingham Commission declared that new immigrants were, in some way, "inferior" to earlier immigrants, a body of scholars had become convinced that those with Anglo-Saxon or Aryan characteristics were inherently superior to other "races."

Prejudice was compounded by the establishment of such pressure groups as the Immigration Restriction League that argued for change in American immigration policies. Their chief political protagonist, Henry Cabot Lodge, focused his efforts on a 22-year campaign to improve literacy standards for immigrants. During those years, the bill passed the House on all five occasions, passing the Senate on all but the first attempt, but was vetoed by successive presidents until 1917, when hostility directed at Germans in particular and foreigners in general was intensified by a propaganda campaign sanctioned by Woodrow Wilson, giving the restrictionists added credibility. Although Wilson had vetoed the literacy bill in 1915, its reintroduction two years later came at a time of heightened emotion, and the House overrode the president's subsequent veto, whereas Wilson himself found little support in the Senate.

The 1917 legislation was the first important immigration restriction to become law. Adult literacy later became a precondition for entry into the United States, although where families were concerned, as long as husbands could demonstrate literacy, wives were not expected to conform to this requirement. The literacy test had a greater effect on southern and eastern Europeans, who experienced higher levels of illiteracy, than it did on immigrants from northern and western Europe; thus, it was effectively tantamount to a quota system. Fears concerning a postwar flood of immigrants added to the general resentment and wartime hysteria, but practically, the test had little effect on immigration as few were excluded as a result of the restriction, although it may have acted as a deterrent. Rising literacy standards in Europe weakened the bill's impact, but it proved to be an important symbolic win for advocates of restriction.

Apart from the literacy test, by 1917, barriers to immigration had been raised in six other areas: a "barred zone" based on latitude and longitude excluded the majority of Asians apart from Filipinos and Japanese, who were covered by the

Table 3.2. Causes of Rejection of U.S. Immigrants, 1909–1917

Cause of Rejection	1909	1912	1914	1917
Idiocy	18	10	14	9
Imbecility	42	44	68	19
Feeblemindedness	121	110	995	224
Insanity (including epilepsy)	167	133	197	146
Constitutional Psychopathic Inferiority	—	—	—	3
Likelihood of Becoming a Public Charge	4,458	8,182	15,784	7,893
Affliction with Contagious Diseases	2,308	1,674	3,143	1,383
Affliction with Tuberculosis	82	74	114	119
Physical or Mental Defectiveness	370	2,228	6,537	1,734
Chronic Alcoholism	—	—	—	10
Criminality	273	592	755	257
Prostitution and Other Immorality	323	263	380	510
Procurement of Prostitutes	181	192	254	371
Contract Laboring	1,172	1,332	2,793	1,116
Inability to Read (over age 16)	—	—	—	391

Source: Derived from *Reports of the Department of Labor, 1917,* Report of the Secretary of Labor, and Reports of Bureaus (Washington, D.C.: Government Printing Office, 1918), p. 126; cited in King, 2000, 172.

Gentlemen's Agreement, an addition to the law covering the political opinions of prospective immigrants, criminals, those whose morals were suspect, those with various diseases, and paupers. Table 3.2 illustrates the causes of rejection of U.S. immigrants between 1909 and 1917.

While the war was not the cause of restrictionism, it had acted as a catalyst that exploited the growing sense of nativism. In 1920, immigration was suspended for a year and a bill was introduced based on the Dillingham quota that effectively ended four decades of new immigration.

Implications of the Dillingham Commission

Several factors combined in the overheated atmosphere at the end of the war, which together meant that the climate was in place for legislation to restrict immigration still further when Congress reassembled in 1920. Nativism increased, fueled by the perception felt by many Americans that the country had failed to fulfill its proclaimed war objectives and that Europe was far from ready for democracy. Compounding these were anxieties regarding perceived threats of subversion by foreign-sounding radicals, the so-called Red Scare, and a press preoccupied with hysterical scaremongering warning of an influx of unwelcome European immigrants.

The realities were rather different. In 1919–1920, 430,000 immigrants entered, but 288,000 who left America balanced this figure. Despite this figure being lower

Ellis Island

From 1892 to 1932, the island off New York, America's busiest port of entry, was the main immigrant reception center for the eastern seaboard, processing nearly 12 million newcomers, and, for those aspirant Americans, a threshold that symbolized their fears and hopes. During the decade 1910–1920, between 5.735 million and 6.347 million immigrants (estimates vary) entered the United States (Carpenter, 1927, 324–25), the majority through Ellis Island. Until 1850, admission of immigrants was casual. By midcentury, the arrival of 4.5 million northern and western European aliens and the growing chaos caused by the sheer weight of numbers convinced major eastern ports officials and the State of New York that a more systematic process and a dedicated center was needed. From 1855 until Ellis Island opened, steerage and third-class immigrants were ferried from their ship to the depot at Castle Gardens. In 1875, immigration administration, until then a question of laissez-faire or, in New York, the responsibility of state and local government, became a federal concern and subject to a uniform system. A former naval arsenal off the New Jersey shore, Ellis Island, was chosen to replace the decaying and corrupt Castle Gardens. Doubled in size by landfill, it opened in 1892 to process subsequent waves of immigrants.

The 1889 Ford Committee report reflects an important change in official American attitudes toward the immigrant, shifting from protection against the rigors of America to protecting America from potentially dangerous immigrants. Immigrants could theoretically be excluded for a number of reasons, but practically, only a relatively small proportion was returned to their country of origin.

On Ellis Island, legislation intended to exclude aliens deemed unacceptable led to the construction of a building complex housing every facility for the efficient daily processing of up to 5,000 immigrants, from baggage handling and inspection and detention areas, to a hospital, laundry, and showers. Inspections were held in the Registry Room, where doctors briefly screened immigrants for obvious ailments, becoming so practiced that by 1916 they could apparently identify many conditions at a glance.

With the decline of immigration during World War I, suspected enemy aliens were held there until the complex was requisitioned by U.S. Navy and Army medical departments. After the war ended, the Red Scare led to the internment of suspected alien radicals on the island. Until unrestricted immigration declined after 1920, immigration officials were joined by a diverse group that included lawyers, doctors, interpreters, ticket agents, and currency exchangers, as well as social reformers and missionaries to protect immigrants from exploitation. As the largest immigration depot in the busiest port, Ellis Island became the template for all inspection depots in America.

than prewar norms, the 1920 bill suspending further immigration for one year was passed with a considerable majority. The bill failed to be ratified by the Senate, however, in part because of pressure by such special interest groups as the National Association of Manufacturers. Republican William P. Dillingham, who had presided over the United States Immigration Commission of 1909–1911, introduced the Dillingham quota bill in its place.

Eastern and Southern Europeans

In general, the sweeping economic and social changes that led to the mass emigration of millions of southern, central, and eastern Europeans after 1880 were those that had stimulated northern and western Europeans earlier in the century. Between 1860 and 1890, however, although the three main areas of emigration (Great Britain, Germany, and Scandinavia) remained the same, several factors combined to move those sources eastward: English, Scots, and Welsh added to the still considerable Irish emigration, Swedes outnumbered Norwegians, while in Germany, emigrants from Prussia and Saxony began to replace Württembergers and Bavarians.

Dramatic falls in the cost of transporting grain by railroad and cargo steamer meant that for the first time American, Russian, Indian, and other distant wheat farmers could compete in Europe. After 1865, the effect on European farming was almost immediate, and this, added to industrial depression in England, Germany, and Sweden along with a flourishing American economy, led to widespread emigration by those affected by agricultural and industrial reorganization. European urbanization, where such cities as Berlin and London attracted some of those displaced, and America, where cities rather than the prairie pulled in the majority of immigrants, contributed to population shifts.

Millions of these emigrants were provided with the practical means to travel by the growth of European railroads that enabled emigrants to reach ports from the most remote regions and by the introduction of steam on transatlantic crossings. New steamship routes made immigration from the entire European continent viable. Better accommodation in passenger-only ships, reduced passage times, prepaid tickets, or fares sent by relatives already in the United States, along with increased competition, especially between German and British companies, stimulated the growth in trade, which continued up to the outbreak of the war. Whereas German lines operating from such ports as Bremen and Hamburg were clearly better placed to exploit the increased emigration from central and eastern Europe, British companies still contrived to keep hold of southern and eastern European passengers by manipulating routes and ferrying passengers so that central Europeans could reach such ports as Liverpool, which had earlier depended on Irish and British emigrants. Services to New York, Boston, and New Orleans from Naples, Genoa, Palermo, and Trieste also increased the flow of new immigrants from southern Europe. By 1907, four ports (Bremen, Hamburg, Liverpool, and Naples) accounted for around 60 percent of European emigration. All except Naples acted as channels for emigrating Europeans, exporting more foreigners than natives.

Italians accounted for the majority sailing from Naples, and between 1880 and 1920, no other country sent so many immigrants, almost 4.1 million. In Italy, particularly the south, years of land exploitation, underinvestment in modern methods, low productivity, problems caused by the overthrow of feudalism, the take-up of land formerly owned by the Roman Catholic Church, the emergence from Spanish and Bourbon neglect, and population increases all contributed to some of the worst poverty in Europe. The eruption of Vesuvius, which buried a town near Naples, and the 100,000 killed in the 1908 Messina earthquake added to southern Italy's problems. Fruit growers were also seriously affected by extremely rapid and increased fruit production in California and Florida and wine tariffs imposed by France. This period of hardship precipitated the first large-scale Italian emigration. These Italians did not go to South America, where there were already significant numbers of northern Italians, but because of epidemics and an unstable political situation there, southern Italians emigrated to North America, chiefly through New York.

Whereas Greek and Turkish immigration only amounted to around 16 percent of the Italian figure, numbers between 1911 and 1920 doubled compared with the previous decade, whereas Italian immigration almost halved. Because ethnic groups and subject nationalities are not differentiated in immigration records, it is difficult to determine the numbers of Arabs, who mainly came from the area around Beirut and Tripoli, and Armenians, from southern Mediterranean Turkey and Russian Armenia, but their numbers became statistically significant in the late 1880s. The number of Armenians arriving between then and the end of immigration in the early 1920s was perhaps around 100,000, increasing during and after the persecution of the 1890s, the atrocities of 1909, and the genocidal massacres of 1915. Although Armenian immigration resembles patterns established by earlier immigrants in that they arrived in New York and settled in eastern cities, Armenians differ in some important ways: almost all adult males were literate, many came from urban regions, and there were significant numbers of artisans and professionals among them. After first settling in Canada, Russian Armenians eventually migrated to Fresno, California.

During the last years of the 19th century and the first years of the 20th, Poles and eastern European Jews began to arrive in the industrial cities of northeastern and north-central America, whereas around five times as many Slovaks as Armenians settled. Until the creation of a new Polish state in 1919, no such country existed. Polish immigrants, who were motivated largely by economic reasons, therefore came from the German, Austro-Hungarian, and Russian Empires. Poles and Jews and more than 20 other ethnic groups, who, although individually small in number, together accounted for a relatively large number, were not recorded

A Polish emigrant carries a trunk on his shoulder as he boards a ship, 1907. (Library of Congress)

in statistics that listed only national origin and not ethnicity. The only way to extract Polish immigration figures from the 1910 census is to examine native language as nearly all Polish immigrants shared Polish as a common tongue. First- and second-generation Polish speakers thus account for some 2.6 million, a small majority of whom came from Russia in the early 20th century, after those Poles from Germany and Austria.

Distinguishing Jewish immigrants from other eastern Europeans is even more difficult as neither immigration records nor the 1910 census recorded religion and Yiddish or Hebrew might be only one of a number of languages spoken. By the early 1920s, there were perhaps 4 million immigrants of Jewish descent, who had come for economic reasons but also to escape growing religious persecution. Because of the distances involved, migration was difficult for eastern European Jews, compounded by having to travel by more circuitous routes to avoid anti-Semitic hostility in some countries. Perhaps because of this, once in America Jewish immigrants had a lower return rate than all other groups. Added to these figures are those from other ethnic groups, among them Magyars, whose numbers peaked at around 450,000 in 1914, encouraged to emigrate by deteriorating Hungarian economic conditions.

Immigration from eastern and southern Europe was halted by the outbreak of World War I and died out altogether following the restrictive legislation of the early 1920s.

Nativism

Nativism in the second decade of the 20th century drew upon many of the same prejudices that had existed since colonial times. In most societies, those who consider themselves "native-born" often exhibit a defensive and generalized hostility toward foreigners, resulting from an awareness of cultural differences, religious differences, or both. A constant in America since colonial times, it is differentiated from a more serious aversion based largely on fear and manifested from time to time in eruptions of widespread xenophobia. These have often corresponded to periods of internal crisis and loss of national confidence, and, in some cases, have been politically motivated attempts to protect American nationality from perceived foreign threats. Deep political fissures, rather than increased immigration, inspired early examples in the 1790s, whereas pre–Civil War nativism was largely directed at the Roman Catholic Church because of its rigid organization, adherence to doctrines, and its close links with European despotism, all the antithesis of political liberty.

Anti-Catholic nativism was compounded by fears over increased immigration and consequent criminality, electoral influence, and dependence on local authority support. Before, and particularly after, the Civil War, concerns were raised that immigrants were incapable of assimilation and that their numbers would result in unemployment, low wages, and the dilution of American homogeneity. Nativism achieved short-lived political expression and success between 1854 and 1856 in the Know-Nothing Party.

The Chinese Exclusion Act of 1882 was significant in paving the way for other restrictions, minor at first, but which cumulatively altered the previously unrestricted immigration policy. Along with the anxieties of the trade union movement that increased immigration would threaten American workers' standards of living and the revival of anti-Catholicism, fears over the influx of southern and eastern Europeans were fuelled by a growing conviction among various groups that those with Anglo-Saxon characteristics were innately superior to those new immigrants. Such groups as the Immigration Restriction League were among those who misapplied Darwinian theories of plant and animal evolution, equating survival of the fittest, which was interpreted as best, to society and pressured for a fundamental change in immigration policy.

The distrust, which at times erupted in demonstrations of overt hatred, was based on the premise that hereditary factors alone would dictate which races would adjust to democracy and free enterprise competition. Using spurious and crude tests, nativists maintained that their prejudices were sanctioned by scientific principles. Following economist Francis Walker, then president of the Massachusetts Institute of Technology and a critic of those from the new areas of immigration, such others as Edward Alsworth Ross concluded in 1914 (from evidence based largely on observation) that immigrants would racially impair the American population if allowed unrestricted entry, inferring an unambiguous association between different and inferior.

Madison Grant amalgamated many of the racial nativist debates in *The Passing of the Great Race; or, The Racial Basis of European History* in 1916, accumulating much scientific material in support of his prejudices. In this widely read tract, he argued that a lower hybrid type resulted from race mixing, the lowest being the eastern European Jew, who, if allowed to enter the United States and intermarry, would undermine the strength of the Anglo-Saxon race. Others produced primitive IQ tests to authenticate these theories, ignoring evidence that demonstrated that the longer a group lived in the United States, the greater the likelihood of an increase in IQ scores.

These warnings did not go unchallenged. A rebuttal in 1911 by the German Jewish immigrant anthropologist Franz Boas showed that environment determined altered "racial characteristics" in second-generation immigrants more than heredity. Despite scientific acclaim, however, lay readers preferred evidence that reinforced their grounds for nativism.

Anti-Semitic nativism was both religious and economic in origin; labor and business leaders fearing the consequences of immigration adduced the example of the usurious and parasitic Jew. In 1914, sociologist Edward A. Ross and others contended that Jews were physically inferior to "our pioneer breed" (Kraut, 1982, 155) and were thus unable to compete in the market or share political power, and that this perceived inferiority was offset by cunning and avariciousness. Despite a lack of evidence regarding the radical nature of immigrants, the few who did participate in labor protests confirmed latent nativist prejudices. Because many unskilled new immigrants competed for jobs with native-born workers, outbreaks of nativist violence were triggered during periods of work shortages. Rising crime rates were also blamed on new immigrants, and despite little evidence, the fiction of immigrant criminality endured.

Although nativist support for restrictive immigration policies was sometimes undertaken in a more formal and organized political arena, most nativists preferred the anonymity of pressure groups that lobbied politicians and manipulated public opinion. One such group, the revived Ku Klux Klan, emerged after World War I, capitalizing on fears of foreign extremists and a renewed tide of European immigration. Although Klansmen did support nativist candidates, they generally preferred public demonstration and acts of violence to active political involvement. There is little evidence that immigrants employed collective violence to counter the attacks, resorting instead to politics and pressure groups; however, enfranchised immigrants, who were ineligible to vote until naturalization, were sometimes reluctant to exercise that right. When they did, they tended not to vote as a bloc. Nor were they an effective enough economic force to counter nativist objectives, whereas organized labor itself, fearing a continued influx of unskilled immigrants, endorsed restriction. Such groups as the Industrial Workers of the World (IWW), or Wobblies, however, whose ambivalent image, part revolutionary activist, part unionist, and part reformist, attracted large numbers of southern and eastern European unskilled immigrants until around 1913.

Recourse to law was often no solution to nativist activities; immigrants found the legal system laborious and unintelligible, and judges were often unsympathetic. World War I was the catalyst that nativists needed to transform the enduring debates on restriction into a desire for national unity. Inspired by awareness of Old World bonds that fostered vociferous demands for loyalty complying with the prevailing national model and often referred to as "100 percent American-

Are Italians White?

In many accounts, northern Italians were historically regarded as educated, cultured, mercantile, and lighter-skinned, whereas southerners, from land adjoining Africa and dominated for centuries by dark-skinned Moors, were the working poor, darker-skinned agricultural and manual laborers; thus, they were discriminated against within Italian culture. In the decades from 1880 to 1920, 80 percent of more than 4 million Italian immigrants were from the South, representing more than 10 percent of America's foreign-born population.

Prejudice followed them to America, where Mediterranean, olive-skinned southern Italians brought with them an ambiguous racial identity, resulting in the U.S. Senate designation of "nonwhite." Immigrant Italians were made to complete a standardized immigration form. Under race, there were two options: North or South Italian. Under color, many wrote simply "white."

This classification reflects the ways in which Italians became white on arrival. Until around 1900, they were regarded as racially inferior; their status was below "native" white Americans but above African Americans and other nonwhites, and even though many suffered racial prejudice and discrimination, it was qualitatively different from prejudice against other groups. The peak of immigration in the late 19th century coincided with an economic recession, concerns that immigrants would take jobs, and the circulation of pseudoscientific, racialist theories alleging "Mediterranean" types were inferior to northern Europeans, resulting in increased anti-immigrant feeling.

Italians lived an in-between existence until they were elevated by social forces and regarded as white, with all that color's privileges, although some claimed their material success resulted from hard work alone rather than advantages consequent on their acceptance as whites.

Jobs often discriminated between whites and European immigrants. Because southern Italians in the southern states resembled African American co-workers, they were subject to the same Jim Crow legislation. Although unions admitted European immigrants more readily than "nonwhites," it was not until the 1940s, when the only option on immigration forms for race and color was "white," that Italians reluctantly began to identify themselves as white.

ism," this xenophobic and isolationist spirit, reinforced by an increase in radicalism and labor unrest, endured into the 1920s, proving to be the central component in the nativists' victory against unlimited immigration.

Immigrant Labor and Mobility

After accommodation, a major priority for immigrants arriving in America was employment. As rapid industrialization in the latter half of the 19th century generated a requirement for cheap, untrained labor, immigrants entering the country could find employment relatively quickly. Already-assimilated and native Americans' hostility toward immigrants often focused on the likelihood that this apparently limitless source of cheap labor would depress wage levels, reduce employment opportunities, and displace earlier immigrants from jobs. These fears were largely unfounded, but they did lead to the immigrant worker becoming stereotyped variously as: talented, resourceful, and ambitious; part of an undifferentiated mass of unskilled labor, vulnerable to exploitation and physical hardship; feckless, inassimilable, radical, and a willing convert to any potentially subversive group.

In truth, immigrants were far from homogeneous, and as individuals within distinct ethnic categories, their ambitions and responses to the American economy varied accordingly. Labor activity was therefore determined by a certain degree of choice, not by the immigrant's previous experience or background, and the economic principles of supply and demand. Because the majority of new immigrants entered America through the Northeast, most entered the economy through industry or commerce there, too. Some 80 percent (Kraut, 1982, 76) of immigrants stayed in the Northeast, the majority in a three-cornered area formed by New England at the apex, Washington, D.C., in the southeast, and St. Louis in the southwest. Around 66 percent remained in New York, the New England states, Pennsylvania, and New Jersey, with a significant number in Illinois and Ohio. Because industry was relatively undeveloped in the South, few immigrants traveled there, whereas those who disembarked in southern ports and elected to stay competed in the labor market with low-paid white and African American laborers. Japanese and Chinese immigrants who landed in San Francisco tended to remain there, and by 1916, some 72 percent of the population considered a foreign language as their principal tongue.

Established immigrant communities in major northern cities meant that immigrants were more likely to gravitate there. These cities continued to sustain such craft trades as the garment industry, and thus provided opportunities for skilled artisans as well as the unskilled. As concentrated population centers, they provided a market for these trades. The largest of these cities (New York, Chicago, Detroit, Cleveland, and Boston) became "immigrant cities"; and the 1910 census shows that about 75 percent of their populations were made up from immigrants, largely from southern and eastern Europe. Because such other cities as Philadelphia were connected to the rest of the industrial centers by rail, significant immigrant communities developed there, too.

Immigrants converged on areas where openings corresponded with their abilities and cultural leanings. Slavs therefore populated the mining and industrial regions of Ohio, western Pennsylvania, Illinois, Michigan, and New York, as well as working in Chicago's slaughterhouses and the construction industry throughout the Northeast. Because many Slavs regarded their stay in America as temporary, many were prepared to tolerate appalling working conditions and long

Early-20th-century view of First Avenue in Little Italy, New York City. (Library of Congress)

hours in exchange for the higher wages that would enable them to return home. Some Slavs (e.g., Poles), who already had capital, acquired small plots of land on which they farmed.

Italians also tended to consider their stay temporary, often returning to Italy in the winter, only to return the following spring. Some returned with families when conditions in the *Mezzogiorno* (the south of Italy, a term derived from the strength of the midday sun) meant a life of servitude. As immigrants with few skills and little accumulated wealth, the majority were manual laborers, often on construction sites. Studies (Barton, 1975, cited in Kraut, 1982, 79) suggest that in common with other ethnic groups, Italians with an artisanal background became acclimatized more readily than those without, and that social background before emigration was an important determinant of their first and subsequent occupations. In Barton's study, almost half were employed in skilled occupations after emigration, and 20 years after arriving in Cleveland, more than 60 percent of Italian artisans were middle class, whereas laborers experienced more difficulty in becoming upwardly mobile.

Employment preferences and areas of colonization for eastern European Jews were also determined by past experiences, cultural biases, aspirations, and individual talents. After 1900, Jewish immigrants tended to be from artisanal or mercantile backgrounds. Because laws in many of their countries of origin prohibited

Jews from owning land, they customarily acquired readily transferable skills that would prove useful should they be required to move quickly. Where Jewish immigrants did not gravitate toward mercantile or craft occupations, they were often employed in retail or as skilled factory operatives. In the period between 1899 and 1914, 66 percent of male Jewish immigrants were categorized as skilled, against an average of 20 percent for all other males. (Kraut, 1982, 82) The high proportion of Jewish immigrants who had been tailors in Europe were drawn to New York's garment trade, where they quickly became predominant, with the industry employing around 50 percent of all the city's Jewish males and two-thirds of Jewish wage-earners by 1910. (Binder and Reimers, 1995) Although influenced in their choice of occupation by cultural bias and personal preference, competition from native-born Americans was also a factor. As native-born workers perceived the garment trade as a less than masculine occupation, there was little competition for jobs. Some young, single women, particularly Jewish immigrants who had had been involved in the labor movement in Russia, became active in labor organization in the garment industry.

Women's occupations were also culturally determined, but in their case, women were often curtailed in their choice of occupation by their group's cultural conventions and proscriptions, as well as by well-meaning reformers concerned to safeguard all women from industrial exploitation. Women thus worked in areas that involved assisting the male breadwinner (e.g., in shops or markets), and although some did domestic work, others (e.g., Italian, Greek, or Jewish women) were prevented from this occupation because it was considered degrading for them to work in any household except her own. Women from all ethnic groups also worked in factories where dexterity was important.

Concern that long hours would affect women's health and safety led social reformers to press for limits on working hours. By 1913, 39 states had legislation in place; however, these initiatives paradoxically often disadvantaged those they were intended to help most. Thus, once already low wage levels were restricted further by limits on hours, many immigrant women were forced to side-step the legislation designed to protect them, and some employers were only too willing to assist them in this. Until at least 1920, when legislation established a minimum age for employment and the requirement for school attendance, children were also employed in factories and mines. Piecework in the garment trade frequently meant that entire families could work together. Homes on New York's Lower East Side doubled as workspaces, but this trend was rarely any more profitable than piecework in factories because employers often reduced the rate. The combination of legislation, increasing mechanization, and sufficient adult labor meant that employing child labor became less viable, but in times of hardship, immigrant families often flouted the law.

By the second decade, almost every sphere of industrial production was dependent on immigrant labor. Among the conclusions in the Dillingham Commission's report was that, in a 21-industry survey, 57.9 percent of all employees were born overseas, and of these, around 66 percent were of southern and eastern European origin, whereas the proportion was even higher in some areas (e.g., garment manufacturing, coal mining, and construction). The effect that this had on the American-born and older immigrant labor force is not clear from the figures. Rapid industrial expansion meant that nativist fears that immigrants would supplant American workers were overstated because industry was absolutely dependent on this source of labor. Geographic mobility and vertical promotion resulting from industrial growth generated by new immigrant labor absorbed much of the displacement of American workers.

A cheap immigrant labor force also gave American industry a competitive edge over its European competitors, and employers exploited this cheap and plentiful source, exposing the workers to long hours, safety hazards, and health risks. Until the beginnings of labor organization, many workers and their families were impoverished as neither government nor employers accepted responsibility for compensation, sick pay, and medical or funeral expenses.

Self-Employment and Mutual Aid

For many immigrants, independence in the form of self-employment provided an alternative to exploitation by employers. In reality, however, any improvement in wage levels was minimal, at best, though self-determination at least gave the new entrepreneurs a sense of control. As in other areas of economic endeavor, past experiences, cultural biases, aspirations, and individual talents determined the choice of activity. At the lower end of the economic scale, Italians and Greeks became shoeshine "boys" and they, as well as Jewish immigrants, adopted the pushcart, which had several advantages over more formal premises. Loaded with foodstuffs, it could be moved between neighborhoods and there were few overheads, other than the purchase of goods. Itinerant merchants were popular with immigrant communities because they often provided for specific ethnic groups, spoke the old language, and sold goods in smaller quantities than traditional shops.

Self-employment both removed immigrants from exploitation by employers and removed Jews (who had often been small merchants in their country of origin) from discriminatory employers. Religious Jews could arrange their work patterns around the observance of the Sabbath or religious holidays. Further up the scale, fixed retail premises provided opportunities for immigrants. Food stores particularly meant that immigrants could take advantage of dietary preferences or strict religious or ritual laws and requirements, so that by 1910, around 80 percent of the wholesale and 50 percent of the retail meat trade was Jewish owned. Significant numbers of bakeries were also in Jewish hands, whereas Greeks and Italians controlled most of the fruit and vegetable trade. Immigrants, who were familiar with ethnic recipes, also flourished as restaurant owners.

*People with carts of goods in New York's Little Jerusalem, ca. 1910. (Library of
Congress)*

The capital required to start a business was seldom easy to raise. After costs
associated with getting to America, few immigrants had the capital necessary to
finance a business. Saving was difficult for those immigrants with large families
to support, and comparatively few had relatives affluent enough to lend them
sufficient capital. Options for hopeful entrepreneurs were also restricted because banks were reluctant to lend money to immigrants with little collateral.
As a result, many new immigrants took advantage of the mutual-assistance associations established to provide business finance. Many of these organizations
(e.g., the Japanese *ken* and the Chinese *tong*) provided social support as well
as financial assistance. Southern Italians, however, proved resistant to the kind
of financial support offered by other nationalities' organizations. Some studies
(Banfield, 1968, and Lopreato, 1970, in Kraut, 1982, 101) contend that southern
Italians arriving in America perpetuated old-world systems of social interaction,
the result of centuries of hardship, geographical remoteness, and feudal behavior. Having faith only in the immediate family meant that cooperative enterprises
and mutual aid were alien to such groups.

Without the security that would convince already suspicious banks that immigrants represented a good risk, immigrants were compelled to develop ethnic
banks that were prepared to advance small loans to immigrants with no experience of credit. One such bank, the San Francisco–based Bank of Italy, founded
by Amadeo Pietro Giannini in the previous decade, was among the first to offer

branch banking, home loans, and installment credit, while the philanthropic Giannini instructed Italians how to negotiate the American economy. Consolidation and expansion resulted in the subsequently renamed Bank of America.

For most new immigrants, material success was only part of their assimilation, however partial, into American life; many were as concerned with preserving familial and religious structures. Nevertheless, occupational upward mobility was a significant factor in how newcomers defined themselves in such a meritocratic and competitive society. Although each ethnic group defined it in different ways, success for most was habitually defined as progression from the ranks of manual labor, perhaps to a white-collar job or, increasingly, to the acquisition of a small business. Another gauge was property ownership, which came to be viewed as a yardstick of how successful a man had been in supporting his family. Margaret Garb (2005) believes that between the 1880s and 1919, immigrant social and economic perspectives regarding the value of property changed from a belief that home ownership boosted family income to a modern middle-class notion that owning a certain sort of house increased both the immigrant's status as well as the value of the property. Families thus forfeited children's educations by sending them to work to maintain mortgages, an irresponsible gamble for poorly paid, fitfully employed working-class families. Moreover, aspirations of home ownership seldom led to enough income to combat low wages and hazardous working conditions. In reality, the additional income thus generated "helped to subsidize and sustain a low wage economy, leaving massive profits in the hands of business owners and bankers," while permitting the reduction of wages to a minimal level, "forcing working-class tenants to work ever longer hours and struggle that much harder to get by." (Garb, 2005, 52) For most immigrants, however, prosperity or personal gratification often went beyond the transition from blue to white collar and beyond wealth, however relative. In most cases, fulfillment was determined by accommodating those principles, beliefs, and concerns that were independent of financial well-being alongside the acquisition of material assets.

Religion and Customs

Those beliefs, along with devotional objects, religious observances, and practices, were the communal and cultural belongings that immigrants brought with them to America. Allegiance to a faith, however, was frequently inextricably enmeshed with parochial and national character. A widely divergent American Catholic community was already well-established, and new immigrants brought to it an array of assorted Catholic groups. Although some of these groups worshipped together, brought together by the new circumstances in which they found themselves and sacrificing differences because of a common faith, those differences more often proved to be barriers to potential unity. Reluctant to sever the link with their communal past, ethnic gatherings preferred their own clergy who could conduct services in ways familiar to immigrants.

Even after the Americanization campaigns, which became widespread after 1915, and in which reformers attempted to inculcate newcomers into accepting English as their first tongue, language remained an enduring barrier in religious services. French-speaking Roman Catholics, for example, regarded services held in English by the Irish-dominated American Catholic Church as an endeavor by Irish clerics to force them to become Americans, whereas Irish churchgoers often regarded anyone speaking a foreign language with suspicion, believing their intentions were to commandeer services for themselves. Contrasting customs heightened national differences among Catholics; during the period when immigration from southern and eastern Europe was at its height, Polish Catholics who rejected the orthodoxies of Irish Catholicism sometimes resorted to a combination of pagan rituals brought from rural Poland and Polish Catholicism. Although apparently at odds with early 20th-century urban life in the Little Italies, folk religion imported from Italian communities often influenced Italian American Catholicism, but these traditions were either forsaken or modified as immigrants became more assimilated.

The sheer diversity of Catholicism exhibited by new immigrants was an embarrassment to clergy who had arrived earlier because they were concerned that tribal conflicts might fracture the Church or, more seriously, weaken their own authority within it. Assistance from the Church was consequently much reduced and often dependent on Americanization, a requirement strongly resisted by immigrants who wanted to preserve their own identity within their interpretation of Catholicism. As a result, they often remained unaffiliated until they could afford their own churches and priests. Anxious to preserve close ties with those from home and to find sufficient spiritual nourishment to cope with the tribulations of immigrant life, many immigrants held to their religions while modifying them to reflect their experience in America. By the second decade, however, second- and third-generation immigrants were frequently less devout than their forbears. Children resisted what they perceived as old-fashioned and irrelevant deference, whereas others, anxious to be accepted as American, quickly forsook religious practices that clashed with the economic or communal realities of American life. By 1914, many second- and third-generation Jews ignored Saturday, their Sabbath, and worked alongside Gentiles for whom Saturday was another business day.

Despite the efforts of evangelists and missionaries, though, few second-generation Catholic or Jewish immigrants chose Protestantism as a route to assimilation, unless forced to do so by marriage to a Protestant reluctant to abandon his or her faith. Dress was also a way of embracing American values and styles, and although married Jewish women were required to wear a *sheitel* or wig as a demonstration of their modesty, by the second decade, many young wives had replaced the wig with a hat that their husbands considered more attractive. Although arranged marriages, at least those prearranged by parents, were far less common in America than in Europe, the practice did survive in the form of "picture" or "mail" brides. At the peak of Greek emigration between 1910 and 1920, for example, many young women were sent to America to marry a man who was often from the same village.

Young women who had been excluded from education in their homeland took advantage of free public schools, particularly after 1918 when national mandatory attendance laws were initiated, whereas those too old for school could attend evening classes in English and practical skills (e.g., housekeeping) often held in settlement houses. Before then, most states had compulsory school attendance requirements so that young immigrants were legally compelled to attend school during the day, whereas evening classes in English, civics, and vocational courses equipped adults for citizenship, assimilation, and employment. Immigrants often found that teachers were condescending, however, and regarded those immigrants slow to acquire English as ignorant, so some held on to their own languages for security. Others felt that schools emphasized American values as a way of eroding traditional systems of family life, and some Italians, Greeks, and eastern European Jews thus sent their children to parochial schools to reinforce the links with their churches and to forestall the erosion of discrete cultures.

Different ethnic groups nevertheless displayed marked differences in their attitudes toward education, and achievement varied widely among groups, too. In a survey of 15 Manhattan schools, Kessner (1977, cited in Kraut, 1982, 139) found that an excessive proportion of immigrant children were left behind one or more grades. Of new immigrants, 23 percent of eastern European pupils were left behind, whereas 16 percent graduated. Thirty-six percent of Italian children were left behind and there were no graduations of Italians who entered high school. Kessner quotes a 1910 survey of New York slums that found more Jews above age 16 remaining in school than any other ethnic category, whereas in 1916, Jewish enrollment in local colleges comprised 73 percent of City College students. It would appear from the statistics that Italians, particularly those new immigrants from the south, undervalued education. Many Italians were temporary immigrants, however, returning to Italy each year until they decided to make America their permanent home. Once they accepted that fact, Italians seemed to be as enthusiastic about education as any other group.

Since the end of unrestricted immigration in the early 1920s, historians have begun to reassess the role that education played in the assimilation and Americanization of new immigrants. Most historians agree that education had a dual role in the assimilation process: providing immigrants with essential skills for upward mobility, while simultaneously eroding cultural differences and promoting a white, homogeneous society as the ideal. Historians like Greer (1976, cited in Kraut, 1982, 137), however, contend that education was not the mechanism that led to economic and social success for immigrants, nor did it aid in the process of Americanization. Instead, schools merely reinforced the social standing and economic status of already established groups, and the main role of education was to perpetuate those groups' relative social positions. Academic achievement was dependent on the socioeconomic status of the child's family, and immigrant pupils frequently failed to achieve their potential because the system was designed to eliminate those who didn't correspond with the white Protestant ideal.

Migration

Like immigrants from Europe and elsewhere, migrants from the southern states decided to uproot for many of the same reasons. The push of environmental, economic, religious, or political pressures that motivate or compel emigration balanced against the pull of forces in the target destination that attract migrants, along with the means that make migration possible, apply equally to both inward migrants and immigrants from outside the United States. Economic considerations formed the basis of much migration from the South, but social factors also played a significant role. Before the Civil War, the majority of African American migration was compulsory as white slaveholders took advantage of the opening of the trans-Appalachian West. After the ending of foreign slave trading in 1808, an interstate slave trade grew as plantations in such states as Alabama, Louisiana, and Texas were worked by these forced migrants. Statistics are far from accurate, but perhaps 1 million African American Southerners were compelled to relocate between 1790 and 1860. After the Civil War and emancipation in 1865, migration was often characterized by the limited degree of autonomy that land ownership conferred. This was to change, however, in the decades after 1890.

Migration from the South at 454,000 was higher between 1910 and 1920 than in earlier decades, and it would increase still further to 749,000 in the period from 1920 to 1930. The Great Migration of the years before, during, and immediately after World War I, however, represented both a phase in the long-term progression of African American urbanization and also accelerated a westward and northward tendency begun in the 1890s. During World War I, however, the trend for migration toward the south and west that had characterized earlier decades declined as the center of African American population moved north.

Four main impulses brought about the mass migration of this period. The westward expansion of cotton cultivation ended in the first decade of the 20th century, and dependency on this single crop left the South vulnerable to the boll weevil invasion, whereas bad weather in the late 19th and early 20th centuries forced hundreds of thousands of agricultural workers to leave the land for southern cities. Disenfranchisement of African Americans and the Jim Crow legislation that legitimized separation left African Americans with few rights and little recourse to law in a South where racial discrimination and violence was common. Industry in the North, which had depended on foreign immigration for cheap labor, was suddenly deprived of this source following America's entry into the war in 1917. This was compounded by the return of some immigrants to enlist in their country of origin and the withdrawal from the labor pool of hundreds of thousands of workers enlisting in U.S. forces. Last, inward investment in a South rich in resources yet poor in capital had led to the transformation of the region into a dependent outpost with few jobs.

In agriculture, opportunities for advancement and land ownership were significantly more plentiful for whites than African Americans, who mainly tended to move from one class of tenancy to another. As industrialization led to more lucrative but less plentiful jobs, whites became more reluctant than in the past to concede them to African American workers. Given the dominance of an all-white Democratic South, the political, social, and economic inferiority of African Americans resulted in their numbers greatly outweighing white migrants during the Great Migration.

Despite the relative isolation and poor communications of the South compared with the North, and restrictive legislation that in some areas prevented African Americans from migrating, African Americans were galvanized into migrating extremely quickly, learning of opportunities through a combination of recruiting agents; family members who had already migrated; employment, housing, and finance organizations; and ethnic presses. Time lags between the decision to leave and departure were usually caused by the difficulty of raising the rail fare, often accomplished by selling property and belongings; however, this became increasingly difficult as more migrants left, seriously depleting some areas. Others relied on family members who had already migrated north sending them money or on prepaid tickets, although some southern rail companies refused to honor tickets issued by those in the North.

Temporary and seasonal migration had already occurred among African American workers, particularly the young and more mobile who found work in southern cites; however, migration in the early 20th century increasingly became permanent as African American workers left the land. Before 1916, comparatively few migrants traveled north immediately, preferring to try southern cities before deciding either to stay or to commit themselves to the industrial cities of the North. This meant that many migrants were urbanized already rather than being the rural displaced that migrants arriving in the industrial North were once believed to be.

Evidence for this, however, is scant because until 1940, the census did not include information other than birth, sex, and age. It is possible, though, to draw reasonably accurate conclusions from such contemporary reports as those undertaken by the U.S. Department of Commerce to examine population turnover in southern cities. Although these reports do not specify duration of residence, it is nevertheless possible to compare population figures with literacy levels from

African American men and boys pose outside the glass factory where they work in Alexandria, Virginia, ca. 1911. Poor wages and working conditions caused many African Americans to flee the South in pursuit of better opportunities provided by jobs in the North. (Library of Congress)

a study undertaken by Stanley Lieberson ("Selective Black Migration from the South: A Historical View"). Lieberson discovered that during the Great Migration "the rate of literacy was actually higher than would have been predicted had there been no out-migration" (Marks, 1989, 42), leading Marks to conclude that there had been "a significant out-migration of literate blacks." (Ibid.) As schools are more widely available in urban rather than rural areas, literacy signifies prolonged urban residence.

It is also possible to deduce levels of skill from reports by the Department of Labor and the census, which both indicate that certain states like Alabama, Georgia, and South Carolina had high rates of skilled and semi-skilled workers in 1910, which had fallen significantly by 1920. States with the greatest out-migration are also those with the highest relative decline in skilled and semi-skilled workers. It is evident, then, that what took place during the Great Migration was far removed from the simplistic deduction that such northern industrial cities as Chicago, Detroit, Pittsburgh, and New York were the destinations for vast numbers of unskilled, rural, illiterate workers. Rather, those who left were, first of all, a diverse and complex range of rural African Americans that arrived in southern cities before the movement of a significant number of skilled, semi-skilled, and unskilled laborers and their families to northern cities.

Racial Conflict

Tensions were inevitable in rapidly expanding northern cities. The influx of African Americans during the Great Migration led to increased hostility between the indigenous white population and the migrants who competed with them for housing and jobs. Racial conflicts emerged in urban communities already affected by the war, and outbreaks of racially inspired violence occurred in East St. Louis, Chicago, and Omaha.

Housing infrastructure in many northern industrial cities was ill equipped to cope with populations swelled by thousands of economic migrants. The crisis in urban housing particularly affected African Americans as discrimination channeled African Americans into poor-quality, racially constricted, and overcrowded areas, denying them access to capital and forcing them into paying high rents. When combined with discriminatory employment and union policies that restricted African American workers to lower-paid, demeaning, and insecure work, these factors played a part in the climate of underlying violence that suffused many industrial centers. The outbreak of violence in East St. Louis that occurred in July 1917 characterized this combination of circumstances. In riots that claimed more lives than any other racial conflict of the 20th century, inflated anxieties over African American infiltration of white districts, fueled by speculation that a mass of African American workers had been recruited for the city's industrial plants, sparked a series of violent and, in some cases, fatal conflicts that resulted in the deaths of at least 39 African Americans and 9 whites.

Chicago, too, was affected by many of the same conditions that exacerbated racial tensions. The city's African American population grew from around 44,000 in 1910 to 109,000 in 1919. The growth of a changed sense of identity for those African Americans who returned from the war was added to the social and labor inequalities that discriminated against African American migrants. Newly aware of the segregated neighborhoods and diminished employment opportunities that faced them on their return, the "New Negroes," as the African American veterans were termed by the civil rights activist and sociologist W. E. B. Du Bois, were less willing to accept discrimination in the cities.

Several theories have been advanced to explain the racial violence that erupted in July 1919. The police were, perhaps, reluctant to make arrests in case they offended powerful political interests, whereas white police racists were blamed for neglecting to prevent the early spread of the riots. In the hysterical atmosphere of the postwar Red Scare, Bolshevik radicals were also blamed for spreading propaganda and fomenting unrest among African American communities in the hope that this might intensify racial tensions as part of a conspiracy to overthrow the government. These claims were dismissed, and it is evident that social conditions were largely responsible for the racial conflicts that broke out in many cities in the so-called Red Summer of 1919.

Following the death of an African American swimmer at a segregated beach, violence spread throughout the Black Belt on the South Side of Chicago on Monday July 27, resulting in two deaths and at least 50 injuries. These incidents escalated on the following day, propelled by the deliberate torching of buildings, a contributory factor in the amount of those left destitute at the end of the conflict. As it became clear that the police could not deal with the scale of the violence, 6,000 National Guardsmen were dispatched as a peacekeeping force. At the end of several days of rioting, at least 38 deaths were reported, more than 500 citizens were injured, and more than 1,000 were left homeless.

Although lynchings in the South and riots in the North had escalated during and after the war, the demographic shift begun in this period had widespread implications. Notwithstanding discrimination by unions, and hostility and suspicion from white residents, increased opportunities for African American mobility and employment did, in some small measure, eventually result in increasing self-confidence and participation in American life in the next two decades.

American Identity

The Melting Pot

King (2000, 14) believes that of all the issues surrounding immigration in 20th-century America, the single most important is how readily immigrants were assimilated. During the decade, those inimical to immigration focused their arguments on how appropriate the new immigrants were for American citizenship. This perceived suitability was evaluated against an Anglo-American notion of American identity, and, arguably, assimilation occurred by means of a melting pot, which has operated to Americanize immigrants.

Although the concept of America as a composite of heterogeneous immigrants had been popular for more than 100 years, the conviction that America was a melting pot that drew on its amalgam of immigrants to form the political way of life was cast in the late 19th century. Although Israel Zangwill's 1908 play of that name gave the term more widespread currency, there were some even then who viewed the concept with some suspicion. German Americans, for example, resisted the idea of being subsumed into American life and were comfortable with being both German *and* American.

As the restrictive legislation enacted before, during, and after the decade demonstrated, the concept of a melting pot proved to be neither unrestricted nor all-embracing. Given that *Anglo*-Americanism was the template on which the idea of being and becoming American was based, the melting pot model also excluded African Americans, whose linguistic and behavioral contributions to the American character were largely ignored. Even though Woodrow Wilson had renounced his earlier discriminatory comments regarding immigrants by 1915, his address to a group of new immigrants in that year concluded that America had been nourished by the "voluntary association with it of great bodies of strong men and forward-looking women of other lands" (cited in King, 2000, 17), thus excluding all such involuntary immigrants as African Americans.

Because the original settlers were Protestant, that religion became irrevocably associated with the innate "Englishness" of that pioneer group, and later immigrants (e.g., Irish and German Catholics) were also immediately singled out on religious grounds. Concerns arose among existing Americans regarding the difficulties of assimilating so many apparently unsuitable eastern and southern Europeans. If anything, these concerns were even more prevalent in the rabid and xenophobic atmosphere of the early war years. These anxieties had their origins in the notion, prevalent in the 19th century, of what constituted American identity. Those early English settlers believed that American characteristics were derived from English roots and were sustained and passed on through the generations. Believing that American identity had been cast between 1776 and 1787, subsequent generations assumed that Americans were essentially homogeneous and thereby immutable, and that assimilation into the existing type was an essential prerequisite for citizenship. The exclusiveness of this view and the consequent emphasis on conforming to certain characteristics thus militates against the idea of an all-embracing melting pot.

Americanization

The use of the term *Americanization* became widespread after 1915, but as formal policy, the Americanization of immigrants was established during and after World War I. Assimilation differs in kind and can be distinguished as, first, that which tends toward imbuing immigrants with Anglo-Saxon principles and concerns; second, where national identity is not dictated by the pre-eminent or longest-present group, often described as the melting pot; and last, where a profusion of ethnic types and identities coexists.

Of these three, it is the first, which King (2000, 85) describes as Anglo-Conformity, which most closely approximates the historical experience of the United States. By the Civil War, a white, Protestant, Anglo-Saxon group, derived from the first English colonists and later northern and western Europeans and who considered themselves as "Americans" and distinguished themselves from nonwhites and non-English, were already a dominant group. These attributes shaped the Americanization impulse in the early 20th century when attempts to define and defend American traits were used politically to control eligibility for assimilation.

Concerns regarding the perceived unwillingness of new immigrants to naturalize as U.S. citizens and their absence of "Americanism" rose during World War I. Legislation thereby allowed for the active promotion of citizenship classes and the dissemination of educational material by public schools, which received names of applicants for citizenship from the Bureau of Naturalization. The role of schools was to promote those values defined as American.

Before American involvement in World War I, the process of assimilation had relatively little effect on a public generally unconcerned with immigrants; however, America's entry aggravated latent tensions, released suspicions about "hyphenated Americans" (Americans whose nationality was prefixed by their ethnic origin, such as Italian-American), and increased pressure by nativists and 100 percent Americanizers on the administration for a more intensive Americanization policy. Education programs to assist Americanization were voluntary at first, reaching a peak only after 1918 when anti-immigration sentiment led to increasing pressure for mandatory Americanization. By supplying advisors, workers, equipment, teaching materials, and some funding of Americanization Committees, the National Americanization Committee made the establishment of education programs in schools and industry possible. This privately funded body also underwrote the Immigration Committee of the U.S. Chamber of Commerce, which also promoted Americanization by employers whose involvement demonstrated a fitting connection between political and industrial motives. Private funding reflects the extent of collaboration between a government agency and the private sector.

There were some, though, like Frances Kellor of the National Americanization Committee, who believed that these initiatives were insufficient to counter what she perceived as anti-American bias, sedition, and dishonest propaganda among non-English-speaking groups and organizations. In 1918, new collaborative initiatives under the umbrella of the War Work Extension, and headed by Kellor, were therefore established and formed the basis for a structured program. In contrast to the political pressures with which Americanization was more associated after the war, the emphasis still was on education and language proficiency. It had been possible as far back as the Revolutionary era to discriminate between various ethnic constituents both by differences in language and by differences in social customs and religions. Americanization initiatives maintained this racial context, with immigrants being differentiated by nationality. Any inadequacies in literacy were discerned as risks to American productivity and war readiness.

The reality of diverse ethnic origins and enduring cultural variations tends to be glossed over in the need to emphasize national unity during times of conflict. This requirement facilitated the growth of such populist campaigns as 100 percent American, whereas the pejorative "un-American" developed after the

31

TO ALL ALIENS

IF the WAR has affected your LIVING or WORKING conditions,

IF you WANT to learn the AMERICAN LANGUAGE and become a CITIZEN,

IF you WISH Employment, Advice or Information,

Without Charge,

Apply to—

Room 1820, MUNICIPAL BUILDING
MAYOR'S COMMITTEE ON NATIONAL DEFENSE
COMMITTEE on ALIENS.

AN SÄMTLICHE NICHT NATURALISIERTEN AUSLÄNDER:

Diejenigen, deren EXISTENZBEDINGUNGEN oder ARBEITSVERHÄLTNISSE infolge des KRIEGES geschädigt sind,

Die die AMERIKANISCHE SPRACHE zu erlernen und das BÜRGERRECHT zu erwerben wünschen,

Die BESCHÄFTIGUNG finden oder RAT bezw. AUSKUNFT einholen möchten, und zwar kostenfrei, sind aufgefordert, sich zu melden im

MUNIZIPALGEBÄUDE, Zimmer 1820
Die vom Bürgermeister eingesetzte Landesvertheidigungs-Kommission
Ausschuss für nicht-naturalisierte Ausländer.

Minden külföldi szülöttnek.

Ha a háboru hatást gyakorolt életmódjára vagy munka viszonyaira,

Ha kivánja megtanulni az amerikai nyelvet és megszerezni a polgári jogot,

Ha foglalkozást, tanácsot vagy felvilágositást kiván

dijmentesen,

Forduljon a

Városház 1820 számu szobájában lévő
Polgármester nemzeti védelem bizottságához
Külföldiek bizottságához.

Všetkým v cudzozemsku narodeným.

Keď vojna mala účinok na spôsob vášho žitia alebo na vaše pracovné pomery,

Keď sa chcete naučiť americkú reč a stať sa občanom,

Keď chcete dostať prácu, poradu alebo vysvetlenie

bez poplatku,

Obráťte sa na

Izbu číslo 1820, v mestkom dome
Mayorov Výbor Národnej Obrany
Výbor Cudzozemcov.

צו אלע אויסלענדער

אויב דער קריג האט אנגערירט אייערע לעבענס אדער
ארבייטס אימשטענדען,

אויב איר ווילט זיך אויסלערנען דיא אמעריקאנער שפּראך
און ווערען אַ בירגער (סיטיזן),

אויב איר זוכט ארבייט, אראט אדער ערקונדיגונג,

אומזונסט,

ווענדעם זיך צו

רום 1820 מיוניסיפעל בילדינג
דעם מייארס קאמיטעל אן נעשאנאל דיפענס
קאמיטי אן איליענס.

A TUTTI I FORESTIERI

SE LA GUERRA ha mutato le vostre condizioni di VITA o di LAVORO,

SE VOLETE imparare la LINGUA AMERICANA e diventare un CITTADINO.

SE DESIDERATE IMPIEGO, CONSIGLIO o INFORMAZIONE,

senza nessuna spesa,

Rivolgetevi alla—

STANZA 1820, PALAZZO MUNICIPALE
COMITATO DEL SINDACO PER LA DIFESA NAZIONALE
COMITATO per i FORESTIERI

Poster showing a small American flag, with text in English, German, Hungarian, Czech, Hebrew, and Italian, 1917. Text reads: "If the war has affected your living or working conditions, if you want to learn the American language and become a citizen, if you wish employment, advice, or information, without charge, apply to Room 1820, Municipal Building, Mayor's Committee on National Defense, Committee on Aliens." (Library of Congress) war's end. It was unclear whether national unity meant consensus of opinion, allegiance to government, or the desertion of all foreign obligation, but the consequences of equivocation were the pre-eminence of an unambiguous official Americanism and, as some reformers grew frustrated with what they saw as the relative impotence of Americanization, the growth of such reactionary movements as the American Legion, founded in 1919.

Concerns regarding the potential threat of radical unassimilated immigrants unsympathetic to American principles led to increasing calls for compulsory registration and education, and Americanization assumed a markedly nativist and patriotic stance. Even though reformers before 1918 assigned the alleged inferiority of southern and eastern Europeans to cultural influences, rather than racial differences, their successors used pseudoscience to justify aliens' "racial" inferiority. For these most fervent activists, Americanization implied leaving behind ethnic diversity and adopting a homogeneous notion of national identity. Breaking up ethnic communities was thought to be essential in realizing this assimilation because assimilation has been markedly slower wherever collective migration and economic and geographic impulses have led to ethnic concentration and isolation.

As language was central to the assimilation process, suspicions fell on foreign-language newspapers, which still circulated widely after World War I. Circulation figures for the largest foreign-language nationally distributed daily, weekly, and monthly papers in the main languages spoken by immigrants (Italian, German, Swedish, Norwegian-Danish, and Polish) amounted to 1.15 million copies. In New York alone, daily papers in Yiddish sold more than 350,000 copies. (King, 2000, 111) The 100 Percent American Committee believed these papers to be "America's Greatest Menace" (Ibid.), advocating legislation to prohibit publication of any newspaper not printed in English, whereas other Americanizers believed that the papers could be exploited by the placement of pro-American stories. At the state level, a great deal of legislation in favor of Americanization was passed between 1919 and 1920, largely as a result of the hysterical responses to anti-immigrant campaigns. By 1919, many states had legislation stipulating some or all of the following: English as a medium of instruction in all schools, instruction in American history and civil government, flying the American flag on school houses, and patriotic exercises in schools. Such steps were instrumental in creating the background to the restrictive legislation of the early 1920s, measures that diluted the argument for regulated Americanization because reduced immigration satisfying national quotas meant that new arrivals were supposedly selected more carefully.

Some dissenting voices, however, believed that Americans would benefit from the legacy of ethnic and cultural diversity, arguing that, should there be a stereotypical American, then he or she was a blend of various traditions rather than the "hyphenated" type from which few could avoid descent. Concerns were also raised about the extent of intrusion that Americanization insinuated, whereas the term itself implied denationalization. Writing in 1920, John Daniels (cited in King, 2000, 118) believed that immigrants' own organizations and societies could assist in the process of Americanization, acting organically as places of transition where newcomers could raise morale and resources before identifying more closely with the surrounding American community. Dissenters from the official view, however, were in the minority.

Americanization concentrated on immigrants, largely excluding some 10 million African Americans who, in 1919, were highlighted by Fred Butler (King, 2000, 122), director of Americanization in the Bureau of Education, for their supposed mental deficiencies, reflecting the eugenic debates then being discussed before congressional immigration committees and which were used to justify increasingly exclusionary legislation in the 1920s.

American Identity in Visual Culture

As part of the process of assimilation, some artists depicted immigrants and their communities with varying degrees of success. Immigrants were perceived as a source of energy by painters of New York's Ashcan School, exploring contrasts between old and new in the first decades of the 20th century. Ashcan realists ignored traditional subject matter, instead depicting life, culture, popular entertainments, the working class, and immigrants in the ethnic communities.

John Sloan's *McSorley's Bar* (1912, Detroit Institute of Arts) and Robert Henri's portrait "types," such as *The Working Man* (1910, whereabouts unknown), have been seen as epitomizing the artists' claims to realism. Many Ashcan pictures, however, such as Sloan's *Night Windows* (1910, last known collection, Delaware Art Museum), reveal contradictory and inconsistent positions about immigrants, representing them as colorful oddities or reveling in their strangeness. By concentrating on immigrants' foreign dress and alien habits, or by depicting immigrants as types rather than individual people, painters often maintained and reinforced enduring stereotypes and popular misconceptions. By emphasizing distinctions between their imported customs and American traditions, and by seeing their culture and neighborhoods as discrete and alien, painters were complicit in immigrants' continued isolation.

Some images do, however, depict immigrants less stereotypically and thus more realistically; Glackens's Washington Square series, 1910–1912, addresses the intermixing of cultures, ethnicity, and class where Italian communities of Greenwich Village were separated from the wealthier neighbourhood on the northern edge of the square.

March Day, Washington Square (1912, private collection) depicts an immigrant woman in a yellow shawl who stands away from a fashionably dressed group. The tension between the more prosperous Americans and the immigrants in this and others, such as *Woman with Baby, Washington Square* (1912,

Night Windows, *John Sloan, 1910, etching. (Library of Congress)*

Museum of Art, Fort Lauderdale), implies the gradual assimilation into every-day life.

In *Parade, Washington Square* (Whitney Museum of American Art, New York) and *Italo-American Celebration, Washington Square* (Museum of Fine Arts, Boston), which were both painted around 1910, Glackens emphasizes small yet significant details by contrasting the dress of newly arrived immigrants with more fashionable older arrivals, and by the conspicuous display in both pictures of Italian and American flags next to each other. *Italo-American Celebration, Washington Square,* shows more dynamism than the remote impression of *Parade, Washington Square,* revealing a greater diversity of participants and emphasizing their ethnicity through dress, movement, and features.

Sloan's *Italian Procession, New York* (1913–1925, San Diego Museum of Art) differs from Glackens's portrayal by depicting Italians as a colorful and pictur-esque group at an Old World ritual.

Glackens shows Italian Americans becoming assimilated into mainstream society, creating a new identity as American citizens while still commemorating their ethnicity. The images expose, rather than conceal or ignore, tensions be-tween immigrants from diverse backgrounds as they become Americanized. At a time when Americanism was proven by observance of societal and cultural standards, evidence of material improvement showed immigrants' desire and capacity to leave behind their origins and to play a role in mainstream society.

Americanization succeeded, in part, because the number of new immigrants was drastically reduced after the early 1920s, by which time around 47 percent of foreign-born immigrants were naturalized. The process endorsed a specific model of American identity that excluded national or ethnic diversity and instead imposed a homogeneous Anglo-Conformity on millions of 20th-century immigrants, thus severely diluting the impact of immigrants' rich cultural and ethnic heritage on America and Americans.

THE IMPACT OF IMMIGRATION DURING THE 1910s

The most visible implications of immigration were demographic and economic. Given the decline in the native birthrate that occurred around the same time that mass immigration began in 1830, it is possible that without immigration the rate of population growth would have diminished even more acutely than it did.

The Dillingham Commission observed that without new immigration the industrial expansion of the 20 years before 1911 could not have taken place; however, its conclusion that immigration had contributed to lower wages, higher unemployment, and the supplanting of native workers from jobs is difficult to defend. Even though immigrant wage levels were below those of native workers, immigrants tended to enter lower-paid occupations. Neither did immigration add to the unemployed as the pull of economic opportunity led to fluctuations in immigration, regardless of conditions in Europe. It is also unlikely that increased immigration led to fewer jobs for native workers because population growth in industrial economies tends to result in increases in the numbers of jobs. In any case, as immigrants tended to occupy lower-paid and less-skilled jobs, native-born and earlier immigrant workers took advantage of increased openings for skilled and managerial employees.

Anxieties regarding potential acts of subversion by immigrant radicals, concerns about the influx of new immigrants, and a generalized feeling about America's failure to achieve its war objectives led to fresh calls for more restrictive legislation to limit immigration. The 1920 Dillingham quota bill, which called for a one-year suspension on immigration, was introduced before the House.

Political influence is harder to determine because many immigrants' first considerations were unrelated to national or local political systems, nor were many early immigrants properly enfranchised. Whereas immigrant numbers significantly altered the political structure, many were politically conservative and inexperienced; therefore, the system was open to potential corruption. Large groups of voters appeared to have little effect on determining foreign policy, as can be seen in the example of the then-largest ethnic group, Germans, who failed to keep America out of World War I.

Immigrants as well as migrants continued to swell northern industrial cities; census data for 1910 and 1920 indicates that the population of New York State, for example, increased from 9.11 million to 10.3 million between1910 and 1920. The 1910 census also shows that "immigrant cities" like New York, Chicago, Detroit, Cleveland, and Boston had an immigrant population of around 75 percent. As discussed earlier in this chapter, in some areas English as a first language continued to decline. Due to the high number of Japanese and Chinese immigrants in San Francisco, for example, 72 percent of the population considered a foreign language as their principal tongue by 1916. New immigrants also affected employment patterns, particularly in the North. The Dillingham Commission found that in a 21-industry survey, 57.9 percent of all employees were born overseas, and that of those around 66 percent were of southern and eastern European origin. A high proportion of Jewish immigrants was drawn to New York's garment trade, where they quickly became predominant, with the industry employing around 50 percent of all the city's Jewish males and two-thirds of Jewish wage earners by 1910. Following concerns regarding long hours in regard to women's health and safety, by 1913, 39 states had legislation in place limiting working hours. Legislation was also enacted stipulating a minimum employment age. Both of these measures particularly affected immigrants.

Self-employment among immigrant communities grew, often among the retail and service sectors, as did such self-help initiatives as ethnic banks, which provided capital for business development and, increasingly, home ownership. Young immigrant women, particularly those from traditional communities, began to embrace more modern American styles and values, abandoning ethnic dress and wigs. In an attempt to assimilate more rapidly, immigrants began to take advantage of education, taking language and home-management classes. After 1918, when mandatory attendance legislation was enacted, increasing numbers of immigrants attended free public schools.

South to north migration had equally obvious demographic and economic consequences, the most marked of which was the growth of African American populations in many northern cities, often beyond the extent to which many cities could absorb such large migrant populations. This led to significant anxiety among the extant populations, both African American and white, about the potentially disruptive impact of large numbers of migrants. Tolnay (2003) discusses discriminatory responses to increases in African American inward migration by the white community in northern cities as they increased their efforts to restrict the residential and occupational opportunities available to African Americans. Racial segregation in northern cities—already evident before the Great Migration—increased as white residents were forced to use still stronger measures to maintain segregation as the African American population expanded.

Department of Labor naturalization class, ca. 1912–1932. (Library of Congress)

A racially and ethnically determined employment hierarchy similarly had limited employment opportunities for northern African Americans before the Great Migration. Within that hierarchy, African Americans came below native-born whites and immigrants with greater access to better-paid jobs, whereas African Americans were clustered in mainly unskilled or semi-skilled jobs.

Racial conflicts emerged in urban communities already affected by the war, and outbreaks of racially inspired violence occurred in East St. Louis, Chicago, and Omaha. The crisis in urban housing affected African Americans particularly as discrimination channeled African Americans into poor-quality, overcrowded areas. The inevitable consequence was the outbreak of racial violence in many cities.

The large numbers of migrants and immigrants, particularly those categorized as "new" after 1880, clearly did affect American attitudes to foreign-born residents, leading to hostility, suspicion, and, ultimately, restrictive legislation after 1920 that drastically reduced the numbers arriving in the United States, creating a conflict between America's self-image of a country open to all regardless of race or circumstances and the reality of a racially based entry policy.

Historians' Debate: New Immigrants and the African American Experience

It may have been inevitable that early debates concerning immigration reflect the historians' own cultural background and ethnic roots. Before 1920, the majority of historians were existing Americans from a white, Anglo-Saxon Protestant background. As a result, they were largely unsympathetic when discussing tribulations experienced by immigrants, and their discourses at times verged on nativism. The first historians to write the history of their own groups were second- or third-generation northern and western European immigrants. As such, they were mainly unconcerned with those new immigrants that by 1910 comprised the bulk of newcomers. One of the first historians to document new immigration, Peter Roberts (*The New Immigrants: A Study of the Industrial and Social Life of Southeastern Europeans in America*) defended rapid assimilation, believing that this process was helped by an understanding attitude from those already settled.

There were others, though, notably Frederick Jackson Turner, whose articles contained many of the discriminatory racial stereotypes typical of the period. Although Oscar Handlin (*The Uprooted*) was among the first writers to concentrate on the new immigrant and what he or she encountered on arriving in America, the book has a novellike structure. It has subsequently been re-evaluated since its publication. Maldwyn Allen Jones (*American Immigration*) renounces the usual division between old and new immigration, preferring instead to underline the progression of a much wider social course of international migration. In doing so, however, he omits the characteristic attributes of each group and the most significant changes in America over the course of successive waves of immigration.

Toward the end of the 20th century, writers began to investigate the subject of the Americanization campaigns of the 1910s more critically. One such writer is Colin Greer, whose *The Great School Legend: A Revisionist Interpretation of American Public Education* investigates the role that schools played in the process. Greer argues that schools operated as instruments of social restraint to manage all of the urban and rural poor, including immigrants, thus impeding their development and so perpetuating the hegemonic class constitution. Alan M. Kraut (*The Huddled Masses: The Immigrant in American Society, 1880–1921*) finds such arguments to be "unpersuasive," although he does accept that schools were "vehicles of assimilation."

The African American experience during the Great Migration and their experience on arrival in the industrial cities of the North are documented by Carole Marks (*Farewell—We're Good and Gone: The Great Black Migration*). Marks argues persuasively that rather than travel north immediately, African American migrants went first of all to southern cities before deciding either to stay or to commit themselves to travel north. Many migrants were therefore already urbanized, rather than being the rural displaced migrants arriving in the industrial north, as many had believed them to be. In a more recent volume (*Making Americans: Immigration, Race, and the Origins of the Diverse Democracy*), Desmond King focuses on the exclu-

> ## Historians' Debate: New Immigrants and the African American Experience, Continued
>
> sion, in both the literature on immigration and the experience of "involuntary immigrants," of African Americans, whose linguistic and behavioral contributions to the American character were largely ignored. King argues that the melting pot model excluded African Americans because writers and politicians had stressed the cultivation of the polity and culture of the United States by "voluntary immigrants."

BIOGRAPHIES

Rose Cohen, 1880–1925

Immigrant Author

Cohen was born Rose Gollup in the Russian empire's Pale of Settlement, emigrating to the United States with an aunt at age 12 to be reunited with her father, who had arrived in America 18 months beforehand. Her vivid and evocative autobiographical portrayal of life in the tenements and work in the garment sweatshops of New York's Lower East Side—*Life in the Shadow*—provides compelling testimony of the divided loyalties young Jewish immigrant women frequently experienced as they made the transition from the customs and life of the Old World to a new identity in the New World.

Before Cohen began the autobiography, at an English language class at the Thomas Davidson School at the Educational Alliance, she had followed her father into the garment trade and, like him, also joined a union. From her account, her father seems to have assimilated fairly readily, trimming his beard and forelocks and adopting such American habits as carrying money on the Sabbath. Although at first shocked by this, within a year Cohen seemed more enthusiastic about Americanization, exhorting her mother, who had joined them in New York along with her siblings, to renounce the traditional kerchief worn by married Orthodox Jewish women.

Family hardship and unemployment forced Cohen into domestic service, a life for which she was barely equipped because she was physically weak and had been cushioned from hard domestic work by her family. The rigors of a life in service, along with the obvious inequities evident in the position, led to her resignation after two months. Her growing alienation from traditional Jewish women and Jewish culture becomes more apparent during a brief arranged engagement to a Jewish grocer, whereas her chance meeting with Lillian Wald of the Henry Street Settlement was instrumental in helping Cohen escape from the almost exclusively Jewish Lower East Side and an environment that was little different from her village in Russia.

Following a stay arranged by Wald in the uptown Presbyterian Hospital, where her health began to improve and where she met New Yorkers other than Russian Jewish immigrants, she felt increasingly out of place and resolved to learn English. Her move outside this milieu, however, was to cause Cohen much internal conflict, and she seems continually to waver between the old and the new worlds. Cohen recovered sufficiently to return to work, but she nevertheless experienced more tension over her apparent inability to integrate successfully into American life. Wald was able to arrange a number of alternatives to the usual options open to immigrant women, such as summer work in a Connecticut retreat for immigrant children as well as work in a cooperative garment shop with the co-founder of the Women's Trade Union League, Leonora O'Reilly.

The subsequent marriage and birth of a daughter before the 1918 publication of the autobiography go unacknowledged in the book, which was followed by several short stories. The cause of her death in 1925 is unclear, but a previous suicide attempt perhaps points to a possible explanation.

Madison Grant, 1865–1937

Conservationist and Eugenicist

Lawyer and conservationist Madison Grant is now remembered as a eugenicist and for one of the best-known works of scientific racism, *The Passing of the Great Race; or, the Racial Basis of European History,* published in 1916. He played an active part in helping to fashion immigration restriction and anti-miscegenation policies.

Although Grant practiced law after graduation, his main interests lay in naturalism and conservation, and he is accredited with the preservation of several species of animals, establishing environmental and philanthropic organizations, and for his work in the development of the field of wildlife management. Much of this has been obscured by his subsequent work on racial hygiene, however, which illustrates the "racial history" of Europe. *The Passing of the Great Race* examines Grant's own interpretation of anthropology and history, centered largely on the notion of race and focusing on his belief in the racial superiority of what he termed "Nordic races." As a highly vocal advocate of eugenics, whereby various interventionist strategies are employed to improve hereditary characteristics, Grant argued for the extermination of "undesirable" characteristics and "worthless race types" from the human gene pool. He also advocated the installation of a dictatorship and argued that "unfavorable" races should be segregated in ghettos.

The book was extremely popular, providing opponents of immigration with "proof" to justify their belief in immigration restriction policies. Grant himself was in favor of restricting immigration, particularly from Asia and southern Europe. He believed that selective breeding should be employed to preserve the "racial purity" of the United States. He served on the National Research Council Committee on Anthropology after World War I, representing the "hereditarian" faction of physical anthropology against the branch that included the German Jewish immigrant anthropologist Franz Boas, who advocated cultural anthropology.

Joe Hill, 1879–1915

Activist

Joe Hill was a controversial labor activist, member of the IWW, and songwriter. He was born Joel Emmanuel Hägglund and was also known as Joseph Hillström. The Swedish American activist emigrated to America in 1902 where, as Joe Hill, he worked as a migrant laborer in various states until 1910 before encountering the IWW in San Pedro, California. Hill was attracted to the IWW by their radical anticapitalist stance. His life is now surrounded by myth, making any definitive biography problematic, but in the letter that he wrote to the IWW newspaper, *Industrial Worker,* in late 1910, he identified himself as Joe Hill, a member of the IWW in Portland, Oregon. In the letter, Hill condemned the tactics of the local police against IWW members and workers. Hill continued to mobilize support and foment labor unrest around the country between 1910 and 1912, and there are often contradictory reports of his activities in several different places at once.

In 1913, Hill traveled to Utah, at that time a state where highly vocal anti-union feelings were evident. The reasons for Hill's arrival in Salt Lake City in the summer of 1913 are unclear, and his activities from then until January 1914 are poorly documented. After rooming with the Eselius family in Murray, Utah, Hill was alleged to have been involved with the fatal shooting of a storeowner after arriving at a doctor's surgery with a gunshot wound. The subsequent trial, at which Hill refused to testify, caused an international controversy. Critics contended that the trial and eventual conviction was unfair, but Hill was executed by firing squad on November 19, 1915, following an unsuccessful appeal to the Utah Supreme Court.

Since his death, Hill's status as a labor martyr has been underlined by both

Joe Hill (aka Hillström), labor activist and Wobbly songwriter (1879–1915). (Library of Congress)

the circumstances surrounding the trial and by the many political songs and satirical poems that he wrote, as well as those written about him.

Oliver Wendell Holmes, 1841–1935

Supreme Court Jurist

Considered to be one of the most influential justices on the Supreme Court, jurist Oliver Wendell Holmes had a long a distinguished career, serving on the Supreme Court from 1902 to 1932. The son of Oliver Wendell Holmes, Sr., a physician and writer, and abolitionist Amelia Lee Jackson, Holmes, Jr., fought in the Civil War, practiced law, and wrote widely on legal matters. Following his nomination to the Supreme Court, Holmes was responsible for a series of important and influential judgments before, during, and after World War I holding that the freedom of expression endorsed by federal and state constitutions merely stated a common-law prerogative to do harm, except where the expression in such circumstances posed a "clear and present danger that they will bring about the substantive evils that Congress has a right to prevent." (Abrams, Floyd, Speaking Freely, 2005, 66)

This judgment had important consequences in the climate of hysteria in the aftermath of the war. In the case of *Schenck v. United States* in which Charles Schenck encouraged recently enlisted men to oppose the draft, an action that led to his subsequent charge under the Espionage Act, Holmes's opinion was that the conviction was constitutional because the circumstances of war allowed greater restrictions on freedom of expression than would be permitted during peacetime. In a subsequent case—*Abrams v. United States,* 1919, again brought under the Espionage Act, which made it an offense to criticize the government—Holmes dissented from the majority view that the Espionage Act did not violate civil rights under the First Amendment because there was no intent to produce a clear and imminent danger.

Holmes was accused of inconsistency and was also criticized for his ideology. He was apparently influenced by Social Darwinism and believed that there were few restraints on the ability of a ruling elite to ordinate their own interests into law. Nevertheless, he was admired by Progressives who shared his opinions—particularly those on eugenics—and critics of the Red Scare and the prosecution of leftist radicals who celebrated his dissenting views regarding freedom of expression.

Frances Kellor, 1873–1952

Sociologist

Frances Alice Kellor, a sociologist and advocate of Americanization initiatives, first encountered immigrants in the Hull House Settlement in Chicago. Daily involvement in the immigrant community gave Kellor first-hand experience of the difficulties frequently faced by immigrants (e.g., employment problems, family issues, and overcoming language and cultural barriers). After 1908, she served on New York's State Immigration Commission, focusing public attention on overcrowded tenement housing and unsanitary labor camps. Galvanized in part by Kellor's work, the state established a Bureau of Industries and Immigration, with Kellor herself as chief investigator. Kellor's own position on the Americanization of immigrants was ambiguous, apparently moving from empathy and a belief in voluntary assimilation to a conviction that Americanization should be mandatory. As immigration from southern Europe grew, Kellor became convinced that rapid assimilation was essential, and with the support of business leaders, she assisted in establishing

Frances Kellor's calls for government action on behalf of immigrants made her a leading reformer of the Progressive era. (Library of Congress)

a network of private organizations like the North American Civic League for Immigrants, whose aim, although ostensibly to aid assimilation, was rather more biased toward preserving American values against the perceived foreign "menace."

Kellor was also convinced that if immigrants learned English as quickly as possible, they would be assimilated more readily, so she began to establish English classes for adults across the country. Following the outbreak of war, many Americans worried about possible divided loyalties because many immigrants came from those countries now opposed to the Allies. Kellor herself became concerned that unassimilated immigrants could pose a threat to national security. Her efforts shifted, therefore, from day-to-day problems to the advocacy of naturalization, citizenship, and national cohesiveness. Kellor believed that early initiatives had been insufficient to repudiate what she perceived as anti-American bias, subversion, and misleading propaganda among non-English-speaking groups and organizations.

Now called the National Americanization Committee, Kellor's organization shifted its emphasis from education to weakening immigrant bonds with the old country. She appeared before the National Security League, a powerful group of financiers and industrialists, to warn them of the potential threat from "subversive" immigrants, and advocated the building of a new interventionist republic of America. In 1918, as anti-immigrant feelings peaked, Kellor addressed the 50 largest employers of immigrant labor at an unadvertised dinner, warning them that Americanization had failed and proposed an alliance of business and social workers to break up the nationalistic racial groups. This alliance, the Inter-Racial Council, would act as an intelligence-gathering unit and propaganda agency. As hostility toward immigrants increased toward the end of the decade, Kellor's strategies included establishing a coalition of advertisers whose aim was to coerce the immigrant press into running anti-radical propaganda.

Abbott Lawrence Lowell, 1856–1943

Academic

Lawrence Lowell, academic and president of Harvard University from 1909 to 1933, was also a historian who has more recently been condemned for his views on ethnic minorities and homosexuals. Concerned that the growing proportion of Jewish students at Harvard was damaging the university's character, Lowell pressed for a 15 percent admissions quota and was responsible for the racial segregation of Harvard dormitories, excluding African Americans from Harvard Yard. Lowell was also on the national committee of the Immigration Restriction League.

The Sacco and Vanzetti trial in 1920 brought Lowell's name to wider prominence. Following widespread international condemnation and campaigns by workers, radicals, and immigrants after the guilty verdict on the two Italian immigrants accused of robbery and murder, the Massachusetts governor, Alvin T. Fuller, assigned a committee to consider executive clemency. The Lowell Committee, so called because its most pre-eminent member was Lawrence Lowell, concluded that the trial had been fair and that clemency was unwarranted. Following the men's execution, Lowell's role in the advisory committee led to Harvard being stigmatized by association as "Hangman's Hall."

Alexander Mitchell Palmer, 1872–1936

Politician

Nicknamed the "Fighting Quaker," Alexander Mitchell Palmer was U.S. attorney general from 1919 to 1921. He oversaw the contentious Palmer Raids. A qualified barrister, Palmer served as a Democrat in the House of Representatives from 1909 to 1915, supporting Woodrow Wilson in the 1912 election. He was not renominated in 1914 and ran unsuccessfully for the Senate. Although President Wilson offered Palmer the post of secretary of war, his pacifist beliefs caused him to decline and he was assigned to the role of alien property custodian (a wartime position whereby the official was responsible for money and property was in the United States of an enemy or ally of an enemy) from 1917 to 1919, resigning to become attorney general.

Although Palmer had earlier been associated with the progressive faction of the party and had supported women's suffrage and labor rights, his moderate stance on civil rights as attorney general appears to have changed markedly. Palmer was in office during the Red Scare and became a fervent opponent of communists and radicals considered to be a threat to the government, thus intensifying the policy of crushing political dissent begun during the war. During his tenure, Palmer was twice the victim of bomb attacks, the more serious of which killed the bomber as he placed the device at Palmer's home. With J. Edgar Hoover as his special assistant, his crusade against insurrection culminated in the flashy and well-publicized Palmer Raids, a sequence of police raids, wiretaps, and mass arrests of suspected radicals, authorized under the 1917 Espionage and 1918 Sedition Acts in which some 10,000 individuals were held. The raids and other measures on such locations as union offices and the headquarters of communist and socialist organizations were undertaken largely without warrants and focused on aliens because they had fewer rights. Contrary to Palmer's belief that a revolution would overthrow the government, no evidence of any such revolution was discovered. Nevertheless, many of those arrested were held without trial for some considerable time, and although the majority were eventually released, 247 were deported to Russia.

There was widespread support for the raids among a public stirred into hysteria by exaggerated newspaper reports. Although civil liberty and leftist groups were highly critical of the policy, the raids did not attract much censure at the time; however, as criticism that Palmer had disregarded basic civil liberties grew, feelings toward him began to change and some opponents claimed that he had fabricated the Red Scare to boost his chances of nomination as the Democratic presidential candidate in 1920.

References and Further Readings

Banfield, Edward. 1968. *The Moral Basis of a Backward Society,* New York: Free Press.

Binder, Frederick M., and David M. Reimers. 1995. *All the Nations Under Heaven: An Ethnic and Racial History of New York City.* New York: Columbia University Press.

Carpenter, N. 1927. "Immigrants and Their Children." *U.S. Bureau of the Census Monograph, No.7.* Washington, DC.

Columbia University Libraries. "Decennial Census Information: The 1920 Census." www.columbia.edu/cu/lweb/indiv/usgd/census/1920.html.

Daniels, Roger. 1991. *Coming to America: A History of Immigration and Ethnicity in American Life.* New York: Harper Perennial.

Foner, Nancy. 2000. *From Ellis Island to JFK: New York's Two Great Waves of Immigration*. New Haven: Yale University Press.

Garb, Margaret. 2005. *City of American Dreams: A History of Home Ownership and Housing Reform in Chicago, 1871–1919*. Chicago: University of Chicago Press.

Greer, Colin. 1976. *The Great School Legend: A Revisionist Interpretation of American Public Education*. New York: Viking Press.

Grossman, James R. 1991. *Land of Hope: Chicago, Black Southerners and the Great Migration*. Chicago: University of Chicago Press.

Jones, Maldwyn Allen. 1969. *American Immigration*. Chicago: University of Chicago Press.

Kessner, Thomas. 1977. *The Golden Door: Italian and Jewish Immigrant Mobility in New York City 1880–1915*. Oxford: Oxford University Press.

King, Desmond. 2000. *Making Americans: Immigration, Race, and the Origins of the Diverse Democracy*. Cambridge, MA: Harvard University Press.

Kraut, Alan M. 1982. *The Huddled Masses: The Immigrant in American Society, 1880–1921*. Wheeling: Harlan Davidson.

Laughead, George. 2004–2007. "WWW-VL: History: USA: 1910–1919." http://vlib.iue.it/history/USA/ERAS/20TH/1910s.html.

Library of Congress. 2002. "Immigration . . . : Introduction." http://memory.loc.gov/learn/features/immig/introduction.html.

Lieberson, Stanley. 1949. "Selective Black Migration from the South: A Historical View." In *The Democracy of Racial and Ethnic Groups,* edited by Frank D. Bean and W. Parker Frisbie (New York: Academic Press), cited in Marks, Carole.

Lopreato, Joseph. 1970. *Italian Americans*. New York: Random House.

Marks, Carole. 1989. *Farewell—We're Good and Gone: The Great Black Migration*. Bloomington: Indiana University Press.

Price, Daniel O. *Changing Characteristics—Negro Population* (Department of Commerce), cited in Marks, Carole.

Stenz, Maggie. "Notes on the Ethnic Image in Ashcan School Paintings." http://www.brickhaus.com/amoore/magazine/ash.html.

Tolnay, Stewart E. 2003. "The African American Great Migration and Beyond." *Annual Review of Sociology* 29 (August): 209–232.

Trotter, Joe William, Jr. 1991. *The Great Migration in Historical Perspective*. Bloomington, IN: University Press.

U.S. Department of Commerce, Bureau of the Census. 1978. *Current Population Reports,* Special Studies Series P-23, No. 80, p. 15, cited in Marks, Carole.

Race and Jim Crow

OVERVIEW

Race

In the 1910s, *race,* the term that differentiates one society or group from another, was contentiously based on visible characteristics (e.g., skin color and facial properties), as well as on genetic origins and self-recognition. Notions of race, and the ways in which people are grouped together racially, change from culture to culture as well as over time. Because of their effect on the ways in which individuals and society determine social identity, notions of race are necessarily contentious. The perception that racial traits could be exploited to establish perceived similarities has more recently become discredited. Race is instead better construed as a social model. It could also be argued, however, that this stance is politically motivated and that classifications of race or ethnicity that result from self-recognition or those that arise from genetic and geographic ancestry are both credible.

Following on from this, the term *racism* relates to the belief that an individual's worth can be established in accordance with a perceived or attributed racial classification and that racial discrimination is thus legitimate. Although the term was largely unknown before the 1930s, the prejudice that a person's expertise, skills, intelligence, physical capability, and moral worth differed according to their race, and that racial classification therefore justified grading (and segregating) races hierarchically, was widespread long before that.

The aim of racial classification could be perceived as perpetuating the concentration of authority, prosperity, entitlement, and land in the control of whites in a white-dominated society. Variations have less to do with biological considerations than with racism and white supremacy (i.e., the social, territorial, economic, and political agendas of any dominant group over its perceived subordinate). This was particularly the case in a 19th-century America in which African Americans, Native Americans, and hyphenated Americans in general were subordinate to a hegemonic white majority. Classifying minorities as racially inferior in this way allowed the white majority to appropriate the lands of Native Americans and to maintain their agricultural labor force. Dominated and therefore readily controlled, African Americans became reduced to the status of commodities.

In the United States, Native Americans, African Americans, and European Americans have long been racially categorized. Before the late 19th century, categories that conferred affiliation to a specific group were, conventionally, visual characteristics, the percentage of acknowledged nonwhite ancestry, and social and cultural grouping. During Reconstruction, however, it was increasingly believed that a person with "one drop" of "black blood" was, by definition, black. By the early 20th century, the concept of indiscernible blackness became legally enshrined in many states and widely endorsed nationally. A "pure" white lineage was a requirement for a person to be considered white. The definition that a black is any individual with any known African black lineage is a legacy of slavery and Jim Crow segregation. The "one drop" rule was first used in the South, but it became accepted nationally by both whites and African Americans, who, in any case, had no choice.

Over time, various terms have been used for individuals with African lineage, the majority being replaced as they became socially unacceptable. From slavery until the 1960s, "nigger" was an informal term for a person of African descent, but it later became coupled to an unequivocal abhorrence, a racist premise of innate black inferiority, making the term highly derogatory. "Mulatto" (in Spanish, "hybrid") originally meant the progeny of a "pure African Negro" and a "pure white," but over time, it began to include the children of whites and mixed Negroes. "Colored" once referred to mulattoes, particularly those of lighter complexion, but came to signify darker Negroes and even unmixed blacks. As racial mixture became more widespread, "Negro" (which is synonymous with "black") was used for any slave or their descendant and is now used in certain historical contexts. It was replaced by "black" with the emergence of the black power movement in the 1960s. "African American," occasionally "Afro-American," or "person of color" have been used more recently in addition to "black"; however, "African American" can also include individuals with European, Native American, Asian, or Latin American ancestry. Further variations arose because of arrivals from the Caribbean and South America, whereas those from Haiti and Jamaica, for example, are more often referred to by their country of origin. It can be assumed culturally, then, that if an individual living in the United States is black and has English as a native tongue, he or she is African American.

TIMELINE

1910   The Committee on Urban Conditions Among Negroes founded by Ruth Standish Baldwin and George Edmund Haynes in New York City to address racial issues in labor, health, and social welfare and to advocate against racial discrimination.

The Crisis, the organ of the National Association for the Advancement of Colored People (NAACP), first published, New York City.

The African American boxer Jack Johnson defeats James Jeffries, a leading white fighter, to win the World's Heavyweight Championship, thus sparking many incidents of white against black violence.

1911   Committee on Urban Conditions Among Negroes, Committee for the Improvement of Industrial Conditions Among Negroes in New York, and National League for the Protection of Colored Women merge to form the National League on Urban Conditions among Negroes (later the National Urban League).

New York hires first African American police officer, Samuel J. Battle.

1912   Woodrow Wilson, the first southern president since the Civil War, elected. Wilson heightens racial tensions by introducing segregation to federal government departments and workplaces, including restrooms and eating facilities.

James Weldon Johnson publishes *Autobiography of an Ex-Colored Man,* a psychological examination of the new Negro movement.

1913   Pioneer of open-heart surgery and founder of Provident Hospital and Training School for Nurses, Chicago, Dr. Daniel Hale Williams, becomes first African American admitted as charter member of the American College of Surgeons.

Darktown Follies opens in Harlem, helping to establish Harlem as an African American cultural center.

1914   World War I, Europe.

1915   Death of the African American author and educator Booker T. Washington.

Buchanan v. Worley and *Guinn v. United States,* respectively, countermand housing segregation statutes and declare the grandfather clause—which held that a man could only vote if his grandfather had voted—unconstitutional.

The Association for the Study of Negro Life and History (now The Association for the Study of African American Life and History) founded in Chicago by Carter G. Woodson and Jesse E. Moorland to "promote, research, preserve, interpret, and disseminate information about Black life, history, and culture to the global community."

1916   Marcus Garvey moves Universal Negro Improvement Association, founded in 1914 to advance African emigration and racial self-esteem, from Jamaica to New York.

Journal of Negro History, the quarterly research journal of The Association for the Study of Negro Life and History, founded by Carter G. Woodson and Jesse E. Moorland.

1917   The United States declares war on Germany. American contribution includes service by 400,000 African Americans.

On Fifth Avenue, New York City, 10,000 African Americans take part in a silent march—"Why We March"—to protest lynching and discrimination.

Riots in East St. Louis and Houston.

Insulted by Jim Crow laws and touched off by the arrest of an African American woman, 150 African American troops in Houston riot, killing 20.

1918   Some 2.3 million African American men register for the draft, and an estimated 370,000 are enlisted into the armed forces, including 1,400 commissioned as officers.

Division of Negro Economics established in the Department of Labor in order to mobilize the African American workforce and to work for the general advancement of African American wage earners.

Oscar Micheaux organizes the Oscar Micheaux Corporation, which went on to make 30 full-length African American films.

Henry Johnson and Needham Roberts of the black 369th Infantry awarded the Croix de Guerre by the French in recognition of their exceptional valor.

1919	Violence, rioting, and destruction of property in Chicago, Washington, D.C., Elaine, Arkansas, and more than 20 other cities in the Red Summer.
	The first African American millionaire, Madame C. J. Walker, dies.
	Associated Negro Press, a news service dealing with events from the African American press, established by Claude A. Barnett.

CAUSES OF SEGREGATION AND DISCRIMINATION

The Legacy of Reconstruction

For the 4 million African American slaves freed after the Civil War, Reconstruction held the promise of both emancipation and land, the franchise, and some measure of equality. They were to be disappointed in all of these. It is a bitter irony that Reconstruction exposed the racial abhorrence masked by the slave system in the antebellum South. Because the perceived inferiority of blacks had been legally designated, a balance existed (albeit an unstable one) between whites and African Americans. Once that balance was destroyed, integration could only occur if a judicious, tolerant, and rapid transition could be achieved. The failure of both presidential and congressional Reconstruction was so shameful and absolute, however, that the reawakening of white primacy coincided with the birth of an even more acute form of racism.

One by one, southern states ratified the Black Codes, which cheated African Americans of their right to vote and assisted and endorsed the activities of such extremists as the Ku Klux Klan. The misplaced exhilaration that African Americans would be given land gave way to a realization, as no scheme for confiscation emerged, that they would have to continue to work on plantations for wages or a share of the crop. Failure to guarantee African Americans the right to land was a significant factor in the curtailment of their political and economic power and the subsequent growth of the segregationist system in the early 1900s.

Reconstruction, which had begun with such hope and possibility for African Americans, ended in disillusion as prospects for southern blacks dissipated, Republican power declined, and constitutional pledges disappeared beneath Supreme Court edicts. Just as slavery had tied blacks to the land before the war, debt enslaved sharecroppers until the Great Migration and, for many, afterwards, too. By 1910, the few African American politicians who had remained in office were all but gone. By this time, the South was marginalized and African

PUCK

FOR THE SUNNY SOUTH.
AN AIRSHIP WITH A "JIM CROW" TRAILER.

Political cartoon from Puck *that satirizes the segregation and discrimination that became prevalent in the South following the Civil War, 1913. (Library of Congress)*

Americans found that they were cut off in penury and oppression as Washington concentrated on industrialization, urbanization, and immigration in the North. As a result, the South was able to implement its own policies on race.

Living Segregation

There is now some debate over the origins of segregation. Until the mid-20th century, it was accepted that racial separation had begun with the end of slavery in 1865. Some historians, however, most notably C. Vann Woodward (1966), have argued that segregation in its most aggressive forms emerged during the close of the 19th century and the beginning of the 20th. States in the South then started to carry through legislation that socially, culturally, and politically would effectively and systematically separate African Americans from whites in almost every form of life. Woodward contended that before this, some whites had advocated a more enlightened, progressive, and racially integrated society, and that race relations were rather more fluid than had been previously suggested.

The African American Family

Despite anti-enticement laws, passed in southern states to prevent unlicensed recruiters, a growing number of northern employers implemented dynamic labor drives, gradually adding African American agents to their white payroll. Railroads offered such incentives as "free" transportation, which nonetheless had to be repaid. Once migrants were settled, they frequently wrote to friends, encouraging them to follow, whereas married men often went north ahead of their families, only sending for them once employment and accommodation was assured. Although the family's destination was generally determined by male employment opportunities, women did have some say in the decision. Moreover, African American women often had other incentives for going north. Intimidation, exploitation, sexual assaults, and verbal and physical abuse often went alongside discrimination and a culture of long hours and low pay for African American domestic workers. Although the North was often the ultimate destination, African American men frequently worked for a number of employers in the South and the North, whereas African American women generally made the journey nonstop.

Although the family was important to most African Americans, slavery did not provide a strong basis for African American family stability or cohesion; rather, in some it had provoked disarray and a contingent, temporary feel to relationships that lacked either emotional closeness or a legal foundation. Migration worsened this tendency as parents moving away individually to look for work split up family units, and families focused on the mother became more common as women who were growing economically more and more viable took advantage of improved pay in the North. Although African American delinquency and crime rates in cities increased, particularly among juveniles, there is little evidence to suggest that increasingly fragmented families contributed to this. It is more probable that crime was a consequence of poverty. In any case, crime in African American ghettoes was often less prevalent than in other disadvantaged urban areas.

Despite early 20th-century increases in the number of families where the male was absent or the woman headed the family, most African Americans still remained in two-parent families. In New York City, for example, despite significant increases in migration there by southern African Americans, the 1910 census records a husband or father in more than 80 percent of African American families, whereas those without men or where women headed the household accounted for fewer than 10 percent.

This argument, however, understates the force of white opposition to integration. To focus on a purely legal basis for segregation would be to underestimate the predomination and acceptance of racial segregation that routinely and habitually separated African Americans from whites that had been in existence from before the Civil War in both the North and South. Jim Crow legislation merely authorized social practices that were already solidly embedded. Nevertheless, both of these positions ignore the possibility that because African Americans had already been excluded from institutions, they frequently demanded separate facilities.

Whatever its origins and whether segregation arose as a result of legislation or practice, by 1910, the racial separation of African Americans and whites was firmly entrenched. Between the end of slavery and the second decade, measures like the Thirteenth, Fourteenth, and Fifteenth Amendments, the Civil Rights Bill, and the subsequent declaration that it was unconstitutional all failed to halt white resistance to any form of integration. In the case of *Plessy v. Ferguson* in 1896, the Supreme Court upheld the "separate but equal" principle, thus accepting the concept of white supremacy and instigated the growth of Jim Crow legislation. African Americans were effectively forced to endure racial segregation in every area from housing to public places, and from the workplace to the armed forces.

Work, Labor, and African American Institutions

During the final decade of the 19th century, the balance gradually began to shift between those African American agricultural workers who still sharecropped in the South and those who managed to acquire tenancies, albeit on largely unproductive and marginal land. African Americans who migrated to urban areas during this period found that labor opportunities were limited to the most menial of tasks. Nevertheless, by the first years of the 20th century, industrial employment for African American laborers did increase slightly in the South. It is not surprising that African Americans—skilled or unskilled—working in areas such as cotton mills, mines, the railroads, and the iron industries earned less than their white counterparts.

As migration from the rural South to the industrial cities of the South, North, and West grew, the percentage of urban African Americans increased from an estimated 5 percent to 7 percent to some 25 percent between 1860 and 1910. These figures, however, mask the fact that in the urban South, African Americans represented around 33 percent of the population, whereas in the North and West, they accounted for far less, around 7 percent. Because employment opportunities were greater in the expanding domestic and service sectors, a disproportionate number of women were pulled toward cities, between 80 and 87 African American males for every 100 African American women in the South and most of the North, although the expanding industrial cities of the Great Lakes attracted greater numbers of young men. As industries expanded in both rural and urban areas, African American workers began to make inroads into mining, railroad, and manufacturing, yet they had to endure discriminatory contract labor systems and pay scales that ensured whites were paid more for the same work; and as industrial unrest increased in the early 20th century, non-union African Americans were also used as strikebreakers.

Strikebreaking was not only the consequence of divisive employment practices, but also reflected African American resistance to discrimination in unions. Still, African American workers gradually began to form their own unions. Moreover, once strikes were settled, African Americans invariably lost their jobs. In many industries in the North, African Americans were outweighed by whites and, following the mass immigration from southern, eastern, and central Europe after 1880, by immigrants as well. In 1910 in Pittsburgh, African Americans comprised around 3 percent of the 300,000 workers in the iron and steel mills, with American-born whites making up 29 percent and immigrants around 68 percent. A similar situation existed in Chicago before 1910; African Americans accounted for only 400 of the city's 16,000 or so meatpackers and even fewer in the steelworks.

Before the war, economic expansion in such cities as Detroit, Cleveland, and Milwaukee boosted the number of African American women who found employment in the domestic and service sectors. Afterwards, however, the number of young men (those aged between 18 and 44) working in these cities exceeded women, sometimes by as many as 120 or 140 to every 100 women. During the Great Migration, and particularly during and after World War I, the majority of southern African Americans who traveled north, rather than south or west, were influenced by the same three factors that influence most migrants: push, pull, and means. In this case, *push* referred to the social, economic, and environmental conditions in the South (the boll weevil invasion, poor weather, disenfranchisement, poor wages, and Jim Crow legislation). *Pull* was the sudden increase in employment opportunities caused by restrictions on immigration and the withdrawal from the labor pool of hundreds of thousands of workers enlisting in U.S. forces. *Means* can be summarized as the ready availability of affordable transport (the railroad) and the absence of restrictions on migrants, either at their point of origin or their destination. During this period, the lure of wages in northern industries that ranged from $3.00 to $5.00 for an eight-hour day, as against agricultural wages as low as 75 cents to $1.00 a day in the South and no more than $2.50 in southern industry, was enough to inspire thoughts of migration. Higher wages were seldom enough on their own, however, to provide the motivation for men, women, or whole families to uproot. Marks (1989, 166) points out that circumstances in sending areas had to be sufficiently volatile to create uncertainty and push migrants toward displacement. The potential for increased opportunity and a better life in receiving areas was similarly necessary before mass migration could take place.

Migration north was never a straightforward option. A complex web of maneuvers, involving wartime federal labor policies, northern African American newspapers, and communal links and associations, had to be undertaken. As the draft accelerated and immigration declined, government promoted the recruitment

Men working in the Oakley Chemical Company making munitions during World War I, New York, 1917. (Library of Congress)

of southern African American workers as a wartime expedient strategy, in which the U.S. Department of Labor assisted northern industries in their recruitment, an initiative resisted by southern employers. Pushed by African American civil rights groups, the Division of Negro Economics (DNE) was established in the Department of Labor to improve urban take-up of African American labor. Although such campaigners as Mary Church Terrell pressed for a Colored Women's Division in the Women's Bureau of the Department of Labor, this never materialized.

As the numbers of African Americans migrating to northern cities increased, there was a consequent expansion in the African American industrial working class. In some cities (e.g., Cleveland, Philadelphia, Pittsburgh, and Detroit), percentages of African Americans in industrial employment increased from around 10 percent to 20 percent in 1910 to an estimated 60 percent or 70 percent by the end of the decade. In most industries, African American participation in the labor force expanded dramatically during the decade; however, although numbers of African Americans employed in such industries as steel and meatpacking did increase—the latter from fewer than 6,000 in 1910 to 30,000 in 1920—employment of African Americans in the Ford Company soon eclipsed all other automobile makers and most other industries, from 50 African American workers in 1916 to 2,500 in 1920. African Americans also benefited from a wider range of supervisory positions at Ford than at other companies. Notwithstanding north-

Table 4.1. Estimates of Black Intercensal Net Migration for Urban and Rural Portions of Regions, 1910–1920 (in thousands; minus sign denotes net out-migration)

Black Population	North		South	West
	Northeast	North Central		
Urban	167	247	588	18
Rural	3	−17	−1,013	8

Source: Daniel O. Price, *Changing Characteristics—Negro Population* (Washington, D.C.: Department of Commerce, 1965); cited in Marks, 1989, 34.

ern mass migration, most African Americans remained in the South, and more African Americans lived and worked in urban areas there after the war than in the North and the West combined, choosing to go to such cities as New Orleans, Memphis, or Birmingham rather than to travel north. A detailed examination appears in the section on migration in the chapter on immigration. As can be seen in Table 4.1, gains in southern cities between 1910 and 1919, the first decade of the Great Migration, surpassed the combined totals for those of the northeastern and north-central regions.

Given that industry was concentrated in specific centers, it is inevitable that African Americans migrated toward those areas. By the end of the decade, almost 40 percent of the African American population in the North was consolidated in New York, Chicago, Detroit, and Philadelphia. Table 4.2 illustrates the African American population and the percentage increase in cities in the South, North, and West.

As labor shortages during the war increased, African American women also moved into industrial jobs, replicating white women's jobs in food production and clothing. They also started working in such heavier industries as steel. Although these jobs were necessarily temporary, some African American women did remain after the war. By 1920, industrial employment comprised around 15 percent of female African American labor, against less than 7 percent in 1910.

As in all other areas, inequality and discrimination in employment were endemic. African Americans were paid less than whites, with 70 percent to 80 percent often working in dangerous and dirty jobs that the U.S. Census identified as unskilled labor. In many northern urban areas, white males comprised more than 50 percent of the skilled and semi-skilled sectors, whereas there were similar figures for white women in clerical and administrative posts. Despite advances in mechanization and mass production, African Americans continued to work in nonmechanized areas (e.g., laboring and the service industries). Southern African Americans confronted similar or worse restrictions, being denied even semi-skilled employment in the tobacco industry, for example, where mechanization had led to cleaner, less-demanding working conditions. In almost every

Table 4.2. Black Population in Selected Cities, 1910–1920

Cities	Population		Percentage Increase 1910–1920
	1910	*1920*	
South			
Birmingham, AL	52,305	70,230	34.3
Washington, DC	94,446	109,966	16.4
Jacksonville, FL	29,293	41,520	41.7
Tampa, FL	8,951	11,531	28.8
Atlanta, GA	51,902	62,796	21.0
New Orleans, LA	89,262	100,930	13.1
Baltimore, MD	84,749	108,322	27.8
Tulsa, OK	1,959	8,878	353.2
Charleston, SC	31,056	32,326	4.1
Memphis, TN	52,441	61,181	16.7
Houston, TX	23,929	33,960	41.9
Norfolk, VA	25,039	43,392	73.3
North			
Chicago, IL	44,103	109,458	148.2
Kansas City, MO	9,286	14,405	55.1
Detroit, MI	5,741	40,838	611.3
St. Louis, MO	43,960	69,854	58.9
New York, NY	91,709	152,467	66.3
Cleveland, OH	8,448	34,451	307.8
Pittsburgh, PA	25,623	37,725	47.2
Milwaukee, WI	980	2,229	127.4
Philadelphia, PA	84,459	134,229	58.9
West			
Los Angeles, CA	7,599	15,579	105.0
Oakland, CA	3,055	5,489	79.7
San Francisco, CA	1,642	2,414	47.0
Alburquerque, NM	244	213	–12.7
Seattle, WA	2,296	2,894	26.0

Source: U.S. Bureau of the Census, *Negroes in the United States, 1920–1932* (Washington, D.C.: Government Printing Office, 1935), p. 55; cited in Marks, 1989, 122, and Holt and Brown, 2000, 128.

industry, African American workers endured discrepant levels of exposure to the worst dangers, difficulties, and pay rates.

Unemployment also disproportionately affected African American workers, with many experiencing periods of between two and four months each year when they were either laid off or finished entirely. As a result, some were concerned less with promotion and more with holding on to the job at all. Some returned south, most stayed, but the economic downturn from 1919 meant that African Americans experienced still more hardship. Even though employers often cited racist, inconsistent, and stereotypical reasons for excluding African American labor (e.g., reluctance to mix whites with African Americans, lack of separate facilities, or that African Americans were "unsuitable" or untrained), African Americans encountered similar prejudice from white workers and public officials. Some unions excluded African Americans or downgraded African Americans to subsidiary lodges controlled by whites, whereas both the government and the army excluded African American workers from contract work. The "work or fight" ordinances issued by the government as a strategy against draft dodgers were often similarly used disproportionately against African Americans, both male and female.

Almost as soon as the Great Migration began, African American workers implemented a range of resistance strategies to counter workplace discrimination. Moving jobs frequently to enhance working conditions, boost wages, and achieve improved recognition of rights worked in some cases, although employers believed that this reflected African Americans' inherent unreliability and inconstancy. Although there were other factors involved in African Americans operating as strikebreakers and establishing all–African American unions, these policies also revealed African Americans' resentment about white discrimination.

Although patchy, African American labor organization did increase. In 1919, the First International Congress of Working Women, which included Helen Burroughs and Mary Church Terrell among its clubwomen, exhorted the convention to cooperate in organizing African American women workers to promote industrial democracy. During the steel strike, the National Urban League encouraged the National Committee for Organizing Iron and Steel Workers of America to employ African American organizers. The National Brotherhood Workers of America, an all–African American organization, was formed in 1919 to organize "every Negro worker into industrial labor or trade unions in all skilled and unskilled occupations" and encouraged African American workers "to exact justice from both employer and the white labor unions." (Trotter, 2001, 393, 394)

Often informal initiatives by African American women were established to resist discriminatory practices in domestic service. In Gainesville during the war, African American women originated a casual agreement to regulate "the amount of work, number of hours, and the wages which they would agree upon with the whites." (Trotter, 2001, 395) Adopting similar strategies to their male, industrial counterparts, domestic employees used absenteeism and high turnover to improve their treatment. The efforts of African American middle-class women— Terrell and Jeanette Carter among them—supported other affiliations established between African American businesses and professionals, and created the Women Wage Earners Association in Washington, D.C., which was intended to help African American working-class women improve wages and conditions. Although employers and authorities repressed many of these initiatives, they did constitute a starting point for the growth of more militant unionism in subsequent decades.

Business and Enterprise

The growth of race awareness among African Americans and aspirations regarding social mobility often led them to start their own businesses. It also had another consequence in allowing African Americans to escape the discrimination that working for white capital necessarily entailed, and it created employment and ensured that their money was reinvested in their own communities. The National Negro Business League (NNBL) was established in 1900 under the leadership of Booker T. Washington and undertook to supply products, services, and employment in African American communities. Self-sufficiency and self-help were prioritized as the organization branched out across the country. League records document the rapid growth of African American enterprises (e.g., the number of banks and retail outlets doubled between 1900 and World War I).

As African American urban employment grew and inequality remained widespread, segregated communities provided opportunities for the establishment of African American enterprises and professional endeavors. It also led to the rise of an African American middle class within broader "New Negro" initiatives to construct the "Black Metropolis." This self-contained municipality within a larger urban area would provide for the needs of African American communities. A growing number of newspapers, most published weekly and aimed at an African American market, both mirrored and boosted this new "black consciousness." Among many that were published in most cities, the *Chicago Defender* stands out as particularly successful. Its circulation increased from 33,000 in 1916 to 90,000 in 1917. It rose to an estimated 250,000 by the middle of the next decade.

Although smaller enterprises predominated, white-collar opportunities also arose in banking and insurance, despite resistance from white-owned companies and discriminatory activities in state licensing agencies. Alongside the ascendancy of an African American middle class, the number of African American professionals also gradually increased. Although African Americans in such professions as medicine and the law increased in number, their growth was overshadowed in education and the clergy. African Americans also began to be admitted to nurse training and social work schemes in increasing numbers. The 1910 U.S. Census of occupations records 500 semi-professional African American religious and charity workers. It is confusing that a decade later the "semi-professional" category had changed to "professional" African American social workers, making comparisons difficult. It is clear, however, that numbers had increased substantially and that the majority were still women. They were augmented by still more semi-professional religious and charity workers, the majority of whom were also women. Despite these advances by African American women, African American men consistently took up the top posts and earned more for the same role.

Traffic on State Street, Chicago, ca. 1910. (Bettmann/Corbis)

During the decade, urban opportunities as an alternative to rural labor gradually increased as many African Americans joined the Great Migration, and the exigencies of war and the downturn in European immigration offered new economic possibilities in the cities. Despite these prospects, African Americans still contended with racial and class discrimination from white workers, employers, and the state. Although African Americans used a variety of strategies to circumvent and frustrate these practices, they nevertheless faced enormous obstacles in the struggle for equality by the end of the decade.

Chicago as the Promised Land

"South State Street was in its glory then, a teeming Negro street with crowded theaters, restaurants, and cabarets. And excitement from noon to noon. Midnight was like day. The street was full of workers and gamblers, prostitutes and pimps, church folks and sinners." (Grossman, 1991, 117)

This was Langston Hughes, the African American poet who was later to play a central role in the Harlem Renaissance, on his arrival in Chicago in 1918. In 1919, an African American newspaper, the Chicago *Whip,* described the center of the hustle, the nucleus of "The Stroll," around Thirty-fifth and State streets, as a "Bohemia of the Colored folks." (Ibid.)

Although migrants in the South may have been unaware of Hughes, they had heard the rumors that circulated about Chicago as the promised land. Although most were unequivocal about their decision to leave the South, not all were certain about their final destination, and many prudently delayed their departure until they had substantiated initial rumors put about by labor agents or relatives, or reports in newspapers. For most, a range of factors determined the destination: geography and whether the place could be reached easily by rail, job opportunities, and whether they had any friends or relatives there influenced the decision. Between 1910 and 1920, the African American population of Chicago swelled from around 44,000 to more than 109,000.

Two contemporary comments from anonymous southern interviewees give an insight into why the city was such a pull. "You could not rest in your bed at night for *Chicago,*" one said, whereas the other recollected that no matter where someone "stopped on the way, the mecca was Chicago." (Grossman, 1991, 4) The choice of Chicago, rather than New York or Pittsburgh, for example, depended on circumstances whose significance changed over time. Early migrants from an area were probably drawn there because of the city's location at the head of the Illinois Central and because of the railroad's penetration into Tennessee, Mississippi, and Louisiana. Discounted railroad fares, word of mouth from early "pioneers," African American baseball teams, its preeminence as a hub of African American business enterprise, and even the fact that it was home to several widely distributed mail-order catalogues all influenced the migrant's choice. The meat-packing industry was almost universally known in the South, so the availability of jobs there and in mills and factories was also a factor. The influence of the *Chicago Defender,* the most popular newspaper in the African American South and one that enthusiastically promoted the city to southern communities as well as carried advertisements from employment agencies, was also significant.

Some migrants, however, left for Chicago by default. As the migration increased, it became essential for those who were bound to their community, either by economic or emotional ties. Districts depopulated by the exodus of whole streets and districts filled up with strangers, leaving those left behind with a sense of alienation and isolation. African American churches lost significant proportions of their congregations, forcing ministers to follow them to Chicago. African American businessmen also went, trailing their disappearing market. Not all of those who remained behind felt the same about the city, either. Some families, divided because men had gone in search of work, were ambivalent about Chicago, which was rapidly gaining a reputation as a center of vice. They feared the possibility that their men would be led astray there.

Nevertheless, for a majority who had already decided to go, Chicago epitomized the promised land. The traditional means of escape (i.e., the train) "had long represented to black Americans an opportunity for movement and change limited only by the seemingly infinite path of the tracks." (Grossman, 1991, 110)

To the young Langston Hughes, a precise destination was embedded in the allure of the railroad because "the railroad tracks ran to Chicago and Chicago was the biggest town in the world to me, much talked of by the people in Kansas." (cited in Grossman, 1991, 110)

Concern regarding what might become of them should they remain behind was also a deciding factor with some migrants. Despite the hesitancy about going, one commented that in Chicago, he "could live with a little less fear." (Grossman, 1991, 110) For many, Chicago became the destination of choice because there the despised southern racial code seemed less important and racial lines were not as rigidly drawn. Although some aspects of the South's discriminatory policies did begin to impinge on African Americans in the North, the pettier day-to-day discriminations that made life so difficult for southern African Americans (e.g., separate drinking fountains and segregated public transport) were less evident in the North. However, the apparent tolerance was largely illusory because there were no laws that actually protected African Americans from segregation; any facility could, if they so wished, refuse access to African Americans, most of whom, in the event, had no legal redress.

THE MAKING OF GHETTOS

The Civil Rights Act of 1875; its subsequent overruling in 1883, when the Supreme Court ruled that only the activities of the government and not those of private individuals or enterprises were protected by the Fourteenth Amendment; *Plessy v. Ferguson* in 1896; and the institutionalization of the "separate but equal" measures all contributed to the situation that existed in 1910: rigid segregation, both in law and in fact, throughout the United States. *Plessy* sanctioned discrimination. After this ruling, every private southern amenity, institution, or facility was largely free to discriminate.

Segregation in the North: No Negroes Allowed

At first, the South was more energetic in legislating against integration. The belief that African American neighbors constituted a threat led whites in such cities as Baltimore and Atlanta to enact local laws that cited the risk to public morals, health, or order if African Americans and whites were to live close together. The laws designated exactly where African Americans could live.

"Segregated district" laws varied in their structure; the most prohibitive labeled whole districts as "white" or "black" and, after the formal imposition of boundaries, restricted occupation to one race, thus effectively ghettoizing the city. It is not surprising that African Americans were frequently confined to poorer, less-developed areas of towns and cities. In 1916, segregation ordinances were finally tested in law by the NAACP, which brought an action in Louisville, Kentucky. In 1917, the court concluded that the statute in Kentucky was unconstitutional, thus addressing the NAACP's action and effectively ending residential segregation laws elsewhere; however, the ruling was applicable more to property title considerations (i.e., the owner's prerogative to dispose of the property to whomever they determined) than it was to racial discrimination.

White supremacists, who were unwilling to concede defeat, devised a new strategy, the restrictive deed covenant, a tactic that would have a significant impact in both the South and the North for some time. Because these covenants were private agreements (and thus not covered by the Fourteenth Amendment), sellers could prohibit sales to African Americans or, indeed, any other group as well. The tactic was legally endorsed and used widely. In some parts of the North (e.g., Chicago), around 80 percent of housing was thus restrained and the strategy became a primary factor in the almost total ghettoization of the city. African Americans paradoxically were more restricted by the covenants than they would have been by boundaries, which would have been unlikely to be drawn so rigidly. City zoning legislation also bolstered residential segregation. In Milwaukee, for example, the whole of the southern half of the city was zoned for commerce by a 1920 ordinance, thus preventing any residential building until World War II.

After World War I, both the size and the number of racially segregated districts in the North grew significantly, all towns and cities there showing considerable increases when the standard measuring tool (the index of dissimilarity) was applied. By definition, ghettos were overcrowded, unsanitary, and rundown. To pay inflated rents, tenants frequently rented out their already crowded and subdivided housing to boarders. The inevitable consequences were radically diminished life expectancy, a higher infant mortality rate, poorer health, and an increased incidence of such illnesses as heart disease, pneumonia, and tuberculosis among African Americans. Of these, tuberculosis was the single biggest killer, with an estimated 202 African American fatalities per 1,000 of the population, against 86 for whites. Although average African American life expectancy for men and women similarly increased by seven to eight years in the early 20th century, against an increase of five to six years for whites, African Americans still lived for some 14 years less than whites, and even in 1930, the average life expectancy for African Americans was only 45 years.

Apart from legal measures to restrict African American movement into white neighborhoods, African Americans were also prevented from transgressing borders by an enduring campaign of terror. African American houses and realtors who sold to African Americans in Chicago sustained attacks at the rate of around one homemade bomb per month. A significant difference existed between the South, where after decades of subjugation, few African Americans would venture beyond their prescribed territory, and the North, where the more affluent African

Americans attempted to move into better neighborhoods and were vilified and attacked.

Before World War I, Jim Crow practices were seldom as overt in the North as they were in the South. The influx of African Americans during the Great Migration altered whites' opinions and led to heightened racial tensions, outbreaks of violence, and discrimination. By the end of the decade, the majority of African Americans were packed into inferior accommodation in northern ghettos, and kept there by a white alliance determined that they should not encroach on their neighborhoods.

Harlem

The considerable growth of the African American population in New York City between 1890 and 1914 was central to the foundation of Harlem as an African American community. The migration from the South and the resulting growth in the African American community meant that one or another part of the city was certain to become an African American ghetto; that it was Harlem was the result of several factors. Throughout the 19th century, New York City's African American population remained relatively low and stable, between 9,000 and 15,000 at midcentury, largely because of a very high mortality rate (in 1890, 37.5 of every thousand against 28.5 for the white population). Until 1915, the death rate exceeded the birth rate. (Osofsky, 1996, 8) African Americans also lived in the most impoverished working-class districts, separated by their color in the margins that, as the city expanded, would be co-opted into new developments, forcing African Americans further out.

By 1900, most African Americans lived in what is now the midtown area, but although they were concentrated in several areas, no one neighborhood was exclusively "black." Despite the high mortality rate, the African American population grew considerably, so that by 1910, there were 92,000 African Americans in the city, the majority of whom were born in the South. In that year, New York City had the second-largest African American urban population in America; by 1920, it was the largest. Most migrants arriving before 1930 took root in Manhattan. By the 1910s, it contained 80 percent of the city's industry, and migrants took many of the unskilled jobs there. Although Jim Crow legislation and discrimination still dominated most African American lives, by 1910, it was less institutionalized in New York, and certainly less harsh than in the South. Increased migration, however, exposed New Yorkers to more African Americans. Whites reacted by reversing the trends in race relations that had characterized the late 19th century so that racial alienation and antagonism had intensified by the second decade.

Harlem's transformation from the affluent suburb of the late 19th century was a consequence of what happened elsewhere in New York City. Population increases from increased migration and immigration and the growth in commerce

North Side of 125th Street and Eighth Avenue in Harlem. (Underwood & Underwood/ Corbis)

and industry led to incursions into formerly residential areas, and the city grew in the only way possible—north. Land and property speculation in Harlem in the 1890s ultimately proved unsustainable, and significant numbers of African Americans began to move in by the early 1900s, joining an already sizeable African American and Italian population. The volatile and fluctuating situation, aided by the construction of subway routes and the elevated railroad, also affected the Jewish community as eastern European Jews, who began to replace German Jews in the garment trade, started to look for homes in lower Harlem that would reflect their newfound status. Further development, largely of better-quality apartment houses, continued in West Harlem, creating what was to become the most opulent African American ghetto in America. The inevitable collapse of the boom around 1904 led to drastic reductions in land and property values, and appreciable numbers of African Americans began to move in to West Harlem as landlords admitted them.

Sharp entrepreneurs, who exploited the possibility that African Americans might rent in the area, coerced whites into buying their property at inflated prices, or they moved African Americans in, hoping that the values of adjoining properties would fall, thereby allowing them to buy at a reduced price. As the city grew, commercial development and the demolition of all–African American blocks in other districts pushed African American families toward Harlem, where for the first time, they could afford reasonable housing. By 1914, the African American population stood at around 50,000; however, to some, the possibility that Harlem should become the focus of New York's most downtrodden and historically worst-housed people, resulting in the perceived despoilment of one of the most modish and discriminative parts of the city, was unacceptable.

Some associations of property owners intent on repelling the African American "invasion" signed restrictive agreements pledging not to rent to African American families. Others drew up covenants limiting the number of African American servants and staff who could be employed in homes. Groups comprising realtors, journalists, businessmen, and local residents with such names as the Anglo-Saxon Realty Corporation and the Save-Harlem Committee attempted to foment controversy and make whites aware of what they called "the greatest problem Harlem has had to face." (Osofsky, 1996, 107) One of the most energetic and vocal of these groups was the Harlem Property Owners' Improvement Corporation (HPOIC), which operated from 1910 to 1915 and urged residents to drive African Americans out to the slums, "where they belong." (Ibid.)

The Corporation was supported by such sections of the press as the *Home News* and *Harlem Magazine,* who frequently used racist and inflammatory terms. The Corporation's founder, John G. Taylor, proposed that whites in properties adjoining African American–owned or –rented blocks should construct 24-foot fences. Other initiatives included attempts to persuade African American realtors to draw a boundary (a "dead line") that would permanently segregate African Americans from whites and campaigns to prevent the licensing of cinemas and the establishment of churches. The efforts of all of the organizations collapsed and none of them prevented African American settlement in Harlem.

The failures can mainly be attributed to the inability of any one group to achieve cohesiveness among the disparate organizations. Some owners persisted in attempts to exploit the situation and it proved impossible to establish a well-coordinated campaign in such a volatile climate. When confronted with the reality of the situation, owners instinctively sold out at often dramatically reduced prices. Panic selling in areas close to or in African American–dominated areas resulted in a glut of property on an already depressed market. Because few African Americans were able to buy, prices spiraled downward and landlords who persevered with restrictive covenants were either unable to find white tenants or were forced to reduce rents. Faced with the alternative of clinging to a whites-only policy and going under or renting to African Americans at a higher rent, most chose the latter.

Harlem's past as an affluent and well-planned neighborhood distinguished it from all other urban ghettos. Although African American families were able to live in accommodations that were of a reasonable or, in some cases, relatively high standard, they paid dearly for the privilege. Rents were higher there than anywhere else in the city, and they continued to increase steeply after the war.

Relative to their 19th-century levels, however, rents had declined, despite increases forced on African American tenants once they had moved in. Nevertheless, before the war, they seldom climbed to their previous levels. As Harlem became predominantly African American, its above-average housing drew many residents away from older African American districts of Manhattan. By 1920, such areas as Columbus Hill were marginalized, shabby neighborhoods populated by African American families unable to manage Harlem's higher rents.

Rapidly escalating mid-Manhattan real estate values after 1910 meant that landlords could sell land and property and reinvest in Harlem. Some African American churches (e.g., St. Philip's) became wealthy through this process, and churches themselves became landlords when they decided to invest their capital in Harlem apartment houses. These buildings, formerly restricted to white tenants, were soon opened up to African Americans who were directed toward African American real estate agents. Early transactions were carried out by stealth because there was still considerable opposition from property owners reluctant to sell to African American buyers. Whites or African Americans sufficiently light skinned to "pass" for white often negotiated for or even bought the property or land and then resold it.

In 1914, the Urban League estimated Harlem's population at 49,555 out of a total of 92,000 African Americans in New York City. That figure grew to 73,000 by 1920, but it was already apparent by 1910 that Harlem was to be predominantly African American on a more or less permanent basis. To take advantage of rapidly increasing numbers of African Americans needing property, African American–owned or –managed real estate businesses were quickly established in Harlem and elsewhere in the city. One, Nail and Parker, became the most successful in Harlem. John E. Nail was the first president of Harlem's Negro Board of Trade and, perhaps surprisingly, vice president of the mainly white Republican Business Men's Club of New York City. He and his partner, Henry C. Parker, had been involved with the Afro-American Realty Company and had founded the business after the collapse of Afro-American in the previous decade. Sometimes known as the "Little Fathers" of black Harlem, they were typical of a new generation of successful and highly visible African American entrepreneurs.

White landlords and businesses began to employ African American managers to handle African American tenants, and by 1914, 37 percent of Harlem tenements were run by African American agents. Despite this, African American landlords owned fewer than 5 percent of these properties. By 1920, more than 20 African American real estate companies had opened up in Harlem, and by the end of the next decade, this occupation accounted for the largest, single, African American professional group. Although white property ownership continued to overshadow African American, their capital investment after 1914 did increase as more properties became available to African American families. Out-of-town agents began to arrive in Harlem as word of financial opportunity spread as far as the South.

National Association for the Advancement of Colored People and The Crisis *magazine offices at 69 Fifth Avenue, New York City. (Library of Congress)*

As part of the commercialization and development of Harlem, almost every major African American institution relocated its downtown base there. Nearly every social service agency, including the Urban League and the NAACP, established local offices, and populist African American newspapers that challenged the traditional and sober *New York Age* were founded. Schools like P.S. 89 on Lenox Avenue, which was 75 percent African American by 1915, began night classes and a community center for African American youngsters, but it quickly became one of the most rundown of all New York's public schools. Elsewhere, P.S. 68, which had earlier been exclusive and respected, became notorious for regular confrontations between white and African American students.

Earlier generations of foreign-born residents (e.g., Germans, Irish, and Jews) moved away. Some retailers and businesses that remained after their customers had gone tried to adapt to changing circumstances, but some resisted change, holding on for a while and eventually selling out. To counter Harlem's reputation as an African American enclave, the Harlem Board of Trade advertised the neighborhood as ideal for the relocation of new industry needing cheap land and labor and good transport. Harlem's ethnically mixed population was promoted as a positive benefit: "Only 17 percent of its people are native white of native parents," a 1917 survey by the Harlem Board of Commerce concluded. (Osofsky, 1996, 122)

Between 1910 and 1920, New York's African American population increased by 66 percent, and from 1920 to 1930, when New York was struggling to deal with the early effects of the Depression, by 115 percent. Harlem's prosperity was not to last. Its decline can be attributed to several factors. Massive African American inward migration and consequent economic and social problems, sizeable outward white migration into other boroughs, growing class consciousness among African Americans from different origins that led to racial tension, the slump of the late 1920s, high rents, and the obvious unsuitability of brownstones that had been built for different times and a different demographic all contributed to its degeneration into the urban slum it became in the late 1920s.

Making African American Urban Culture

Given the importance that such secular forms of music as jazz and the blues played in the formation of African American culture, it is ironic that the African American church was prominent in its construction. After Reconstruction, the Black Codes, legislation, and increasingly strict segregation resulted in African American mobility, trade, civil rights, and creativity becoming progressively restricted. As a consequence, the African American public realm became an equally constrained and therefore isolated sphere of African American interests. The establishment of social spaces that were inconspicuous and undercover, yet still public, became central to the formation of African American culture and, thus, identity. Neal (1999, 4) observes that during this period, the embryonic elements of the African American public realm were most frequently seen in the development of the African American church and in casual locations of pleasure (e.g., the juke joint, or "jook"). Before Reconstruction, gatherings of slaves were illegal and African Americans therefore cultivated social activities that challenged and undermined white control, thus creating an enduring tradition of undercover social activity. The urge to transpose these surreptitious activities to an urban environment led to the first secular cultural establishment, the jook.

Because segregation precluded African American access to public spaces, the African American church became a surrogate public space, accessible to both the religious and the secular. Leisure activities, social welfare, and commercial activities for African Americans were found there. In part, this provided a space for such newly emergent forms of expression as popular music and dance, which, at a time when popular culture, consumption, and leisure were still rare among the American working class, was viewed by a dominant white society as antagonistic and subversive. These institutions, particularly the jook, prefigured the appearance of more conspicuous spaces (e.g., theaters, clubs, and dance halls in Harlem and elsewhere).

In New York, the honky-tonk became an early expression of the juke joint in an urban context. These, and other mainly covert and improvisatory spaces, nourished an illegal underground economy and the development of ragtime, which had migrated north from Memphis and St. Louis. James Weldon Johnson writes of a dozen or so clubs in this black Bohemia that were frequented by whites as well as blacks. (Neal, 1999, 8) For Johnson, music played a central role in the formation of African American community and culture.

Alongside music, African American urban culture was formed by the African American press, which had flourished in a relatively unrestricted African American sphere in New York before Reconstruction. The resistant, intellectual, and critical tradition established by *Freedom's Journal* was carried on by such others as Frederick Douglass's *North Star* and, later, the *Chicago Defender* and *The Crisis*. In an increasingly fragmented and dispersed society, when migrants left the rural South and attempted a new life in the alien territory of the urban North, the African American press became an important conduit and cohesive force in African American culture. As cities became more industrialized, a new urban-based working class emerged whose identity was, in part, predicated on their participation in mass popular and consumer culture. Alienation and isolation frequently led African Americans to the need to establish a "South in the city." Along with the enduring requirement for underground spaces, this resulted in a profusion of African American southern culture in the North, although that culture was modified in the transposition.

The "South in the city" was manifested in urban blues and jazz, the lingua franca of the jook, the club, and the rent party. Rent parties were a means of compensating for the discrepancy between white and African American rents, which could be as much as double that paid by whites for similar, or worse, accommodation, whereas African American wages were also less. They were also a public and cooperative activity that stimulated creativity and expression, and many well-known African American artists took part in rent parties in Harlem and Chicago, giving working-class African Americans access to acts that they would have little opportunity to see in clubs. Performers from all over the United States began to create a style that was distinctively urban as they conflated and synthesized regional styles, whereas lyrics reflected their experiences during migration, the impact of the city on them, and their impact on it.

As African American music emerged from the underground, it influenced subsequent forms of American music. Its commercial success, perhaps inevitably, led to its appropriation and dilution by whites for a white audience and helped to foster the development of the recording industry in the next decade. Musical forms like jazz and blues that were originally considered transgressive by whites were similarly abjured by aspirational urban African Americans—the new generation of New Negroes that identified themselves with a more bourgeois sensibility and felt that African American popular music was too closely linked with the rural South and, thus, slavery.

The Impact

The growth of urban America and the creation of an African American public sphere created new audiences, and with them increasing self-confidence for

Film

Mediated mass culture in the form of film and the movie theater, which had emerged in the late 1880s and 1890s, developed during the decade. Eyerson (2001, 85) observes that film drew on conventions that had been established in minstrel shows and vaudeville depicting African Americans as stereotypes, reinforcing the view that they were stupid, submissive, irresponsible, lazy, and cowardly. African Americans' involvement lent an element of veracity to these characters. Movie theaters, like every other public institution, were segregated, but African Americans comprised an increasingly important audience in the African American communities expanding in the newly industrialized cities of the South and the North. In response, a parallel African American film industry grew alongside the white, stimulated by a white-controlled industry, which excluded African American film producers in 1910. By the end of the decade, there were 300 theaters showing narrative and documentary films to African American audiences.

Although African American performers were involved from early on, there were few, if any, African American producers and distributors before 1910. William Foster in Chicago is an early example. During the decade, African American–controlled companies appeared, some with names that evoked earlier times (e.g., the Lincoln Motion Picture Company in Los Angeles, 1916, and the Frederick Douglass Film Company in New Jersey, 1919). Films seldom went beyond superficial comedies or celebrations of the middle class (e.g., *Realization of a Negro Ambition,* 1916). A few depicted African American soldiers and were exhibited in schools and church halls as well as theaters. Films made by African Americans that portrayed slave history were rare; however, perhaps because commercial exigencies were less important than political convictions, some white independent companies challenged the mass-market representation of slave history, using all–African American casts to attract an African American audience. *Injustice,* 1919, by The Democratic Film Corporation, was made as a response to *The Clansman,* itself adapted from the novel from which D. W. Griffith's racist *Birth of a Nation* was derived.

Mainstream white films portrayed African Americans as racial stereotypes, loyal slaves, or self-sacrificing servants. In marked contrast, Eyerson notes, African American–produced films (e.g., those made by Micheaux Film and Book Company, established in 1918) generally ignored the rural southern past, concentrating on narratives that reflected the New Negro market (politically astute, race-conscious, and culturally aware urban African Americans who condoned the African American retaliatory response to white hostility and were less willing to seek white approval). As a more distinctive African American culture evolved, popular culture and entertainment, not the more-elevated culture that Du Bois had visualized, provided a conduit into the dominant society.

African American writers, performers, and intellectuals. This new realm extended but also rivaled the smaller and more exclusive coteries established and sustained by the educated African American bourgeoisie of the previous generation whose book clubs, concerts, and theaters depended on small networks maintained by intimates and initiates in contrast to the anonymous, collective enterprise of the new African American public. The emergence of a consolidated and literate African American population made possible and accelerated the appearance of new cultural tendencies, whereas engagement with a distinctively urban culture politicized and radicalized African Americans whose activities were informed by and reflected in such publications as Garvey's *Negro World,* founded in 1918, and the socialist *Messenger,* founded in 1917, as well as *The Crisis,* which remained under Du Bois, a progressive and challenging outlet for African American writing and visual culture.

The decade closed with the emergence of a new generation of artists, the Harlem Renaissance, and the advent of recorded music to augment live performance in clubs, honky-tonks, and juke joints, which, in any case, increased in popularity during Prohibition because they were a source of bootlegged liquor. The tensions apparent at the end of the 1910s between this new generation and an older grouping would intensify in the next decade. Older African Americans continued to stress "culture" as a conduit for acknowledgment and acceptance by a dominant white society into which they sought either assimilation or distance, emphasizing that true culture was, for them, high culture, undertaken by trained and educated musicians, painters, or writers. The judgmental tone evident in many of the pronouncements on music by the older African Americans echoes that used to evaluate literature. Whereas an earlier generation of African Americans favored narratives of protest or moral redemption, the new writers turned to introspection, the impact of racism, and realistic depictions of urban life for African Americans.

For new African American intellectuals and performers, the achievement of racial identity became central to their work. Unlike the older generation, who largely avoided realistic depictions of the urban masses because they believed it would buttress negative racial stereotypes, younger African Americans nurtured on mass culture rejected these constraints. More responsive to more forms of reproduced and mediated culture than their predecessors, the close of the decade saw the beginnings of a new African American public sphere that exemplified and manifested the penetration by consumer society of African American life.

THE QUEST FOR EQUAL RIGHTS

Although the Civil War was fought over such other issues as tariffs or states' rights, its provenance lay in slavery. If African Americans and reformers believed that they would achieve equal rights alongside whites after the war, however, they were largely to be disappointed. Although emancipation freed slaves from bondage, it did not lead to a society in which racism, discrimination, and white supremacy were absent. Although the *institution* of slavery had been abolished, the recipients of slave labor were quick to reestablish a kind of antebellum master–slave relationship. The resulting legislation, the Black Codes, regulated almost every feature of African American life and would, a few decades later, solidify into formally ordained legislation, the Jim Crow system.

In general, the Codes meant that in the South, African Americans were forbidden from testifying against whites or from serving on juries; many did not allow African Americans to enter towns without police permission, whereas others disbarred them from remaining overnight in specified locations; public transport was frequently segregated or African Americans were even completely excluded from any form of transport. Most facilities (e.g., theaters, hotels, restaurants, and shops) were off-limits and, perhaps most restrictive to any hope of future advancement, African Americans were excluded from many schools.

Although the notion of "equality" enshrined in the Fourteenth Amendment effectively wiped out the most severe aspects of the Codes, it was by no means the "color-blind" solution some hoped, and neither the 1875 Civil Rights Act, outlawing Jim Crow practices, nor the Fifteenth Amendment, which "ensured" the enfranchisement of African Americans, helped much as the Act was subsequently ruled unconstitutional. African Americans were disenfranchised with it as well by the end of Reconstruction. Segregation spread throughout the South and the states that bordered on the North with no effective political opposition, and by spreading, it *became* the law. Where segregation was not possible, African Americans were excluded.

This happened mainly because whites, those with power, wanted it to; because northerners abandoned their attempts to prevent it; and because the federal government and courts, institutions almost wholly made up of whites, failed to prevent it. It was in this context of segregation, discrimination, and the belief by white supremacists that *any* white was superior to *any* black that such organizations as the Niagara Movement and the NAACP set out to challenge the gross inequalities at the beginning of the 20th century.

The National Association for the Advancement of Colored People

Formation

The NAACP has been termed "the most important agency for the Negroes in their struggle against caste" (Myrdal, 1962, 819) and "the organization that most fully and comprehensively attempted to further the interests and improve the living standards of both northern and southern blacks. (Ellison, 1974, 71) Although African American radicalism had already found a voice in the Niagara Movement

Silent Protest parade in Harlem on July 28, 1917. The parade was organized by the National Association for the Advancement of Colored People and religious leaders in Harlem to protest violence against African Americans throughout the United States. The parade organizers also denounced the United States' use of African American troops in World War I, as these same men were often denied the rights for which they were supposedly fighting. (Library of Congress)

(the precursor to the NAACP), the catalyst for its formation was the growth of anti–African American feeling in the industrial centers of Illinois, which erupted into violence in August 1908 when white laborers felt that African American migrant workers threatened their livelihood.

Spurred by the violence, which left scores of African Americans killed and injured, with many driven out of the city, the white Kentucky socialist William English Walling devised the idea of an interracial organization that would revive the abolitionist spirit and promote and defend African American rights. Mary White Ovington, a white socialist from an abolitionist background, joined him first, followed by others that included Oswald Garrison Villard, who drafted a conference proposal in February 1909. A Committee of Forty was established to pursue the aims of the organization at this first conference. In a weak attempt to avoid angering Booker T. Washington, neither William Monroe Trotter, one of his more outspoken critics, nor Ida Wells-Barnett, who had opposed Walling's accommodationist stance, was nominated. There was little real resolve, however, behind these attempts to mollify the accommodationists, which were inspired more by the reality of Washington's disruptive influence. Mass meetings took place after the conference, pamphlets were widely distributed, and recruitment drives were initiated. The 1910 conference, at which a merger was completed between African American liberals from the Niagara Movement and white abolitionists, adopted a policy for the NAACP that was almost identical to its predecessor.

Among the organization's policies were complete equality of opportunity, the condemnation of economic subordination of African Americans, and the fact that, in reality, such civil rights legislation as the Fourteenth and Fifteenth Amendments were largely ignored. Within the Fourteenth Amendment was the tenet that no state should "deny to any person within its jurisdiction the equal protection of the laws." The Fifteenth Amendment stated that "the right of citizens of the United States to vote shall not be denied or abridged by the United States or by any State on account of race, color, or previous condition of servitude." The organization thus resolved that the right to vote underpinned all other rights.

Although the initial inspiration for the NAACP had come from whites and whites constituted all the early appointments of officers for the organization, by 1914 there were 13 African Americans on the board of directors, the majority of whom had come from the Niagara Movement. The one exception to the bias toward whites as officers was William Edward Burghardt (W. E. B.) Du Bois, who, in his role as director of publicity and research, edited *The Crisis*.

The NAACP and Discrimination

Woodrow Wilson's presidency brought about further grounds for the NAACP to oppose what they saw as the gradual and systematic erosion of African American civil rights. Despite 100,000 African American votes for Wilson, segregation was implemented in the civil service and government by 1913, and separate working and rest areas had been introduced in the Treasury and Post Office Departments. Applicants for civil service posts were required to submit photographs, and Wilson's allegedly progressive views were countered by the strictest and most explicit discrimination for more than 50 years. At the beginning of Wilson's presidency, African Americans filled 13 significant federal offices and 11 diplomatic and consular positions. By the end of 1915, this had been reduced to 4 and 8, respectively. The NAACP was resolute in its opposition to what had been until then a largely southern problem. Leaders like Villard called for such retrogressive and inflammatory policies to be rejected, and Wilson's assertion that such policies benefited blacks gave the association sufficient cause to call for nationwide protests.

Although support came from those previously indifferent to NAACP campaigns, the opposition was never robust or coordinated enough to be successful. No significant retractions occurred, and by 1914, those slender connections that did exist between African American radicals and the Wilson administration were cut. Although the NAACP still lacked the strength and coordination to combat the prejudices of a deeply entrenched establishment, the experience that it gained in so doing provided a basis for later, more successful campaigns.

Membership numbers increased during these years, from 329 in January 1912 to 1,000 in 11 branches by the end of the year. By 1919, there were 91,203 members in 310 branches, and southern membership at 42,588 outweighed northern at 38,420 for the first time. From the outset, it had been clear that there was a North–South split in the NAACP; at the 1916 Amenia conference in New York, disagreements over policies occurred between southern leaders and their northern counterparts, and it was evident that southern leaders did not want the level of social, political, or economic transformation that the radical northern impulse contended was their right. The level of activity in 1919, however, demonstrated that the NAACP had begun to achieve its original goals of improving the lives of southern African Americans.

The prevention of miscarriages of justice was among important advances achieved by the Association. In 1910, Villard was instrumental in having the death sentence against the sharecropper Pink Franklin commuted to life imprisonment, although *The Crisis* argued that he should have been acquitted. As a result, a legal redress department was founded, and during the decade, several more important legal victories were won. The NAACP established a policy of holding meetings and lectures intended to educate northern whites and assist in eliminating discrimination. Branches in New York and Boston had some local successes in such issues as preventing the exclusion of African Americans from swimming pools, whereas committees successfully dealt with cases of discrimination in theaters and police brutality. The 1910 Baltimore ordinances, providing for residential segregation, stimulated both national and local opposition. In 1917, the NAACP took a case of residential segregation in Louisville to the Supreme Court, which ruled in the plaintiff's favor, thus demonstrating (at least in principle because the triumph turned out to almost meaningless) that legal, peaceful protest could be at least as effective as agitation.

The Association had fewer successes in their attempts to redress imbalances in education. Campaigns against the Smith-Lever and Smith-Hughes bills were unproductive, as were regular demands for impartial federal aid to assist state provision of vocational and agricultural education, the improvement of rural schools, and the eradication of illiteracy. In certain northern schools, however, local branches successfully campaigned against segregation, whereas the NAACP was instrumental in successfully challenging discriminatory practices at such universities as Cornell and Johns Hopkins. Less productive were attempts by the Association to end discrimination in the legal profession. The achievement of overturning the decision to rescind the appointment of three African American lawyers to the American Bar Association proved a hollow victory when few were subsequently elected, and despite attempts by the NAACP to thwart discrimination in insurance, banking, hotels, and restaurants, it remained widespread and entrenched throughout the decade.

The NAACP had some success in amending state civil rights legislation, but compliance was patchy and cases brought against segregated transport had varying degrees of success. The right to vote was an area in which the Association made repeated and concentrated efforts, and it had some success in Oklahoma in 1910 in challenging the "grandfather clause," which disqualified most slaves and their descendants from voting because they could not satisfy statutory requirements, and which the Supreme Court ruled was in violation of the Fifteenth Amendment. A victory in a test case, however, did not always mean that individual laws were repealed elsewhere.

The nature of the criticism aimed at the Association varied and depended on the agenda of the source. Some regarded its emphasis on publicity, the right to vote, and civil liberties while neglecting a more structured and scientific approach as superficial. Critics of its policies in the South viewed its attempts to change entrenched attitudes as futile. To the more radical activist, the NAACP's policies evaded the more fundamental problem of the economic causes of poverty and discrimination. Such criticism, however, ignored the very real gains the Association did effect. James Weldon Johnson, at one time NAACP secretary, observed that "there is a school that holds that these legal victories are empty. They are not. At the very least, they provide the ground upon which we may make a stand for our rights." (Myrdal, 1962, 832) Johnson describes the legal status of African Americans when the Association was founded, and the worsening situation, as the only basis for appraisal, arguing that "its work would be of value if only for the reason that without it our status would be worse than it is." (Ibid.)

W. E. B. Du Bois

Born and raised in a largely white community in New England, the civil rights activist William Edward Burghardt Du Bois, was perhaps the most eminent and most formidable opponent of Booker T. Washington's policies, but this role was by no means the limit of his achievements. As a sociologist, teacher, historian, writer, editor, and more besides, Du Bois was a key figure, perhaps the key figure, in the struggle by African Americans against discrimination.

Educated in America and Europe, Du Bois became the first African American to receive a PhD from Harvard. On his return from Europe to the United States, he taught at several universities and established the department of sociology at Atlanta (now Clark Atlanta) University. Following the publication of Booker T. Washington's *The Souls of Black Folk,* in which he argued for African Americans to adopt a policy of accommodation, to cooperate with the white southern elite, and to forgo politics, Du Bois spoke out against these views, urging African Americans to persevere with the fight for equal rights, in particular, the franchise and admission to higher education.

The growth of anti–African American sentiment and the ensuing climate of violence against them in the years after 1905 prompted the formation by Du Bois of the Niagara Movement, an organization that characterized African American radicalism in the Progressive era. In addition to his role as a prominent spokesperson for the Movement, Du Bois also edited *Horizon,* the Movement's journal. Although he was not responsible for the establishment in 1909 of the successor to the Niagara Movement, the interracial NAACP, he became director of publicity and research and the editor of its journal, *The Crisis*. As editor, Du Bois was largely responsible for determining the content of the journal, and throughout the decade and Du Bois's 25-year tenure as editor, it included editorials on racial discrimination, segregation, African American education policies, and the role of the church. Du Bois was also a vigorous promoter of the arts, publishing work by, among others, James Weldon Johnson and writ-

W. E. B. Du Bois, called the father of pan-Africanism for his work on behalf of the emerging African nations, devoted his life to the struggle for equality for African Americans and all people of color. (Library of Congress)

ers associated with the Harlem Renaissance. He also wrote weekly columns for a number of other publications, including the *Chicago Defender* and the *Pittsburgh Courier,* and until his death in 1963, he published a wide range of books and articles, including three autobiographies. It is as a radical activist who challenged the white status quo, however, that Du Bois will perhaps be best remembered.

Church Groups

Before emancipation, although African Americans worshipped in the same churches as whites, they did so in the same conditions of inferiority as in every aspect of life. Even though whites occupied places at the front of churches, African Americans were generally contained in separate balconies or, at best, at the back of the church. The minister or preacher was invariably white. Following emancipation, segregated religion spread quickly throughout the South as

The Crisis

Founded in a period of a still embryonic African American press and a white press that made little attempt to present news about the Negro, *The Crisis* (its name was taken from James Russell Lowell's poem "The Present Crisis" and then sub-titled *A Record of the Darker Races*) was the NAACP's propaganda vehicle from 1910. Du Bois was adamant that a vocal, dynamic publication was indispensable to the success of the NAACP, and although some board members resisted the initiative, the publication went ahead. Based in New York City, Du Bois stated in the first issue that it was primarily a nonpartisan newspaper in that reports would reflect the impact on interracial relations, specifically those that affected the "Negro-American." It would review literature and opinion on the "race problem" and commission articles, whereas its editorials would speak out for the rights of people, regardless of color or race. Although the periodical had almost no capital at the start, it was able to commission copy from such established writers of both races as James Weldon Johnson and H. L. Mencken, as well as from those that were young and still unknown. Its monthly circulation rose rapidly from an initial printing in November 1910 of 1,000 to 16,000 a year later, 24,000 at the end of two years, peaking at 104,000 in 1919. In the first years of its publication, the circulation exceeded NAACP membership. In addition to its coverage of NAACP news, under Du Bois, who largely determined the content, *The Crisis* featured his own polemics on racial prejudice, segregation, inferior education for African Americans, and his perception that churches were inherently and secretively segregationist.

These editorials sometimes mirrored Association ideology, but senior figures there feared that criticism directed at the church might be damaging, and Du Bois' independent stance and his defiance regarding NAACP dictates led to Villard's resignation from the chairmanship in 1913. Other leaders were dismayed at the bluntness and speed implied in editorial demands for complete equality. Du Bois' uncompromising and dismissive attitude also aggravated African American newspaper editors, on whose support the Association depended. The Association thus attempted to placate the African American press by passing a conciliatory resolution at the 1914 annual general meeting. There was little dissent, however, between the board and Du Bois over his regular critiques of Washington's policies of appeasement. During this period, the NAACP was stridently anti-accommodationist, and whatever conflicts there may have been between Du Bois and other leaders over policies, its radicalism found a mouthpiece in *The Crisis,* which was linked to the Association by its fundamental base of ideological conformity. Nevertheless, Du Bois acknowledged the difficulties he faced in achieving a balance between his own views and those of the NAACP, but he was also aware that, for two decades at least, his opinions and objectives coincided with those of the periodical.

In addition to its role as the "house" journal of the NAACP, regular promotion of the arts was evident early. The periodical featured photographs and paintings, literary contests, and poetry, and there were annual editions dedicated to children and education. Nevertheless, its primary function was to challenge bigotry

---

The Crisis, *Continued*

and prejudice, and, as George S. Schulyer observed in the 40th anniversary edition, "the whole concept of white supremacy then nationally accepted."

Regular features of these early years were accounts, in pictures as well as text, of lynchings. The first reports were compiled from newspaper articles, but NAACP investigators (frequently whites sympathetic to the cause) wrote later accounts from first-hand observation. After persistent pressure by the NAACP, in 1918 Wilson came out against lynching in public, but lynchings continued throughout the decade and thereafter.

---

well as the North. African Americans found that they were unwelcome in white churches, and that they were frequently excluded by legislation. Athough theologians might have attempted to justify discrimination by asserting that racial segregation was ordained by the Creator, it was less a divine ordinance and more another example of whites' determination to exclude African Americans from every area of their lives. As African Americans established their own places of worship, those churches became the most significant social structure after the family itself.

Relationships between family members historically were deeply embedded in African American religious faiths and social systems and customs. These beliefs inspired the search for education, power, a more cohesive community, and, ultimately, equality and civil rights. This pursuit achieved its expression in the institutional growth of the African American church. African American churches gradually began to expand and gradually to disassociate themselves from white congregations. By 1890, the U.S. Census noted the presence of some 1.3 million African American Baptists, nearly 1 million of whom lived in the South. By 1914, that figure had reached 3 million in some 22,000 churches. As in the white church, the number of African American churches far outweighed ministers, particularly in rural areas. Because the Baptist church had a largely decentralized structure and did not insist on a rigid program of formal training, wider access to the ministry was possible, and these factors enabled rapid expansion and the emergence of new churches.

This swift growth involved a complex fragmentation process, often caused by doctrinal, financial, or social differences that resulted in ministers establishing new congregations and led to a great many splinter churches and movements. The African Methodist Episcopal (AME) churches, for example, expanded into the South, opening up new conferences in Georgia and Florida. AME membership increased from around 4,000 after emancipation to some half a million in 6,600 churches in the North and the South by 1914. Formal participation in the AME

Zion and the Colored Methodist Episcopal churches, the third- and fourth-largest African American denominations, simultaneously increased to 300,000, in around 2,700 churches each. (Trotter, 2001, 353)

Segregation and Jim Crow legislation stimulated churches to augment their programs of spiritual, ethical, and emotional aid with an increasing array of endeavors intended to support the economic, political, educational, and social welfare needs of parishioners. By the second decade, the AME church ran 25 schools and colleges, whereas the African American Baptist orders maintained 14. In addition to education, some of the institutions provided theological instruction. Churches also established their own publishing houses.

African American women, who outnumbered men in churches, were instrumental in developing the spiritual and social welfare endeavors of the church. The National Training School for Women, founded by the Convention in Washington, D.C., began accepting students in 1909. By World War I, increasing numbers of young African American women were educated to high school and junior college levels there. Students were trained in domestic science, clerical and administration work, agriculture, and printing.

The African American Church in the North

In such urban areas as Harlem, churches performed an increasingly important part in the community's development. The church was historically always among the most stable and financially sound African American institutions. The wealth, authority, and influence of the church grew as the African American population grew rapidly in the early century. By 1914, participation in long-established churches increased by as much as 300 percent, forcing them to move to larger premises. As these churches expanded and as such new churches as Seventh Day Adventist, Roman Catholic, and evangelical were founded, white denominations moved from the neighborhood, selling their property to African American Baptists, Methodists, or others. To cope with this increased participation, bible classes were often held in such commercial premises as theaters, whereas Mass services were sometimes conducted in gospel tents on vacant lots.

Ministers encouraged their more affluent parishioners to buy property in Harlem while prices were still low. Many churches achieved considerable profits by selling property in the midtown districts and relocating uptown where land and property prices had become depressed before the war. More affluent congregations built new churches and invested in real estate as well, in the process becoming the largest African American property owners in Harlem. By becoming landowners, African American churches aided in the transformation of Harlem into a predominantly African American neighborhood.

African American churches implemented a range of programs intended to help migrants. In many of the destination cities (e.g., Chicago, Cleveland, and Detroit), health, leisure, and child care, as well as employment and housing, agencies were established. An active and motivated group of women organized and implemented the social welfare activities in African American churches. The enterprises were closely linked with the endeavors of such national organizations as the National Association of Colored Women (NACW) and the Women's Baptist Convention (WBC). As more migrants arrived during the war, the NACW accelerated its development and implementation of centers that provided many, or all, of these activities, whereas the WBC instigated social scientific investigations intended to improve African American health and life expectancy as they moved from rural life and employment to an urban and industrial environment.

Lynching and Racial Violence

Although the great influx of African Americans into the industrial cities of the North occasionally resulted in a more tolerant attitude among whites that originated from understanding and experience, more often whites felt intimidated and vulnerable. Many felt that their perceived innate superiority might be lost or that their cultural identity could be threatened. Migrants' color was also physically different, too different for them to be tolerated and to be integrated as European immigrants (perhaps) had been. Underneath the apprehension and suspicion, deeper and more intangible fears prevailed, fears that were possibly sexual in origin. Although miscegenation was legal in the majority of the North, marriages and liaison between African Americans and whites were rare and profoundly deplored.

Hostility inevitably arose in the cities and towns most affected by migration and the war. With the outbreak of war, immigration from Europe declined and this, along with vacancies caused by native-born workers who joined the armed forces, created employment opportunities for African Americans. As they competed with whites for jobs, tensions emerged. Such urban infrastructure as housing and welfare in many northern cities was unprepared for the arrival of thousands of migrants. African Americans were particularly affected by the subsequent problems in urban housing as they found themselves forced into high-rent but substandard housing in racially defined and overcrowded areas. Discrimination in the work place further disadvantaged African Americans as they discovered that the only jobs available to them tended to be low paid, frequently temporary, and often dangerous and dirty. This potentially inflammatory combination of circumstances almost inevitably erupted into racial violence in some places.

Although racially inspired disorder had already taken place in Illinois in 1908, when workers believed that their jobs were at risk from African American migrants, the incidents were relatively isolated compared with the violence that began in 1917, which signaled the start of a series of race riots that continued into the 1920s.

Race Riots

There is now some disagreement over whether the term *riot* is appropriate for interracial conflict. Myrdal preferred "terrorization or massacre, and [considered] it a magnified, or mass, lynching." (Myrdal, 1962, 566)

The first confrontation took place in East St. Louis where fears among white workers were fueled by rumors that African American labor was being recruited for industrial facilities. These were combined with heightened, and probably exaggerated, anxieties that black migrants were penetrating formerly white-dominated neighborhoods. The unrest began with the accidental shooting of a white by an African American and was quickly put down by police and military. Although this first affray was serious enough, it soon erupted into riots in which more lives were lost than in any other subsequent racial conflict.

The violence that ensued was exacerbated by several factors. White fears concerning jobs were heightened by a corrupt committee's suggestion that African Americans were responsible for the first confrontation, whereas the police did little, if anything, to curb racially motivated attacks on African Americans. Several warnings about an impending crisis went unheeded, and the killing of two white detectives on July 2 led to a riot, unprecedented in its scale and inhumanity. Estimates of deaths vary between 39 and more than 100 African Americans and 9 whites. More than 200 African American homes were burned, along with some people, and others were lynched.

Despite national condemnation, little legal redress took place in East St. Louis. Relatively few convictions resulted from the subsequent brief trials, and although the later inquiry blamed the employers, the labor organizers, and the politicians for creating the circumstances, no further prosecutions ensued.

Although many of the conditions that heightened racial tension in East St. Louis (increases in the African American population, social and employment discrimination, welfare inequalities) also existed in Chicago, the situation there was worse, too. In part because of their experiences during the war, by 1919, African Americans who returned from Europe had become conscious of the segregated neighborhoods and reduced employment options that confronted them, and they were less disposed to accept discrimination.

The catalyst for the July riot was the stoning by whites and subsequent drowning of an African American swimmer, but specific conditions in Chicago also contributed to the outbreak. Evidence of police corruption and their apparent reluctance to act in case they antagonized powerful political factions emerged; white, racist police officers were condemned for failing to prevent the escalation of riots; and in the febrile climate of postwar anticommunism, extremists intent on increasing racial antagonism that would help provoke the eventual uprising against the government were accused of distributing propaganda intended to stir up unrest among African American communities. Although these allegations were refuted, it is clear that social conditions were at the root of the racial violence that erupted in many urban areas in the Red Summer of 1919.

A police officer provides protection to black residents of the South Side of Chicago, moving shortly after the riots of 1919. (Bettmann/Corbis)

The death was followed by five days of rioting in which at least 38 were killed, 500 injured, and 1,000 left without homes as houses were set on fire. Six thousand National Guardsmen were sent in when police were unable to cope. A marked difference between the Chicago and East St. Louis confrontations was that, when provoked, African Americans in Chicago retaliated fiercely. Although a governor's commission drew predictable conclusions and recommended more tolerance on both sides, as well as more equitable allocation of welfare and educational resources, few tangible changes occurred.

Although worse in terms of lives lost and property destroyed than the violence perpetrated in other towns and cities, the conditions that sparked the racial unrest in East St. Louis and Chicago were echoed elsewhere in places where resentments that had simmered below the surface spilled over into open confrontation. At least 15 were killed in Washington until the riots there were quelled by a large contingent of troops. There was little agreement among opposing factions in later analyses. The NAACP accused whites of African American victimization, and the failure to establish a formal investigation into the causes left blacks to nurse their animosity and whites resolute in their determination to smother black independence and civil rights. As in Chicago, newly radicalized African Americans, who were now keenly aware that their contribution to America at home and in the war had been largely ignored by whites, retaliated forcefully.

Although it was clear that in its evident prowhite bias the white press in Washington had inflamed the situation, director of Negro economics at the U.S. Department of Labor, George Haynes, observed that segregation had been a more significant causal factor in polarizing the two sides. Other factors, more local in nature, had also contributed to white resentment. Some African American families were felt to have become too affluent and socially assured, and there was also constant animosity among whites over growing African American militancy.

Racial violence was not confined to the North. In October 1919, concerns among whites that African Americans were establishing a black progressive union led to the murder of African Americans in Elaine, Arkansas. Although local police were explicitly implicated in the killings, the riot resulted in markedly restricted rights for many local African Americans. Twelve African Americans were convicted of murder in the subsequent trial and sentenced to death and only intervention by the NAACP prevented their executions.

Although serious riots occurred in only a handful of cities and towns, they embodied a widespread and profound antipathy between African Americans and whites permeating much of America. Most commentators agreed that much of the unrest could have been avoided had there been less discrimination, if the police had been less evidently partisan, if there had been greater attempts to reconcile opposing factions, and if the largely white offenders who had escaped the law had been brought to justice after the unrest. Given that the underlying problems of inequality, discrimination, segregation, and poverty were never really addressed, resentment among African Americans similarly continued to simmer for decades thereafter.

For the rest of the decade, and in the next, too, conflicts broke out in places as far apart as Philadelphia, Charleston, Omaha, Duluth, Houston, Springfield, and Tulsa. In each of these, there were different local factors that led to the unrest, but in all, there were underlying social and economic inequalities given pseudoscientific justification by contemporary racist sentiments. The same spurious eugenic theories that had been cited to claim that immigrants were racially inferior were used to "prove" the inherent inferiority of African Americans. "Evidence" of racial inferiority by such racist writers as Eggleston and Mayo were reported in the popular press, articulating and reinforcing the part-formed prejudices of significant numbers.

Although the war afforded some temporary relief in African American unemployment, African Americans were antagonized by the enduring problems that persisted afterwards. Resentment was strengthened by the bitter irony that African American servicemen who had fought for democracy were disallowed that very quality on their return. The optimism exhibited by the African American press that the war might lead to more equality and civil rights for blacks turned to disappointment and resentment afterwards, whereas prejudicial attitudes among whites laid the foundations for the resurgence of the Ku Klux Klan in the 1920s.

Lynching

Although race riots were essentially an urban phenomenon, lynching took place in predominantly rural areas. The term is generally used to describe an extralegal system of summary justice, almost always resulting in the death of the victim. In the late 19th and early 20th centuries, so-called lynch law became an institutionalized (and criminal) process of social control by which African Americans were tyrannized, perpetrated by white mobs to preserve white supremacy. Although lynching occurred elsewhere, it has become associated with the southern and border states in the period between Reconstruction and around 1940. The executions usually took place in public and victims were frequently hanged or shot, sometimes both. Many, though, were compounded by the mobs that burned victims at the stake or dismembered or tortured them.

Because lynching was illegal, statistics on how many were carried out are unreliable, particularly before 1882. Nevertheless, three main sources of statistics do exist. From 1882, the *Chicago Tribune* systematically began to record lynchings, and in 1892, Tuskegee Institute collected and tabulated the statistics. From 1912, the NAACP documented lynchings independently. Statistics were largely gathered from newspaper accounts, but because of the scattered nature of habitation in the South and because communication between rural districts and city newspapers was infrequent, it is almost certain that a great many lynchings eluded the notice of the press. There are inconsistencies in numbers between each of the three sources, with those recorded by the NAACP being slightly higher than the Tuskegee figures. Historians now believe that the latter err on the conservative side. In a sample year, 1914, Tuskegee Institute recorded 52, the *Tribune* accounted for 54, and *The Crisis* put the number at 74. Differences can be attributed to differing interpretations of what constitutes a lynching and mistakes in the figures.

In opposition to recent popular notions, lynching was not only inflicted on African Americans, particularly during the 19th century when a considerable minority of the victims were white. After 1900, however, the great majority was African American and Tuskegee Institute figures indicate that the ratio was around two-and-one-half African American to white. (Myrdal, 1962, 560–561) Although the crime occurred throughout the United States (apart from four states: Massachusetts, Rhode Island, New Hampshire, and Vermont), most were carried out in the southern states, accounting for approximately 90 percent. More than 66 percent of the remaining 10 percent took place in the border states (West Virginia, Ohio, Indiana, Illinois, Kansas, and Maryland). More than half occurred in Mississippi (the highest), Georgia, Texas, Louisiana, and Alabama.

Lynching of Leo Frank, Marietta, Georgia, August 17, 1915. (Library of Congress)

Lynching was carried out for "crimes" that ranged from serious offences to minor misdemeanors, and often for no other motive than racial bigotry. A racist orthodoxy to defend or justify the practice has grown up in the South that it happened solely in retribution for the rape of white women and murder, but this is not borne out by statistics. The relatively high figures for rape and attempted rape were probably inflated, Myrdal believes, by the all-embracing southern definition of rape, which includes all sexual relations between African American men and white women, and because the accusation of rape ("the nameless crime") left the mob safe from any further investigation and perpetuated the myth that African Americans were overcome with an insatiable urge to rape women. (Myrdal, 1962, 561) The majority were for "felonious assault," according to Tuskegee records, with around 19 percent carried out for rape. A significant minority occurred for miscellaneous, usually trivial, "crimes," such as "disputing with a white man," "unpopularity," or "asking a white woman in marriage." Lynch law often ignored whether the victim was guilty of the alleged offence, and mistaken identity was sometimes a factor.

Lynchings often occurred in isolated, rural areas and smaller towns where there was a high incidence of poverty and illiteracy. Mobs were frequently made up from the same, albeit white, economic strata as their victims: laborers and tenant farmers who feared what they perceived as economic competition and African American progress, although sometimes, more affluent whites took part. Given the hysterical atmosphere surrounding interracial relationships, inciting a mob was often easy and the practice was looked upon as a form of local amusement. Although the majority occurred late at night, some of these illegal and brutal spectacles took place during the day and were publicized beforehand in newspapers. Many of these crimes were photographed and postcards depicting lynchings were frequently sold, allowing the photographer to profit from the activity. Such postcards became sufficiently popular to become an embarrassment to the government, and the postmaster general banned them in 1908; however, they continued to be circulated until at least the mid-1930s. The police frequently turned a blind eye to, and even participated in, the illegal practice, whereas lynch law was condoned, and often supported, by many southern politicians who rose to power on a race platform. Because small communities were often wholly in favor of lynching and the judicial system, from judges to witnesses, was white, participants were seldom brought to justice.

Although by 1910 the practice had declined from its peak during the later decades of the 19th century, they still occurred (and the percentage of lynchings among African Americans increased), and according to the NAACP, the figures increased again after World War I, from 58 in 1916, to 63 in 1918, to 77 in 1919. Accounting for the decline is difficult, but it probably stemmed from a number of factors. As some sectors (most notably, women) of southern communities became more affluent and educated, they gradually began to regard the practice as distasteful. Increasing urbanization and communications could also help to explain the decrease, as well as the growing use of statewide police forces and the National Guard to oppose lynching mobs. In addition, newspapers in the South began to condemn the practice. Statistics recorded by the NAACP made people more aware of lynching, but the organization also carried out a highly vocal campaign against the practice, investigating and publicizing these and other offences carried out against African Americans. *Thirty Years of Lynching in the United States, 1889–1918,* published by the NAACP in 1918, articulated the causes and the circumstances surrounding the crime. The publication made many more people aware of the atrocities and laid the foundations for the organization's support of antilynching legislation in the following decade.

The African American Reaction

African Americans reacted to racial oppression and violence in a number of ways, either in kind, by migration, or by organized peaceful resistance. Although violence in retaliation was ultimately counterproductive because it frequently led to more beatings and lynchings, it was nevertheless supported by a number of prominent African American activists, among them W. E. B. Du Bois. In 1911 and 1916, Du Bois urged blacks not to be passive and, if necessary, to arm themselves against lynch mobs. Also an advocate of physical resistance, the editor of the combative *Socialist* publication, A. Phillip Randolph, encouraged African Americans to fight back, whereas the NAACP defended the use of African American self-defense in retaliation. By the beginning of World War I, increasing numbers of African Americans were prepared to carry arms and to use them if necessary. It is probable that many riots were exacerbated by African American retaliation, and that in most of these, African American resistance proved to be abortive because whites heavily outnumbered them.

Because of violence, intimidation, and discrimination, many thousands of African Americans migrated from the South; however, some campaigners felt that peaceful protest, raising public awareness about lynching, and promoting antilynching legislation were more appropriate responses than either revengeful violence or becoming complicit in the Great Migration northward. Central in the organization of crusades against lynching was Ida B. Wells, who along with editing the Memphis *Free Speech,* campaigned tirelessly, acting as chair of the Anti-Lynching Bureau of the Afro-American Council and publishing a number of pamphlets in which she revealed the savagery of lynching. The best known of these was *A Red Record* of 1894.

Along with the publication of statistics, the NAACP began an energetic campaign against lynching and all other forms of racism. *The Crisis* published a monthly account of lynchings and was indefatigable in its advocacy of African American equality, whereas the organization's Legal Redress Committee fought cases of segregation and discrimination in the courts.

Impact

The decade 1910–1919 was significant in the history of African Americans. The Great Migration, the enduring legacy of Jim Crow and segregation, the growth of urban ghettos, race riots, lynchings and violence, the emergence of such organizations as the NAACP, and characters like W. E. B. Du Bois and Marcus Garvey all contributed to a very different picture for African Americans at the end of the decade.

For migrants who traveled north, the so-called promised land did not always fulfill their expectations. Regarded as cheap labor, they were never conceived by northern employers as coequals in the mainstream of the labor pool, and they were almost always employed within the rigid confines of management's own dictates. Skilled or unskilled migrants in a labor pool that was both replaceable and disposable had few opportunities to advance in a profit-orientated system. Unlike many immigrants, African American migrants were forced out, not up. Although the wartime drive for an available and cheap source of unskilled labor partly explains the transformation of capital, northern industry thrived because cheap labor could be circulated at will. Once the demand disappeared, large numbers of black migrant workers could not be reabsorbed. Unable to return to the South, African Americans were usually demoted to the more-or-less permanent position of being forced into the worst jobs, and, given their perceived differences from the ruling majority, assimilation was also unlikely.

A combination of factors (migration, federal and state policies, declining prices, and environmental emergencies) had a profound, if predictable, impact on the southern economy. African American–owned farms throughout the South declined in number during the decade, whereas such African American businesses as banks suffered a similar fate. The white reaction to migration was less predictable. Given the downturn in cotton and the boll weevil invasion, the reduction in the labor force did not lead to widespread concern because restructuring would probably have been necessary in any case. Moreover, white fears of African American political influence diminished as more African Americans migrated. Despite mass migration, the majority of African Americans remained in the South, and after the war, more African Americans lived, and worked, in urban areas there than in the North and the West combined, choosing to go to southern cities rather than travel north.

By 1910, segregation and discrimination were firmly lodged in almost all areas of African American life. Industrial expansion meant that African American workers began to make inroads into most areas of employment, yet they had to endure discriminatory contract labor systems and lower pay than whites for the same work. African Americans were frequently used as strikebreakers and found that employers had little use for them once the strike was settled. Wartime labor shortages led to opportunities for African American women, who replicated the jobs of white women in food production and clothing, as well as in heavier industries.

Moreover, African Americans were also more frequently unemployed, but during the decade, African Americans began to develop such resistance strategies as unionization and changing jobs frequently to counter discrimination. Women also resisted discrimination in domestic service by regulating working hours and conditions and by creating affiliations and organizations to help improve African American working women's wages. Despite increased African American employment, inequality remained far-reaching and pervasive, so segregated communities where African American enterprises and professional ventures could be established provided alternatives to employment by whites and facilitated the growth of an African American middle class. The new African American consciousness was reflected in the growth of African American newspapers. Nevertheless, despite increases in white-collar jobs in such areas as insurance, banking, and social work and advances by African American women, whites still regularly achieved better promotion prospects and earned more for the same roles at the end of the decade.

As migration increased, so too did the African American populations of urban areas. Attracted by its reputation and employment and leisure opportunities, Chicago became the preferred destination for many migrants, and the African American population there grew from around 44,000 to more than 109,000 during the decade. As migrants left the increasingly depopulated communities in the South, businessmen faced the alternative of following their clientele or losing their business. Many northern urban areas struggled to cope with the influx, and as cities expanded, whites reacted to the new experience of a vastly increased African American population by implementing progressively more rigid segregation laws, restrictive deed covenants effectively limiting African Americans to specific neighborhoods.

Total urban ghettoization resulted in many cities, which increased in size and number after World War I. Many tenants sublet apartments because they were unable to pay inflated rents. The resulting overcrowding and unsanitary conditions inevitably led to increases in diseases, which in turn resulted in reduced life expectancy and higher infant mortality rates among African Americans.

Massive African American inward migration and growth from European immigrants meant that many cities increased in both size and population. By 1910, New York City had the second-largest urban African American population; by 1919, it had the largest. As the city expanded northward and property values collapsed in the first decade, the formerly affluent and comfortable Harlem gradually became the neighborhood in which African Americans eventually settled. Alarmed whites intent on preventing a perceived African American invasion formed associations of property owners, signing restrictive covenants that prohibited selling to African Americans. The collapse of these attempts and economic and social factors contributed to Harlem's decline into the urban slum ghetto that it would become by the late 1920s.

Throughout the decade, several organizations [e.g., the National Association for the Advancement of Colored People (NAACP)] were established to support African Americans struggling against the inequalities of race. The NAACP had some notable successes in preventing miscarriages of justice and in addressing civil rights issues. Despite criticism, it is evident that the NAACP did achieve some very tangible gains in this and subsequent decades. African American urban churches established social and welfare programs, and with increased migration, the National Association of Colored Women and the Women's Baptist Convention helped migrants in the transition from rural to urban life.

Social and economic consequences caused by large numbers of migrants were determining factors in the outbreaks of violence that occurred toward the end of the decade. Failure to address the causes of the riots (inequality, discrimination, segregation, and poverty) led to continuing and lasting resentment among African Americans. Wartime reductions in African American unemployment were temporary, and demobilized African American servicemen faced the

Historians' Debate:
The Great Migration

Two issues tend to dominate debates regarding the Migration: first, whether African American migrants left the rural South for purely personal reasons, and, second, whether their lack of education, perceived individual shortcomings, and rural origins were linked in earlier studies to what Marks refers to as "the disappointment of the exodus": the discrimination, segregation, and abuse that African Americans suffered following migration.

In migrations like this, Marks believes, it is unlikely that the motivation for leaving depends solely on the migrants. It is, as Burawoy (in Marks, 2000, 167) proposes, "institutional activity beyond the scope of individual experience that sets the stage for mass migrations," although, as Marks observes, individuals are not unrelated to the experience. Certain types (e.g., young, literate, educated men with some industrial experience) are among the most probable migrants, whereas wives supported married men during their search for work. Migrants were not a homogeneous mass, nor were they "displaced rural peasantry" or "bewildered country folk." (Marks, 2000 169) Rather, they were a disparate group that included artisans, urban nonagricultural laborers, and farm owners and tenants whose common experience were the effects of the economic metamorphosis of the South.

Although Marks argues that many migrants came from urban, often skilled backgrounds, and that their eventual hardship was little or no different from their rural counterparts, others considered that the unskilled and illiterate were disadvantaged when the demand was for the skilled and literate. Yet, *urban* workers, whatever their level of education and experience, did not progress either, particularly when compared with European immigrants. Is it possible, Marks asks, that African American migrants were less literate than Europeans? Research (Lieberson, 1980, 20) suggests the opposite is true. A more probable reason is that once the demand for African American labor disappeared after the war, African Americans could not be absorbed, nor could they return to the South. Thus, they were relegated to what Marks calls "a permanent urban-based industrial reserve, called underclass."

same discrimination, hostility, and inadequate housing that they had left behind; they returned from the war in competition for jobs and accommodation with migrants from the South, demobilized native-born soldiers, and European immigrants returning from the war. African Americans became increasingly unwilling to tolerate racial oppression and violence, and in many of the riots, violence was met with African American retaliation.

In cultural terms, the impact of a new generation of African American artists and intellectuals who were increasingly unwilling to accept the strictures of an older generation and a white-dominated society was felt toward the end of the decade and would be intensified in the next as African Americans everywhere in an increasingly urbanized and industrialized sphere stamped their imprint on America.

BIOGRAPHIES

Marcus Mosiah Garvey, 1887–1940

Journalist and Campaigner

Marcus Garvey was a prominent crusader for African American nationalism, a publisher, journalist, and entrepreneur, and, as founder of both the United Negro Improvement Association and African Communities League, one of the most important postwar African American militants. During his early life in Jamaica, Garvey was apprenticed in the printing trade, and he first experienced labor organization during a printers' strike in 1908. Blacklisted because of his involvement, he worked briefly for the Government Printing Office before moving to Costa Rica in around 1910. His travels throughout Central America exposed him to the harsh working conditions and lives of blacks there. While in Central America, Garvey started several newspapers and organized labor, campaigning for better conditions and pay. Although there are conflicting reports of this time, his activities and his involvement with the Costa Rican newspaper *La Nacionale* brought him to the attention of the government and he was expelled.

Marcus Garvey launched the first mass movement of African Americans in the United States that was based on racial pride, self-help, and separatism. (Library of Congress)

Garvey began to plan the United Negro Improvement Association after returning to Jamaica. In 1912, Garvey moved to London, England, with his sister. While there, he worked on *The African and Orient Review,* attended college, and traveled in Britain and Europe. Garvey returned to Jamaica in 1914 and became convinced that unity was the only way to improve conditions for blacks and, to achieve his aims, founded the United Negro Improvement Association (UNIA). Established on the motto, "One God, One Aim, One Destiny," the objective of the organization was to unite as one all people of African ancestry with their own country and government. The promotion of the spirit of race, pride, and love; support for the needy; the establishment of colleges, universities, and schools for the education and culture of boys and girls of the race; and the creation of a global industrial and commercial intercourse were included among its aims.

Following correspondence with Booker T. Washington, Garvey arrived in the United States in March 1916 for a lecture tour and the ambition of establishing a school in Jamaica based on Washington's Tuskegee Institute. Garvey established himself in Harlem and exhorted African Americans to take after their heroes, dignify their own women, value their blackness, construct their own institutions, and work toward the liberation of the motherland, Africa. Although the Harlem branch of the UNIA gained momentum only slowly, his reputation and his followers expanded so that he could claim 2,000 members by 1918. As the Garvey movement expanded across the United States and further afield, it claimed some 2 million members by 1918, increasing to 4 million in 1920.

Garvey is also remembered somewhat controversially as a central proponent of the "Back to Africa" movement, which encouraged African Americans to return to their ancestral native land. Because most African Americans had no experience of their homeland, this initiative was less than successful. The Black Star merchant fleet was founded in 1919. Its ships were intended to transport returning African Americans, but the enterprise was later the subject of a mismanagement scandal. The Negro Factories Corporation of the same year was created to construct factories across the Americas and Africa to manufacture goods. Other initiatives included shops, restaurants, and a publishing house.

Although he was vehemently opposed to integration, which he viewed as the concern of a minority, African American, middle-class elite, some have argued that he was not necessarily a devotee of African American supremacy. Nevertheless, he appears to have advocated racial segregation and racial autonomy. His reputation has been marred by the controversy surrounding the steamship line and his subsequent imprisonment for mail fraud.

George Edmund Haynes, 1880–1960

Sociologist

The social worker and educator George Haynes was one of the co-founders of the organization that became the National Urban League. Haynes developed an interest in social problems surrounding African Americans who had arrived in Chicago as part of the Great Migration while studying at the University of Chicago. Further study followed at the New York School of Philanthropy, and in 1912, Haynes became the first African American to receive a PhD from Columbia

University. His doctoral thesis was subsequently published as *The Negro at Work in New York City.*

Along with the reformer Frances Kellor and the philanthropist Ruth Standish Baldwin, Haynes was central in the merging of the American Association for the Protection of Colored Women, the Committee for Improving the Industrial Conditions of Negroes in New York, and the Committee on Urban Conditions Among Negroes into the National League on Urban Conditions Among Negroes (NLUCAN), later renamed the National Urban League. Between 1911 and 1918, Haynes operated as the organization's executive director. Visiting African American colleges while still a graduate student, Haynes encouraged students to strive for academic excellence and worked to help colleges establish high standards. He founded the Association of Negro Colleges and Secondary Schools and acted as secretary from 1910 to 1918. He also established a collaborative project during this period between the New York School of Philanthropy and NLUCAN that resulted in the first social work training center for African American students at Fisk University, directing the center between 1910 and 1918.

After 1918, on leave from Fisk, Haynes served as director of the Division of Negro Economics in the U.S. Department of Labor. His role there as special assistant to the secretary of labor involved him in issues concerning racial conflict in the work place, housing, and recreation. Haynes also maintained his earlier research into the exclusion of African American workers from certain labor unions, interracial conditions in employment, and child labor. Research in these areas resulted in a number of important scholarly publications, including *The Negro at Work during the World War and during Reconstruction.*

James Weldon Johnson, 1871–1938

Novelist

James Weldon Johnson was a prominent novelist, diplomat, poet, civil rights activist, songwriter, journalist, and educator. He was a contemporary of W. E. B. Du Bois. Like Du Bois, his activities extended over several historical and literary tendencies. After a childhood in Jacksonville, Florida, where he was educated at the Stanton School (where he later returned as principal) and Atlanta (now Clark Atlanta) University, Johnson established the *Daily American,* a short-lived publication that reported on matters of interest to the African American community. Although the paper was only published for one year, it did bring Johnson to the attention of Booker T. Washington and Du Bois.

After a brief spell practicing law, when he became the first African American to be admitted to the Florida state bar, Johnson began to provide lyrics for music written by his brother, Rosamond. This led to a successful period providing music for Broadway musicals with Rosamond and songwriter Bob Cole as the Johnson Brothers and Cole. The brothers' best known composition, "Lift Every

Voice and Sing," originally written for a celebration of Lincoln's birthday, was later adopted by the NAACP as the "Negro National Anthem." Johnson's eclecticism is epitomized by his next decision, to pursue a career as a writer, coinciding with his appointment as U.S. consul to Venezuela, a post that he secured through his connections to Booker T. Washington. During his three-year tenure, Johnson published his only novel, *The Autobiography of an Ex-Colored Man* in 1912, in which he documents the life of a man light enough to pass as white. Though assumed by many to be a work of nonfiction, Johnson revealed later that the work had been fictional. Although Johnson was praised for his role in assisting U.S. Marines in the 1912 Nicaraguan revolution, where he had moved as consul in 1909, he left the Consular Service in 1913 because he felt that there would be scant opportunity for an African American in the Wilson administration. He

James Weldon Johnson left his mark in so many areas of African American culture during the early part of the 20th century that he is not easily categorized: he was a songwriter, poet, novelist, scholar, diplomat, and civil rights activist. (Library of Congress)

continued to write during this period. Several poems were published in nationally distributed publications, including "Fifty Years," which honors the anniversary of the Emancipation Proclamation.

Following his appointment as field secretary to the NAACP in 1917, Johnson was, in large part, responsible for founding local branches throughout the South and for the growing membership. He became the first African American secretary to the organization in 1920. He was instrumental in bringing the NAACP to national prominence as an organization equipped to undertake a successful crusade against segregation.

Jesse E. Moorland, 1863–1939

Minister, Civic Leader

Jesse Edward Moorland is most notable for his activities in African American social organizations, such as the National Health Circle for Colored People and as co-founder of the Association for the Study of African American Life and History with Carter G. Woodson in 1915, and for his work with the Young Men's

Christian Association (YMCA). Over 25 years, he was instrumental in the establishment of modern YMCA buildings for African Americans.

Following his appointment as secretary of the "colored" branch of the Washington, D.C., YMCA, he subsequently served as administrator and fundraiser for African American YMCAs across the country. Under Moorland's stewardship, the institutions were transformed, becoming sanctuaries and promoters of education, religion, and health for poor and undereducated African American migrants in large cities. Realizing that the majority of associations did not own the buildings in which they met, Moorland began a campaign targeted at mainly white philanthropists to raise funds for purpose-built premises. The new YMCA in Washington, D.C., was thus funded with money from, among others, Julius Rosenwald and John D. Rockefeller, Sr., as well as $25,000 from the community itself.

Although Moorland was a vocal opponent of racial segregation within the YMCA, he acknowledged that the provision of facilities to train young African Americans was beneficial, and as Moorland increasingly devoted himself to the expansion of YMCA work among African Americans, the number of exclusively African American branches grew. The educational, recreational, and religious facilities that these institutions provided were among the first for a population formerly excluded from activities only available to whites. The donation of Moorland's private library and personal papers, then believed to be one of the most important collections of African American–related materials, to Howard University inspired others to become involved in the recording, conservation, and interpretation of African American culture and history, and established a foundation for one of the world's largest archives for the history of African Americans.

Julius Rosenwald, 1862–1932

Clothier and Philanthropist

The son of German Jewish immigrants, Rosenwald amassed a considerable personal fortune as president of Sears, Roebuck and Company. His friendship with a senior partner of Goldman Sachs, Paul J. Sachs, and his growing conviction that the predicament of African Americans was among the most serious problems in the United States, led to a meeting with Booker T. Washington and William H. Baldwin, then among the leading advocates of African American education. Rosenwald served on the board of Washington's Tuskegee Institute from 1912 and also contributed significantly to the Institute's funds.

Subsequent funding provided for six schools in rural Alabama in 1913 and 1914. Constructed by and for African Americans, the enterprise prefigured his philanthropic involvement in education, a role focused on the provision of decent educational facilities for African Americans. Inspired by the social reform agendas of such progressives as Jane Addams and Grace Abbott, he established the Rosenwald Fund in 1917, which donated $70 million to educational institutions, museums, Jewish charities, and African American institutions. As one of the largest parts of the Fund, the schools building program was responsible for providing matching funds (because Rosenwald insisted that communities that benefited from the Fund contribute to the project) for more than 5,000 Rosenwald schools throughout the South. Rosenwald also donated $1,000 to each of the first 100 counties to take on county extension agents. His offer of $25,000 to any city willing to raise $75,000 to establish an African American YMCA led to the construction of 24 such facilities between 1911 and 1933. Throughout his life, he was convinced that financial donations alone would be of little use; education was key to helping African Americans out of poverty, and philanthropic generosity should not be restricted by geography, race, or religion.

Mary Church Terrell, 1863–1954

Writer and Activist

The daughter of former slaves, Mary Church Terrell was a writer and notable civil rights activist. She was one of the first African American women to be awarded a bachelor's degree, after which she traveled extensively in Europe, where she became fluent in several European languages. A career in education followed her return to the United States, and she became the first African American woman to be appointed to the District of Columbia Board of Education, a position she held until 1911. As one of two African American women (the other was Ida B. Wells-Barnett) to become charter members of the NAACP, Terrell was an active campaigner against racial segregation and discrimination, particularly against African American women.

Mary Church Terrell, an African American suffragist, was president of the National Association of Colored Women and a charter member of the National Association for the Advancement of Colored People. (Library of Congress)

Her continuing role as an academic led to her assistance in the formation in 1914 of the Delta Sigma Theta sorority at Howard University, where she was an honorary member, subsequently writing the Delta Creed, a code of conduct for young women. During World War I, Terrell became involved with the War Camp Community Service, an organization that assisted in recreation for African American service personnel and their later demobilization. Terrell also became active in the African American suffrage movement, which promoted the ratification of the Nineteenth Amendment.

Along with other African American middle-class women, Terrell formed the Women Wage Earners Association in Washington, D.C. The improvement of working conditions, pay, and housing conditions for African American working-class women was among its aims. As a speaker at the Quinquennial International Peace Conference in Zurich in 1919, Terrell achieved international recognition. She was also the first president of the NACW.

Carter G. Woodson, 1875–1950

Historian

As the founder of *Black History Month,* the African American historian, author, and journalist Carter Godwin Woodson is notable for being the first to pursue a scholarly undertaking to popularize African American history. After receiving a PhD from Harvard in 1912, Woodson and the African American minister Jesse E. Moorland co-founded the Association for the Study of Negro Life and History in Chicago in 1915, the result of a conviction that the role of African Americans in the nation's history was being marginalized or distorted, and that research into the overlooked past of African Americans was essential.

That same year, Woodson published *The Education of the Negro Prior to 1861* and *A Century of Negro Migration* in 1918. The *Journal of Negro History* (subsequently renamed the *Journal of African-American History*) was first published in 1916. During this period, Woodson became associated with the Washington, D.C., branch of the NAACP but became dissatisfied with certain aspects of the organization. His suggestion that the organization should cease patronage of businesses that did not treat races alike was rebuffed by the NAACP, and differences of opinion led to the end of his association with the organization.

Along with other like-minded individuals, Woodson co-founded the Association for the Study of Negro Life and History, serving as the Association's executive director. Woodson's belief that African Americans should be treated as a distinct race frequently brought him into conflict with the majority of African American educators, who felt that African American history should be taught as part of general American history. As a result, Woodson's attempts to have a discrete African American culture and history included in the curricula of institutions were often frustrated.

REFERENCES AND FURTHER READINGS

The Crisis Online. "About *The Crisis*." www.thecrisismagazine.com/about.htm.

Davis, F. James. 1991. *Who Is Black? One Nation's Definition*. University Park: Pennsylvania State University Press.

Drake, St. Clair. 1993. *Black Metropolis: A Study of Negro Life in a Northern City*. Chicago: University of Chicago Press.

Ellison, Mary. 1974. *The Black Experience: American Blacks since 1865*. London: B. T. Batsford.

Eyerman, Ron. 2001. *Cultural Trauma: Slavery and the Formation of African American Identity*. Cambridge: Cambridge University Press.

FindLaw. "U.S. Constitution: Amendments to the Constitution of the United States of America." caselaw.lp.findlaw.com/data/constitution/amendments.html.

Gibson, Robert A. "The Negro Holocaust: Lynching and Race Riots in the United States, 1880–1950." Yale-New Haven Teachers Institute. "Race Riots." www.yale.edu/ynhti/curriculum/units/1979/2/79.02.04.x.html#c.

Grossman, James R. 1991. *Land of Hope: Chicago, Black Southerners, and the Great Migration*. Chicago: University of Chicago Press.

Harley, Sharon. 1995. *The Timetable of African-American History*. New York: Simon and Schuster.

Hine, Darlene Clark, William C. Hine, and Stanley Harrold. 2003. *The African-American Odyssey*. Upper Saddle River: Prentice Hall.

Holt, Thomas C., and Elsa Barkley Brown, eds. 2000. *Major Problems in African-American History*. Vol. 2, *From Freedom to "Freedom Now," 1965–1990s*. Boston: Houghton Mifflin.

Horton, James Oliver, and Lois E. Horton. 2001. *Hard Road to Freedom: The Story of African America*. New Brunswick: Rutgers University Press.

Lieberson, Stanley. 1980. *A Piece of the Pie: Black and White Immigrants since 1880*. Berkeley: University of California Press.

Marks, Carole. 1989. *Farewell—We're Good and Gone: The Great Black Migration*. Bloomington and Indianapolis: Indiana University Press.

Myrdal, Gunnar. 1962. *An American Dilemma: The Negro Problem and Modern Democracy*. New York: Harper and Row.

Neal, Mark Anthony. 1999. *What the Music Said: Black Popular Music and Black Popular Culture*. New York: Routledge.

Osofsky, Gilbert. 1996. *Harlem: The Making of a Ghetto, Negro New York, 1890–1930*. Chicago: Ivan R. Dee.

Packard, Jerold M. 2002. *American Nightmare: The History of Jim Crow*. New York: St. Martin's Press.

Trotter, Joe William, Jr. 2001. *The African American Experience*. Vol. 2, *From Reconstruction*. Boston: Houghton Mifflin.

UNIA-ACL. "UNIA History." www.unia-acl.org/info/historic.htm.

Wikipedia. "W. E. B. Du Bois." en.wikipedia.org/wiki/W.E.B._Dubois.

Wikipedia. "*The Crisis*." en.wikipedia.org/wiki/The_Crisis.

Woodward, C. Vann. 1966. *The Strange Career of Jim Crow*. Oxford: Oxford University Press.

Rural America at the Crossroads

OVERVIEW

As America entered the second decade of the 20th century, the rural landscape, both visually and in the way that farms were worked, was much as it had been for hundreds of years. Of course, there had been changes, but these had been relatively small. In America in 1910, the rapid transformation of the economy, society, and politics occurred in the urban-industrial North, not in the largely preindustrial rural heartlands. The inconsistent and paradoxical nature of agriculture meant that a very few producers efficiently worked large farms that might amount to several thousand acres with still primitive machinery. Others planted using lunar cycles, while more still raised crops of global importance according to a semi-feudal system that relied on manual labor and serfdom. Isolated by geography and resolutely local, American farmers were nevertheless affected by events outside their control; wars or economic disasters across the world or the shift of monopoly capital closer to home could affect the farmer's livelihood. By this time, American farmers had become complacent, momentarily prosperous and still independent. They only grudgingly began to change their financial, cultural, or political conventions and organizations.

Still, by 1910, rural America had begun to change. As a percentage of the labor force, farmers comprised 31 percent, down from 38 percent in 1900, and that figure would fall still further, to 27 percent in 1920. Moreover, fewer numbers of farmers owned the land on which they farmed. The relative shortage of good land meant that in many places a long period of tenancy was necessary before a farmer lacking in capital could own the land. Good land was still available, but it was generally in marginal areas. Although expansion carried on, the prosperous period of plentiful land and mass ownership and the cultural, political, and economic practices thus created were over.

Agricultural life was frequently unremittingly hard for farmers and their families, largely because producers had to strike a balance between self-sufficiency and commercial viability (i.e., making enough to pay the mortgage and taxes and to buy machinery, appliances, fertilizer, clothing, and other items that they could not produce themselves). In 1910, farmers still carried out many tasks on the farm without the assistance of machinery, and their wives labored in the farmhouse without the labor-saving devices her urban counterparts took for granted. Such commitment and hard work was seldom adequately rewarded. Few reliable statistics exist on the amount the average farmer earned; indeed, farmers themselves frequently did not know the extent of their annual income or even whether they made a profit. Although the size of the average investment might have defined a farmer as middle class, income was less than the average urban middle-class employee.

Researchers also discovered that even in the middle of the decade, ignorance regarding sanitation was widespread in rural areas, and that factor, as well as a poor diet and primitive waste disposal practices, were major contributory factors in the spread of such diseases as typhoid, dysentery, and malaria.

Yet, despite the hardship and poor conditions, until after World War I American agriculture was extremely prosperous. Just before the start of the decade in 1909, Secretary of Agriculture James Wilson remarked that the value of farm products was "incomprehensibly large" (Saloutos and Hicks, 1931, 20), whereas *Wallace's Farmer* commented on the earning power of the farmer and the comforts and advantages available to him. (Ibid.) In the 1910 report, the secretary observed that if the index of the value of farm products in 1899 was assumed as 100, it stood at 189.2 by 1910. (Saloutos and Hicks, 1931, 21) High produce prices did not entirely explain the farmer's affluence. The price of land had increased by 118.1 percent in a decade, according to the 1910 census, and was also a major factor. Farmers who did own the land on which they worked, however, grew prosperous from the unearned increase that resulted from the ownership, and not from farming.

Although there were difficulties and anxieties for the farmer in 1910, agriculture had seldom been so prosperous. At least until 1918, farmers would benefit from high prices for produce and rising land values, and such problems as increased levels of tenancy, insufficient labor, and the exodus to the cities and towns were caused by affluence, rather than misfortune.

TIMELINE

1910–1919   Agricultural exports: $1.9 billion—45 percent of total exports. Commercial fertilizer consumption: 6.1 million tons per year.

1910   In the U.S. Census, the farm population is estimated at 32,077,000 with farmers comprising 31 percent of labor force. The number of farms is put at 6,366,000 with an average acreage of 138.

1911   Farmer's Equity Union organizes to improve rural economic and social conditions and provide agriculture with a program of security and equality with other types of industry.

First Farm Bureau established, Broome County, New York, to provide education and advice on good farming practice.

1912   The first legal action in the United States to prevent the introduction of pests from foreign countries—the Plant Quarantine Act—establishes a network of inspection stations at principal ports of entry and authorizes the federal government to establish border quarantines and prevent entry of any infested goods.

1913   James F. Wilson, U.S. secretary of agriculture from 1897, is replaced by David Houston, who undertakes the position until 1920, when he takes over as U.S. secretary of the treasury.

Federal Reserve Act, U.S. Department of Agriculture's (USDA's) Office of Markets created to boost agricultural marketing.

Rural Organization Service created.

Rural parcel post added to Rural Free Delivery service, stimulating the national economy by allowing rural Americans to buy previously hard-to-get commodities (e.g., foodstuffs, medicines, and dry goods), which were mailed directly to their homes. In return, agricultural producers could ship smaller produce (e.g., eggs) directly to the consumer.

1914   Following the passage of the Smith-Lever Act, the Cooperative Extension Service institutes trials in African American agricultural education and provides funds for cooperative administration of agricultural extension education by the USDA and the state land grant colleges, in order to increase agricultural productivity and improve rural life.

Cotton Futures Act passed, subjecting the Cotton Exchange to constant regulation by the federal government.

Congress passes Federal Trade Commission Act, authorizing a presidentially appointed commission to supervise industries (e.g., the meatpackers) participating in interstate commerce.

1915   Non-Partisan League formed, advocating state control of mills, grain elevators, banks, and other agriculturally related industries in order to diminish the power of corporate political interests.

National Agricultural Organization Society (NAOS) established.

1916   Congress passes Stock Raising Homestead Act, allowing ranchers to homestead, or privatize, lands originally designated as having no value except for livestock grazing or forage. Under the Act, which effectively privatized some 70 million acres, surface rights were granted to homesteaders, but mineral rights underneath were retained by the federal government.

Rural Post Roads Act passed, providing federal aid for the construction of "rural post roads" (any public road on which the government had a monopoly of carrying mail and over which the U.S. mails were transported).

Federal Aid Road Act enacted, providing for the improvement of roads and having the added social benefit of enhancing life in rural America by concentrating on rural post roads, rather than either long-distance roads or those in cities.

Congress passes Federal Farm Loan Act, making both low-interest, long-term loans and short-term credit to meet recurring needs available to farmers through a system of agricultural banks.

Railroad network peaks at 254,000 miles.

The U.S. Warehouse Act, passed in 1916, establishes a federal licensing system for warehouses including provisions for financial security (e.g., loans on the security of staple crops) and record keeping. Warehouses thus licensed were inspected and audited by the federal government and required to conform to regulations intended to guarantee the facility would properly store and care for agricultural commodities delivered by farmers and others.

1917	Herbert Hoover appointed head of U.S. Food Administration by President Wilson and succeeds in reducing consumption of food needed overseas, while avoiding rationing and keeping Allies fed.
	Smith-Hughes Vocational Education Act passed, providing for the promotion of vocational education in agriculture and its isolation from other parts of the curriculum.
	Federal Food Control and Production Acts passed, stimulating the wartime production of agricultural commodities and significantly increasing the number of extension agents.
1919	The lobbying organization, the American Farm Bureau Federation formally constituted in Chicago to improve productivity and, thus, profitability by organization rather than individual effort.

RURAL LIFE

Causes

By 1910, rural America had already undergone important changes. Since the early settlers began to farm their own land, the interconnectedness of society and economics and the attachment between family, locality, community, and labor had been masked by the fiction of the family farm, a fabrication that implied an integrated unit (i.e., the family) functioning in an economically and geographically isolated context (i.e., the farm). In reality, that family was an interdependent unit whose individual components did not always share interchangeable considerations. Although it may have been geographically remote, the farm itself was nevertheless part of a network of community bonds and commitments linking families and farms in rural areas.

Unlike urban America, where industrialization involved a neat division into paid labor in the workplace and domestic labor that was unpaid and undertaken in the home, rural America retained a labor structure based on unpaid cooperative family and community-reciprocated work for women and men. Agriculture structured in this way meant that there was no straightforward equation between products and cash because goods could be used by farm or family or had exchange value in the locality. Because farm people had little control over prices and none over the weather, returns from cash transactions were less reliable than those from personal use or local exchange, and these latter helped to ensure survival. Analyses of the social and economic changes that, increasingly, affected every aspect of American life in the late 19th and early 20th centuries

Steam plow in Kansas in 1910. (Library of Congress)

have traditionally focused on the changes brought about by urbanization and industrialization, neglecting much consideration that, even in 1910, the farm population was still some 32 million out of 92 million and that some of these broader changes were determined to a significant degree by developments in rural communities.

As Neth (1995, 3) observes, "in rural America, the development of industrial capitalism directly collided with a family-based labor system" and rural America itself was revolutionized by an economy that by the early 20th century was increasingly defined by capitalist mass production economic systems and processes. Farms focused on and produced for the market by then, yet domestic and unpaid labor remained central to their efficient operation. Farms were still largely self-sustaining, and although machines began to supersede farm people's own labor and farms underwent a process of amalgamation, agriculture is not readily transferable to assembly line production processes and the division of labor. The seasons determine which tasks must be completed and in which order. Nevertheless, agricultural production by the flexible family unit was transfigured by the growth of industrial capitalism.

The transformation that took place in the early years of the 20th century when rural America stood at the crossroads between tradition and progress happened in that "golden age" between the depressions and political upheavals of the 1890s and the 1930s. In this period, rural America, particularly the Midwest, seemed affluent, secure, and calm, untouched by the race issues and poverty of the South or the strikes of the industrial North. For the first time, or so the orthodoxy would suggest, farm people could afford consumer goods to relieve the grind of farm life, to buy newly available automobiles or more productive farm equipment (e.g., tractors).

This reading, however, masks the reality that during this period, the underpinning was established for what would, in later decades, become modern agribusiness. In the decade 1910–1919, farmers began to understand how mechanization and increased costs could quickly outstrip income. Despite overproduction, government edicts still advocated increased production. Notwithstanding the instability of incomes, consumption began to take the place of home production. Depopulation began to have a significant effect on communities dependent on family-based labor. Interventionist policies by the state and newly established agencies promoted the increased use of technology and the consolidation of smaller farms into larger units to increase efficiency and thus production; however, unlike the industrial economy, the fragmented nature of agriculture did not lend itself to the same economies of scale. Nevertheless, rural America did begin to change and farm people were not wholly resistant to those changes, instead adopting a pragmatic approach and combining the advantages of scientific agriculture and a modern, consumerist way of life with their rural, family-oriented community.

Progress seemed to imply that there also should be fewer but larger farms with decreases in the farm population. Even though advocates maintained that this newly consolidated structure would lead to greater affluence, such an ideology was at variance with that promoted during the 19th century. Overall, the pattern of change occurred slowly; statistics indicate that rather than farm numbers decreasing, they actually rose, although the rate of increase slowed toward 1920.

1900 farm population: 29,414,000 (est.); farmers 38 percent of labor force; number of farms: 5,740,000; average acres: 147

1910 farm population: 32,077,000 (est.); farmers 31 percent of labor force; number of farms: 6,366,000; average acres: 138

1920 farm population: 31,614,269; farmers 27 percent of labor force; number of farms: 6,454,000; average acres: 148 (www.agclassroom.org/textversion/gan/timeline/1910.htm)

These figures suggest that the changes that did occur had little immediate effect on the numbers or size of farms; rather, it was the social impact that affected rural America. Although the number of farms *appears* to increase during the two decades, the figures do not indicate whether people living on farms

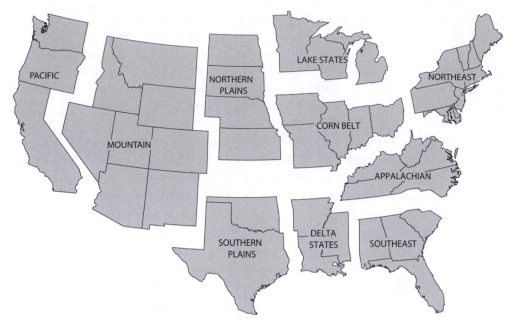

Map 5.1 *Farm Production Regions.*

actually worked on them as well. In fact, during this period, the growing requirement for additional income brought about by fluctuating prices and increased capital and consumer expenditure compelled family members to seek wage labor elsewhere. The preceding figures also mask the fall in the rural population as a percentage of the whole: 59.5 percent in 1900 to 53.7 percent in 1910 to 48.3 percent in 1920. Farm people confronted the harsh economic realities of the decade with means that were frequently below those of the urban middle class, and the period between 1910 and 1914 was probably the last time that the prices paid by farmers for manufactured goods equated to what the market paid for crops.

Farm Production Regions

The map above depicts the main regions responsible for agriculture. Although change in the early 20th century affected farms throughout the United States, for various reasons, the social, economic, technological, and political changes that occurred more widely can be mapped in the Midwest (loosely, the Corn Belt, the Northern Plains, and parts of the Lake States) more productively than elsewhere. Agriculture was molded by the topography (the plains and prairies), whereas progressive consolidation of farms and the predominance of a market economy and of small family farms characterized the Midwest in the late 19th and early 20th centuries. Although families were pivotal to all types of agriculture, there are important differences between the midwestern farm and family structure and those in other regions. Sharecropping and slavery in the South emerged from entirely different social structures than tenancy in the Midwest. Ranching in the West developed in highly mechanized and capital-intensive ways and was supported by a high proportion of migrant labor. In the East, industry was sufficiently close to change the form of agriculture there, and although small family farms could be found in all these areas, agriculture based around a labor structure founded on unpaid cooperative family and community-reciprocated labor, complemented by hired hands, distinguished the Midwest from the rest of rural America.

By 1919, the midwestern farm population (except for Illinois at 17 percent) extended from 35 percent to 61 percent, compared with a national average of around 30 percent. Most colonization occurred throughout the 19th century and, in some states, the early 20th century. Settlement generally followed the expansion of the railroads, which stimulated growth, but settlement was also anchored to and, to some extent, dictated the only freight routes to progressively rationalized and centralized markets. Rural America was thus controlled by urban forces whose corporations owned the transportation and frequently the mills and stockyards as well.

The Farm as Home and the Farm Wife

Structurally, and in the way in which labor was organized on the thousands of family farms scattered across the rural Midwest in the early 20th century, agriculture differed significantly from labor organization in urban industries. Moreover, farm people viewed their rural way of life, as well as their traditions and principles, as peripheral to the commercial and social center of industrial and urban America. Although this description of how a farm woman perceived this separateness was captured in the 1920s, it mirrors other recollections from the previous decade: "You don't think of your home on a farm . . . as just a space inside four walls. The feeling of home spreads out all around, into the garden, the orchards, the henhouses, the barn, the springhouse, because you are all the time helping to produce live things in those places and they, or their products, are all the time coming back into your kitchen from garden, orchard, barn, or henhouse, as a part of the things you handle to prepare for meals or market every day." (Neth, 1995, 17)

Neth believes that there were few, if any, separate spheres for men and women on the family farm. The distinctions between work for financial gain and domestic labor, and between goods or produce for the market or for the family, similarly had less significance on the family farm. Whatever was produced on the farm or in the home fulfilled the same function, benefiting and maintaining the family farm and its members. Although notional distinctions between men's

Woman milks a cow in a barnyard as a child watches, 1907. (Library of Congress)

work and women's work existed on family farms, such divisions seldom operated in practice, and where separate functions based on gender did occur, they
emerged from the physical environment of the farm. Thus, women's work was
focused on the house and men's outside. When men did help out with household duties, which were almost always described by farm people as women's
work, it was because no women were at hand. Women's duties included maintaining the house (although its repair was the man's responsibility), feeding and
clothing the family, often including making and mending clothes, and child care.

Women were also responsible for everything directly encompassing the
house (e.g., gathering eggs or maintaining vegetable gardens), for family consumption or for the market, or carrying water, coal, or wood for heating and
washing. Although men could have undertaken these tasks, women carried out
the majority, according to a 1920 USDA survey. (Neth, 1995, 21) Women were
also more active in caring for dairy animals, as well as for such associated tasks
as making butter and washing equipment. Although the survey does not specify,
children could have carried out some or all of these tasks. In any case, women
usually supervised children and other farm people who helped in the house and
its surroundings.

As farm people's lives were increasingly affected by the climate of change
happening throughout rural America in the 1910s, urban professionals started
to concern themselves with economic performance and society outside the
cities. As modern methods and attitudes began to transform agricultural labor
and the communal basis of small farming began to diminish, women's roles and

their status also began to change. The Country Life Movement and the Commission on Country Life, which had been appointed by Theodore Roosevelt in 1908, had already focused attention on rural life. As some farms became more successful and prosperous, the modern farmer's wife came to signify the class status of the farm family; however, physical labor, by both men and women, conflicted with any perception that urban dwellers might have had that farm people were acquiring a foothold in the middle class. Women who worked on the farm were seen as somehow inferior to their urban opposite numbers whose purely domestic role was to provide for the family.

Popular magazines began to reflect a more widespread interest in rural matters and to offer farm women advice on aspects of rural domestic life, as well as to carry discussions on the role of women in modern agriculture. One such, *Farmer's Wife,* was an enthusiastic advocate for improving farm women's lives and the Country Life Movement. From its establishment in 1905 to the middle of the next decade, the magazine ran articles on women's suffrage and women's organizations, alongside which were such more populist items as advice on dressmaking, household remedies, and marital guidance. Nevertheless, *Farmer's Wife* was an important forum for women on farms and contained a balance between more lighthearted articles and others that attempted to establish the sort of work that was suitable for women in the farm home and on the farm itself. It also included features that offered advice on the dairy and poultry keeping. From 1915, *Farmer's Wife* reflected the growing emphasis on professionalizing domestic activities and the intervention of agricultural institutions into farm women's home routines. Features on poultry and the dairy began to command less space in favor of increased allocation to items on child care and domestic issues. As the emphasis shifted from the farm to the home, women were perceived as homemakers, and the journal ran articles on how rural women could improve culturally and how they should entertain. Although the editorial agenda became more reactionary on farm procedures, labor matters, and women's issues, supporting the American Farm Bureau Federation (AFBF) and criticizing the labor unions, it nevertheless continued to promote advances in farm women's status.

Professionals recommended that women should follow certain policies to enhance their status. Reconfiguring the association between women's work on the farm and their role in the home was regarded as essential, while simultaneously eliminating the perceived inequality between the divisions of labor on the farm and in the home where women's physical labor was often more strenuous than that of men. Writing in 1912, the columnist and lecturer, Nellie Kedzie Jones argued that women's work should be separated from men's because women were expected to work in the field, whereas men seldom reciprocated in the house (Neth, 1995, 230). Advisers also criticized women's inclination toward self-denial, believing that women, in spite of evidence to the contrary, could (and should) be able to afford labor-saving devices and should not persist in making such readily available items as soap.

Sears Catalog

Although the Sears catalog was not the first mail the order organization to focus its retail activities on rural America, the "farmer's wishbook" was perhaps the best known and the one that encouraged the greatest number of imitators. America in the late 19th century was still a largely rural country. Out of a total population of 76 million in 1900, the farm population was around 29 million and farmers comprised 38 percent of the workforce, working on 5.7 million farms. By 1910, the total population had grown to 92 million and the farm population was 32 million on 6.3 million farms. Rapid agricultural expansion in still relatively isolated areas meant that farmers had little time and, given the inadequate stocks at general stores, few opportunities to buy better equipment. Sears, Roebuck filled this gap by bringing an urban, mass-produced way of life to rural communities. Such other factors as the growth of the railroads, lower postal rates for catalogs, and Rural Free Delivery were also important in the expansion of the catalogs, which, by 1910, were being distributed to nearly 4 million homesteads and included more than 10,000 different items. These covered every feature of the cradle-to-grave cycle, including sewing machines, firearms, bicycles, and patent medicines, although these were dropped in 1913 when the catalog came out against home remedies.

Although price and the wide range of goods were important factors in the increasing popularity of catalogs, mail-order houses also succeeded because they helped determine taste, recommending to rural households what should be bought and how it should be set out, presented, or worn. By the second decade, Sears had helped the rural economy to move from one based on barter or extended credit to one constructed on and preoccupied by money. Rural consumption thus depended on acquiescence to urban criteria. Sears, Roebuck prospered partly because they advertised goods that they knew rural people would want and because economies of scale and efficient distribution made them affordable and available quickly.

Professionals also contended that the substantial contribution that women made in the home made them eligible for a more equitable share of farm earnings. They also believed that as agriculture became more scientific and mechanized, women should be regarded as managers and included in its newly professionalized status. As in so many assumptions that professionals made about farm women, these were frequently at odds with the reality of farm life. Women disputed the extent and pace of mechanization and that any ostensible expansion or acceleration meant that they could thus relinquish home production for consumption and cultural improvement. Women valued the contribution that they made to the home and to farm income, and even if farm budgets had allowed them to substitute one for the other, they believed that their status was sufficiently enhanced by their existing role. The perceptions of the professional advisers too often coupled any improvements in farm women's status with a fundamental shift in gender roles as well as in women's roles, rather than in the improvement of the economic circumstances of small farmers.

Religion

The Decline of Rural Religion and the Country Church

Although by the second decade there were signs that the rural church suffered from rather less commitment from parishioners than was the case in the 19th century, it was nevertheless still an important establishment in rural communities. In 1913, an anonymous Missouri clergyman grumbled that "there is in all our rural churches a general indifference toward religion" (Danbom, 1979, 16), while there were some 1,200 deserted churches in that same state and another 500 in Illinois. Many of these buildings had been requisitioned by farmers for other uses (e.g., hay and tool storage), further diminishing their religious status. Despite the increasing appropriation of fresh agricultural land, even in these newer areas, many churches were neglected or deserted altogether, and research undertaken between 1912 and 1916 indicated that in most areas congregations were increasing in fewer than half of the churches, and significant proportions of the population did not attend church at all.

Nevertheless, rural people did attend church more regularly than urban dwellers. There were many thousands of very small churches in country areas, many of them geographically isolated and most with very few members. The majority of these lived a hand-to-mouth existence; some survived by maintaining a strong connection with racial or ethnic groups, but others, which had come into being as the result of some age-old rift or barely remembered revival, limped on as tokens of community disunion or religious grudge. Like the rural school, the country church was more appealing in myth than in reality, and like schools, churches were often small, insufficiently lit and heated, inadequately maintained, and poorly financed. To survive, clergymen invariably had to undertake services in several churches and were often forced to work on farms or do odd jobs to boost their incomes.

The decline of the rural church and the consequent penury in which many rural ministers lived forced some urban commentators to conclude that the most able clergymen inevitably found their way to the cities, thus abandoning the rural church to pastoral beginners or to function as refuges for the ancient or the incompetent. Nevertheless, to many country people, the church remained an important institution and retained its appeal largely because parishioners themselves stayed in control, whereas many contributed significantly to ethnic and social distinctiveness. All were important centers of social diversion and entertainment in an environment where very few such hubs remained. Like rural schools, country churches in the early years of the century were highly localized

Children in their Sunday clothes pose in front of an adobe church, Alamo National Forest, New Mexico Territory, May 13, 1908 (now Lincoln National Forest). Photo by A. M. Neal. (National Archives)

and simple, echoing rural distinctiveness in their creeds, the ways in which they fragmented along sectarian lines, and in their reluctance to collaborate with each other.

The Solution

Concerns regarding the decline prompted urban professionals in the Country Life Movement to advocate radical restructuring to combat what they perceived as a descent into "paganism and barbarianism." (Danbom, 1979, 59) As a central component in the industrialization of agriculture and one of the few rural institutions to play a decisive role as an agent of social control, the church was celebrated by Country Lifers and critics, who argued that rural compliance to religious jurisdiction located it in a unique position to shape rural customs and opinions. Religious leaders felt that the source of religious and ethical life of the nation itself lay in the country church and located the reasons for its decline in the dissolution of faith, deterioration they attributed to rural people themselves.

Country Lifers, however, blamed the churches for the decay. Because country churches were mainly attended by women and the elderly, this group believed that the country church was too bound up with "technical religion, formal piety, [and] small and empty social duties" (Danbom, 1979, 59) and thus lacked appeal to more manly citizens. Most critics agreed, however, that individualism in the rural church had weakened it as an institution uniquely placed to act as an organization of social cohesion. In a period when many reformers believed that only cooperation could bring about increased efficiency, the church remained steadfastly rooted in individualism, a problem that many churchmen felt led to sectarian divisiveness and multiplication with too many small churches serving too few people. In turn, this weakened them and reduced their potential as effective social institutions.

The rural style of preaching emphasized revivalism, a style that appealed to individuals more than it did to groups and hampered social coordination and participation. Sensing that rural religion had declined for many of the same reasons that caused the decline of urban Protestantism in the 19th century (largely the irrelevance of religion to everyday life), critics advocated a return to the Social Gospel, a post–Civil War Protestant tradition that underlined obligation to the community and the economic and social present, rather than some unknowable future. By focusing on social ethics rather than personal morality, and by growth and change, it was hoped that the churches could meet modern rural necessities, reaffirm their social guidance, and, consequently, modify rural social and economic conduct.

As part of the drive to renovate the church's social mission, it was hoped that churches could hold gatherings and entertainments that would reinforce parishioners' bonds with the church itself as well as meet the needs of those more sociable members of the community. Clergymen were especially concerned about the social welfare of the young and tenants, who, it was thought, were in most need of social management. Collective pursuits and organized diversions would thus bind them to the church and help to ward off any tendency toward immoral activities. In addition, these activities would help to make rural folk more satisfied with their lives and begin to halt the drift to towns and cities. Rural modernizers also hoped that this expanded social function for churches would weaken individualism and promote collectivism at every stage in people's lives, but especially in the economic phase.

Central to Country Life reformers' program for the country was the assumption that ministers themselves would promote the modernization of agriculture, becoming advocates for increased agricultural efficiency and productivity; however, they acknowledged that ministers were unlikely to possess the relevant skills themselves. Instead, they anticipated that ministers would try to generate some enthusiasm among farming communities for the scientific agriculture promoted by others. Toward this end, Country Life Movement churchmen relied on their clergy to underline the greater morality of this new way of farming, founded as it was on increased productivity, scientific management, and economic collaboration. This expanded role, which amounted to a form of social engineering, would transform the church into "a social-service church, or an institutional church, or again . . . a 'country church industrial.'" (Danbom, 1979, 61) They were helped in this zeal for reform by the Young Men's Christian Association (YMCA), which by 1910 was an enthusiastic advocate for social Christianity through its recreational projects.

The reformers also acknowledged that existing church buildings were unlikely to be suitable for their expanded role as a social center *and* as a place for religious worship, and that the expansion would also require the service of full-time ministers, fully trained in all aspects of industrializing the countryside. To bring about these reforms, and to tie them in with the unification of rural neighborhoods and the reduction of wasteful and unproductive sectarian fragmentation and multiplication, some reformers advocated church consolidation and interdenominational cooperation. As Danbom (Ibid.) notes, the future for rural churches, then, was to be founded on nonsectarian social lines, managed by social engineers in expanded or new social centers. It was to be based on an essentially urban perception that all rural social organizations had to be redesigned to comply with an urban-industrial norm of economic and social efficiency.

Impact

The mechanisms suggested by social reformers for regenerating the rural church proved to be largely ineffectual in the face of the almost wholesale rejection of what country people perceived as unnecessary interference in a trusted and valued institution. The Social Gospel, which had seemed so appropriate in regenerating urban churches, was less relevant when applied to rural religious problems and the stubborn individualism and self-sufficiency of farm people. Even when applied to urban-industrial society, the Social Gospel was subjected to highly vocal disagreements over whether its purpose was the salvation of souls or society. Doubtful that the solutions proposed by the reformers could be applied to the problems of the church in the countryside, rural clergy were particularly troubled that the focus on consolidation and efficiency would rob the church of its distinctive social function and its divine calling.

Throughout the decade, ministers warned that entertainment, enjoyment, and social engineering should not be the main concern of the church. Instead, what was needed was that the church, and only the church, should provide "the moral and religious basis for the development of the heart and the soul." (Danbom, 1979, 82) Disdainful of the Country Lifers' vision of turning "the house of worship into a dance-hall and the preacher of the Gospel of Jesus Christ into the director of the dance" (Ibid.), ministers also suspected their motives, believing that if the reformers persisted with their attempts to increase productivity through religion, it would actually be counterproductive, turning the farmers against the church.

Diary Entry

Farm people kept diaries to chronicle those aspects of their lives that they regarded as most significant. Many surviving diaries were kept by women, and it was they who were responsible for household finances. Even though diarists recorded outings to town, they seldom detailed stores visited or purchases in the way that they would describe farm work or family life. They were workers, members of and contributors to the community, and constituents of the family, but they were also consumers. A rare example of a diary in which the details of purchases are documented to the same depth of detail as work and family is that of Bertha Gabelmann from Iowa.

Gabelmann's record for November 22, 1912, itemized what happened that day and includes the butchering of a farm animal and notes that her parents sold some produce, but she also listed the purchases of commodities by the family on a visit to town. These were incorporated into comments about other aspects of farm life. Gabelmann described less-routine purchases that were made in more detail, however, demonstrating that buying these items afforded an interlude in farm schedules. Outings to the closest city or catalog purchases culminated in longer accounts, but they were still integrated with other events.

Among the more regular purchases (e.g., a brush and comb and a baking dish), the entry for September 14, 1918, includes the news that Gabelmann took films for developing. The purchase of a modern item like a camera, which, like the diary, was another method of recording daily life, reflects the changes in rural lives that arose from modern technology. The images that Gabelmann made with the camera depict the same concerns of the diary (e.g., family, work, community), but also includes less-common purchases (e.g., automobiles and tractors). These symbols of change and modernity, which are obviously significant, are nevertheless located within established systems of work and community life, rather than being depicted as radical deviations.

Attempts to turn rural churches into social and recreational centers also met with hostility. Far from believing that dancing and leisure activities were the route to social cohesion, fundamentalist groups were more likely to believe that such recreations were sinful and should be abjured. In these concerns and prejudices, parishioners and clergy alike were in agreement, and this resistance to change maintained the churches' traditional role. Rural church members were equally hostile to the suggestion that churches should be consolidated. Parishioners seemed contented with small, poorly equipped churches as well as with ministers whose duties were spread around a circuit because this gave clergy and parishioners alike the opportunity to hear news from elsewhere. Separate denominations were a fact of life in the countryside; the few churches that did experiment with federation frequently found that it aggravated, rather than solved, their problems. In the process, they discovered that arguments over physical resources, ministers themselves, and beliefs and principles outweighed any gains, and institutions often broke up in the face of these overwhelming disputes.

By 1917, even those rural churchmen most in favor of reform despaired of ever changing what they perceived as a moribund and enfeebled church. The example of the Presbyterians, perhaps the largest sect that had been most energetic in their reforming zeal, proved to be no stimulus to dominant rural sects. Reforms undertaken by the Baptists and Methodists were comparatively insignificant, whereas the more powerful Lutheran and Catholic churches, skeptical at what they saw as empire building, ignored any entreaties for reform. Rivalry and jealousies between denominations led to mistrust of the Social Gospel, and it gradually became clear that the rural church was not a particularly appropriate model for rural change. This private and deeply conservative institution had been founded on the principles of self-control and voluntary change, and the rural church proved to be almost entirely resistant to those who promoted the church as the agent of industrialization.

Food and the Farm

The balance struck between self-sufficiency and commercial viability depended in no small measure on tactics adopted by families that would sustain them outside of the times when the value of cash crops could be realized. Because income was tied to factors outside of the farmer's direct control (e.g., the weather and fluctuations in the market), adopting strategies that counterbalanced these variables was essential. Despite an apparently enduring and unbreakable connection between the market and income, farm families were nevertheless largely self-sufficient concerning food, valued making do, and abhorred waste.

Families with long experience of hard times developed ways of surviving by passing on skills like milking, preserving, smoking, and canning and also used the milk to make butter and cheese. They extended the garden, giving precedence to vegetables whose use could be extended by keeping them in the cellar. Home production, basically undertaken by women, was central to family farming, providing food for the family themselves, as well as making a significant contribution to farm income. Although not all food came from the farm, studies of Iowa families undertaken in the 1920s noted that overall the farm had provided around 60 percent of food throughout the previous decades, including 95 percent of poultry, eggs, and dairy products, 81 percent of meat, and 43 percent of vegetables. (Neth, 1995, 31) Income level did not appear to be a significant determining factor in whether or not families practiced self-sufficiency, although the proportion of produce provided by the farm for home consumption fell away at higher income levels.

*Tupelo, Mississippi, cooking and canning club at work at the town community
building, 1919. (Bettmann/Corbis)*

Markets close by where women sold and exchanged products also provided
a valuable extra source of income, which subsidized the purchase of items that
could not be made (e.g., groceries and clothes). Many families kept poultry, and
in addition to selling the birds themselves, they also sold the eggs, often paying
for all the groceries with this income. Farms sometimes sold produce to callers
at the farm as well. Some families sold milk door-to-door in the neighborhood,
which also subsidized necessities and proved to be a strategy that allowed income from other parts of the farm to be used for improvements and modernization. Cash transactions were not the only method by which families raised
extra income. By the second decade, small farms that in earlier years had grown
a wide range of produce, perhaps keeping livestock as well, had begun to spe-
cialize in some produce to sell in the larger markets in more distant towns. Many
farms also still produced other commodities that could be exchanged locally. The
system of exchange allowed for a wide range of alternative "payments," extending from exchange for cash, to barter for other goods or services, to loans or gifts.

Exchange and barter conformed to the same gender boundaries that characterized all of the farm's income-generating activities. Men were nominally,

economically, and legally the head of the family, and they presided over commercial enterprises, usually taking responsibility for selling to larger markets.
Women typically operated at a more local level, selling to local markets or
trading communally. This pyramid of economic activity, with men at the apex,
masked the reality that women's smaller, more localized and personal activities
were as central to the economic well being of the farm as were the larger, more
impersonal transactions.

RURAL POLITICS

The Aftermath of Populism

When, in 1896, the editor of the Kansas newspaper the *Emporia Gazette,*
William Allen White, attacked the People's, or Populist, Party's claim that "the
rights of the user are paramount to the rights of the owner" (www.nytimes.com
query.nytimes.com/gst/ abstract.html?), he encapsulated the views and prejudices
of America's economic and social elite, who believed that populism constituted
a serious threat to respectability and order. The People's Party had by then become significant in the challenge for power in the South and West as voters dissatisfied with the two main parties migrated to the party, which claimed to meet
the needs of the "common people." Populists were hardly the undisciplined mob
that the other two parties claimed. Most were middle-class property owners
whose politics recalled the moralistic and democratic inclination of Jefferson,
Jackson, and Lincoln. They believed that the two main parties had undermined
America's potential by adopting a laissez-faire, free-enterprise economy, a social creed based on the survival of the fittest and the doctrine of wealth.

Moral and industrious farmers beset by poverty worried about such issues as
their loss of independence as some were forced into tenancy; the inequities that
arose from middlemen, speculators, and monopolies, who continued to profit
from a declining market; and a government that appeared to have little interest
in their plight. It was they who enthusiastically adopted third-party politics and
agricultural radicalism.

Cooperatives seemed to provide a challenge to the power of the monopolies,
but because they were frequently underfinanced, a solution appeared to be for
the government to create warehouses to store crops and produce. Those items
could be stored rather than unloaded onto a glutted harvest-time market. It
could then be used as collateral against a government loan. Further demands
from increasingly resistant farmers included calls for land to be set aside for settlers, not speculators; government-owned transport; a flexible monetary system
based on greenbacks, rather than silver; a graduated income tax; and the democratization of politics.

Falling crop prices following the 1893 Panic caused much rural hardship. Divided and weakened, populism was effectively over after 1894. As the economy recovered, efforts to regain national electoral support in 1900, 1904, and 1908 proved ineffectual, and there were no populists in Congress after 1903.

Nevertheless, populism had more success in later years. White, who had been so vocal in his condemnation in 1896, referred to the overdue successes thus: "They abolished the established order completely and ushered in a new order." (Saloutos and Hicks, 1931, 421) In 1914, the campaigner Mary E. Lease reflected that her work in the early period of populism had not been in vain: "the Progressive Party has adopted our platform. . . . Direct election of senators is assured. Public utilities are gradually being removed from the hands of the few and placed under the control of the people who use them. Woman suffrage is now almost a national issue." (Ibid.) There were some who continued the fight for equality by joining Eugene V. Debs's Socialist Party, whereas others allied themselves to the reform elements of the mainstream parties.

Acts were passed during the Progressive era to regulate monopolies, reform the banking and currency system, and bring in a graduated income tax. The populists' warehouse plan has its parallels in the 1916 Warehousing Act, but the populists' demands for direct democracy, which were addressed in the initiative and referendum, were undermined by reduced electoral turnout. Populist reforms were really only endorsed selectively and sporadically, and by the end of the decade, the result was scarcely the democratic populist vision of the previous century.

Midwestern Politics: The Farmer-Labor Connection

The Midwest, which was originally agricultural and self-reliant, was subject to rapid industrialization in the mid- to late 19th century that effectively separated one region from another. Its diverse population mix, the result of immigration from all over Europe and America, donated a distinct quality to the culture of the region, whereas the post–Civil War agricultural revolution resulted in an enviably productive record so that by 1900, the Midwest could supply the entire nation and still have a surplus for export.

Since it was settled from the East, the Midwest inevitably suffered from a mild colonial complex; however, the Midwest was by no means the political backwater that some in the East imagined it to be. Midwesterners were thoroughly and quickly informed of political and cultural developments. Midwestern politics had a social agenda since at least the 19th century; politicians endeavored to impose decisive and planned control by the state on the economic and social life of the people. The political philosophy of the state consistently prioritized economic and social reform for the collective good. Parties, factions, and alliances from Anti-Monopoly to Reform, Populist, and Progressive advocated compensation for workers, conservation projects, labor laws that protected the rights of women and children, unemployment insurance, programs for agricultural modernization, state policy, education reforms, and pensions. From the outset, midwestern reformers tried to adapt government to the necessities of the people.

A benign self-interest came to characterize the endeavors of the midwestern politician. From just after the Civil War, the three-way alliance (in reality, a number of cartels) of railroads, banks, and businesses protected from tariffs dominated the economy in the Midwest. Confronted with speculators, moneylenders, railroads, high-tariff industries, trusts, and mortgage keepers, the Midwest and such parties as the Grangers, the Populists, the Non-partisan League, and the Socialists became an arena for radicalism and a legitimate and powerful force in American politics. Despite its reputation for radicalism however, the Midwest and the midwesterner was conservative in outlook, preferring the legitimate political process rather than revolution.

Self-interest took the form of opposition to railroads that overcharged, for example; a grain elevator monopoly provoked moves to set up a state alternative; overpriced farm machinery stimulated the foundation of a cooperative that would buy or make it; and deflation initiated a call for currency regulation. For the most part, midwestern radicalism comprised logical and rational attempts to discover a levelheaded way of eliminating specific hazards to midwestern interests. As a result, it was an inherently practical, agrarian, frontier militancy, a local, home-grown synthesis of assorted elements of midwestern history, heritage, and tradition.

The Farmer-Labor Connection

Along with enduring concerns regarding the tripartite alliance, the continuing decline of the rural population worried farmers, reformers, and politicians. The second decade was one of increasing prosperity and high prices for both land and produce. Rural prosperity paradoxically contrasted sharply with both relative and actual declines in farm population. More unsettling still, the decline was even more marked in wealthy states that depended almost wholly on agriculture and where the land was worth the most in terms of agriculture. Iowa experienced a fall of almost 6 percent in rural population in the decade, whereas its urban population increased by roughly the same proportion.

Several factors account for this drift. Increasing dependence on machinery meant more goods from fewer farmers, but rising land prices also meant that farmers sold out to speculators or neighbors and either retired or relocated to areas of lower prices, thus concentrating agriculture in states where land prices had not increased by so much. Farm laborers, particularly the young, were also seduced by the high wages and shorter hours, and the excitement, opportunities, and comforts that cities could provide. Farm laborers, who had mainly grown up on the farm, were experienced and accomplished, making their loss to industry particularly serious. Although city wages appeared to be higher, there was seldom much real financial advantage for young laborers to migrate to the cities when board, heat, laundry, and sundry expenses were taken into account.

Attempts to direct the influx of overseas immigrants toward the farms were often frustrated by Europeans' lack of experience in American farming methods. In any case, immigrants frequently preferred to remain in cities. As a result, farmers consistently lobbied government to make rural life more attractive. Farmers also began to become more active in such political parties as the Non-partisan League, which, in 1917, attracted some politically motivated Wisconsin Equity members. Speculation regarding a farmer-labor alliance also surfaced in 1918. From the outset, the League was heavily influenced by organized labor, and in a period of rising farm prices, it attracted disaffected growers from the Midwest. Aware of the success of organized labor in challenging unemployment and low wages, farmers in areas like North Dakota supported similar policies to counter low farm prices, high freight rates, and monopolistic practices.

Many senior League figures believed that national growth was only achievable with the assistance of organized labor, but even though a fusion of agriculture and labor occurred in North Dakota, its growth was only made possible by the predominantly agricultural population there. The alliance was more tenuous in other states where the proportions were more evenly balanced, and it became apparent that electoral cooperation between the two was vital if national growth was to be achieved. The purpose of the 1917 St. Paul conference, which brought together consumers and producers, was chiefly to engage the support of labor. High on the agenda was price fixing "so that the rich speculator and the powerful trust may be compelled to bow to the same level rule as the toiling farmer and wage-worker." (Saloutos and Hicks, 1931, 180) Delegates also declared that the Food Administration should assume control of elevators, mills, bakeries, and factories for the people's benefit. Farm organizer and League president, Arthur C. Townley, noted the political potential of cooperation, observing that nationally farmers commanded 35 percent of the vote, whereas labor controlled about 27 percent.

The League initially had exploited the difference between rural and urban America. This policy inevitably aroused hostility among urban dwellers excluded from the organization who believed that the League would benefit the farmer to their cost, and this exclusionary policy eventually weakened the organization. Opposition to the League's aims centered on the organization's alleged pro-German stance and disloyalty. The League vociferously refuted these accusations, citing its patriotism in supporting the Liberty Loan drive, increases in productivity by League farmers in the wheat states, and its legislative accomplishments in North Dakota, which in 1916 and 1917 supported farmers attempting to meet the demands for increased production who had been affected by the drought, and crippled by lack of funds and the inability of banks to provide credit.

The League discovered that farmers, some of whom had supported the Grange, the Alliance, the Populists, and the Equity, were responsive to their ideology. Despite early electoral success in the 1918 primaries, however, the farmer-labor alliance failed to capitalize on the victories in the general election. Membership campaigns followed, emphasizing the necessity for more productive cooperation between agriculture and labor at the ballot box. Despite the lack of tangible success outside its electoral heartland of North Dakota, however, the 1918 general election secured earlier advances by the League and majorities were gained in both houses of the legislature. Complete control in North Dakota encouraged the League to press ahead with its industrial program. Passed in its entirety in 1919, the program included the creation of a commission to direct the state industries, which would be financed by the Bank of North Dakota; the building of a mill and elevator, as well as affordable housing for farmers and laborers; an experimental creamery; and bonds to finance agriculture and the industrial projects. All of these initiatives would be self-financing, rather than being supported by increased taxes.

A combination of opposition by conservative forces, former supporters of the League, and those opposed to the League's leadership, however, led to the gradual erosion of its support. By 1920, the industrial program had been emasculated. The situation was compounded by a series of well-publicized financial irregularities, and votes were sacrificed as women in rural areas who took advantage of the recently adopted Nineteenth Amendment failed to vote in enough numbers. Nonetheless, the League did manage to attract more than 1,200,000 votes in the 1920 election, against 230,000 in 1918. In 1918, however, a new and persuasive opposition (the Independent Voters' Association) began to campaign on a platform largely appropriated from the League. Public endorsement of the program allowed them to gain control of the lower house.

Internal dissent, the agricultural slump, the apparent lack of League interest in urban areas, the growth of alternative farm organizations, which divided support among farmers, and League leader Townley's later imprisonment for disloyalty and sedition all contributed to the demise of the League. The League had grown rapidly thanks in part to the application of aggressive sales techniques to politics. Its decline, though, rested on somewhat lax financial control and the absence of a secure economic foundation, the unwillingness of members to assume real responsibility, and the apparent eagerness of its leaders to venture into new projects without the necessary expertise or resources, all exacerbated by the postwar depression.

Nevertheless, some reforms advocated by the League were adopted by Republican or Democratic candidates and League ideologies endured in the sentiments of many farmers in the Midwest despite its collapse.

The Politics of Race

By the second decade of the 20th century, out of a total of some 6.3 million farms, around 893,377, or 14.04 percent of the total, were African American operated. By the end of the decade, the number operated by African Americans had risen to 925,710 out of 6.4 million, or 14.34 percent. (U.S. Department of Agriculture, 1997 Census of Agriculture, vol. 1, pt 51) Around 89 percent of the African American population lived in the South, making up 35 percent of the region's population. Around 73 percent of African Americans were located in rural areas, mainly on farms. Despite an increase in the percentage of African American landowners to around 14 percent and some 15 percent of the total agricultural acreage, African American agricultural workers' ambition of "40 acres and a mule" remained out of reach for the majority, most of whom were tenants, mainly sharecroppers. At the start of the decade, the average acreage farmed by African American tenants was around 50 acres against 138 for white farmers, a figure that rose to 77 acres by the end of the decade. Most tenants stayed in debt and were tied by a perpetual contract that obliged them to stay on the land and work off their debt to the landowner or furnishing merchant. Between 1910 and 1920, the average value of African American farms rose from $799 to $1,588, compared with $2,140 and $3,911 for white-owned farms during the same period. African American farmers were also confined within severely constrained territorial limits, frequently defined by racism rather than by physical boundaries.

During the Great Migration of the period before, during, and after World War I, some half a million African Americans left the rural South, 20 percent from Alabama and Mississippi alone. Migrants were mainly pulled by the promise of jobs in the northern industrial cities and were pushed by a combination of poverty, exclusion from the political system, racism and violence, the boll weevil infestation, and poor weather. Those who stayed had little alternative other than to go to another landowner who might offer better conditions and credit. African Americans were frustrated in this ambition, however, by anti-enticement laws and violence, which severely restricted their ability to move.

Although physical restrictions were the most visible manifestations of segregation and discrimination, African Americans were also limited in other ways. Discrimination operates when the established social order, through government, devises policies to maintain the livelihood of certain types of farmers, while excluding farmers from certain races. When administrative institutions designed to modernize and advance the agricultural sector were established, African Americans were largely excluded from the policy-making process. The USDA was initially a small federal agency, which nevertheless had a wide remit, including the distribution of plants and seeds and information on the most effective ways in which they could be used. In addition, the USDA was committed to

African American farmer plowing with an ox, in Virginia, ca. 1901. (Library of Congress)

a scientific program to improve agricultural production. Higher education institutions were established to educate farmers in the latest agricultural methods, whereas federal experimental stations were introduced close by to carry out scientifically based procedures to advance agricultural modernization.

The 1914 Federal Extension Service, established to provide farmers with scientifically dependent agricultural methods and products, proved to be of little interest to African American farmers, especially those subsistence farmers who could have benefited from scientific intervention. The unprecedented number of agricultural laws in place by the beginning of World War I, many of which were motivated by scientific principles and consequently aimed at increasing productivity in a more advanced and technologically developed agricultural sector, largely excluded African American farmers, the majority of whom were based in the South and thus beyond the limited reach of agricultural institutions. This constituency was mainly uninterested in attending southern colleges (which in any case were segregated), distrusted new farming methods and Extension agents, and was not generally market oriented. Small-scale farmers, both white and African American, confronted institutions, and the circumstances created by those institutions, which created and then encouraged larger-scale producers. African Americans, the majority of whom were tenants, were therefore disadvantaged by the consequences of initiatives by institutions whose intentions had been largely benevolent.

African Americans and the Cooperative Extension Service

Although the agricultural institutions that evolved before World War I seemed for the most part to be irrelevant to African American farmers, there were, nevertheless, African American Extension agents whose responsibility was to convey the Extension program to African American farm owners. The modified program had been created by white bureaucrats and was originally aimed at African American farm owners, but it became clear that if the program were to succeed in transforming southern agriculture, then sharecroppers would have to be included. Following the passing of the Smith-Lever Act in 1914, the Cooperative Extension Service instituted trials in African American agricultural education. These trials emerged from both white and African American colleges. Certain, mainly private, African American institutions had already undertaken the task of agricultural education. In the way that agents were allocated to counties and were responsible to district agents, who were themselves accountable to the state director and answerable to the state agricultural and mechanical college, the African American agent structure mirrored the white system, at least up to director level, where both African American and white district agents reported to a white director. It grew more slowly, however, because counties who were at first slow to acknowledge the value of agricultural education directed toward African Americans frequently refused to fund the system.

There seems to have been little relationship between white and African American agents, and the three African Americans who were made responsible for several states each in 1918 had little influence in policy decisions. Thomas M. Campbell, J. B. Pierce, and E. L. Blackshear, who controlled all of the Gulf and South Atlantic states among them, developed the African American agent system by demonstrating that it met the objectives of the Cooperative Extension system. They did so by showing that the role of African American farmers was pivotal in the agricultural modernization program in the plantations of the southern states. Underproduction, overintensive soil cultivation, the boll weevil infestation, and the migration of large numbers of rural African Americans meant that the outlook for plantations was bleak by the middle of the decade. Because African American sharecroppers carried out most of the farming on plantations, African American educators contended that any successful policy depended on getting through to them.

Exposed to the mass migration of African American agricultural workers from the rural South, the labor-intensive plantations were among the first to be affected, and the Extension Service was compelled to rethink its modernization policy and to find ways of curbing the mass migration. In the racially sensitive South, any suggestion that conditions for African American workers could be improved, thereby allowing them more independence, would have been met with outright hostility from white plantation owners (who wielded substantial influence within the USDA) and officials, so the Extension Service had to accomplish this by advocating the Extension program as one solution to the African American migration.

Harvesting sweet potatoes at Claflin University, Orangeburg, South Carolina, ca. 1900. (Library of Congress)

Structured and managed along the same lines as the farm program, the initiative for improving conditions for the African American farm home and family involved sending African American Home Demonstration agents into the field to offer advice on food preparation and domestic matters. Because of mass migration, however, the program assumed particular importance. Moreover, conscription of African American soldiers exposed serious shortcomings in the southern diet. African American Home Demonstration agents therefore undertook responsibility for teaching families how to avert diet-related and other diseases and how to practice better hygiene. Unlike the white program, which focused its efforts on encouraging women to supplement farm income by marketing their own garden produce, African American farm women were instead convinced that produce should be directed toward the home. Jeannie Whayne (2003, 157) cites a study providing evidence that white women were steered toward consumption and "a farm home based on the suburban white middle class model," whereas the program for African American women "rarely emphasized consumption."

Reluctance to disturb the fragile racial status quo that existed in the South motivated African American agents to be pragmatic. They did not attempt to interfere with white power structures. African American farmers were only too aware that any action, whether collective or individual, would threaten their livelihood and, possibly, their safety and that of their families. They were therefore more responsive to programs that would improve their daily lives. Rural African American churches were also important influences. In 1911, the African American county agent in South Carolina noted that "the negro rural church and the negro preacher constitutes the two important factors in the negro's social and economic development, therefore, whenever feasible, farms have been selected [for demonstration] near churches and the negro preacher" (Whayne, 2003, 159), indicating that the agent was sufficiently aware of the significance of religion and that that knowledge should be exploited in generating support for the Extension program.

Nevertheless, the aims of the Department of Agriculture and the white planters were frequently at odds with the requirements of African American farmers and their families. The priorities of the Extension program were to salvage the southern agricultural economy through the advocacy of improved farming procedures and so to generate greater profits for landowners. It was the duty of African American agents to translate those priorities into forms that would be acceptable to African American farmers without making it disagreeable for planters or to recommend a program that the white administration would be unlikely to endorse.

The system of debt that prevailed throughout the South inevitably led to stasis among African American laborers. Unable to move without first settling the debt, which many found difficult to do, laborers became trapped. Improving farming methods and thus increasing profits for African American sharecroppers eroded the system of indebtedness and also weakened financial sharecroppers' dependence on the plantation. Moreover, by encouraging African American farmers to supplement farm income by growing vegetables and tending cattle and poultry, families became progressively less reliant on the plantation commissary.

Although African American agents were urged to do nothing to disrupt the fragile racial equilibrium in the South, African American leaders did take the initiative in campaigning for measures to support the production of sufficient agricultural goods for the war effort. Although white agencies hesitated, a state commission suggested that a department be established to "induce the Negro man and woman who has left the agricultural section of the South to return" (Whayne, 2003, 169), recommending that an African American should head the department. Others began to petition for a new division within the USDA, also to be headed by an African American, and not merely for the duration of the war or to halt the African American migration, but to "look after their [black farmers] needs." (Ibid.) Although the administration remained deaf to these petitions, the entreaties did lead to an increase in the number of African American county agents. Thus, while acknowledging the importance of African American agents' attempts to arrest the flow of migrants away from the plantations, officials did little, if anything, to address suggestions that African Americans could be located in policy-making positions.

Cooperatives

Two problems were central in preventing agricultural expansion for much of the 19th century: insufficient credit and ineffective and inadequate markets. The requirement for cheaper credit, more relevant credit forms, economic strength to participate successfully in markets stacked against them, and the need to identify ways in which they could contend with the strength of such monopolies as railroads and the mills were uppermost in farmers' concerns. Early efforts to develop cooperative marketing associations to regulate the marketing of agricultural commodities were largely unsuccessful. Strategies begun in the early 20th century under President Roosevelt, who's Country Life Commission supported a fairer credit system, were more successful. By 1912, the three major political parties had advocated measures by government regarding agricultural credit. Following President Wilson's appointment in 1913 of a commission to report on agricultural credit and cooperation, the Moss-Fletcher bill, which proposed a system of privately funded, profit-making agricultural credit and cooperative associations, was put before Congress in 1914.

Roundly criticized by special interest groups who preferred the "pure" system of credit then favored by Europeans, and those who wanted loans to be made direct to farmers by the government, a compromise bill—the Farm Loan Act—was eventually passed after two years of arguments. The Act ratified a cooperative structure of 12 land banks and a privately capitalized joint stock land bank, the government part funding the cooperative sector and regulating interest rates for both systems. Because farm revenues between 1916 and 1920 were high and farmers had fewer requirements for credit, the system of long-term agricultural credit was slow to develop, whereas the cooperative system was sufficiently complex to require the education of some farmers before they could become involved.

Criticism of cooperative marketing and buying centered on how rural merchants, and hence rural towns, would be affected. Critics were really concerned, however, that organized producers in control of the food supply could hold the nation ransom and drive up prices, whereas those critics concerned about the loss of rural individualism saw cooperation as essentially anti-individualistic. Advocates of efficiency nevertheless argued that progress without cooperation was impossible and that mutuality would benefit consumers and the nation as a whole by furthering education in scientific agriculture, accelerating crop standardization, and modernizing supply sources. Acknowledging that reorganization would heighten rural political influence, advocates also contended that it would lead to political stability, and by providing farmers with a stake in the countryside that they would necessarily want to safeguard, it would make farmers more moderate. Establishing mutual interests would lead to compliance, allegiance, and respect for authority, thus diminishing the more flagrant examples of rural individualism. Reflecting the trend toward cooperation, which even the more immutable Country Lifers were beginning to accommodate, the USDA created the Rural Organization Service in 1913 to promote all kinds of rural organization. Following concerns that USDA involvement could lead to a conflict of interests, the National Agricultural Organization Society (NAOS) was established in 1915. Operating as a part-public, not-for-profit organization, the NAOS assisted farmers who hoped to initiate and run cooperative ventures, and such cooperative measures were seen by the NAOS as a cure-all for rural economic ills and disproportionate living costs.

Increasing numbers of economic cooperatives and political movements organized by farm people themselves paralleled government initiatives during the decade. Some were community-centered local groups that had originated in the 19th century in the Grange and Populist Party, and which included whole families among their members. Within these organizations were small economic cooperatives that echoed larger initiatives in the market. In the small, community-based groups, educational projects and social pursuits, as well as fund-raising activities, helped to unify the community behind the agricultural and political organizations. By the second decade, cooperatives and smaller political associations had grown in importance in many rural areas.

The network of farm bureaus, Homemakers' Clubs, and 4-H clubs established by the Extension Service during and after 1914 tended to focus on the interests of individual family members, rather than the family as a whole and the part it played in the community. This inevitably meant that a man's interests were characterized as agricultural and a woman's as domestic. Young people's corn, pig, canning, tomato, and poultry clubs were created in around 1902 to provide applied, hands-on education for young people to connect formal learning with country life. The young were perceived as being more amenable to new agricultural methods, and it was therefore hoped that they would then share their experience and enthusiasm with adults, thus introducing adults to new agricultural technology. The clubs were incorporated into the Coalition of Essential Schools (CES) charter in 1914 and soon became coordinated as 4-H clubs.

The economic cooperatives of the decade, which were enthusiastically promoted by the Country Life Movement, had their roots in the informal neighborhood trading organizations or "rings" of the early to mid-19th century. Before World War I, many cooperatives were highly localized and responded to local market circumstances. Set up to combat the monopolistic practices of such organizations as the grain elevator companies, which all paid farmers the same price, cooperatives were able to negotiate higher rates for grain sent to Chicago. In the increasingly centralized economy of the early 20th century, farming communities were thus afforded greater economic power, and gains made in grain, for example, led to the expansion of these initiatives to other agricultural commodities, as well as livestock.

In addition to increased economic power, local cooperatives served community needs and dealt in a growing range of commodities and services. Farmers

Some of the "Caesar Gang" boys demonstrating how to cull chickens to improve the quality and the quantity of the product, Charleston, West Virginia, 1921. Lewis Hine photo. (Library of Congress)

typically traded in eggs, dairy, and grain products. Services included a telephone company, community threshing and silo-filling cooperatives, and cattle-testing associations. Cooperative elevators combated the cartels and monopolies that had previously exploited individual farmers. By 1913, six midwestern states had set up grain associations; by 1914, 380 cooperative creameries were operating in Wisconsin; and by the following year, there were 718 cooperative cheese factories. Until World War I, livestock transportation was still largely in the hands of several large companies; however, from 1914 to around 1920, when the number peaked, this activity also had started to be undertaken by cooperative organizations that could negotiate lower prices with the railroads. During World War I, cooperatives started to expand into areas that offered more marketing scope and geographic range, but by 1920, some 90 percent of existing cooperatives remained local.

From Local to National
Despite their local emphasis, many cooperatives became aligned with regional or national cooperative associations. The decline of the Populist Party, which had emerged from the Farmer's Alliance in the 1890s, was the effective end of

wide-ranging agricultural political activity; however, economic cooperatives continued to grow in number and in scope. Farmers propelled the American Society of Equity (Equity) into new activities, investigating sharing crops, collaborating with labor unions to exclude intermediaries, and advocating farmer-owned warehouses and grain exchanges. In addition to withholding activities to obtain better prices, the Farmers' Union promoted education, whereas their political activists lobbied for improved agricultural legislation.

There were also disadvantages to widespread cooperation. Larger and more geographically remote organizations could not command the same degree of loyalty as local cooperatives. Nevertheless, local associations could only confront local, privately run companies, and if local cooperatives wanted to engage with unfair practices or deliberately low prices in larger organizations, alignment with larger cooperatives was essential to combat the increasingly centralized and bureaucratic culture of the decade. Cooperatives were legalized in 1914 when they were granted immunity from antitrust laws under the Clayton Antitrust Act. Following this, larger cooperatives were able to combat corporate interests.

Political agricultural groups simultaneously lobbied government to increase legislation aimed at eradicating abuses in the cartels and monopolies of shipping and marketing companies. Perhaps the most militant of these, the Nonpartisan League, challenged companies and intermediaries in the period before and after World War I. Centered in the Dakotas, Minnesota, and Wisconsin, the organization advocated state control of grain elevators, banks, and utilities and urged an affiliation with the unions. Economic cooperatives aligned themselves with unions to elect candidates more disposed to advance agricultural interests than the major parties.

The formation of the AFBF in 1919 was a direct response to the emergence of alternative, politically engaged cooperatives, a national farmers' organization supportive of agricultural institutions' interests and less censorious of corporate interests. Like the Extension Service, which had resulted from the passing of the Smith-Lever Act in 1914 and through which county farm and home demonstration agents promoted agricultural efficiency through adult education, local farm bureaus employed agents and promoted scientific agriculture. They also had financial links with such companies as International Harvesters and Sears. Their members, who were more closely aligned with the more prosperous landowners, were frequently funded, at least in part, by bankers and railroads. Before World War I, the composition of local Farm Bureaus was diverse, but by 1919, they were closely associated with county agents and land-grant colleges.

Criticism from commercial farmers leveled at corporate agriculture led to increased interest in marketing during World War I. The AFBF, USDA, and colleges therefore started to include marketing in their educational concerns, aiming to establish centralized marketing structures that would, it was hoped, modernize agriculture, stabilize prices, and align farmers to business, rather than labor, thereby eradicating radicalism. In these endeavors, they were backed financially by business. Undermining and changing the prevailing marketing system was not the aim of the economically and politically conservative AFBF, but by complementing the economic aims and the policies of agricultural institutions, the Farm Bureaus effectively opposed rural community-centered institutions. Organized from the top down, rather than the bottom up, Farm Bureaus stressed marketing and production and had few local or neighborhood affiliations or loyalties. Farm Bureaus were not compelled to compromise with local interests, nor were their programs centered on socializing or community; rather, they were biased toward business and education.

As the official spokespeople for farmers, Farm Bureaus were effectively a business organization that promoted agriculture as an industry. Largely unconcerned with the preservation of small family farms, the AFBF complemented Country Lifers' aims of administering and promoting an affluent, educated, and stable middle-class constituency.

The Farm Bureaus were popular regionally in the midwestern corn and livestock areas, in part because their ethos appealed to livestock farmers who had invested heavily and who had already changed to the mixed agriculture advocated by the agencies. These producers were less dependent on exports than were those in the wheat regions further west. Because they were less affected by the boom-bust cycles of the war years, they tended to be more conservative. Further west, in the Great Plains and dairy regions, farmers tended to be aligned with such alternative organizations as Equity or the Non-partisan League. Although the Farm Bureaus had more members than many other organizations, not all farmers, even those from among their constituency, supported their policies. Because participation in the larger shipping associations and markets in such "destination" cities as Chicago was frequently dependent on membership of Farm Bureaus, farmers joined for pragmatic reasons rather than from social loyalty or commitment. Monopolized by professionals and large landowners with little empathy with small family-owned farms, the AFBF did eventually comprise a more diverse membership, but their management and composition meant that the organization was always securely bonded to the aims of production-focused, centralized agriculture.

FARM ECONOMICS

The Price and Its Effect

Following one of the most acutely economically depressed periods of the 19th century, the 13 years before 1910 were a period of prolonged growth for American agriculture. Although there was no striking upsurge, farm prices increased consistently year on year, rising by more than non-farm prices. In the so-called golden age that followed (between 1910 and 1914), farm prices had increased and, equally important, had remained stable. Before war broke out in Europe, the world appeared secure; terms of trade favored farmers, and, it could be said, a degree of complacency had set in among agricultural producers. Many Americans were taken by surprise when war in Europe was declared in 1914. Isolated in almost every way, American farmers, along with the majority of the population, believed that their lives would be largely unaffected by the conflict. Both in real terms and in relation to urban workers, farmers in general prospered in the period. Net farm income more than doubled in the decade, and although the data collected in the two censuses differs because the total value of farmland was only added in the 1920 census, thus making valid comparisons difficult, it is probable that the value of the average farm, which remained less than 150 acres during the decade, increased by an amount similar to farm income. Farmers therefore banked upon the rise in the value of their farm augmenting their relatively meager income.

The substantial increases in the export and import demands for foodstuffs that the war stimulated provoked abrupt increases in farm prices in 1916, which, by the end of the decade, had resulted in the doubling of farm prices. By 1915, land that was relatively easy to cultivate had become scarce, and farmers competed with each other for better cropland. The price of farmland increased by 70 percent between 1913 and 1920 for the whole nation, and by 60 percent between 1916 and 1920 alone. In such intensive areas as Iowa, where the land was of good quality and the transport infrastructure already developed, the price increased by more than 100 percent between 1914 and 1920.

By 1910, the convictions of such observers as Bolton Hall and other advocates of a back-to-the-land policy, who had already maintained that population would surpass increases in food production, appeared to have been confirmed. Agricultural prosperity had in part been maintained by imbalances between supply and demand. As long as there was an adequate supply of fertile land that could be exploited, agricultural output would increase. Between 1870 and 1900, the acreage of farmland had increased by more than 100 percent, with resultant increases in crop production. By the early years of the 20th century, however, the majority of the best, and most accessible, land was already cultivated and producing. By 1920, acreage had increased by a mere 12 percent. To compound the slow growth in acreage, the majority of the new land was either of relatively poor quality or in areas far from established transport links and markets (e.g., the arid High Plains, the Great Basin of Nevada and Idaho, and the Oregon desert).

Modest growth in acreage was exacerbated by mediocre farmer productivity. Between 1910 and 1919, agricultural productivity grew at barely 1 percent per year, and although population growth had slowed from the previous decade, it had increased by some 15 percent in the decade 1910–1920. Farm prices, perhaps predictably, increased more rapidly than general prices, and farmers extracted a greater proportion of the economic whole. Farm incomes also flourished because

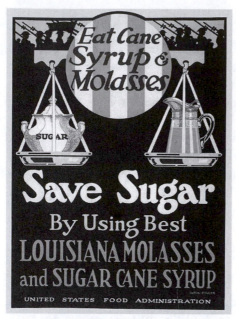

Food Administration poster encourages the use of domestically produced sweeteners like cane syrup and molasses as a means of conserving sugar, 1918. (Library of Congress)

the situation in America was replicated in the rest of the Americas, and in Russia, Australia, and Africa, where the marked agricultural growth of the late 19th century had decreased noticeably by the second decade. American farmers found themselves in the fortunate position of being able to supply a home market at inflated prices, as well as an export market where the overall volume remained static, but whose worth had increased by almost 400 percent. Because America would have to maintain food production to feed its own population and also provide the Allies with foodstuffs once war was underway, the government doubted the farmers' capacity to meet these needs, given the torpid growth in agricultural efficiency before the war.

Legislation to ensure adequate production was passed in the early stages of the war. The Food Production Act was followed by the Food Control Act, overseen by the U.S. Food Administration, a new agency led by Herbert Hoover, which stimulated food production, distributed scarce supplies, and controlled consumer prices. The husbandry of limited supplies was reinforced by a program that encouraged the population to make savings wherever possible and was furthered by the Food Administration's control over a wide spectrum of the food chain, from processing through retailing and exports. The agency attempted to guarantee that consumers were not overcharged by establishing the prices for a few staples (e.g., wheat, pork, and sugar). Those producers affected by the capping complained that the prices of commodities not included in the measures were permitted to rise, but a balance was generally achieved between ensuring that prices were sufficiently high to stimulate production and low enough to safeguard consumers' interests.

Shortages were experienced in Allied food supplies in early 1918, and the United States increased its freights of such crops as wheat. Because of U.S. Grain Corporation operations (e.g., establishing a fixed price for wheat) between September 1917 and May 1920, wheat production and farm acreage escalated, whereas exports of foodstuffs grew markedly. Agricultural land values increased sharply, as did farm debt. Table 5.1 illustrates activity in these areas between 1913 and 1919.

Table 5.1. Wheat Output, Acreage, Exports; Farm Value, Farm Debt, 1913–1919

Year	Wheat Output (millions of bushels)	Wheat Acreage (millions of acres)	Ratio Wheat Export to Net Output	Value Farm Land and Buildings ($ billions)	Farm Debt ($ billions)
1913	751.1	52.01	23.2	38.46	4.3
1914	897.48	55.6	42.6	39.58	4.7
1915	1,008.63	60.3	27.3	39.59	4.9
1916	634.57	53.5	39.8	42.27	5.2
1917	619.79	46.78	26.4	45.53	5.8
1918	904.13	61.06	37.3	49.98	6.3
1919	945.4	73.09	26.9	54.53	7.1

Source: Adapted from Hacker and Zahler, 1952, 206.

Although prices did not drop immediately with the cessation of hostilities in 1918, the subsequent reduction in postwar relief measures brought about a fall in prices by the end of the decade. These falls were to be the precursors of the more far-reaching and sharper declines that were to come in the 1920s. Before that, though, farm people reacted to their affluence by participating in the market more eagerly. Increasingly, they concentrated on saleable goods, rather than those that contributed to family self-sufficiency. The USDA gauged that by the end of the decade, on average, only 40 percent of the commodities a farm family consumed were produced by them, a reduction of 20 percent in 20 years. Some farmers did convert surpluses into farm improvements (e.g., machinery, more land, newly available fertilizers, livestock, and farm buildings), as well as purchases of labor-saving appliances and new technology (e.g., telephones, automobiles, and furnishings). They also improved roads and schools, and some invested in their children's high school or college education.

In general, though, relatively few farmers invested in more land, which meant that the average farm acreage remained comparatively static. Many farmers recalled the recurrent troughs of the late 19th century and were thus reluctant to expand and risk potentially extravagant behavior that might damage the business when hard times returned. The false optimism among farmers that the high prices might endure led some of those hesitant to expand before the war to pay inflated prices for land, equipment, and stock. Those who incurred the most debt were perhaps the hardest hit when prices did fall.

Debt

Although some farmers may not have recognized the term *capital,* the farm that they worked represented a significant capital investment. Although self-sufficiency took priority, the farms were nevertheless commercial ventures, and prosperity relied on how much income above expenditure could be achieved. The cost of starting a farm in 1900 was around $3,000. Even allowing for the relatively modest inflation of the early century, the cost in 1920 would have risen significantly year to year, but during the second decade, inflation rose from 2.5 percent in 1910 to 9.1 percent by the end of the decade. The amount it did cost depended largely on the cost of the land, which fluctuated from area to area and from time to time. A characteristic northwestern farm would have constituted an investment of $12,000, made up of $1,400 for buildings, $350 worth of machinery, and $1,400 in livestock, with the remainder being the cost of the land. (Saloutos and Hicks, 1951, 13) There are few reliable statistics on the amount the average farmer earned, and many farmers themselves often did not know the extent of their annual income or even whether they made a profit. Nevertheless, an investment of this size would require financing from one or another source.

In most circumstances, the original purchase was funded by a short-term mortgage. Approximations of the average mortgage debt per farm are not straightforward. In 1920, however, after the increases in land values initiated by the affluence of the period during and shortly after the war, the average amount of all new loans was $4,270. In Iowa, however, where land was particularly valuable and speculation was rife, the figure was closer to $11,000. (Shover, 1976, 123)

Apart from the cost of land, farmers also incurred such other expenses as chattel mortgages to buy draft animals or machinery. Wages for hired labor, taxes, medical expenses, veterinarian charges, and possibly insurance policies all ate into any profit from the sale of crops, livestock, or produce. The report published by Roosevelt's Country Life Commission had encouraged farmers to cooperate through marketing associations, both to negotiate better prices for goods that they bought and to force up commodity prices and thus receive a higher level of income. Lending also became easier and cheaper as banks promoted loans to compete with such alternative sources as new farmer's savings banks.

The 1914 Federal Reserve Act provided some degree of financial stability, whereas the 1916 Rural Credit Act supplied low-interest loans to alleviate agricultural debt. Supplying an expanded market as population increased, exporting to parts of the world affected by the war, and inflated land and building values (up from $35 billion to $66 billion between 1910 and 1920) all conspired to drive up prices, and many farmers were deceived into overproduction and a false sense of security. Younger farmers, seduced by the notion of greater profits, began to buy out neighboring farms as an older age group who had endured the hard times of earlier years took the opportunity to profit from the sale, retire, and move away from the countryside. The speculation and avarice that the war engendered distorted the fragile economic structure, and farmers who took on more debt paid a high price when the inevitable falls in prices and land values came.

In 1914, agricultural production was an unexceptional $6 billion, but this figure rose to $14 billion in 1918 and peaked at $16 billion in 1919. Commodities increased by similarly impressive percentages. Between 1914 and 1919, the index for wholesale prices increased by 127 percent, with the most marked gains in midwestern states. (Saloutos and Hicks, 1951, 90) Farmers accumulated debt on the assumption that they would be able to repay loans out of the profits from high prices, and banks promoted loans that extended borrowers beyond any reasonable safety margin. Agricultural mortgages increased from $4.7 to $10.2 billion between 1914 and 1920. (Benedict, 1953, 168) The amount that banks had outstanding to farmers (e.g., loans on personal and collateral security) increased from $1.6 billion in 1915 to around $3.8 billion in 1920. (Saloutos and Hicks, 1951, 103)

In 1918, *Wallace's Farmer,* concerned at the rising levels of debt, warned farmers that "cost-plus" (any costs associated with operation and production) had to be factored into any equation of profit and loss. Those costs were not static, and for an acre of corn, for example, they had risen by 130 percent between 1913 and 1918. The journal estimated that after taking these costs into consideration, farmers actually made less net profit. Because price levels remained high in the period immediately after the war when Europe was still importing foodstuffs, few farmers anticipated the inevitable downturn if exports declined, government support was withdrawn, and there was a change in policy by the Federal Reserve System.

Although loans from the Federal Farm Loan System were forthcoming at slightly lower interest rates, rural banks were the principal lenders during the boom, with some funds coming from life insurance companies. Novices such as retired farmers who used their wartime profits as capital established many of the 1,700 new banks that sprang up in 11 representative agricultural states, some duplicating the banks already there. Even in times of prosperity, the high land values could not be justified by returns earned from even the most efficient and profitable farms. Average farmers saw a return of around 3 percent on their investment. The Federal Reserve System saw the warning signs and put a check on credit, government subsidies were withdrawn, and exports did decline when European crop yields increased again and labor was once more available. Consumption at home also fell as consumers' eating habits seemed to have been permanently changed by wartime exigencies. Increased taxes, which rose every year except 1918, contributed to the farmers' problems. Such costs as farm wages and freight were further expenses that continued to rise. Moreover, modernization meant that farmers who did not invest in new machinery (e.g., tractors to replace horses and mules) were at a serious disadvantage. Many farmers began to believe that the modernizing initiatives preached by the USDA actually made them worse off.

Many farmers were forced to dispose of land that only realized enough to pay off their debts now that land values had fallen. More than a few ended up as tenants on farms they had once owned. Others were forced into bankruptcy.

Tenant farmers, Corsicana, Texas, 1913. The entire family worked in the 50 acres of cotton fields for a meager return. (Library of Congress)

Between 1910 and 1919, there were 12,000 such disposals. The lower value of the farms that escaped such a fate meant that the reduced equity would not support the mortgage. A predictable consequence was the failure of many small banks that had lent unwisely, a situation that began in the late years of the decade and accelerated until 1926. Failures like these affected farmers who had resisted speculation just as much as those who were overextended.

The overall despondency that necessarily goes alongside multiple bank failures meant that almost no individual remained unscathed in the Midwest particularly, but elsewhere as well, and as the decade ended the farmers' problems were really only beginning.

Sharecropping

Debt of a different, and more permanent, kind affected African Americans, as well as some whites, in rural areas of the southern states. Sharecroppers and tenant farmers were both farmers who did not own the land on which they worked. Payment to a landlord typically entitled a tenant to grow crops on a piece of land, which might extend in size to the norm for this decade, up to around 140 acres. Tenants also mainly owned some livestock and equipment. Sharecroppers, though, were further disadvantaged and impoverished by having little or no cash and few resources. Sharecroppers were therefore compelled to farm a plot of land, which rarely achieved the average size of farms for the period, in exchange for an agreed share of the crops. Freed African American slaves who had no cash or access to credit to purchase land comprised the majority who worked the land in the late 19th and early 20th centuries.

The perpetual cycle of landlessness, debt, and impoverishment endured by sharecroppers trapped them in what became known as the crop-lien system, which stipulated that landowners could exact a lien on the crops for any debts run up during the growing season. Because sharecroppers needed supplies to raise the crop and to sustain their families, debt was inevitable. Taking the crop as collateral, "furnishing merchants"—frequently the landowner or perhaps a neighboring merchant—would supply sharecroppers with food and supplies. Further supplies acquired throughout the year were added to the total, and by "settlement time," the charges were deducted from the sharecroppers' share of the crop. Because the debt frequently exceeded the value of the share, sharecroppers were forced to sign on for a further year or move on to another farm, thus perpetuating the cycle of debt.

Lack of proficiency among former slaves, who knew how to grow little else beside cotton, along with a lack of capital ensured that cotton had become the South's major cash crop. There was scant information on the importance of fertilizing and crop rotation. In any case, poor African American farmers lacked the capital to invest in new techniques, further ensuring that they depended almost entirely on a single crop. The price of cotton gradually rose between 1898 and 1913, and the simultaneous increase in African American–owned acreage meant that by 1910 (the peak year for African American ownership) African Americans owned around 15 million acres, with 175,000 properties wholly owned, 43,000 part owned, and 670,000 sharecropped. The outbreak of war in Europe in 1914, however, temporarily halted most exports, devastating the cotton market. Financial hardship was aggravated by such legislation as the 1916 Federal Farm Loan Act, established to provide farmers with credit at affordable rates, which routinely discriminated against African American farmers. The failure of many of the African American banks that had been established in the previous decades plunged African American clients still further into debt. A combination of the boll weevil invasion, which ravaged the cotton crop in many areas, poor weather, racially inspired violence, and discrimination resulted in the Great Migration north in the period before, during, and after World War I and provided many sharecroppers with a means of escape, but the system prevailed in the South for many years after.

Machinery

By the second decade of the century, urban-industrial America had already been mechanized to a significant extent. Farmers, by contrast, benefited little from the

Table 5.2. Value of Implements and Machinery in 1909

Divisions	Average per Farm (in dollars)	Average per Acre of All Farmland (in dollars)
New England	269	2.58
Middle Atlantic	358	3.88
The North		
East North-Central	239	2.28
West North-Central	332	1.59
The South (three divisions)	72, 88, 127	0.71, 0.92, 0.95
The West (two divisions)	269, 350	0.83–1.29
The U.S.	199	1.44

Source: Adapted from www.marxists.org/archive/lenin/works/1915/newdev/7.htm

improvements and progress in factories. The farmer's year was a constant and largely unchanging cycle of hard, long days, toil that was, in the main, unrelieved by much agricultural machinery. Table 5.2 reflects the value of machinery.

Even in 1909, the average farm operated on less than $199 worth of machinery. (Census Reports, Twelfth Census 1900, Vol. V: Agriculture, Wash., 1902; Thirteenth Census 1910, Vol. V: Agriculture, Wash., 1913) This average, however, masks the fact that the figures for the South, which in the census was divided into three divisions, are much lower ($72, $88, $127). For the most machine-intensive area, the Middle Atlantic, the figure is $358. The figures also have to be approached with caution for two other reasons. First, because the census did not distinguish between machinery and implements, and, second, the American statistical method of assessing the value of machinery and other assets (e.g., land, livestock) by acre of all land, not by acre of improved farmland, underplays the predominance of the "concentrated" northern areas. The differences between the different regions regarding proportions of improved land are extensive; 26.7 percent for the Mountain states and 75.4 percent for the East North-Central states, for example.

Improved land is clearly of great importance economically. Whereas the proportion of improved land in New England decreased from 1880, machinery was heavily used, and the value of machinery per acre of improved land was particularly high. The region with the smallest farms by acreage similarly had the largest capital investment in land in terms of machinery.

Comparison between different census years at the beginning of the 20th century is difficult because the preceding figures are abstracted from different parts of the census because the 1910 census did not enumerate the value of implements and machinery. In the 1920 census, the value is given as an average of $557.47 for all states, which may not be a valid comparison. Nevertheless, it is clear that the average did increase significantly between the two census dates.

It is evident, then, that even by 1910 farmers had not invested significantly in machinery to lessen the drudgery of farm tasks, and most work was undertaken with traction animals and rudimentary equipment. If country life was hard for farmers, however, it was more arduous still for farmers' wives, who, for the most part, carried out their work without hired labor. Unlike farmers, whose work slackened off in the winter, farm wives' tasks continued undiminished and the cycle of housework endured, unaided by even token modern household appliances. For women in the towns and cities, life had been transformed by technological advances, but rural women still labored with the implements common 100 years earlier. Agricultural modernization seldom touched women's lives either, and as farm sizes increased, and more labor was hired, women's work increased correspondingly. In hard times, too, women were expected to work in the fields, as well as carrying out their regular work in the dairy, the vegetable garden, and the hen house.

Machinery in the Farm Home

It would be wrong to assume, though, that the absence of modern household appliances or the expectation that women would work in the fields turned them into subordinate drudges. Many farm women regarded their work as intrinsic and indispensable, *part* of the farm rather than separate from it, and believed in the self-esteem that resulted from *all* their work. Women prized their capacity to make do and be frugal, to prepare commodities for the family and the market, to look after the family, and to undertake work on the farm when necessary. Like farm men, farm women chose and modified new technology to match their work patterns; however, because many women regarded their work as essential to the survival and expansion of the farm and prized most the activities that contributed most to the farm, any economies that resulted from labor-saving devices were more likely to be plowed back in to the farm rather than into consumption.

Budgets permitting, farms were more likely to purchase new technologies that reduced the physical effort of household chores. Because central generating power was unavailable, electricity was still relatively rare in many rural areas. This effectively prohibited access to a range of devices taken for granted in urban areas. When it was available, it was used for lighting because it dispensed with kerosene lamps, which were difficult to clean. Water pumped into or near the house similarly meant that it no longer had to be carried for long distances. Despite the belief among some professionals that labor-saving appliances would increase farm women's time for recreation, they frequently used the time saved to add to other kinds of farm work. Intermittent and spasmodic farm income, and the need to pay for farm and home modernization, kept the majority of farm women working on farm tasks. Activities that centered on home production were valued more than daily tasks, and, given the economic means, few women persisted with washboards, for example. Even after tinned goods became more

Men in an automobile in a wheat field on the farm of Benjamin Martin, July 24, 1910. Photograph from volume one of a series of photo albums documenting the construction of Pathfinder Dam and other units on the North Platte Project in Wyoming and Nebraska. (National Archives)

widely available in stores, however, women continued to preserve and can produce because it was appreciated for the expertise it required, its financial contribution, its significance for family consumption, and the part that it played in women's social life.

The aspirations that advocates of rural modernization had for improving country people's lives were often at odds with the realities and priorities of rural life and perhaps reflected professionals' own lives more than they did the lives of farm people, who were unable to buy all the essentials of a modern farm. Farmers, and farm women, had to offset any upgrading on the farm with improvements in the home. The census enumerated the underlying yardsticks of agricultural modernity and listed connection to a water supply, machinery such as automobiles and tractors, communication technologies like the telephone and, later, the radio, and electricity. Farm people were generally slow to adopt new technology because their choices were molded by economic pragmatism.

Statistics indicate that a high priority for farm people was to communicate with others, whether in person, by automobile, or by telephone. The 1920 census, which listed purchases during the decade 1910–1920, shows that these two items outstripped all other purchases. Percentages of ownership of both items varied widely, from 47 percent for the telephone in North Dakota to 86 percent in Iowa, whereas the automobile achieved a penetration of 31 percent in Missouri to 76 percent in Nebraska. Both of these lessened the remoteness of farm life in both real and psychological terms and reduced the physical distance between farm people and family, neighbors, and markets. Advertising the telephone to potential rural customers frequently focused on its practical advantages (e.g., determining market prices), its use in emergencies, and its capacity for saving time by ordering by phone. All other aspects of modernity were present in percentages varying from less than 10 percent to no more than 20 percent.

Automobiles

The extent of automobile ownership reflects its importance in rural life. In 1900, there were only a few thousand automobiles in the whole country; in 1920, rural ownership alone amounted to 2.5 million, and more than 30 percent of farmers had bought at least one. At least until 1920, the Model T Ford was the farmer's car of choice. In terms of its price and its ability to answer rural needs, Henry Ford had designed and marketed the model with the farmer in mind. It was rudimentary enough to allow for simple and inexpensive repairs, whereas its tight turning circle, high gravitational center, and relative light weight made it popular in areas of unimproved roads. Automobiles were also appealing because they made farm work more manageable. Access to a quick means of collecting spare parts, for example, increased their appeal, whereas the increasing availability of trucks after World War I made marketing produce easier. Imaginative adaptations of internal combustion engines to carry out such tasks as sawing, washing, and even towing farm implements increased their appeal.

The automobile was appealing largely because it became a method of entertainment for rural families, allowing them to take part in community life outside the immediate neighborhood. It also facilitated the consolidation of churches and schools and gave farm children access to the high schools unavailable in many small rural communities. The price that rural communities paid for increased ownership was the gradual decline of small shops because families preferred the wider range of goods in larger towns. As driving for pleasure and recreation became more popular, it also began to replace attendance at church and other community activities. The major investment that the purchase and running of an automobile represented was also a significant strain on rural finances and limited farmers' ability to improve their farms or homes in other ways. Moreover, as Jellison notes, although the Model T would "revolutionize transportation during the next decade," for many farm families, it was not yet affordable in 1913. (1993, 13)

The take-up of modern technology was determined both by people's individual circumstances, as well as by economic patterns, settlement trends, and availability. Farm people in such states as Iowa, which had been settled earlier and had enjoyed affluence rather longer than, say, North Dakota, adopted a broader range of improvements for both farm and home. Supply systems also determined the adoption of new technology. Before 1915, competition between phone-line companies increased access to telephone lines, but as American Telephone and Telegraph's monopoly in urban districts grew and the company increased rural rates or marginalized rural markets, access dwindled. Nevertheless, there was no deterministic link between the availability of technology and its adoption. In the 1910s, the notion that technology dramatically altered most farm homes distorts the reality of the rate of take-up, even in the more affluent regions. The only items to be adopted by the majority of farm people were the automobile and, later, the radio. People in rural areas still bought cautiously, often spacing the purchase of major items out over several years, planning and managing their expenditure rather than rushing into buying on credit.

Farm Machinery

Despite the slow adoption of new machinery at the beginning of the 20th century, innovations and improvements were taking place that would, in the decades following, transform agriculture in the United States. Developments that resulted from agricultural modernization during the 1910s were mainly mechanical. Steam-powered combines and tractors were still in widespread use early in the century, and the combines were capable of harvesting up to 100 acres a day; however, they were widely regarded as ineffective and unsafe. It was evident that a more efficient source of power was required to tow and run the increasingly large machines. Steam engines dissipated enormous amounts of fuel and water to little effect, and the machines that they powered (e.g., tractors and combines) were heavy and, consequently, laborious to move and maneuver. As a result, even in 1910, some 24 million horses and mules, around three or four to an average farm, supplied almost all the power on farms.

Early gasoline-powered engines lacked sufficient power to tow a plow, but constant improvements meant that by 1910, manufacturers had increased their power and reduced their weight and the size of the frame that carried the engine. Economic production methods meant that by the start of the decade, around 30 manufacturers were producing around 2,000 tractors a year. Advances in the design and effectiveness of the gasoline-powered tractor during the decade led to their prompt adoption by farmers, and numbers increased from around 4,000 in 1910 to about 246,000 in 1920. As standardization of parts became more widespread during the decade, farmers who were unwilling to invest in machinery that required custom-made spare parts became more responsive to the relatively high capital investment required for their purchase. The high capital cost of tractors, however (at the end of the decade, an average of $785, outweighing the total for all other machinery), and shortages in supply during the war meant that they were used on fewer than 4 percent of farms by the end of the war. Because male laborers were in short supply, the war did mean that there were minor changes in who drove the tractor. Agricultural institutions prompted women to carry out field work, and a 1918 USDA article contended that women made better tractor drivers because driving involved "skill and close attention and ability to follow directions." (Neth, 1995, 234) The writer argued that a woman would presume that she knew nothing and would follow instructions; conversely, a man would assume he knew everything and would "monkey with the machinery" (Ibid.) and be careless.

Nevertheless, it was evident that the increased output that resulted from their use and secondary benefits (e.g., the release of millions of acres from the production of grain and forage to sustain horses and mules—land that could subsequently be used for the cultivation of food for people—and the replacement of a labor force that was in increasingly short supply) meant that most observers saw tractors, and gasoline-powered machinery more generally, as the key to efficient agriculture in the future.

Truck Farming, Migrant Labor, and Immigration

Throughout the United States during the late 19th century, migrant labor (men, women, and children who arrived at harvest time and left shortly after) became increasingly important. Two factors were instrumental in changing agriculture: first, farmers' growing reliance on mechanization; second, the rapid growth of urban populations who needed to be fed. These two factors compelled farmers to find new plants and to plant them in different ways, and to discover new supplies of labor.

Mechanization had unforeseen disadvantages, however. The absentee farm owners of "bonanza farms" in the West capitalized on developments in farm machinery and symbolized the expansion in agricultural production that would engulf world grain markets. Although mechanization greatly increased the size of some farms and also increased the yield per acre, the quantity that farmers could plant was always limited by the amount of labor available to propagate and harvest the crop. Because nature imposed an immutable schedule on agriculture, farmers needed very few workers for much of the time and very many more at harvest time, and on very large farms, it was impractical to borrow labor from neighbors. Harvesting crews therefore traveled northward from farm to farm, following the ripening wheat.

Although wheat production increased beyond all forecasts, wheat farmers did not experience any consequent growth in profits. Overoptimistic expectations by speculators, falling prices, and rising taxes were among the factors contributing to the disappearance of the large estates. The small, fragmented farms in the East that resulted from their break-up were unable to compete with produce from the West and, against the national trend, northeastern farm numbers and production declined. Although eastern growers were close to urban markets, they were unable to compete with the quantities and prices of western produce. Although some left their farms, those who remained managed to survive and even prosper by going over to dairy or truck farming, "the intensive production of vegetable and fruit crops for commercial markets." (Hahamovitch, 1997, 20)

In such northeastern states as Pennsylvania, New York, and New Jersey, market gardeners or truck farmers drastically increased the worth of each state's vegetable and fruit crop, supplying perishable goods to nearby urban markets where the increasing mass of people and their close proximity to each other made urban cultivation impossible. Truck farming increased the value of land devoted to intensive farming, but it also increased its productivity. The land was used extremely intensively; crops were planted successively, and soil enervation was counteracted by copious use of newly developed commercial fertilizers. Growing under glass and irrigation meant that production could continue year-round. Truck farming spread from the Northeast down the Atlantic coast to the South, where more affluent farmers who could afford the relatively high capital outlay could exploit rapid freight and refrigerated cars and export produce to the North, particularly in winter.

Migrant Labor and Immigration

Because of the high capital expenditure, relatively few farmers in the South could take advantage of truck farming, but it saved enterprising farmers in the Northeast, especially in New Jersey. In addition to leaving behind old ways and crops, truck farming also meant identifying new pools of labor because the system created its own labor problems. One such problem was that truck farms were unable to provide enough work throughout the year to prevent rural labor from migrating to cities. By the 1910s, farm families were no longer wholly self-sufficient and no longer depended on both family members and hired help to produce the raw constituents for such items as clothing or soap. The attractions of small industries that could provide laborers with work in winter and, later, urban manufactories that offered year-round employment and which were, in any case, close to northeastern producers gradually deprived the countryside of available labor.

The turn to truck farming exacerbated this migration because hired labor was only required at peak times. Growers were unable to compete with urban wages and mechanization only worsened the problem, reducing the labor requirement to the point at which the crop was harvested when machinery became irrelevant. It was possible in some areas to stagger the harvests, but not all soils could sustain a variety of crops, and as more and more producers switched to this way of farming, labor shortages became worse. A rural community at hand for short-term employment had been relinquished. Growers would have to attract a more distant labor pool if they were to prosper.

Sources that East Coast growers began to draw on included migrant workers, who sometimes worked in one area, whereas others traveled to a number of harvests. The Great Migration provided African Americans from the upper South, whereas urban Italian families worked in south Jersey. Because wages were lower than industry and the harvest season was shorter, agriculture proved less attractive to many migrant workers, and although immigrants from southern and eastern Europe often had agricultural backgrounds, they avoided agriculture for the same reasons. Italian immigrants, many of whom either returned to Italy once they had saved enough money or who harbored dreams of doing so, provided a more permanent source of labor once they settled in areas like New Jersey. Those who stayed did so because land values in Italy rose as more immigrants sent money home, thus increasing the amount required to buy land and prolonging their stay in America.

Married women and children who worked in such industries as garment manufacture and artificial flower making used those industries' slack periods to work on farms, thereby providing the families with more than subsistence wages. Women often left their husbands in the city to take up agricultural labor. The men who did work on farms were commonly seasonal or temporary laborers who lost little by leaving industrial work for some months. Although the irregularity of women's work, the often temporary nature of male employment and their vulnerability to lay-offs, and the emphasis on Italian children to be cared for by the family themselves made the Italian family well suited to the requirements of New Jersey's producers. The Dillingham Report observed that of that state's Italian population, only 5 percent were employed in agriculture.

Given New Jersey's racial history (it had one of the most uncompromising slave codes and had failed to ratify the Thirteenth, Fourteenth, and Fifteenth Amendments), it is ironic that more African American migrants chose the state than any other, perhaps because growers there were prepared to advance their fares. Although many returned south after the harvest, a great number remained, tripling New Jersey's African American population between 1870 and 1910. Nevertheless, 75 percent of the state's African American residents were urban by 1910. For the majority of Italians and African American laborers, agriculture was an expedient, a temporary solution to a financial problem.

For growers, however, migrant labor was a more permanent, albeit unreliable, answer to labor shortages. The circumstances involved identifying, hiring, and controlling often-large bodies of laborers whose outsider status changed the relationship growers had traditionally had with employees. Where earlier hired hands had received the majority of their wages in board and often ate with the family, migrant workers were lodged in frequently overcrowded and unsanitary barns or stables, paid by the day, and the arrangement ended as soon as their role was fulfilled. Because labor costs were often the only outlay over which growers had any control, some sought out the cheapest sources of available labor: the South and the urban tenements. Anxious to shave costs wherever they could, growers rarely reinvested any profits into building purpose-built accommodation, and although these conditions attracted the concern of reformers, they were more opposed to the use of child labor.

Child berry carriers on Newton's Farm in Cannon, Delaware, 1910. (Library of Congress)

Reformers focused their criticism on the system of "padroni," the labor organizers who mustered, shipped, and controlled Italian farm workers. Growers contended that they were unable to compete with industry for adult male labor, and that abolishing child labor would deprive them of adult women as they almost always came with their children. By the 1910s, the role of the padroni had changed from the earlier intermediaries who acted as agents for American companies, recruiting laborers in Italy and binding them by paying their passage and charging a recruitment fee. Twentieth-century padroni took over responsibility from growers for the supervision, accommodation, and payment of laborers, and because most growers could not speak Italian, they were also interpreters.

The system was not as exploitative as some reformers imagined; without the padroni, laborers would have had to find work, transportation, and housing for themselves, and most were prepared to relinquish a proportion of their wages for that service. The Dillingham Report observed that in many instances the system worked well as the padrone or his hireling knew the laborers, could communicate with them, could apply more discipline than the grower, and became a genuine go-between to defend laborers' interests. In other cases, however, they noted that the padrone was merely interested in collecting the commission. Problems associated with recruiting migrant labor did not become any less difficult during the decade; as migrants were constantly attracted by better opportunities, growers usually had to contend with a fresh batch of raw beginners each year. By 1910, expenditure on labor was 66 percent higher than it had been at the beginning of the century, with the difference frequently being swallowed up by the padroni. By 1914, up to 70 percent of producers in states like New Jersey hired laborers, and as long as they were Italian, growers relied on the padroni. Although growers called for the state to intervene and establish a padroni system of its own, their requests were largely unheeded. Nevertheless, reformers did succeed in establishing an expanded role for themselves as witnesses and surveyors of conditions for workers.

As Hahamovitch observes, "it was the experience of becoming employers, more than changes in methods, markets, and crops, that made a business of farming." (1997, 36) For migrant workers, it was frequently the only way of remaining solvent.

THE IMPACT OF CHANGES IN RURAL AMERICA IN THE 1910s

Many of the changes that occurred in these early years were outside of the farmers' control. Always resistant to change, American farmers by 1910 had nevertheless been forced to accept that modernization in the form of mechanization was already beginning to transform the rural landscape. Moreover, demographic changes (e.g., the reduction in the percentage of farmers in the labor force) had also begun to affect life in the countryside. Shortages of good land also increased the numbers of tenant farmers. Despite the more widespread use of agricultural machinery, its contribution in 1910 was minimal and many farmers still relied heavily on draft animals and primitive equipment. However, the widespread replacement of steam-powered engines by the internal combustion engine meant that the average value of agricultural machinery had increased significantly by 1920, whereas millions of acres of land, used earlier for growing feed for draft animals, could be released for producing foodstuffs for human consumption.

Farm women, however, had far fewer labor-saving appliances than did their middle-class urban counterparts. Any new technologies bought when budgets allowed were more likely to reduce physical effort in farm tasks than for consumption of leisure goods. In any case, rural electricity was still relatively rare in 1910, further reducing the potential for new appliances. As mains power became more widely available, farm people began to replace labor-intensive kerosene lamps. As more rural exchanges were connected, they began to buy telephones. The increasing availability of affordable automobiles meant that the remoteness of rural life had been diminished by the end of the decade. Many communities paid for such benefits as small shops began to decline in popularity, church attendance suffered, and community cohesion weakened as families began to drive for pleasure more and visit larger towns.

High produce prices, brought about by the rise in value, if not volume, of exports, and demand from the growing population led to rising farm income from 1910. Land scarcity led to average prices rising by 70 percent, and problems were aggravated by sluggish productivity, growing at barely 1 percent per year. Production of commodities for home use fell. Despite increased prosperity, there was relatively modest investment in improvements or modernization. By the beginning of World War I, farmers were prosperous and complacent, and falling prices as government subsidies were withdrawn and production resumed in Europe caught many by surprise. Prewar speculation caught up with farmers with substantial mortgages and loans, and as their land value depreciated, bankruptcies rose and many were forced to dispose of land and whole farms, frequently becoming tenants on farms they had once owned. Many of the newer banks established during the boom, frequently run by inexperienced owners and which had lent unwisely, failed during these years. Although the economic situation in the last years of the decade seemed grim, these years were a foretaste of a deepening depression in the 1920s.

As modernization and new attitudes began to transform agricultural labor and the communal basis of small farming began to diminish, women's roles and status also began to change. Urban professionals concerned with rural life and farm women's status and role reflected a more widespread interest in the countryside. Despite a perception that rural women should be less self-sufficient and should use ostensible increases in "leisure" time, there was little significant realignment in gender divisions of labor, however, and women continued to be central to survival strategies during periods of fluctuating income.

Although the rural church was still important in the life of the community, parishioners' commitment toward this institution had begun to weaken by 1910. Many small and isolated churches closed, appropriated by farmers anxious for more storage. The same professionals who had encouraged farm women to improve their status urged churches to modernize and clergymen to promote modernization in agriculture. Nevertheless, rural churches remained resistant to change as parishioners rejected what they saw as unnecessary interference.

The decade was characterized politically by the aftermath of Populism, increased links between agriculture and labor, and the growth of alternatives to the two mainstream parties (e.g., the Non-partisan League). Despite significant success in some largely rural states, a combination of factors put an end to the League. Some of its policies (e.g., the 1916 Warehouse Act) were belatedly adopted, but most were assumed sporadically and selectively.

The number and percentage of African American–operated farms increased during the decade, but despite this, African American aspirations for an increased

Historians' Debate: The Role of Women in Agricultural America

Until at least the 1970s, the majority of texts on American agricultural history (e.g., John L. Shover's *First Majority–Last Minority: The Transforming of Rural Life in America* and Steven Hahn and Jonathan Prude's *The Countryside in the Age of Capitalist Transformation*) overlook farm women entirely, or discuss them only tangentially. Farm women's experiences in agricultural communities in the 18th and 19th centuries have been examined more recently by a relatively small number of historians, but they have generally neglected any examination of the issue in the 20th century, leaving any such investigation to sociologists and anthropologists (e.g., Sonya Salomon, *Prairie Patrimony: Family, Farming, and Community in the Midwest*). This is in marked contrast to the urban historians who have documented the ways in which urban women's work was transformed by mechanization in the Progressive era.

Although, as Joan Jensen has observed, women have been "active participants in every stage of agricultural production and in every period of agricultural history" (in Jellison, 1993, ixx), compared with the role that men played, their role has been marginalized or misinterpreted. Even during their own lifetimes, their contributions frequently went unrecognized, and their absence has been further compounded "by historians' failure to examine the history of farm women's experience." (Ibid.) Historians like Katherine Jellison, *Entitled to Power: Farm Women and Technology, 1913–1963,* and Mary Neth, *Preserving the Family Farm: Women, Community and the Foundations of Agribusiness in the Midwest, 1900–1940,* have begun to compensate for histories in which, as Jellison describes, farm women were "invisible." This is not, Jellison argues, because of an absence of sources; rather, it has been the consequence of historians who have neglected to recognize the importance of farm women's experiences. In contrast to most historians, Jellison demonstrates the significance of farm families' adoption of technology for American social history.

share in the period's prosperity and more influence remained largely unattainable. The value of African American–owned and –operated farms increased, but they did so by rather less than white-owned businesses, and African American farmers remained within strictly confined territorial limits. Modernization promoted by a largely white establishment was of little interest to the African American farmer, although the Cooperative Extension Service had some degree of success with African American agents.

Industrial capitalism's development in a progressively centralized and incorporated market economy meant that many farmers were severely disadvantaged by their lack of individual negotiating power against the monopolies. Initiatives like economic cooperatives were established to strengthen farmers' ability to challenge prices set by effective cartels, whereas such government initiatives as the 1916 Farm Loan Act and the Rural Credit Act reduced interest rates and helped alleviate debt. The 1919 AFBF was less helpful to small farmers because professionals and large landowners with little empathy for smaller producers dominated the agency. Although many cooperatives consolidated, spreading out to achieve national coverage, cooperatives generally retained their relatively local and community-based focus.

The perpetual cycle of landlessness, debt, and impoverishment continued to dog African Americans trapped in the sharecropper system, a situation aggravated by the outbreak of World War I, when exports were temporarily halted, devastating the cotton industry. The effects of the boll weevil invasion, poor weather, and racially inspired violence and discrimination led to the Great Migration north in the period before, during, and after the war, and although the migration provided many sharecroppers with a means of escape, the system prevailed in the South for many years thereafter.

Although prosperity had touched the rural communities of America in the second decade, many farmers ended the decade significantly worse off than in 1910. They had only grudgingly begun to change their financial, social, and political conventions and organizations. Still rooted in habit, conservative, inefficient, self-reliant, and unorganized, farmers faced the next decade and an uncertain future in which adaptability, progressiveness, proficiency, interdependence, and organization were prized over the very individuality that had brought them to this point.

BIOGRAPHIES

David Franklin Houston, 1866–1940

Politician

David Houston was an academic, businessman, and politician, serving President Woodrow Wilson as U.S. secretary of agriculture from 1913 to 1920. Following a period as president of the Agricultural and Mechanical College of Texas, and as chancellor of Washington University in St. Louis from 1908 to 1913, Houston was appointed secretary of agriculture, during which period a record number of agricultural laws were passed by Congress. The Smith-Lever Act, the Farm Loan Act, the Warehouse Act, and the Federal Aid Road Act were significant among these.

Houston supervised the expansion of production of food for domestic and foreign consumption while also addressing problems of rural life. In the depressed climate following World War I, Houston was in office during Herbert Hoover's initiatives to provide Europe with food from American farmers. Just before his tenure as secretary of agriculture ended and later, in his role as U.S. secretary of the treasury, Houston had become concerned that America should avoid the inflation experienced by European allies. Predicting the fall in U.S. agricultural prices after the optimism of the end of hostilities subsided, he pressed for easier credit for farmers while simultaneously urging them to reduce production. The dramatic falls in prices were accompanied by virulent criticism of Houston's policies and the accusation that he had deliberately destroyed agricultural prosperity. Although the allies favored the cancellation of war debts, Houston, along with the U.S. Congress and President Wilson, restructured the short-term debts into long-term loans.

David Franklin Houston, secretary of agriculture (1913–1920). (Library of Congress)

Nellie Kedzie Jones, 1858–1956

Columnist and Lecturer

A nationally acknowledged home economics pioneer, Jones was an advocate for rural women homemakers, alerting them to the latest scientific research through her capacity as state leader of the University of Wisconsin home economics extension and in her "Country Gentlewoman" column for *The Country Gentleman*.

Born and raised on a farm, Jones followed an academic career, becoming Kansas State's first female professor in 1887, leading the new home economics department and lecturing to farmers' institutes on the importance of home economics until a change in policy led to the closure of the school faculty. Jones's subsequent moves culminated in various academic roles, after which she and her second husband settled on a farm in Wisconsin in 1911. Jones began writing a series of articles for *The Country Gentleman* in 1912, adopting the role of a fictional aunt, as well as writing practical and commonsense advice columns, which appealed to rural women all over the country.

In these columns, which continued until 1916, Jones wrote on the "country code," on neighborliness, on the importance of borrowing and lending, which she believed made the allocation of economic resources possible, and on home economics. Jones also wrote on the inequities of farm work, believing that men's and women's work should be separated because women too frequently worked in the field, whereas men seldom helped in the house. She refused to teach girls in agricultural college to milk, arguing that it was not women's work, and, to counter what she perceived as male dominance of a rural life that was becoming increasingly capital-intensive, advocated for more help and technology to assist farm women in the home. She also believed that women should buy clothing and household requisites so that their time was given monetary value.

Jones was appointed home economics extension leader at the University of Wisconsin in 1918 and traveled widely throughout the state, talking to groups of women and clubs and organizing homemakers' clubs. She was also an active member of the Women's Christian Temperance Union.

Arthur C. Townley, 1880–1959

Labor Organizer

Arthur Townley was an organizer for the American Socialist Party and is best known as creator and later leader of the Non-partisan League. Born in northwestern Minnesota in 1880, Townley first taught in a country school. He tired of the vocation after two years and tried farming in a marginal area of North Dakota. His organizational skills soon became apparent after he became impatient with the slow progress of working with horses, and he convinced farmers to cooperate in buying a tractor. After establishing a neighborhood syndicate, Townley backed out when the likelihood of a good harvest looked doubtful, leaving other members to prosper. After a year drifting around the Pacific Coast, he returned to North Dakota to farm in the Golden Valley, a region where returns were high. After two good seasons, his third year, 1912, was catastrophic. Despite a dry season, a poor harvest, and low prices, Townley blamed his failure on speculators and "grain gamblers," disowning any personal responsibility for the collapse.

This perspective became part of his "campaign of education" of the Non-partisan League. Price fluctuations, agricultural inefficiency, and variable weather were not the responsibility of the farmer for the circumstances in which farmers found themselves. This attitude and his failure as a farmer made him an ideal subject for conversion to socialism in North Dakota, a state where agricultural disaffection was intensified by contact with monopoly capitalism, semi-arid farming conditions, and widespread lack of awareness and inexperience of the need for diversified farming to compensate for the vagaries of farming.

There is some doubt about whether Townley was a member, and his early success as an organizer for the party was brought to a premature end when the 1915 socialist convention recommended the termination of the organization department. Townley was encouraged to establish a nonpartisan organization, the Non-partisan League, by an associate, A. E. Bowen, and the party was founded in February 1915. The unconventional strategies employed in the League's organization represented a mixture of socialism and aggressive salesmanship. Dominated by a committee chaired by Townley, whose tenure was assured by a policy that excluded the election of successors, the party was initially highly successful in recruiting disaffected farmers in North Dakota.

Townley was adept at galvanizing agricultural support by warning farmers of the consequences of the failure of the League to win at the ballot box. Opposition in several quarters encouraged him to take the campaign for electoral success directly to farmers and to advocate closer links between agriculture and labor. His attitude toward America's involvement in World War I, however, prompted accusations against the League of pro-Germanism and disloyalty. During the six years of League successes, Townley acquired something of a national reputation and was extensively denounced as a dangerous "leftist" radical. The collapse of the League brought Townley down in its wake, although he had forfeited effective control some months earlier. He was subsequently imprisoned in 1921 on rather questionable charges of sedition and disloyalty. He resigned as leader of the League following his release.

Henry (Harry) Cantwell Wallace, 1866–1924

Politician and Editor

Editor of *Wallace's Farmer* from 1916 to 1921, Wallace was also U.S. secretary of agriculture from 1921 to 1924. He graduated from Iowa State College (now Iowa State University) and was subsequently professor of dairy science there. He farmed close to Orient, Iowa, where his son, Henry Agard Wallace, was born. Harry Wallace dealt with the majority of the daily aspects of *Wallace's Farmer,* assuming the editor's role after the death of Henry Wallace, the founder of the journal established to promote scientific agriculture and to safeguard the farmer's role in the national economy. Harry Wallace helped to establish 4-H, the youth program created to provide applied, hands-on agricultural education for young people, Extension programs in Iowa, as well as assisting in the creation of the Iowa Farm Bureau.

Henry C. Wallace was one of the most successful secretaries of agriculture in American history. Wallace served during the Harding and Coolidge administrations. (Library of Congress)

Henry Agard Wallace, 1888–1965

Politician and Geneticist

Son of Henry Cantwell Wallace and geneticist, economist, editor, businessman, and, later, U.S. secretary of agriculture, Henry, Jr., graduated from Iowa State College in 1910, and from that same year until 1924, he worked on the editorial staff of *Wallace's Farmer*. During this period, he undertook tests on corn that provided high yields and wrote widely on aspects of agriculture. The first corn-hog charts devised by Wallace in 1915 specified the probable course of markets. Wallace's scientific, political, and social views were molded by his religious beliefs. Raised a Presbyterian, the right-wing columnist Westbrook Pegler called him a "spiritual window shopper" (www.cooperativeindividualism. org/schlesinger _wallace_bio.html), and he subsequently investigated Catholicism, Judaism, Buddhism, Islam, Zoroastrianism, and Christian Science, settling eventually on Episcopalianism. Wallace inherited a fervor for the modernization of agriculture, as well as a talent for genetics, agricultural research, and statistics. He specialized in hybrid corns and the econometric analysis of farm prices, but his scientific views were always underpinned by strong religious and even mystical beliefs. These beliefs are exhibited in a letter he wrote to a friend: "Fundamentally, I am neither a corn breeder or an editor but a searcher for methods of bringing the 'inner light to outward manifestation.'" (Ibid.)

James Wilson, 1835–1920

Politician

James F. Wilson was U.S. secretary of agriculture from 1887 to 1913. Born into a Scottish farming family in 1835, Wilson's family emigrated to the United States in 1852, eventually settling in Iowa. Wilson became professor of agriculture at what is now Iowa State University and became nationally known when President William McKinley appointed him secretary of agriculture. The longest-serving American cabinet official, Wilson's tenure coincided with a period of modernization of agricultural practices. Wilson also sponsored legislation that would increase the agricultural export trade while simultaneously acknowledging the necessity of a strong organization that would unify rural interests. He was responsible for organizing improved food inspection procedures, as well as for the development of roads across the country. Under his supervision, the Department expanded its activities, establishing experimental stations throughout the United States, initiated farm demonstration work in the South, began cooperative extension work in agriculture and home economics, and sent expert representatives all over the world to accumulate data for the promotion of agriculture. Legislation relating to plant and animal diseases, insect pests, forestry, irrigation, conservation, road building, and agricultural education was also sanctioned. Presidents Roosevelt and Taft retained Wilson as secretary; however, following

Woodrow Wilson's electoral success in 1913, James Wilson retired at age 78 to contribute toward several noteworthy movements directed at spreading agricultural knowledge. Along with Henry Wallace, Wilson was appointed to examine agricultural conditions in Great Britain. He died in 1920.

REFERENCES AND FURTHER READINGS

Benedict, Murray R. 1953. *Farm Policies of the United States: 1790–1950: A Study of Their Origins and Development*. New York: Twentieth Century Fund.

Cochrane, Willard W. 1979. *The Development of American Agriculture: A Historical Analysis*. Minneapolis: University of Minnesota Press.

Cochrane, Willard W. 1958. *Farm Prices: Myth and Reality*. Minneapolis: University of Minnesota Press.

Danbom, David B. 1995. *Born in the Country: A History of Rural America*. Baltimore: Johns Hopkins University Press.

Danbom, David B. 1979. *The Resisted Revolution: Urban America and the Industrialization of Agriculture, 1900–1930*. Ames: Iowa State University Press.

Grigg, David. 1995. *The Transformation of Agriculture in the West*. Oxford: Basil Blackwell.

Growing a Nation. "Growing a Nation: The Story of American Agriculture." www.agclassroom.org/textversion/gan/timeline/1910.htm.

Hahamovitch, Cindy. 1997. *The Fruits of Their Labor: Atlantic Coast Farm Workers and the Making of Migrant Poverty, 1870–1945*. Chapel Hill: University of North Carolina Press.

Hacker, Louis M., and Helene S. Zahler. 1952. *The United States in the 20th Century*. New York: Appleton-Century-Crofts.

Hahn, Steven, and Jonathan Prude, eds. 1985. *The Countryside in the Age of Capitalist Transformation*. Chapel Hill: University of North Carolina Press.

Hicks, John D. 1961. *The Populist Revolt: A History of the Farmer's Alliance and the People's Party*. Lincoln: University of Nebraska Press.

Jellison, Katherine. 1993. *Entitled to Power: Farm Women and Technology, 1913–1963*. Chapel Hill: University of North Carolina Press.

Lenin, V. I. "New Data on the Laws Governing the Development of Capitalism in Agriculture. Part One: Capitalism and Agriculture in the United States of America—7. Machinery and Hired Labour in Agriculture." www.marxists.org/archive/lenin/works/1915/newdev/7.htm.

Marble, Manning. 1979. "The Land Question in Historical Perspective: The Economics of Poverty in the Blackbelt South, 1865–1920." In Leo McGee and

Robert Boone, eds. *The Black Rural Landowner—Endangered Species: Social, Political and Economic Implications*. Westport: Greenwood Press.

Miller, Robert Worth. 1995. "Farmers and Third Party Politics in Late Nineteenth Century America." In Charles W. Calhoun, ed. *The Gilded Age: Essays on the Origins of Modern America*. Wilmington: Scholarly Resources.

Miller, Robert Worth. "Populism." history.missouristate.edu/wrmiller/Populism/Texts/populism.htm.

Neth, Mary. 1995. *Preserving the Family Farm: Women, Community and the Foundations of Agribusiness in the Midwest, 1900–1940*. Baltimore: Johns Hopkins University Press.

Nye, Russel B. 1959. *Midwestern Progressive Politics: A Historical Study of Its Origins and Development, 1870–1958*. East Lansing: Michigan State University Press.

Saloutos, Theodore, and John D. Hicks. 1931. *Twentieth Century Populism: Agricultural Discontent in the Middle West, 1900–1939*. Lincoln: University of Nebraska Press.

Schlesinger, Arthur Jr. "Who Was Henry A. Wallace? The Story of a Perplexing and Indomitably Naïve Public Servant." Reprinted from the *Los Angeles Times*, 12 March 2000. www.cooperativeindividualism.org/schlesinger_wallace_bio.html.

Shover, John, L. 1976. *First Majority—Last Minority: The Transforming of Rural Life in America*. DeKalb: Northern Illinois University Press.

Taylor, Brian. "The Century of Inflation." www.globalfinancialdata.com/articles/Century_of_Inflation.doc.

U.S. Census Bureau. "Urban and Rural Population: 1900 to 1990." www.census.gov/population/censusdata/urpop0090.txt.

U.S. Department of Agriculture, 1997 Census of Agriculture, vol. 1, pt 51.

U.S. Department of Agriculture. "Data Sets: Farm Income." www.ers.usda.gov/data/farmincome/finfidmu.htm.

Whayne, Jeannie. 2003. "I Have Been Through Fire: Black Agricultural Extension Agents and the Politics of Negotiation." In R. Douglas Hurt, ed., *African American Life in the Rural South, 1900–1950*. Columbia: University of Missouri Press.

Leisure, Popular Culture, and Metropolitanization

OVERVIEW

America's apparently limitless capacity for enjoyment, the inventiveness associated with leisure activities, and the ways in which business found new ways of parting consumers from their money did not begin in the 1910s. However, the growth of an urban, industrialized society and the changes that were forced on Americans did mean that people in the city and the country found new ways to distract themselves from work and their living conditions.

Popular culture emerged as part of the urbanization and industrialization of America. Vaudeville, the follies, and burlesque were still popular, but the lure of the movies—now irrevocably associated with Hollywood—transformed people's experience of this extraordinarily popular art. People started to see their favorite stars in nickelodeons in the early years of the decade, and by the close of the decade, lavish movie palaces had begun to emerge, and increasingly they displaced those earlier attractions. The emergence of independent working women was a significant factor in the growing popularity of dance halls. The halls, and the culture that surrounded them, offered opportunities for social and sexual experimentation and a liberating space where young people could step outside familial and social boundaries.

Americans in the 1910s were at the juncture between an economy based on production and one centered on consumption and leisure in which such traditional values as the desire for emancipation from life's privations and the lure of entertaining distractions combined with 20th-century technology. Commodities proliferated and a mass market, one expanded by increased leisure time and disposable income, developed to consume them. The decade was characterized by attempts to cultivate that market. Technology, and its increasing application to leisure activities from amusement rides to movies, was explicitly designed to expand the audience for those commodities and entertainments.

TIMELINE

1910   The height of the nickelodeon's popularity.

The operas *Pagliacci* (Ruggero Leoncavallo) and Pietro Mascagni's *Cavalleria Rusticana,* as well as parts of Puccini's *Tosca,* broadcast live for the first time from the Metropolitan Opera House, New York.

With the Kinetophone, Edison attempts to create motion picture talkies.

Hallmark Cards is founded.

1911   Following a change of name from Follies of the Day, the vaudeville revue the Ziegfeld Follies becomes the most famous of the era.

Photoplay and *Motion Picture Story Magazine,* effectively the first motion picture fan magazines, first published.

The animated film *Little Nemo in Slumberland* by animator Winsor McKay appears.

Irving Berlin's *Alexander's Ragtime Band* first published. Sheet music sales top 1 million copies.

1912   Motion pictures, previously registered as photographs, added to classes of copyright-protected works.

Billboard magazine publishes its first list of most popular songs.

Universal Pictures founded.

1913   The first crossword puzzle, created by Arthur Wynne, published in the *New York World*.

The Palace Theater opens at 1564 Broadway, New York. Built by theater owner Martin Beck and operated by the Keith Circuit, the theater describes itself as the "Valhalla of Vaudeville."

1914	The first transcontinental telephone line finished.
	The American Society of Composers, Authors and Publishers (ASCAP) established.
	The Perils of Pauline establishes Pearl White as a star.
	Charlie Chaplin creates one of the movies' most enduring characters, the little tramp.
1915	D. W. Griffith's *Birth of a Nation* released to critical acclaim and, because of its racist premise, great controversy.
	Van Wyck Brooks publishes *America Comes of Age,* which includes the influential essay "Highbrow and Lowbrow."
	National Board of Review replaces the National Board of Censorship for films.
	The Sea Beach Line to Coney Island upgraded to a subway, followed in 1919 by the building of the New West End terminal, heralding the resort's busiest era.
1916	Norman Rockwell draws his first cover for the *Saturday Evening Post.*
1917	Trench Pen puts pellets of ink into fountain pens to aid writing by soldiers.
1919	*Zorro* appears as a character in Johnston McCulley's serialization *The Curse of Capistrano.*
	First wax recordings appear.
	First tabloid newspapers published in New York City.
	New York's Capitol Theater opens. It was then the largest movie theater in the world with seats for 5,300.
	Mary Pickford, Charlie Chaplin, Douglas Fairbanks, and D. W. Griffith found United Artists.
	Short-wave radio invented.
	RCA, the Radio Corporation of America, founded.

THE ORIGINS OF POPULAR CULTURE

New patterns of leisure emerged as the social and cultural changes that had begun late in the 19th century began to filter down to the middle and working classes. These were enabled in part by reductions in the working week and, as wage levels increased, a rise in disposable income. America began to kick off the claustrophobic constraints of late Victorian morality to an extent that it was difficult to retrieve any sense of the previous era. The flux and upheaval of early 20th-century America was of such concern to the self-appointed moral reformers that they felt duty bound to impose their moral and cultural authority on the emergent masses and, as Kasson (1978, 4) observes, "to inculcate the Victorian values of 'character'—moral integrity, self-control, sober earnestness, industriousness."

By the second decade of the century, enough people had enough discretionary income to want to alleviate the rigors of working lives, poor conditions, and overcrowded accommodation in an increasingly urbanized America. Popular culture (e.g., movies, theaters, amusement parks, and dance halls) provided distractions from life's obligations.

Although the beginnings of mass or popular culture are difficult to date precisely, it did not exist at all until the 19th century because popular culture is dependent on a modern working class to support it and to carry out a decisive role in its creation; however, there are many dissenting views regarding its origins. These vary from 18th-century England, when affordable treatises became widely available, to late-19th-century France, when methods of mass communication emerged. Other writers, such as C. Wright Mills (in Kammen, 1999, 164), believe that the 19th-century public was transformed into a modern mass audience. Still more critics (e.g., Richard Slotkin and Neil Harris in Kammen, 1999, 165) date the appearance of mass culture from the beginning of the 20th century because of "pulp publishing, vaudeville, silent film, pop music, and spectator sports." Film historians might argue that D. W. Griffith's 1915 *Birth of a Nation* gave rise to mass culture because it appealed to a broad audience that transcended class distinctions. Whatever its origins, however, most discussions fail to discriminate between mass and popular culture. The two terms merely become conflated.

To a significant extent, *popular culture* is determined and augmented by mass production. Lawrence Levine defines it as "the folklore of industrial society" (in Cullen, 1996, 21), with industrial society being an umbrella term for those changes (e.g., the migration of populations to urban areas and the exponential growth of technological change) that occurred in the West from the 18th century. All of these are pivotal in the establishment and growth of popular culture.

Although urbanization has been a precondition for popular culture, popular culture is not purely urban culture because it is informed by rural inward migration, and, as it develops, it migrates outward again, initiating the process again. Nevertheless, cities do provide a shared environment for often diverse groups and are where population mass and capital allows for the establishment of comparatively complex institutions to generate and disseminate cultural materials. Popular culture is also informed and enhanced by immigration. As this process increased in the late 19th and early 20th centuries, immigrant cultures supplemented indigenous forms, becoming diluted as they did so and, in some cases, leading to entirely new popular pastimes.

Patrons stroll along the boardwalk in Luna Park at Coney Island. Mechanical rides,
sideshows, and amusements line the walkway. (Library of Congress)

For various reasons, the period when American popular culture was at its height seems to have been between 1885 and around 1935. For example, attendances at Coney Island in 1909, adjusted for population, surpassed the combined 1989 attendance at Disneyworld in Orlando and Disneyland in Anaheim. (Cullen, 1996, 130) This is the era when a significant increase in leisure time took place. In addition, the commercialization of organized activities to entertain the working and lower middle classes reached an unprecedented level. Improved transportation and technological innovations also enabled these commercial activities to reach these audiences. The gradual relaxation of social conventions allowed forms of behavior and interchange that would have been unconscionable in polite mid-19th-century society. Finally, this was possibly the last era when popular cultural activities were still mainly participatory and active, rather than the largely passive culture that emerged after World War II.

That era was one in which an almost dizzying variety of types of entertainment became accessible to the middle and working classes. These new diversions were cheaper, more entertaining, and more appropriate to their experience and education than the more elitist activities that appeared exclusive and unwelcoming. It is also an era when many impresarios, businessmen, and promoters realized that they could make more money by providing affordable entertainments for this huge demographic than by catering to a relatively small elite.

At first, many of these activities (e.g., circuses and fairs) traveled from place to place. As the railroads became more widespread, these entertainments could reach a larger number of communities more rapidly. Although circuses remained a temporary diversion in most people's lives, more permanent attractions (e.g., amusement parks, movie theaters, burlesques, dance halls, theaters, and vaudeville) began to replace minstrel shows and Wild West shows.

Technology

Technological innovation, which after the mid-19th century meant the rapid growth of mechanical reproduction of text and image, moving images, and such developments as electricity and mechanization, also played a decisive role in the formation of popular culture. Although it is evident that technological developments were significant in disseminating popular cultural activities, it is equally apparent that there is no causal link between those innovations—on which the activities depended—and their widespread use. Thomas Alva Edison was doubtful about the commercial potential of his "zoetropic device," so it was left to his competitors to exploit the financial potential of the movie camera. Decades passed before the phonograph was in widespread use, whereas wireless telegraphy (i.e., radio) was initially thought to be more applicable to shipping and warfare than to mass broadcasting. This unpredictability of cause and effect characterized the period, but all of these examples, and more, were ultimately exploited for commercial gain.

Most inventors and entrepreneurs paradoxically were certain that it was what is now known as "hardware" that would make their fortunes, whereas most innovations only became commercially successful when "software" was developed. Although manufacturers attempted to profit from the sale of cameras, the industry only became profitable when an audience for films was established. The technology was mainly developed by those more privileged and educated innovators who were able to exploit sources of capital and equipment. Their enduring success, however, depended on their accessibility and affordability to working- and middle-class buyers and audiences. The medium on which the equipment depended (e.g., films or records) also had to be sufficiently appealing to bring about relatively small returns that would reap much greater rewards when applied to potentially huge audiences. Although the equipment tended to emerge from a privileged elite, its viability and success depended on talented working-class individuals who created much of the most popular software.

Popular culture, then, emerged for a number of reasons: social, technological, cultural, and economic. All of these are interdependent and it is impossible to single out any one as being more significant. By the second decade, most innovations and social changes had already brought about major shifts in people's leisure habits, and many of the changes that occurred between then and the end of possibly the most flamboyant and productive period in the history of American popular culture, around 1935, happened as a result of their further refinement.

POPULAR AMUSEMENTS

Time and Money for Entertainment

As new patterns of leisure arose in the 1910s, facilitated, in part, by increases in free time and discretionary income for the working and lower middle classes and, in part, by social and cultural developments that began to work down from above, American workers and their families emerged from their overcrowded tenements, enthusiastically shook off the restraints of the previous century, and began to take advantage of new forms of popular amusements. In print, syndicated comic strips quickly caught the public's imagination, and, as technology developed, many were adapted into animated films.

Staged entertainments like vaudeville and burlesque were still popular—particularly after vaudeville was made respectable for a family audience—and were supplemented in the larger cities by the follies. As the decade wore on, however, and expenditure on leisure more than doubled, motion pictures replaced vaudeville as the primary entertainment medium for the masses. Although big-time vaudeville still drew crowds throughout the decade (and would continue to do so as long as movies remained silent) and provided stars for the nascent motion picture industry, smaller venues were increasingly under threat from the lower priced nickelodeons. By the end of the decade, vaudeville's audiences and performers were eroded by motion pictures.

Vaudeville

Vaudeville, a form of entertainment characterized by the variety of acts that took part, was most popular between around 1880 and 1920. The form developed from 19th-century stage sources (e.g., stage plays, comedy, variety shows, freak shows, minstrelsy, and burlesque), and although all of these, and more, coalesced into vaudeville after around 1880, the show remained as a succession of discrete, unconnected acts, each showcasing a different kind of entertainment. Its popularity in the 20th century stemmed largely from its migration from the saloons, with their disreputable reputation, to vaudeville theaters and the consequent opening up of the form to a more general audience and, particularly, to women.

Family of vaudeville performers, Grand Rapids, Michigan, 1917. The youngest child performer is only 21 months old. Photo by Lewis Hine. (Library of Congress)

The "cleansing" of the old variety theaters and concert saloons and the early success of vaudeville can be attributed to Tony Pastor, who, after 1881, did much to improve vaudeville's reputation. There were other later impresarios (e.g., B. F. Keith and Edward Albee) who had started in the circus and who popularized vaudeville still further. They accomplished this by assembling a chain of theaters in the Northeast, manipulating audience behavior through ticket pricing and strict regulations, and lending the form an air of splendor and extravagance through their strategy of providing luxurious theaters and helpful staff. Performers were also warned that if they broke the strict rules regarding impropriety or the use of bad language, they faced banishment from the rest of that week's features. Despite this, performers habitually disregarded such warnings, often to the joy of the very audiences that demanded such strictures in the first place. Further refinements (and hence, respectability) came when the theaters were opened from morning to night. Consecutive performances thus enabled them to become acceptable and proper distractions for families and women on shopping expeditions.

These policies and others (e.g., transforming the content of shows into a highly regimented lineup that included singers, dancers, lampoons, and animal and magic acts) made vaudeville legitimate and respectable. By the 1910s, Keith and Albee and their successors had made vaudeville a family-orientated, escapist entertainment medium. Other vaudeville circuits grew rapidly following the success of the Keith and Albee enterprise, which, in addition to reducing competition from smaller enterprises, reconciled complex touring circuits and ensured the domination of the medium by a few large, corporate organizations. The widening of vaudeville's appeal and the development of circuits were the two most important factors in the growth of the industry. In an era characterized by the consolidation of industry, chains of affiliated vaudeville theaters ensured the medium's economic strength. The consolidation of vaudeville meant that groups were no longer tied to the chaotic system of booking artists into individual theaters. Instead, acts were tied into contracts on a regional and national basis for periods that could be as long as two years. As the circuits became more rigidly structured into a hierarchy of "small, medium, and big time," the most popular performers inevitably gravitated toward the top end of the industry.

Perhaps the most successful of the big time venues, and arguably the most famous, was the Palace Theater at 1564 Broadway in New York City. The Palace was built in 1913 by Martin Beck and operated by Keith. Complex negotiations over stock, complicated by a monopoly that meant that performers on that part of Broadway could only be booked through Oscar Hammerstein, contributed to a slow start for the theater. The appearance of the French actress Sarah Bernhardt, however, guaranteed the success of the theater, and it became the most sought after venue for performers.

Although a growing proportion of the audience came from the middle classes, vaudeville's roots were firmly working class, and, as vaudeville's popularity during the decade increased in cities swelled by immigrants, working-class patrons eager to make the most of their leisure time provided the theaters with a ready-made audience. One of the few surveys of the period, completed in 1911 (in Cullen, 1996, 133), concluded that 60 percent were working class, whereas another 36 percent were "clerical." Although the scope of the survey was relatively narrow, it is evident that working-class families constituted a significant proportion of the audience, particularly in the smaller theaters in residential neighborhoods. Moreover, almost all vaudeville performers came from the same background. Many, like Sophie Tucker, who was the daughter of Jewish immigrants and spent a large part of her career in mainly working-class Yiddish theater, retained their allegiances to their communities.

Along with class, ethnicity was an important factor in the growth of vaudeville. Vaudeville provided the rapidly growing number of immigrants with a venue where communities could gather for entertainment and, importantly, social cohesion. Race was also central in some districts. Although African American

The Follies

Follies were musical and comedy reviews that were highly popular on Broadway during the first two decades of the century. Although there were several revues in New York between the early 1900s and the late 1920s, the Ziegfeld Follies seem to have embodied the spirit of Broadway more than any other and became the most expensive productions there. Above all, Florenz Ziegfeld was a supreme self-publicist, and like most aspects of his life, the birth of the Follies is surrounded by some hard facts and much rumor and publicity. It is clear that Ziegfeld based his shows on the Parisian *Folies Bergère.* Anglicizing its name to *Follies of the Day,* Ziegfeld nevertheless continued the French pretension by using the French term *revue,* and the show opened in 1907 in the roof garden of the New York Theater, renamed "Jardin de Paris."

From then until its demise in 1931, Ziegfeld provided audiences with a seductive mix of spectacular visuals, comedy routines, and beautiful chorus girls. Throughout the life of the revue, Ziegfeld presented a succession of performers who made their name there, often capitalizing on their Follies success in later productions and films. Sophie Tucker made a brief appearance in the 1909 Atlantic City tryout. In the Follies of 1910, Ziegfeld used Bert Williams, the first African American performer to star on Broadway with a white cast, and Sophie Brice, both of whom became key figures in the reviews. Later stars included W. C. Fields and Eddie Cantor and the songwriter Irving Berlin. From 1911, the annual revues became known as the Ziegfeld Follies and in 1913 moved to the 42nd Street New Amsterdam Theater, where it would remain for most future performances. Drained of most of its audience by the stock market crash and the Depression, the Follies struggled to keep its doors open, finally closing in 1931.

acts were popular, the widespread practice of one African American act per show restricted opportunities. Even after the decline of minstrel shows, many white *and* African American performers—Bert Williams, Eddie Cantor, and Sophie Tucker among them—continued the tradition of blackface. African American influences found their way into other ethnic cultures, too; Al Jolson and Sophie Tucker were among many performers who brought Yiddish and African American components into their acts. African American audiences, as well as Yiddish speakers and immigrants from all over Europe, had their own smaller circuits.

Vaudeville donated one more innovation to the modern era. After around 1900, managers constantly searching for new moneymaking features introduced a "chaser" (an act that would indicate the close of the show) to the main program. This usually involved moving images of, for example, horse races or parades projected onto a screen. Although only a curiosity at the time, these "movies" were soon to become one of the most significant forms of popular culture. The opening of the Palace Theater in 1913 coincided with the beginning of the decline of vaudeville. The increasing popularity of lower-priced cinema in the 1910s dealt a fatal blow (from which it never recovered) to small-time vaudeville when it's predominantly working-class audience was drained off by nickelodeons. Big time vaudeville, however, still attracted an audience through its emphasis on color, spectacle, sound, splendor, and top-quality live entertainment through to the 1920s. Vaudeville remained popular as long as films remained silent—and studios with massive investments in silent films were reluctant to invest still more in the technology that sound recording entailed—because it could provide something that films could not. Vaudeville suffered a double blow, however. As its audience was eroded by films, so, too, were its performers, who now had an alternate opening for their talents.

Burlesque

American burlesque's roots lie in the mid-19th century. It developed alongside vaudeville, but on separate and competing circuits. Early burlesque featured comic sketches, parodies of middle- and upper-class mores and high cultural values, and dance routines. More often, however, the common perception of burlesque is encapsulated by A. J. Goldstein: "Stop 10 people on the street and ask what's their idea of burlesque and if only one of them says anything but striptease, I'll forfeit a month's salary." (Allen, 1991, 241)

In marked contrast to its later development, burlesque was originally dominated by women. The performers as well as the writers and producers adopted the attitude of one of burlesque's early stars, the Englishwoman Lydia Thompson, who toured America in 1869. Toward the end of the century, however, as America became more professionalized and the classes became more stratified, burlesque was taken over by male impresarios, theater owners, and agents. What had once been an art form characterized by wit and the undermining of conventions about how women were expected to exhibit their bodies became debased into a progressively unsavory means of exploiting women in an often mute and eroticized parody of "bump and grind" dancing, beginning with the 1890s "cooch" dance and the striptease of the early 20th century for an almost exclusively male audience.

Allen demonstrates that burlesque's assimilation of the ways in which the female body had been displayed in other entertainment forms (theater, photography, and early cinema) and its influences from dime museums, concert saloons, minstrel shows, and circuses defined it as "low." Nevertheless, in its early manifestation, women at least had the chance—and the power—to challenge and subvert society's expectations about women's roles. By the early 20th century, however, burlesque had become institutionalized, another wing of American show business controlled by a relatively small number of operators employing several thousand personnel. As the form became more disreputable, its original audience deserted it for the more genteel attractions of vaudeville and later early cinema. Alcohol was often sold, either in burlesques themselves or in saloons nearby. In contrast to the relatively sophisticated wit of early burlesque, often-crude comics provided the comedy, frequently using the women performers as the butt of their jokes.

Burlesque also contrasted markedly with what Allen terms "the acceptable face of feminine sexual spectacle," the Ziegfeld Follies. (Allen, 1991, 245) As part of America's newly assumed mantle of spectacular bourgeois consumption (the culture of the show, the department store, and "showing off"), the managed sexuality and elegant costumes of Ziegfeld's *show*girls are perfectly in tune with the bourgeois consumer culture of the early 20th century. Ziegfeld packaged staged eroticism in a way that avoided public opprobrium and censorship partly because he managed to make audiences think of the cultivated cultural sophistication of Paris rather than the low sexuality of burlesque. Even though Ziegfeld's costumes became progressively briefer, there was seldom anything other than the wholesome sexual appeal of the girl next door.

The Decline of Burlesque

As burlesque began to lose both audiences and performers to movies and revues, the venues struggled to maintain their core working- and lower-middle-class male audience. Because the industry was dominated by a few tightly controlled organizations and franchises, there was little incentive for innovation and new producers rarely penetrated the walls. By the middle of the 1910s, however, some resourceful producers developed "stock" burlesque, a cost-cutting innovation that effectively reduced burlesque to its essentials and increased its suggestive and ribald nature beyond the level that the organizations were prepared to go. To diminish the risk of prosecution, a warning system at the box office was installed so that stage managers could revert to the clean version should any potential trouble arise. In any case, even if the show was closed down, the financial loss was minimal.

As vaudeville became progressively more consolidated in the 1890s, and entrepreneurs realized the advantages of organization into circuits that would streamline touring schedules and tie performers into longer-term exclusive contracts, effectively limiting competition by parceling out the country into protected territories, burlesque owners followed much the same route, although not nearly so successfully. Some became known for more risqué shows that often pushed the limits of what the authorities were prepared to tolerate, whereas others promoted shows as "clean," but rapidly adopted the strategies and style of its competitors when the more sanitized versions proved financially unsuccessful.

Burlesque's popularity peaked during the 1910s and then swiftly declined. By 1912, around 70 touring burlesques could employ as many as 5,000 personnel and fill around 100 theaters across the country, although with the exception of San Francisco, it was mainly centered around the East Coast and the Midwest.

Seven young women of the burlesque theater, ca. 1916. (Library of Congress)

Moral and religious concerns meant that burlesque was never popular in the South. It was effectively a big city phenomenon, and in terms of luxury and opulence, a few theaters could compete with the best of vaudeville, most notably the 47th and Broadway Columbia Theater. Most, though, were not in the same league, their owners correctly assuming that a typical burlesque audience was less interested in this aspect than they were in what was on offer.

A typical burlesque audience could comprise largely white, working- and lower-middle class males, groups of family men on a night out without their wives, and rural out-of-towners in search of excitement entirely unavailable in small-town America. Because all the troupes were highly managed and regularized, patrons could expect dependable variations on the same theme: crude comics, variety performers, and—the main attraction—(mostly) young women prepared to reveal at least some of themselves. Unlike earlier burlesque, by the 20th century, burlesque theaters seldom showed any other form of entertainment, which, although it made economic sense, further ghettoized the medium, isolating it from the largely middle-class respectable mainstream of American theater.

Stock burlesque proved to be a process of diminishing returns as the more salacious the shows became, the more the comedy acts and variety turns became subsumed into what the producers believed the patrons really wanted—

striptease. Although some persevered with "clean" burlesque, others attempted to satisfy the demand for more ribald shows. Declining returns then encouraged the owners to experiment with "hotter" shows, but this strategy failed to stem the drain of patrons to other attractions. Burlesque was effectively over after the demise of all the major circuits by the late 1920s and early 1930s.

The 1919 Actors Strike

Before the foundation of the Actors' Equity Association (A.E.A. or Equity) in 1913, the iron grip of the producing managers and the consolidation of the industry into rigidly controlled circuits meant that, apart from a few big names, performers were routinely abused, forced to rehearse without pay and pay for their costumes and travel, and frequently suffered abysmal working conditions. An early attempt at organization—the 1896 Actors' Society of America (A.S.A.)—was more a club than a union, and it had little success at negotiation. Following its disbanding in 1912, four A.S.A. members established the A.E.A. under the presidency of Francis Wilson. Concerns over the erosion of audiences anxious about the war and the continuing intransigence of producing managers led the A.E.A to conclude that affiliation with organized labor was the only solution. To avoid conflict between unions, however, the American Federation of Labor (AFL) would only grant one charter to any profession, and in entertainment, the vaudeville performers union, the White Rats Actors' Union of America, held that charter.

Following the formation of the Producing Managers' Association (P.M.A.) and its refusal to recognize Equity, the union's contract with producers expired. Equity demanded recognition from management, improved rehearsal pay, a maximum of eight performances per week, and holiday and Sunday pay. These demands were vigorously resisted by the producers. As tensions grew, the White Rats agreed to surrender their charter in July 1919, permitting the AFL to establish the Associated Actors and Artistes of America (AAAA). All professional performer unions were affiliated with organized labor through the AAAA, and among its first acts was the granting of the charter to the A.E.A. By August 7, a resolution was ratified that unless the P.M.A. recognized the A.E.A. and adopted the contract, no member would work for any P.M.A. manager. That evening, the casts of 12 shows refused to perform. This radical action, however, was unpopular with those performers who felt that individual ambition (the driving force behind show business careers) was incompatible with the mutual ethic of unionism and collective bargaining.

From the outset, Equity had been a relatively exclusive and hierarchical union, denying membership to most vaudevillians (apart from a few big names) as well as the chorus line. Producing managers could draw on a large pool of nonunion performers, so even with the closure of some two-thirds of New York's theaters

Comics and Animation

Popular culture found another outlet in comic cartoons. Two factors are significant in the development of comics as mass entertainment. The first is syndication, whose origins lie in William Randolph Hearst's 1902 sale of the rights to reproduce comic strips from his newspapers to other publications, thereby initiating a national market. "Funny papers" or the "Funnies" became popular extremely rapidly, helping to accelerate the growth in newspaper sales in the first decade. By 1910, there were at least nine chains, but because America was still in a transitional period between a rural and an urban society, artists had to bridge a still-diverse nation.

The first comic cartoon, the 1895 "Yellow Kid" in the New York daily *World,* was of uncertain ethnic origin and caught the public's imagination so quickly that Hearst poached the artist, Richard Outcault, for the *New York Morning Journal.* Because Outcault neglected to copyright "Yellow Kid," imitations soon proliferated in other urban papers, generally centered around the same formula of lower-class urban youngsters at large in the city. Despite the ethnic background of several of these comic characters—the Katzenjammer Kids is just one example—ethnic humor appealed to a relatively narrow audience and the "Kids" strip was modified so that their adventures took place in a semi-rural location, thus maximizing their appeal. The popularity of comics and their hand-drawn format over several frames made their transition to animated images almost inevitable. It took several decades, however, before they reached a sufficiently high level of technical quality to widen their initial appeal.

Little Nemo in Slumberland by the earliest animator, Winsor McKay, appeared in 1911, followed in 1914 by *Gertie the Trained Dinosaur.* By 1915, other animated shorts (e.g., Mutt and Jeff) became popular. By the end of the decade, the majority of cartoons—the Katzenjammer Kids and Krazy Kat among them—were animated versions of popular, usually New York–produced, comic strips.

Licensed merchandising proved to be the second factor that ensured the widespread popularity of comic cartoons. Outcault's "Buster Brown" was among the first to exploit the popular appeal of a comic character by selling the right to replicate the character's image onto a diverse product range, which included toys, games, and watches. This initiative proved financially astute as the merchandise provided better returns than the syndicated comic.

and the spread of the dispute to such other cities as Chicago, where all theaters had closed by August 17, the strike was by no means as solid as some had hoped. To overcome this, Equity began to relax the strict membership criteria and accept members formerly excluded from joining the union. Nevertheless, the dispute came at a time of unprecedented industrial action and public and commercial support for the striking actors was high. A week of benefit performances at the Lexington Theatre with stars like Eddie Cantor and Lionel Barrymore followed.

Twelve-frame comic strip shows Little Nemo and his companions, the dwarf, Flip, and the cannibal, Impy, flying into New York in their dirigible spaceship from a trip to Mars, ca. 1910. "Little Nemo," first published by Winsor McCay in October 1905 in the New York Herald, *featured a small boy who traveled in his dreams each night to another world, Slumberland, where he had fabulous adventures. (Library of Congress)*

Sensing public hostility, producing managers began to resort to similar tactics exploited by other adversaries (e.g., threats of court action and adverse publicity). This strategy proved counterproductive, however, as it merely antagonized other theatrical unions. Backers, too, who had provided substantial funding for the massive theatrical expansion during the early 20th century could see their investments disappearing and had little appetite for a prolonged dispute. Faced with pressure from investors, the P.M.A. had little choice but to negotiate and announced that they would agree to all the union's demands except the closed shop. After a month of strikes, 37 closed productions, 16 shows prevented from starting, and an estimated $3 million loss to producers, the strike was settled with a five-year contract and recognition for the union. Membership had increased from a prestrike 2,777 to 14,000 members afterwards. Because conservative artists did not see themselves as industrial workers or wanted to align themselves with other theatrical unions, however, there was little incentive to change the prevailing economic order. Despite the relatively short-term benefits that resulted from the new contract, the structure of the industry remained largely intact.

DANCE HALLS

A New Independence for the Young

Between the late 19th century and the first two decades of the 20th, commercial amusements (movie theaters, vaudeville, dance halls, and amusement parks) emerged and expanded rapidly, and they began to play an increasingly important part in urban centers across the United States. In addition to increasing opportunities for recreation, dance halls in particular were a liberating environment that provided men and women with the possibility of escaping parental supervision and joining a peer group culture. Other venues were popular locations for rehearsing dating routines, but they also attracted other age groups, whereas dance halls tended to attract more younger men and women, and because hooking up on the dance floor was actively encouraged there, they were doubly appealing. Although such family-oriented attractions as picnics in the park still played an important role, a new commercial realm where the mingling of the sexes was actually sanctioned presented new opportunities to young people tentatively moving away from neighborhood and community.

Stepping outside familial and community ties frequently involved challenging parental and societal boundaries. Because dance halls provided opportunities for sexual experimentation, flirting, and flaunting the latest styles, middle-class reformers and parents alike were quick to oppose what they perceived as unimpeded social intercourse. Rules and regulations that limited much of the

Couples on the dance floor at the Pavilion, Catalina Island, California, ca. 1911. (Library of Congress)

original appeal—and, consequently, some of young people's longed-for independence—were quickly drafted. Despite these setbacks, ways of avoiding and subverting them were found, and in the process helped to establish a culture that consolidated the various halls and palaces and provided the patrons with guidelines to govern the niceties of behavior on and off the floor, even though class, gender, and racial divisions remained in evidence.

The Creation of the Hall

Community dance halls and balls connected to educational projects and political organizations were among the first places where young people met to dance. As urbanization and immigration grew in the 1890s, however, the urban working class gradually began to organize their own clubs where dances or "rackets" were held. Just as early movie theaters took advantage of impromptu venues, so too were dances held in rented halls, saloons, or stores. Participants also gathered in their own tenement basements, often to dance, but also to gamble, smoke, drink, and generally take part in the more clandestine and disapproved-of activities.

Treating

Treating refers to the practice whereby men paid for various "treats," usually drinks. In order to impress women, many men would persuade them to order more expensive drinks (e.g., whiskey) rather than cheaper drinks like beer or soft drinks. Treating could also extend to fares and such gifts as scent or even dresses. More expensive gifts were rare, though, away from the hostesses employed in taxi-dances, and although some women did exploit the practice, they were sometimes labeled "charity girls" to distinguish them from prostitutes, who traded sexual favors for money, not gifts.

Because few patrons of dance halls in working-class neighborhoods could afford an expensive night out, far less the cost of extravagant treats, the policy of pairing up helped reduce the expense of a night dancing and drinking. That way, women were always guaranteed a companion should they not "catch on" and, thus, not be treated. The practice of a treat for both women in a pair was generally understood, even if only one was successful in getting a date. That practice did not, however, ensure that men hunting in pairs would be treated, but it did help men to pay for them.

Men usually expected something in return for a treat. That "something" was generally felt to involve intimacy of some sort, and the evening frequently became a contest between men who were determined to get something for "showing a girl a good time" and women who were equally determined that they would not "come across," often engaging in elaborate strategies to outwit their escorts and making sure that they did not see them a second time. Notwithstanding reformers' beliefs that working-class young women were inherently promiscuous, treating was a complex ritual, involving a balance between the desire for social inclusion and deference to cultural embargoes on premarital intimacy. Although women may have received treats from men, they nearly always paid for their own entrance because they arrived at dance halls with female friends. Men complained that even after treating their escorts all evening, the women left that way, too, or with other men. Women found ways of "clearing out" before closing time and found a female companion with whom they could leave for home.

As dance halls proliferated, they were joined by dance academies (commercial venues unaligned with any club where classes were held during the day and regular dance nights later on). Although these academies helped to counter dance halls' poor reputation, in the early part of the century, many were still next to saloons, frequently owned by breweries, and derived the majority of their income from alcohol. As late as 1915, many of Chicago's dance halls were still adjuncts of saloons, seating was meager, and drink was the main attraction. Elsewhere, dances could be held almost anywhere—even on the roofs of buildings and frequently in venues joined to movie theaters to capitalize on the

Independent Working Women

Before World War I, an elite class of women and the more adventurous had already made substantial advances in gaining economic autonomy. Less privileged women, however, accepted that marriage would not necessarily restrict their ability to undertake wage labor, but probably meant a job that was less stimulating, fulfilling, and important. Female emancipation after the war encouraged a sense of potential, whereas smaller, less fixed families inspired women to look outside the home for work. Other factors (a reduction in the live birth rate, fewer adult dependents living at home, and easier access to birth control) helped to engender an impression of liberation and control over one's destiny. A new (relative) prosperity was characterized by the ability to afford a few of the new domestic appliances and an increase in leisure time, whereas movies came to represent glamour and escape for a new generation.

The postwar period inspired a climate of acquisition and ambition. Once outside the strictures of the home, young women, both married and single, took advantage of new types of jobs (e.g., clerical, administrative, sales, and marketing), whereas employment and social mobility became viable options. As the *expectation* of waged labor became more widespread, for many women marriage and employment began to appear less incompatible. Single women entering the labor market were encouraged not to halt their career on getting married or to disdain marriage for a career. By 1920, the academic Rhoda Elizabeth McCulloch could write that "encouraging women to have careers with or without marriage offered them something more than child bearing." (Kessler-Harris, 2003, 229) By then, 25 percent of wage-earning women were married, and postwar increases in the percentage reflected a growing change in the social realities that enabled women to seek independent paid labor.

crowds flocking there. By 1910, dance palaces were established by resourceful promoters and businessmen keen to exploit the fashion for dancing. One of the first, New York's Grand Central Palace, opened in 1911 and was joined by Roseland—where the quarter-acre dance floor could hold 2,000 patrons—and others like the Aragon in Chicago and Los Angeles' Paramor. Before long, smaller towns throughout America had their own exotically named venues. Like movie palaces, the huge dance palaces in major cities were brightly lit advertising beacons, often located in some of the more affluent districts or, as in New York, in the already-established amusement districts like Broadway and 42nd Street. More extravagant than earlier dance halls, palaces frequently incorporated saloons, pool halls, and smoking rooms because smoking was usually forbidden on the floor. They were lavishly decorated and many had one or more orchestras.

Although closed or taxi-dance halls did not grow in number until the 1920s and 1930s, they originated in the 1910s, probably along San Francisco's Barbary

Coast. Elsewhere, as larger and more lavishly appointed halls grew in popularity, older halls were compelled to pare their already sparse facilities, provide supervision, and modify behavior criteria to find a new clientele. Taxi-dance halls, which were predominantly aimed at men, often masqueraded under the guise of dance academies, but in reality they provided hostesses (or dime-a-dance girls) with whom men could dance for a fee, from which the hostesses were paid a commission. Smaller, frequently difficult to find, and less well furnished than regular halls, taxi-dance halls flourished in the margins of urban areas.

Inside the Dance Hall

Although larger halls did become more widespread, they were by no means the norm. Thousands of smaller halls with few amenities still existed, and many of them were garishly decorated in an effort to attract customers. Nevertheless, in people's enthusiasm to go dancing in the decade, neglected or sparsely appointed dance halls appeared to make little or no difference to the numbers who crowded into them throughout America. Cleveland, for example, had around 130 for a population of some half a million in 1910, and these figures were repeated elsewhere. In such cities as New York and Chicago, annual attendances were in the millions. Although dance halls appealed to patrons from a wide range of backgrounds, they were often to be found in working-class neighborhoods with high proportions of immigrants. In Chicago, for example, halls in Gaelic Park, near the city's stockyards, attracted mainly clients from Polish, Irish, and Slavic backgrounds. Saturday night crowds, particularly in larger halls, tended to be more diverse than on other nights. Despite this diversity, dance halls were strictly racially segregated. African Americans could perform on the bandstand, but "mixed" dancing and dancing by African American couples alongside white was prohibited. African American "joints" proliferated in predominantly African American neighborhoods, but the more expensive clubs also catered to white "slummers" who, in some areas, constituted a significant—and profitable—minority.

Changes in the working week, particularly to women's hours, were partly responsible for the growth in recreation facilities. By 1914, legislation to restrict women's working hours had been enacted in 27 states, and by 1917, only 9 had no such legislation. Reductions in the number of women in domestic service—where they frequently found leaving the house difficult—and the growth of clerical work for women led to the increasing separation of the worlds of work and leisure as women's expectations that their recreation should consist of more than a few stolen moments grew. New social spaces led to new opportunities to explore different relationships and to try on new identities. New circumstances led to such new dances as the turkey trot and the Boston Dip—often with regional variations—that replaced the formality of the waltz. Many of these styles were deliberate expressions of youthful sexuality. Sexually provocative "tough" dancing became popular and, much diluted from its original form in Barbary Coast brothels, became the foundation of a dance craze, the one-step, in the 1910s. Although the middle classes were enthusiastic participants in the dance crazes that swept the nation, appearing to adopt the same sensual poses as working-class dancers, the styles were, as Peiss points out, "carefully controlled and refined to meet middle-class standards of respectability" (Peiss, 1986, 103), and most stopped short of dancing "tough."

Regional differences in dance styles also fragmented further between different neighborhoods, whereas subtle social gradations existed between small neighborhood halls where youngsters could try out their skills before graduating to larger halls and palaces. Many halls had cliques who had known each other for some time and were accomplished at the more intricate dance steps, effectively excluding casual outsiders. Dance halls were frequently organized around ability levels. Because certain styles and skills were predominant, men and women could judge what was required of them, thereby avoiding any concern regarding identifying a partner of equivalent ability.

Dance culture in the 1910s was largely segregated by age: smaller, neighborhood halls attracted young and old; the larger venues attracted a younger clientele. Although traditional halls continued to be popular throughout the decade and into the next—many catering to families—situations where young people could gather with the same age group were much more in evidence than they were in earlier decades. Even in traditional venues, dancers began to imitate styles that had become popular nationally.

Policing the Dance Hall: Morality and Reform

A more informal atmosphere also provided opportunities for young people to approach each other, unrestricted by parental conventions. Even though they were far from being the "brazen petting party" (McBee, 2000, 68) some reformers claimed them to be, they did act as the "parlor of certain classes" (Ibid.), providing a space where young people could begin their courtships. Halls in working-class and immigrant neighborhoods were more liberated places, where the combination of more uninhibited dancing, alcohol, and crowds of single youngsters free from parental supervision resulted in a shared sexual atmosphere, and patrons could spurn their parents' attempts to regulate their sexual conduct and orchestrate their relationships. Middle-class venues, however, were rather more sedate.

As dance halls grew in popularity, they became the focus of regulatory legislation and were targeted by moral crusaders who associated them and the new dance styles with a relaxation of moral standards, almost always singling out women as the cause of the decline. After 1910, national ordinances that restricted opening hours, specified minimum ages, introduced licensing fees and regulations on sanitation, and policed dancing styles were rapidly enacted. Although further legislation was largely suspended during World War I, it was restarted afterwards. Although increasing legislation clearly affected the everyday running of dance halls, the possibility that the police, anxious to curtail certain types of dancing, could unexpectedly interrupt their activities was more serious for young patrons. Policewomen and sometimes police matrons trained in social work were authorized to deal with cases involving women and children.

Supervisors from agencies like Chicago's Juvenile Protective Association oversaw the halls, whereas larger venues provided their own custodians or floor men who looked out for alcohol, "immodest" dancing, close contact between couples, and any person behaving in a rowdy manner. In some halls, unescorted women and men were prohibited. Because "vice investigators" were not always particularly diligent, not all these initiatives were successful. In any case, by mid-decade dance halls had proliferated beyond the resources available to police them. Anxious to maximize profits, hall owners were less concerned with regulating conduct than they were with inciting drinking and encouraging dancing, and some employed spielers on the lookout for wallflowers with whom to dance. Other initiatives included special dance nights (e.g., masques, or costume balls) to stimulate trade. Between dances, which could be as short as five minutes, dancers were encouraged to buy drinks in intermissions lasting up to 45 minutes, another source of revenue for owners who sometimes also provided facilities for after-hours drinking.

Some halls ran special contests, either for dancing or, occasionally, beauty contests. Prizes for these were usually relatively wholesome, but some halls, especially before Prohibition, gave away alcohol. Larger, more conspicuous halls were usually owned by companies and run by a manager responsible for dancers' behavior. In smaller halls, however, especially those where the venue was hired for the night, responsibility was often delegated to the hirer and behavior clearly depended on that organization's integrity.

Despite increasing legislation and reformers' efforts at regulation, many owners operated a double standard when it came to operating the hall. Anxious to promote the impression of propriety, they nevertheless were keenly aware that a moral and demure environment was not what attracted most young dancers, who, in any case, habitually thwarted dance hall regulations and purchased alcohol for later consumption or even while dancing. Unwilling to pay the often extortionate prices charged by halls, others simply smuggled in their own alcohol or left using pass-outs to drink in nearby saloons. Even Prohibition did not halt the sale of alcohol entirely because men selling bootleg liquor would come into the halls. Women also felt they were put under undue pressure to drink, either from men or from hall owners.

Although "promiscuous" styles of dancing were largely prohibited, couples found ways of avoiding the watchful inspectors by hiding in the middle of the dancers. Some orchestras were primed to play certain tunes when invigilators arrived, whereas other couples merely left the floor and took advantage of adjoining rooms. Few halls provided anywhere near enough seating, so couples intent on a quick dalliance left the hall and found a toilet or cupboard, or simply went to a dark corner. The balconies of larger halls became known as the "great lover's lane of the dance halls." (McBee, 2000, 79) Middle-class attempts at regulation were thus defied by working class dancers intent on a good time and, in the process, creating a collective character and shared intimacy among a like-minded culture. Experimentation and independence increased despite reformers' and parents' best efforts.

Sexuality and Dance Hall Girls

During the decade, young women emerging from the strictures of domestic service and those who took advantage of increased leisure and more disposable income played an important role in defining dance hall culture. In dance halls, women began to achieve autonomy and an identity independent of the family or the workplace. Autonomy was gained in small, incremental steps, but it was power nonetheless, achieved by declining invitations from men to dance, attending dances unescorted, and rebuffing entreaties to step out between dances or to be escorted home. Such devices permitted women to challenge assumptions that commitment was the inevitable outcome of fraternization and to dismiss familial efforts to govern relationships and orchestrate marriages.

Moving outside the immediate neighborhood and into the world of commercialized leisure provided young women with opportunities to meet young men (men they would not meet in the course of day-to-day life) they found attractive and who in turn were attracted to them. Dance halls were also popular because for women there were relatively few alternatives. Here, young women could shed their habitual domestic or workplace selves and try on new identities, thus testing the limits of working-class conventions. Dress, Kathy Peiss observes, was a "potent way to display and play with notions of respectability, allure, independence, and status." (McBee, 2000, 85)

As the most visible aspect of women's identity, dress attracted the most criticism from reformers—it both conferred a front of self-confidence, and it seemed to reformers to mirror more dubious styles. As Peiss observes, "by the 1910s, it was often difficult to distinguish the dress and style of respectable women from prostitutes at dances." (1986, 98) Although the brash, highly colored, slashed, and abbreviated styles of the 1920s were a few years away, young women who went dancing in the 1910s still presented onlookers (notably, the male habitués of dance halls) with a marked contrast from their late-19th-century predecessors. Young women imitated contemporary screen heroines, but they also (despite the popularity of the hobble skirt) opted for looser, brighter-colored, and lighter fabrics with lower necklines. In Chicago, working women put powder puffs in their stocking tops, whereas in New York high heels, ball gowns, extravagant pompadours, and elaborate make-up were used to attract men. Dressing up allowed women a reckless form of expression proscribed in other parts of their lives.

Although most parents felt that traditional neighborhood dances were comparatively safe places for their daughters, for young women, parents, and moral reformers, public dance halls were a source of danger and transgression. Claims that dance halls were closely associated with prostitution were exaggerated, and figures advanced by reformers as evidence of moral decline were largely groundless and based more on opinion than fact. Claiming that dance halls "had been the origin and chief recruiting station for [the] traffic in women," it was also argued that out of 1,000 girls in New York's Bedford Home for Women in 1910, all "had got the downward start from a dance hall somewhere." (McBee, 2000, 87) Although baseless, specious declarations like 163 out of 200 "bad girls" had fallen "from the Ballroom to Hell" (McBee, 2000, 87) did little to alleviate parents' fears.

Although claims that dance halls led inexorably to damnation were exaggerated, parents, particularly immigrants, worried about their daughters' assimilation of American ways. Customs considered "fresh" (e.g., smoking, which was still a dubious form of behavior for women in the 1910s, and drinking whiskey) accelerated the loss of gender-based differences so conspicuous in their country of origin and were considered masculine traits. Dance halls provided women with public spaces in which they could test their sexual magnetism and so undermine ethnic cultural virtues. Dancing was physical, often suggestive, and defied male assumptions about female sexuality and conduct. Many of the dances by women dancing in same sex pairs were perceived as deliberately provocative and asserted women's power and sexuality. Reformers also criticized the way that men could—notionally, at least—walk up to any woman and invite her to dance, further undermining behavioral conventions that required a previous introduction.

More than amusement parks or movie theaters, dance halls became the preferred venue for women because there they could have a good time away from the strictures and tedium of family life, experiment with romance, lay claim to public space and undermine gender conventions, and challenge parental expectations about relationships. Out on the floor, women expressed their sexuality in the way they dressed, danced, and acted. Yet for all this notional independence and reformers' beliefs that women were instrumental in the moral decline of America, the majority of women had very traditional expectations (i.e., ultimately, a steady relationship leading to marriage). Women also had to balance the desire to have fun with men's expectations that they would "come across." In any case, in the heterogeneous society of the 1910s, social, cultural, and sexual norms were by no means uniform, and what might have caused friction in one community (e.g., an Italian girl who came home late) would have caused little comment in another.

Concerns regarding women's alcohol consumption were justified in some cases, but most remained sober enough to look after themselves and adopted numerous strategies to avoid men's overly enthusiastic advances. Moreover, by taking control, women both challenged societal and parental norms as well as definitions of masculinity. Although men still exercised their prerogative of asking a girl to dance, they had few other "rights" beyond that. The collective nature of dance hall culture, whereby women relied on each other, allowed them to advance and reinforce their own definition of recreation and intimacy.

AMUSEMENT PARKS

Audience Participation

One of the most telling manifestations of the changing face of America in the early century, the amusement park, evolved from 19th-century, end-of-trolley-ride pleasure parks and urban midways. They were an amalgam of earlier entertainments and technological innovations (e.g., the 1893 World's Colombian Exposition in Chicago and a significant influence on emerging forms of mass amusement from the late 19th century onward). The Exposition failed to attract sufficient visitors until the opening in June 1893 of the Ferris wheel. Included in its attractions were the freak shows (under the guise of anthropological exhibits) as well as the Ferris wheel, and, as the midway, the separate area has donated its name to all subsequent segregated amusement zones.

Amusements parks were exceptional, however, because of the new mechanical entertainments and the crowds' reactions to them. Amusement parks were distinguished from such other forms of mass entertainment as sports, theater, the movies, and vaudeville—all essentially spectator activities—by the extent to which the boundaries between entertainment and audience were blurred. Spectators *become* the entertainment. The amusement park provided an environment and entertainment that influenced behavior and undermined existing conceptions of public demeanor and social propriety—in other words, all the institutions and standards of the dominant culture.

Origins

The origins of amusement parks lie in the 19th century, when pleasure parks were created at the end of the line by transit companies anxious to increase the number of passengers traveling during quieter times. The addition of mechanical amusements during the late 19th and early 20th centuries greatly increased their popularity, so that by the end of the 1910s, their number had swelled enormously. Increasing urbanization, inward migration and immigration, and a younger, more

Roller coaster at Coney Island, Cincinnati. (Library of Congress)

affluent population provided a ready-made clientele for the amusement parks. "Thrill" rides like roller coasters and sideshows in enclosed parks (e.g., Coney Island) acted like magnets for the burgeoning urban populations eager to escape the confines of work and overcrowded dwellings. Social psychologists and critics viewed America's pleasure economy with apprehension, despairing of the masses' inexorable slide into a new barbarism. Ignoring their censure, the masses flocked to amusement parks in the millions.

The Development of the American Amusement Park

In addition to urbanization, industrialization, immigration, increased leisure time and wages, the gradual relaxation of moral constraints, and the emergence of a younger, more mobile urban population with fewer responsibilities and more disposable income, other changes took place that, in part, can help explain the appearance and rapid growth of amusement parks.

Electric trolley lines began to appear in most larger American cities in the 1890s. Because transit companies were frequently compelled to pay a flat rate for electric power irrespective of the amount of electricity used, owners began to devise methods of maximizing the use of street railways in quiet times, evenings, and weekends. One solution was to provide an attraction (in most cases, a pleasure park) at the end of the line. These quiet parks quickly grew in

The Freak Show

Although freak shows were a popular and ubiquitous attraction in amusement parks by the 20th century, their origins lie in the dime museums of the 19th century and sideshows in traveling circuses. New York alone had 50 such museums, and most large cities had at least one. The growth of vaudeville in the 1890s lured patrons away from the museums, their numbers dwindling rapidly after 1900. Their central attraction had always been the human curiosities, the shows migrating then into circuses and amusement parks. Just as traditional carnivals and fairs had displayed the grotesque, so too did amusement parks. Dwarves, giants, fat ladies, and the excessively tattooed or hirsute—ambiguously described as ape-men—were all on display, where they were disparaged and celebrated in equal measure as freaks.

Spectators were attracted by the way they were exhibited as anomalies and aberrations in a conventional world, with the abnormal becoming a freak when their difference is made the basis for the commercial exploitation of this distinction. The freak's capacity simultaneously to captivate and to repel was central to their appeal: Siamese twins beguiled visitors because they were neither a single unity, nor two separate bodies; hermaphrodites were often exhibited so that a bearded male appeared in one profile, whereas the other profile was a distinctively smooth-faced and made-up woman. Various physical abnormalities became the foundation of half man–half animal freaks: persons with vestigial limbs became seal children, whereas all manner of deformities and disfigurements were the basis of human–animal amalgams (e.g., frog/snake boys or mule women). Animals with abnormalities (e.g., two-headed sheep) also appeared in freak shows.

After amusement parks began to decline in popularity, freak shows transferred to traveling carnivals, helped in part by the growing use of automobiles for excursions. Their numbers declined as medical and scientific advances explained the "freakishness" as deformities or genetic mutations. The term *freak show* increasingly became a pejorative and was replaced by *sideshow*.

number as mechanical amusements, dance halls, water activities, and other resort attractions were added. Although sources disagree regarding their number, by 1919, there were between 1,500 and 2,000 amusement parks in the United States.

The success of these ventures meant that the extra passengers often subsidized transit companies, particularly during the summer months. People enjoyed riding in the quiet, clean electric cars, which contrasted markedly with the steam railroads. Fares were usually low (around 5 cents in the early years) and admission to the pleasure park was free. By the early 20th century, there was one or more trolley park in every major city: Palisades Park in New Jersey, Willow Grove Park in Philadelphia, and Cheltenham Beach in Chicago were just some of the best-known.

Table 6.1. Percentage of Total Consumption Expenditures Allotted to Selected Products and Services between 1909 and 1919

	1909	1914	1919
Recreation	2.9	3.0	3.6
Alcohol	6.2	6.0	3.3
Tobacco	2.2	2.2	2.4
Medical	3.6	3.6	4.3
Transportation	5.2	6.4	8.1
Insurance	0.06	0.07	0.07
Education	1.4	1.5	1.2
Religion/Welfare	2.8	2.5	2.4

Source: U.S. Bureau of the Census, *Historical Statistics of the United States: Colonial Times to 1970* (Washington, D.C.: Government Printing Office, 1975), ser, G470–494; adapted from Adams, 1991, 63.

Other factors were also significant in the growth of leisure activities. The average five-and-one-half-hour reduction in the working week for low-skilled wage earners coupled with an average rise in annual earnings from $558 to $1,358 between 1910 and 1920 were important contributory factors. Clerical workers enjoyed similar improvements in wage levels and reductions in the working week, but although these were partially offset by rises in the rate of inflation, statistics for the period show a decrease in expenditure on such essentials as housing, clothing, and food, along with a corresponding increase in the percentage available for discretionary activities and purchases. Table 6.1 shows the percentage of total consumption expenditures allotted to selected products and services between 1909 and 1919.

Recreation increased slightly, whereas alcohol consumption dropped when Prohibition was introduced; however, the highest expense was on transportation. In 1914, the mass production of automobiles was having a marked effect on their cost (as little as $400 in some cases), whereas technical developments led to reduced maintenance costs. As sales of automobiles increased from 2 million in 1914 to 9 million in 1921, they were used more and more for recreation.

Because statistics for amusement parks were not included as a separate category in census data until 1935, it is difficult to distinguish expenditure on those from other forms of recreation. Nevertheless, data on estimated consumer expenditures for selected products and services shows a total increase of some $288 million between 1909 and 1919, and that by the end of the decade, expenditure on vacation travel and amusement admissions (e.g., movies, theaters, etc.) overshadowed all other categories.

Table 6.2. Attendance at Various Leisure Activities

	1909	1914	1919
Amusement Admissions			
Motion Pictures	—	—	—
Theaters, Concerts	—	—	—
Other[1]	—	—	—
Total	286	327	574
Nightclubs	—	—	4
Social/Athletic Clubs	20	24	41
Firearms	29	31	64
Music/Instruments			
Sheet Music	10	12	25
Pianos	109	103	204
Phonographs/Records	26	54	339
Photographic Equipment	15	24	45
Books/Magazines	95	120	182
Sporting Goods/Attire	17	51	78
Toys and Games	20	32	65
Vacation Travel[2]			
Trunks/Suitcases	32	31	74
Auto Operation	59	115	568
Railroad/Air Fares	126	156	265
Other (Domestic)	150	200	350
Foreign Travel	130	140	40

[1] Includes amusement parks as well as dance halls, billiard parlors, bathing beaches, sporting events, race tracks, fairs, etc.

[2] Weinberger calculates recreational and vacation use of automobiles, railroads, and airways from estimates by the American Automobile Association, and by analyzing summer-month passenger revenues for railroads and airlines for a number of normal years.

Source: Julius Weinberger, "Economic Aspects of Recreation," *Harvard Business Review* 15 (Summer 1937): 452, 454, 456; cited in Adams, 1994, 64.

Technology and Play

The Roller Coaster and Other Daring Rides

As Adams (1991, 9) observes, "mechanized thrill machines are the essential and central components that transform a sylvan retreat . . . into an amusement park." Examples like the carousel and the roller coaster symbolize a good time, excitement combined with fear, and an escape from the everyday. Unlike the machines that many patrons operated each day, which to an extent they resembled, those in amusement parks were essentially unproductive, providing nothing other than delight in the activity itself. Technology transcended mere function and became spectacle.

One of the first attractions, Ferris's 264-foot-high wheel that dominated the 1893 Chicago's Exposition, was "the first large-scale harnessing of technology solely for the purpose of fun" (Adams 1991, xiii) and demonstrated the attraction of mechanical rides. By the early 20th century, elaborately decorated carousels, complete with galloping horses, were in many of the leading amusement parks, including Chicago's Riverview Park and Luna Park in Coney Island. Compared with the thrill machines, the carousel is relatively sedate, attracting its riders with rococo embellishments, often-delicate carvings, mirrors, and seductive organ music.

No attraction better embodied the atmosphere and look of the amusement park than the roller coaster. The "gravity railway" system, apparently inspired by industrial switchback railways, was introduced at Coney Island in 1884 and rapidly became popular, covering the original investment in just three weeks. Nearly 50 additional rides were subsequently built, and the introduction of the chain elevator system, which raised cars up the first incline, led to the development of the giant coasters that were to dominate later amusement parks. Further refinements and safety devices followed: two cars were joined together, doubling the capacity, while the track was partially covered with a tunnel that plunged riders into a terrifying darkness that was then lit by the recently introduced electric lights. This combination of apparent—and sometimes actual—danger, speed, lights, and technology proved a winning formula with patrons who demanded more precipitous descents, faster rides, and greater capacity. The trend toward steeper and higher rides and greater speeds led to the development in 1912 of the Zippin Pippin, formerly the Pippin, in East End Park, Memphis. More wooden coasters followed, but higher speeds also required higher safety standards. Despite increased safety measures, however, consumers' demands for heightened thrills did lead to some dangerous experimentation in coaster dynamics. The vertical loop coaster was first introduced at Sea Lion Park, Coney Island, followed by the Loop-the-Loop at Oletangy Park, near Columbus, Ohio, but these proved to be too unsafe and were soon dismantled.

The Enclosed Park

Just as the roller coaster came to symbolize the American amusement park, so, too, did Coney Island become synonymous with 20th-century amusement and thrills for the urban masses. A conflation of mechanized rides and amusements and an atmosphere of excess, disorganization, and artifice was central to Coney Island. The paradox that created disorder out of the ordered precision and unvaried reliability of mechanical devices and electricity also brought fun and amusement to a burgeoning urban working class, swelled by immigrants, whose lives were increasingly regulated by the exigencies of time and the machine.

Coney Island, 1910. (Library of Congress)

The success of Brooklyn's Coney Island was partly because the railroad enabled passengers to travel there cheaply and partly because of the astute exploitation of a young, single clientele who were drawn in by advertisements in working-class newspapers and whose main aim was to have a good time and, however briefly, escape from the era's moral constraints. The rides were thus contrived to propel youngsters into close but blameless contact and to expose legs to eyes that had seldom seen such sights.

For an all-in-one price of 25 cents, patrons could enjoy all the amusements, including the steeplechase, a mechanical ride rather more sedate than the roller coaster. Other attractions relied on the customers' willingness to be humiliated in front of other patrons, thus becoming the entertainment as well as the clientele. Thus, social decorum was demolished and inhibitions released. The attractions proved irresistible to young New Yorkers. Another spectacularly successful enclosure Luna Park followed, but in the culmination of extravagance, Dreamland, in which the owners attempted to graft a façade of culture onto the amusements, they misjudged a public whose priorities were fun, unruliness, and deception. Returns came nowhere near the original investment, and in 1911, Dreamland, along with many other attractions, was destroyed in a catastrophic fire. The disaster ironically merely increased the crowds, drawn out of New York in the following days to take in the devastation.

Coney Island benefited from the massive population growth in New York City in the first two decades of the century, the result of immigration and inward migration. Between 1910 and 1920, the population there grew by 850,000 to around 5.62 million. Of these, the majority were under 40 years old, with a spike between 20 and 24, the very age range to which Coney Island appealed. At the same time, mechanization and organized labor resulted in a national reduction in the working week of five-and-one-half hours while wage levels and disposable income also increased. Available statistics show that between 1903 and 1905, from an average family annual income of $836, $13.17 was spent on leisure. By 1918, income had increased to $1,505, from which $33 went on recreation. (Adams, 1991, 54–56)

1910 represents the peak of Coney Island's early popularity when a crowd of some 1 million could be there on a summer Sunday. In 1920, the arrival of the final terminal for all the subways—with fares of only a nickel—paradoxically, perhaps, was instrumental in the Island's gradual decline in popularity. As Adams (1991, 56) observes, despite greatly increased numbers, the crowds flocking to the island insisted on amusement at subway prices, and although numbers remained high for some time afterwards, its eventual decline was probably inescapable.

Visual Culture and Recreation

Nevertheless, its heyday was marked by the attentions of artists, writers, and critics. Among critics, the resort provoked uncomfortable debates concerning crowd behavior, the ultimate (and perhaps pernicious) influence of mass entertainment, and its effect on the dominant culture in an increasingly urbanized and industrialized era. Its representational potential did not go unnoticed among painters. Its vulgarity and tawdriness made it unacceptable to the sedate establishment artists, so it was first captured by applied artists: photographers such as the Byron studio and the Detroit Photographic Company and illustrators who had no such reservations. Their work was intended for widely distributed popular magazines like *Everybody's* and *Cosmopolitan,* rather than the galleries and exhibitions of the cultural elite.

Painters who rejected the genteel subjects favored by society artists soon found in Coney Island a subject epitomizing a modern America transformed by technology, urbanization, and popular culture. Realists and modernists alike depicted the amusement park for precisely the reasons that their academic counterparts rejected it—it was, as Kasson (1978, 88) notes, "stunningly technological, urban, populous, egalitarian, erotic, hedonistic, dynamic, and culturally diverse."

In the 1913 *Battle of Lights, Coney Island* (Collection: F. M. Hall, University of Nebraska Art Galleries), the Italian American Joseph Stella captured the onslaught of impressions and emotions that assailed him, building, as he observed, "the most intense dynamic arabesque that I could imagine in order to convey in a hectic mood the surging crowd and the revolving machines." (Ibid.) In the upper half, the whirling, knotted shapes of the rides, signs, and lights predominate, crowned by Luna Park's electric tower. The painting is a combat zone of competing forces in which, Stella believed, crowds and machines generate "violent, dangerous pleasures . . . a carnal frenzy." (Kasson, 1978, 88 and 90)

Bracketing Stella are the realists, John Sloan, who writes of Coney Island's "tawdry, gaudy, bawdy beauties" and the "crowds [who] watch the people coming down the Bamboo slide in Luna Park—lingerie displays bring a roar of natural 'vulgar' mirth" (Kasson, 1978, 91), and Reginald Marsh, whose paintings are "crowded with a rich profusion of human forms and exuberant girls displayed

as curvy Coney Island burlesque queens in a spirit of voyeuristic detachment."
(Constance Schwartz at www.tfaoi.com/aa/2aa/2aa662.htm)

Although Coney Island has become synonymous with the American amusement park, such others as Oletangy Park, near Columbus, Ohio, which was at one time the world's largest, rivaled it for size, daring rides, and innovative amusements. After early development, including the relatively tame Figure Eight roller coaster, by 1910, the park had a zoo and enclosed rides like the Tunnel of Love, as well as America's then-largest theater. Electric lighting was introduced throughout and the local trolley now came directly into the park, making Oletangy one of an increasing number of American "Trolley Parks" that brought visitors from all over the city. Two other coasters (the Whirlwind and the Red Devil) replaced the dangerous Loop-the-Loop, the latter being located only feet from the nearby main road. A large dance hall and Shoot-the-Chutes, a water slide then popular at many amusement parks, were also added during the decade. Ever anxious to provide visitors with extra titillation—and following a trend for the exploitation of animals that would be quite unacceptable in later years—an elephant was trained to descend the slide, while at Luna Park, an old elephant past its prime was executed in full view of the crowd.

Moral Anxieties: Losing Oneself in the Crowded City

Although all of the amusement parks that emerged and flourished in the period began to provide amusements like the Ferris wheels and roller coasters that had made Coney Island so popular, most were in conservative communities and abjured the more sensational aspects common in Coney Island. Most banned alcohol and gambling, largely to foster a family atmosphere. Many families, correspondingly, treated the visit as a special occasion, dressing formally and behaving demurely.

Amusement parks mirrored the increasingly democratic and relaxed nature of society and provided "a safety valve, a mechanism of social release and control that ultimately protected existing society." (Kasson, 1978, 109) There were some, however, who regarded their popularity as symptomatic of the decline in moral standards in early 20th-century America. Because Coney Island provided the template for many amusement parks, particularly those in the Midwest, the self-appointed custodians of moral welfare attempted to eradicate the degenerate activities they identified with it.

Kansas City is typical of this tendency. During the 120 days of the 1911 season, the city's two amusement parks Electric Park and Forest Park attracted more than 1.3 million visitors, which, given a population of only 248,381 in 1910, demonstrates the popularity of the parks. Entrance charges were low (10 cents and 5 cents, respectively) and the parks were readily accessible by streetcar. There were those, however, like investigator Fred R. Johnson, at the city's

Board of Public Welfare and Recreation Department, and Recreation superintendent Fred McClure, whose censure of the parks' "immoral climate" was expressed in warnings that "unsupervised bathing results in undue familiarity" and that in the dance halls "prostitutes and men seeking prey mingle with those seeking innocent amusement." The rides also incited moral abandonment, as they "usually disarrange the clothing and throw members of the opposite sex into close proximity in darkened enclosures." Johnson claimed that "public dances, questionable picture shows, poorly regulated amusement parks, and burlesque houses" were "prolific sources of corruption," (Adams, 1991, 65, 66) and by 1913, his inspectors permitted only those dances not involving close bodily positions, improper baring of the limbs, or indecorous hands placed upon the partner.

Looking over Dreamland from the top of the Shoot-the-Chutes, Coney Island, New York, ca. 1904. (Library of Congress)

Despite various legal and educational measures intended to halt the development and consequences of what they believed were debasing, uncultured, and vulgarly commercial amusements, McClure and Johnson's efforts were unsuccessful, and amusement parks and other attractions thrived simply because of their magnetic attraction for the masses. It is here, in the divide between the views of the traditionalists, the reformers, the educationalists, and the custodians of moral propriety, and those of the public who flocked to the new attractions, that tensions arose: between those who wished to shape the masses, prepare them for a modern America while still preserving the decorum and standards of an antebellum era, and the masses themselves, who were more engaged with having fun than with maintaining values and standards.

Although there were critics who welcomed the democratic melting pot of the new pastimes, imbued as they were with the spirit of the carnival, the unconstrained hedonism was profoundly worrying to others. Following a visit to Coney Island in the 1910s, critic James Gibbons Huneker called for its abolition, seeing it as a "disgrace to our civilization" (Kasson, 1978, 96), believing that the experience released man's primitive nature. In his belief that America was experiencing the emergence of a new barbarism and that people reverted to savages once they gathered in crowds, Huneker was voicing anxieties often fostered by behavioral scientists of the era. In their rejection of the values of propriety, industry, caution, frugality, and self-control (values that ensured the prosperity and endurance of both family and society), the crowds would jeopardize the foundations of society itself.

Some social psychologists of the early 20th century maintained that participation in a crowd provoked a release of habitual constraints and repressed desires. Rationality was disabled, and screened by anonymity, the liberated individuals would vent their intense emotions. Huneker felt that in the crowd, the primitivist tendency was exacerbated by the growing presence of immigrants, affectionately remembering a time before New York had become "the dumping-ground of the cosmos." (Kasson, 1978, 97) The debates around Coney Island mirrored wider concerns: that in modern, urbanized America, the devotion to work and the pursuit of profit overrode any consideration for the community and the provision of leisure. As small-town values and constraints were sacrificed in the move to cities, people were left with nothing to put in their place. For those migrants, communities where personal relationships necessarily curbed behavior were abandoned for metropolitan anonymity. Ignoring the social networks established by newcomers to the city, pessimistic reformers saw only the breakdown of society.

Viewing the "pleasure economy" of America with alarm and despondency, they believed that in the dearth of edifying mass recreation, individuals exhausted by the demands of industry inclined to the crass commercialism of amusement parks, dance halls, brothels, and cheap movie theaters, paradoxically exchanging the noise and crowds of the city for those of the attraction and the resort. From this perspective, these attractions constituted a desecration of play where the innocent and unsophisticated were cynically exploited for profit and the surrender of their decency.

To re-establish the sanctity of play, reformers advanced a policy of government dictate, open-minded local initiatives, and specialist direction through which recreation could act as a vigorously productive force in social (re)integration and moral growth. Public parks and exercise facilities would replace city streets, community centers would displace saloons to assist in the assimilation of immigrants, and recreation courses would facilitate the fulfillment—and, hence, productivity—of factory workers. Commercial amusements would thus be replaced by more disciplined and regulated entertainments, and the ordered and productive community would replace the unruly and unproductive crowd.

Notwithstanding reformers' concerns that popular amusements would bring about, or at least accelerate, the collapse of society, they did assist in the displacement of a polite, provincial, and prissy culture with a mass, popular culture. In any case, the middle classes—for whom the amusement park was such a liberating experience—were very different from the working classes, who merely incorporated the parks into a culture that already included excursions and outings. In the passage from a production-based economy to one centered on consumption and leisure, 19th century virtues like hard work, frugality, propriety, and self-discipline allied to 20th-century technology had produced a wealth of commodities, requiring a developed mass market to digest them. The decade saw the emergence of attempts to cultivate that market. The growing application of technology to leisure activities from amusement rides to movies was explicitly designed to expand the audience for those commodities and attractions. In this radically altered environment, old-fashioned and outmoded virtues and the benefits they presaged (social mobility and the anchor of the family) meant little as new opportunities promised more rapid gratification.

In the minds of middle-class critics, a worrying consequence of the growth of a popular culture was the loss of deference for traditional arbiters of taste and standards. On the other hand, for patrons of this new culture (the working and lower middle classes and, particularly, the immigrants), it offered the chance to take part in American life on a revised basis. Mass culture thus depended for its success on its inclusivity. Yet for others, the masses merely exchanged one form of subjection for another; the mechanization and standardization of mass culture simply augmented and replicated work, whereas for those working in the attractions, it *was* work. From this perspective, the safety valve of mass distractions merely reinforced society's existing values, promoting passive acquiescence of the persistence of production and consumption.

Amusement park entrepreneurs faced a perpetual challenge to provide new distractions for visitors, while maintaining the distinction between the park and the world outside. This was to prove increasingly difficult by the end of the decade as the potential for popular entertainment was more plentiful than ever before. Other forms of popular culture (e.g., the movies that depicted illusion more convincingly and cheaper than the amusement parks could) had made amusement universal. The arrival of the subway meant that visitors would demand prices equivalent to those on the subway, and it also reduced the contrast between city and resort. Although amusement parks were heralds of the new mass culture, the values they introduced were instrumental in their decline.

MOVIES

Theaters and a Celebrity Culture

By 1910, vaudeville had begun to lose its appeal for an audience captivated by the novelty of moving pictures. The embryonic motion picture industry responded by turning out longer pictures with more complex narratives. Film programs changed more regularly as renting films became the norm. Entrepreneurs converted existing halls and buildings of all kinds to exploit the new audience. The number of nickelodeons grew rapidly, and theaters in working-class neighborhoods provided a wide mix of patrons (families, single and married women, and workers) with affordable, escapist entertainment. Combination

Jewish and Immigrant Theater

Immigration led to extensive changes in American culture. From early settlement areas, ethnic theater was dispersed throughout the country, sometimes becoming, alongside religious centers, a communal home for ethnic groups. In addition to staging their own theatrical activities, ethnic communities, particularly those with Irish, Italian, and German roots, made important contributions to the growth of an American theater with distinctive characteristics. A key factor in the development of the entertainment industry is the role of Jews. After the first influx of mostly German Jews in the mid-19th century, between 1880 and 1910, New York in particular was inundated by Jews from central and eastern Europe. German Jews, who had assimilated more readily than eastern European Jews, were embarrassed by Yiddish theater and frequently attempted to suppress its development.

Despite animosity between the two groups, a dynamic and popular Yiddish theater flourished in New York and other cities for two generations after the 1880s. Yiddish theater also contributed many performers to the English-speaking theater. Jews played a major part in the development of vaudeville and musicals, as well as in the emergent motion picture industry, both as performers and as directors, producers, technicians, and entrepreneurs. In attempting to list the major players in all areas of popular culture, it would almost be easier to catalogue non-Jews. In theater, musicals, and vaudeville, Ziegfeld, the deMille family, Irving Berlin, and Sophie Tucker were all Jewish, whereas the Hollywood studio system that began to emerge in the latter years of the decade was created, built up, and controlled almost entirely by such Jewish entrepreneurs as Adolph Zukor, Louis Mayer, and the Warner brothers. By the end of the decade, and well into the 1920s and 1930s, the presence of Jewish ability, dynamism, and finance transformed American popular theater and the motion picture industry.

theaters showing a mixture of live entertainment and movies catered to those unable to afford vaudeville but reluctant to attend nickelodeons, and as exhibitors began to realize the enormous potential of an audience put off by the shabby and poorly appointed nickelodeons, they began to open full-size theaters with better facilities. By the end of the decade, enormous movie palaces had begun to open, with some seating as many 5,000.

As moviegoers began to identify with actors, a star system developed as studios promoted performers alongside the films. The birth of a celebrity culture resulted in huge earnings and more autonomy for the most popular stars (e.g., Mary Pickford). Studios also realized that an East Coast base, where weather and light were less predictable than on the West Coast, restricted their activities, so most relocated to California. As Hollywood became synonymous with moviemaking, studios grew in size and became much more technically sophisticated. American filmmakers capitalized on the collapse of European production during the war years, and by 1920, the apparatus was in place for America's subsequent global domination of the industry.

The Creation of Popular Film

By 1890, all of the technical prerequisites upon which a modern cinema depended were already in place. Of more importance, it was unclear how to unite the essential elements of cinema and capitalize on the technology to exploit a potentially sizeable audience. How would technical achievements be transformed into commercial success?

Despite competing attractions (e.g., amusement parks, circuses, and vaudeville), there was a great deal of public interest in the novelty value of moving images. Because moving theater productions between different locations was expensive and people often had to travel long distances to visit attractions, the cinema offered a more viable means of providing visual entertainment to mass audiences. Because the United States had more theaters per head of population than any other country, it was potentially the largest market for motion pictures. In the decades before 1910, both American and foreign films competed energetically for this audience. Once films could be watched by more than one viewer, which is something that was previously impossible with Edison's Kinetoscope, film exhibition in amusement parks, vaudeville theaters, small, storefront theaters, even churches extended across the country fairly rapidly. Exhibitors rented or bought the projector, but distribution was difficult to control because films themselves were not subject to copyright. Copying was fairly widespread because until 1912 the United States had no motion picture copyright law. By the early 20th century, audience numbers increased as filmmakers developed fictional stories with more sophisticated narratives, as well as elaborate special effects copied from such European directors as Georges Méliès,

Nickelodeons

By 1910, as fiction films became the industry's mainstay, renting, rather than selling, a film to an exhibitor was increasingly the norm, effectively dividing the industry into production, distribution, and exhibition. Permanent film theaters, usually with between 100 and 200 seats and a single projector, increased in number and spread to all larger and many smaller urban areas. Admission was typically a nickel (hence, "nickelodeon"). Although there is scant evidence to support it, early audiences seem to have been largely middle class. As the working week shortened, moviegoing became more commonplace and less of a novelty. Within a few years, it had become the entertainment medium of the working class. Renting films meant that the film no longer had to be shown until the cost had been recouped; thus, the program could change more regularly,

Patrons outside the Leader Theater in Washington, D.C., ca. 1922. (Library of Congress)

sometimes daily. Audiences therefore began to come back equally regularly. Nickelodeons were not seasonal (a major drawback with amusement parks), and they were cheaper than vaudeville theaters as costs in the sparsely furnished and barely advertised venues were minimal. Compared with vaudeville at twenty-five cents or more, which was beyond the reach of most blue-collar workers, nickelodeons were cheap and opened cinema up to a mass audience, capitalizing on the growth of urban populations and the growing number of immigrants looking for cheap, escapist entertainment. Because early films were silent (Edison's dream of coordinating sound with images would not be realized until the 1920s), the language barrier in ethnically diverse audiences mattered little.

Growth in the number of nickelodeons happened extremely rapidly. Within five years of their first appearance, they numbered 10,000. New York alone had 600, and daily attendance was estimated at between 300,000 and 400,000. (Cullen, 1996, 142) Many were located in working-class neighborhoods and business districts, so that workers could go to a venue close to home, and since most opened from late morning, office workers could go during lunch or after work. Women and children could also go during a shopping trip. A nickelodeon might be the only popular entertainment in a small town, and audiences there often consisted of a wide range of different classes. As older venues were transformed into nickelodeons, women's attendance rose correspondingly, to 40 percent of the working-class audience in the early part of the decade. Unlike dance halls, where the crowd was largely single and predominantly young, female movie audiences were mixed along marital and generational lines. Despite this diversity, single working women nevertheless integrated moviegoing into their other leisure habits. Although movie houses provided a cheap—and dimly lit—venue for meeting men, perhaps because of its intergenerational appeal and its neighborhood location, it was perceived as a safer environment by anxious parents, so it was adopted by both middle- and working-class young women.

Despite their popularity, nickelodeons were not universally liked. To attract an audience unable to afford vaudeville and scared away from nickelodeons, promoters like Marcus Loew opened combination vaudeville and picture theaters. At around 10 cents for cheaper seats, combination houses proliferated, and there were hundreds by 1910. Convinced that they were yet to tap into a huge potential audience, exhibitors felt that if movies were to become an acceptable and permanent part of popular entertainment, they would have to appeal to people who wanted something cheaper than theater, less crude than vaudeville, and better appointed than nickelodeons. In attracting a huge audience of moviegoers who could afford no more than a nickel, cheap movie houses alienated a middle class unwilling to mix with the working classes. To appeal to this potentially enormous audience, full-size theaters would have to differentiate themselves from the saloon bar reputation of nickelodeons. Although not as lavish as the later picture palaces, the new theaters were nevertheless closer to playhouses than storefront venues; therefore, they attracted an audience who made an occasion of dressing up and going out, rather than dropping in. Some were built in the new suburban neighborhoods to attract white-collar workers unwilling to travel into town, whereas others often boasted air-conditioning and restrooms.

The Development of the Industry

In 1909, Edison had formed the Motion Picture Patents Company (MPPC), often known as the Trust, forcing those who wanted his films to employ only his cameras. After 1912, when the monopoly of the MPPC—members of which effectively controlled the industry—was investigated under the 1890 Sherman Antitrust Act, several members of the industry's independent sphere, who had aligned themselves against the MPPC, established a new structure that would form the basis of the Hollywood film industry. By this time, the Trust was largely irrelevant because its interests lay in protecting the equipment rather than in addressing the emergent movie culture, the real source of growth in the industry.

The independents who challenged Edison and finally achieved his aim of controlling the industry were mainly eastern European Jewish immigrants. Because the Trust believed that certain sectors of the industry (e.g., production and exhibition) were relatively inconsequential, former movie theater owners like Adolph Zukor and Marcus Loew were able to bypass the Trust and, through legal challenges and the ability to anticipate public taste, gradually eat away at the Trust's influence.

Cinema was only part of a new, industrial, urban society that was unmistakably throwing off the residues of late-19th-century restrictions. Cinema's mass popularity, however, brought consequent social pressures, focused mainly on reforming the medium. Reformers believed that films depicting violence and adultery, for example, were a malign influence on the young and impressionable, and following the creation of the private Board of Censorship in 1909 (a voluntary strategy aimed at achieving more respectability and frustrating federal national censorship), the National Board of Censorship, later the National Board of Review, was created in 1915. In attempts to enhance the medium's status, the industry began to produce more noteworthy films that would attract a better class of spectator. Films became longer and narratively more complex, with scripts sometimes derived from classic literature or depicting significant historical events.

By 1915, some nickelodeons still operated, but audiences increasingly wanted better facilities. Exhibitors catered to this demand by building or converting larger, more ornately decorated theaters with consequent increases in admission prices, up to 25 cents or more for longer, multireel programs. As twin projectors became more widely used, singing acts, which had been used to cover the change of reel, gradually disappeared, whereas orchestral or organ musical accompaniment became popular. These improvements were calculated to provide increasingly demanding and sophisticated audiences with a very different environment from that of the nickelodeons.

As audiences increased, distributors needed more titles. One theater showing three films in a program changing three times a week would need around 450 films a year. As competition from imported multireel foreign films increased, American producers were compelled to release longer films, and by mid-decade, the "feature" film had become the norm in all the more prominent theaters with a consequent decline in the programs of short films more common in nickelodeons. Apart from big, first-run venues, which showed the same film for a week, most theaters changed the program more frequently. In 1916, *Motion Picture News* reported that the average number of changes was five. (Koszarski, 1994, 34) As soon as feature-length films were established, some houses began to move from daily to weekly changes, thus ensuring better returns if a theater was prepared to double their budgets for film rental and advertising. Nevertheless, by 1919, the majority of theaters still made frequent changes to their programs. Publicity was of little use in such venues. Many exhibitors felt that patrons would turn up whatever was showing, attracted more by the physical certainties of the venue (e.g., the seating or the music) than the quality of the film. Because programs changed so frequently, there was little time for negative audience reaction to circulate. In any case, the film would be replaced within a few days. Given the number of competing theaters, however, the drawing power of certain stars became increasingly important.

The Star System

Once nickelodeons became popular, films began to be promoted by brand name (Edison, Vitagraph, and Pathé were well known among moviegoers), but unlike opera, vaudeville, and theater, where the star system was well established, film actors and filmmakers were still not credited, partly because it was feared that screen credits and subsequent fame would lead to demands for more money. Most actors did not appear regularly enough before 1910 to be recognized, but after this, actors began to be tied to longer contracts; audiences started to recognize those that appeared more frequently and, consequently, to show an interest in familiar faces and ask theater managers for names and to write to studios for photographs. Writing reviews was also difficult if actors were anonymous. Studios therefore began to promote actors alongside films, often providing publicity stills for display in theater lobbies. Personal appearances by actors became more frequent, and in 1911, *Motion Picture Story Magazine,* effectively the first motion picture fan magazine, was published. Other promotional activities included photo postcards of popular actors, but actors were seldom credited on screen until 1914.

East to West: The Move to Hollywood

Location in New York or Chicago might have provided an embryonic film industry with ready access to audiences and capital, but as early films were shot outdoors or in light glass studios, overcast weather conditions could delay production schedules. As a result, after the establishment of the MPPC, some companies wintered in Florida or the West. One of the first to establish a permanent base in Los Angeles was the Selig Company, followed shortly after by Ince's New York Motion Picture Company. In 1910, American Biograph sent D. W. Griffith there. Los Angeles, which became the industry's main production center during the early 1910s, had certain advantages over other areas. Shooting outdoors was possible for most of the year in the clear, dry climate there, whereas Southern California more generally provided a wide diversity of landscapes, from ocean to deserts and mountains. Because the Western was beginning to break through as one of the most popular genres, shooting in western locations appeared rather more authentic in California than it did in the East.

Studios were established in Hollywood, then a small, relatively unknown sub-urb, as well as in other areas of Los Angeles. However, it was Hollywood that became a synonym for American motion picture production, despite the fact that the head offices of many companies were still in New York. During the decade, the industry grew rapidly from small, open-air stages to complex facilities with large, indoor studios.

The War Years and After

The growth of popular cinema until the outbreak of World War I followed a trajectory that could be summarized as, first, action as novelty; second, the development of narrative; and last, filmic techniques that enabled the audience to follow increasingly complex narratives more easily. The outbreak of the war, however, brought about major changes in international cinema, severely limiting film production in the two main producing countries (France and Italy). As a result, America became the dominant producer of films to the world market, and the isolation of several countries led, in part, to the emergence of discrete and specialized national cinemas.

Content until then to satisfy domestic demand, following the decline of film production in Europe, Hollywood grasped the initiative to satisfy overseas demand. Because a film's production budget was dependent on what the film was expected to earn, domestic production budgets before the war were relatively unexceptional. Once American films began to be exported, however, budgets could be increased proportionately. As a result, sets became larger, costumes grew ever more extravagant, and equipment and special effects were developed in line with these changes. American film stars like Mary Pickford and William S. Hart also received global exposure, achieving worldwide fame and adoration.

Pickford, the most popular female star of the Nickelodeon era, was one of a small number of actors who could command enormous sums for her roles in silent films, partly because she went on to produce and supervise distribution of her films, and partly because of the emergence of independent companies, sidelined before 1912 by the MPPC. In 1919, Pickford, along with Charlie Chaplin, Douglas Fairbanks, and D. W. Griffith, formed United Artists (UA). Responsible only for film distribution, UA did not produce films, providing filmmakers with access to its own screens and temporarily vacant theaters owned by other companies. At the time, Hollywood was vertically integrated (i.e., they both made and distributed films). Filmmakers were thus dependent on studios for bookings. UA broke the rigid stranglehold exerted by such companies as Fox, Paramount (which controlled many silent era stars like Gloria Swanson, Pickford, and Fairbanks and directors like Griffiths and DeMille), and Warner Bros. by providing filmmakers, who became genuinely independent for the first time, with unprecedented control over their films.

At the same time, studios began to initiate the system of block booking (a strategy whereby theaters were forced to take all of a studio's films even if they only wanted some), increasing the process of vertical integration through the development of national theater chains that would dominate the industry in the next decade. Block booking provided studios with income that financed increasingly lavish movie theaters and the inflated salaries of the stars. It also nurtured new talent because studios were able to make cheap films ("B movies") with comparative unknowns that were then sent out with the higher profile films that exhibitors really wanted.

Mary Pickford on the beach with a motion picture camera, ca. 1916. (Library of Congress)

Hollywood film production during the decade had much in common with the contemporary mass production assembly lines: division of labor between specialist writers, set designers, editors, and technicians who might never meet became more and more common. Studio sets became progressively larger with the control of lighting effects a key factor in film production. Studios also began to invest in huge outdoor "back lots" where elaborate sets were constructed that could be reused to save expense. As films became more homogenous and audiences more heterogeneous, filmmakers established guidelines for making plots more readily understandable to a diverse range of filmgoers whose first language may not have been English.

Features, by now the staple of movie production, became standardized at around 75 minutes, and stars like Pickford and Chaplin could command as much as $10,000 a week as a result of the intense competition between studios anxious to exploit the public's growing fascination with actors. As readily adaptable vehicles for these stars, studios increased their purchases of literary classics. Perhaps the most ambitious film of the decade, and subsequently one of the most notorious, was D. W. Griffith's 12-reel epic, *The Birth of a Nation,* which, although condemned at the time and since for its bigoted portrayal of southern history, was enormously successful and its style and Griffith's techniques were extremely influential and widely imitated.

Many successful filmmakers came to prominence during the decade, among them Cecil B. De Mille and John Ford, who began to exploit the popularity of Westerns in 1917, whereas such others as Mack Sennett, Harold Lloyd, and Chaplin capitalized on the fashion for slapstick comedy. Among actors, Tom Mix and

William S. Hart became the decade's most popular cowboy stars. Motion pictures were also where immigrants hoping to break into show business could flourish. Many of the early stars were first- or second-generation immigrants: Theda Bara, who was Jewish; Pola Negri came from Poland; and Rudolph Valentino's appeal came, in part, from southern Europeans trying to assimilate into everyday life. Stars from older stock (those whose forebears had arrived in America rather earlier) helped immigrants by providing visual signals on being "American."

Animation, which was also increasingly popular with audiences in the 1910s, benefited from a number of technical advances that speeded up the process. Discovering that animation could be done more cheaply and faster if the process was subjected to the same division of labor as the assembly line, filmmakers exploited the process whereby the main animator would design and supervise, while a team of animators could draw most of the images required for the film's movement. Once backgrounds could be printed mechanically and "cels" (separate, transparent celluloid on which moving figures were drawn while the background remained constant) used, the processes of such early animators as Winsor McKay, who had produced huge numbers of drawings, could be greatly simplified and speeded up.

Film production during the decade underwent critical technical and structural changes, and these, as well as new cinematic conventions, were to make the films of the late 1910s closer to the films of the present than to films only 10 or 20 years earlier. This turning point marks the decade out as a transitional decade between early cinema and the highly sophisticated and complex industry it was to become in the next decade. Hollywood's domination of global film production, which it achieved almost by default during World War I, would have far-reaching implications during subsequent decades.

The Silent Films

Although films had no synchronized sound until the late 1920s, attempts were made from the very early days of cinema to link the image to mechanically reproduced sound, most often on phonograph records. Most of these attempts failed because of the problems of synchronization and because existing amplifier and speaker technology was incapable of coping with theater auditoriums. Nevertheless, most silent films had a live music accompaniment provided by a pianist or organist, or sometimes a full orchestra.

Although by the mid-1910s feature length films were increasingly popular, most longer features failed to exploit their increased length in any significant way. Films generally maintained the same successful format of the nickelodeon era—they were simply longer and contained more detail on characters and plot. Melodrama continued as the most popular dramatic style, mainly because it

Crane Wilbur and Pearl White in The Perils of Pauline, *directed by Donald Mackenzie, 1914. (Bettmann/Corbis)*

dominated the stage, but also because characterization and, indeed, any subtle nuances were all but impossible given silent film's restricted narrative capabilities. Melodrama meant that filmmakers could characterize heroes and villains by employing a visual shorthand, where simple dramatic confrontations substituted for more nuanced interpretations. Although some films did gain from the extended length made possible by multi-reel formats (e.g., Griffith's *The Birth of a Nation* benefited from a richness of detail that demonstrated his ability to expand the most dramatic elements of the short film), most other filmmakers failed to exploit the potential of longer running times, sacrificing coherence in the extra footage. Certain genres were ideally suited to melodrama. Westerns (probably the most popular of silent genres) and traditional family melodramas that used recurring situations, locations, and characters were films readily understood by audiences.

Many of the principles that were later codified as classical Hollywood cinema were, in fact, already evolving before most filmmaking was located there. Because early audiences were unfamiliar with complex and multiple narratives, filmmakers thus had to ensure that films were straightforward enough for audiences to follow. Various techniques such as editing, continuity, and explanatory intertitles, which increasingly included dialogue, were developed by filmmakers during the decade so that most audiences could follow the story.

Although the feature-length film gained in popularity during the decade, short films did not disappear. Distributors and exhibitors demanded a continuing flow of silent shorts to bolster the program and to provide the diversity that they believed would attract audiences. Although news, animated films, and comedies dominated short films, some theaters continued to offer a dramatic production, frequently a Western. In the period between 1913 and 1915, filmmakers anxious to avoid problematic long and complex narratives attempted to overcome this by making serials. Acknowledged as the first genuine serial film, *The Adventures of Kathlyn* in 1913 contained a narrative thread running through succeeding episodes, whereas in 1914 *The Perils of Pauline* established Pearl White as a star.

Makers of dramatic films generally abandoned the short-film format, leaving it to children's serials, newsreels, Westerns, and comedies. Relatively few feature-length comedies were made before 1920, and the short-film market was dominated by "low comedy," a form developed from vaudeville that continued the slapstick tradition of the early years and was ideally suited to silent films.

Musical Accompaniment

Music was used from its earliest days when silent films were first exhibited to audiences as part of vaudeville either to accompany the film or as a separate performance. The majority of theaters, whether large or small, provided music of some sort. The number of players varied widely, ranging from a single pianist or organist to larger ensembles ranging from 2 to between 25 and 50, with the majority consisting of 5 to 10 players. (Koszarski, 1994, 41) Unless the film was a more prestigious release, where producers offered guidance, the choice of music was largely left up to the theater itself. Because the program changed regularly, arrangers needed to have appropriate music for every new film. Many larger theaters had a music library, but smaller venues were able to draw on such works as *Motion Picture Moods,* indexed according to subject alongside the type of music suggested. An original score was only rarely written, and some combined original and stock melodies. Most arrangers attempted to synchronize the music with the action on screen.

Some films came with a choice of familiar selections that, with minimal rehearsal, could be adapted by the theater arranger, but "musical cue sheets," which contained approximate running times and brief descriptions for scenes, were a more popular alternative. This format became the most widely provided by the end of the decade, and because a careful reading of the sheets would avoid the need for an advance screening, it was popular with arrangers coping with frequent program changes. Although works by the best-known classical composers like Beethoven or Liszt were found in music libraries, some exhibitors felt that the average audience was incapable of appreciating such music, preferring instead more populist works. Others decried the poverty of choice available in smaller theaters as well as the quality of musicianship and instruments. Accompanists, whether solo or in groups, in large and small theaters, were usually expected to accompany the shorts, provide an overture, and, if a "prologue" of live performers was part of the program, support them as well.

Perhaps in an attempt to maintain audiences and concentrate their attention on the screen, or possibly to "enhance" what they believed were weak films, some exhibitors recut features or speeded them up during slower parts. Until the advent of sound, there was no agreed projection speed, nor was the physical permanence or intactness of a film sacrosanct either. The speed at which the film was projected (ideally, the same as that at which it had been filmed) and the presence of every (intact) reel clearly affected the audience's experience, but the practice of slowing down or speeding up the action, carried over from late-19th-century moving-picture toys and such mechanical devices as the Zoopraxiscope, was one that projectionists in the nickelodeon era saw no reason to change. The practice became the subject of much heated debate, with most protagonists believing that it diminished the audiences' experience and that speeding the film up was an attempt by unscrupulous managers to squeeze in more shows.

Despite tests carried out by the Society of Motion Picture Engineers throughout and after the decade, the society persisted with a shooting speed of 60 feet per minute and a projection speed of 80 feet per minute throughout the silent era. There was no requirement for theater managers to adhere to these standards, however, and as films increased in length, projection speeds (and cutting by theater managers) rose in tandem. In any case, because hand-cranked cameras were notoriously variable and some cameras had no film-speed indicator, a great many films were the result of guesswork. After the larger theaters had recut, hand-spliced, and removed entire reels, films were often in very poor condition by the time they reached smaller theaters, many being badly scratched, marked in places by projectionists, and damaged by overspeeding or even fire.

Audiences could experience moviegoing throughout the silent era, either in their convenient local and affordable neighborhood theater, albeit with the attendant problems of mutilated prints, hackneyed and often amateurish musical accompaniment, and indifferent projection, or, should they venture further to one of the lavish movie palaces, they could see a film with fewer scratches and less damage, but which had been cut at the whim of the manager and speeded up so radically as to make any comprehension of the filmmaker's aspirations almost impossible.

The Movie Palace

"Please do not turn on the clouds until the show starts. Be sure the stars are turned off when leaving."

This notice (Hall, 1961, 102), beside the switchboard in the Paradise Theater in Faribault, Minnesota, embodies the atmosphere of the movie palaces that by the end of the decade had begun to complement the nickelodeons of the early years of the movies, albeit in relatively small numbers. Between the emergence of movie houses from the fairgrounds of the late 19th and early 20th centuries and the exotic "atmospherics" of the late 1920s, "there was an age when the cinema became a dream palace, a building which embodied escape and fantasy, a temporary relief from the mundane and repetitive world of work," (Heathcote, 2001, 9) providing a level of opulence seldom experienced by their patrons.

Before the movie theater as a new building type arrived in the second decade, films were exhibited in rented halls, theaters, or music halls hastily converted to exploit the boom, and fairground booths. The purpose-built movie palaces of the 1910s combined elements of these earlier building types. Several were inspired by such ornate turn-of-the-century spectacle venues as the New York Hippodrome, which, in 1905, opened at a cost of some $4 million and combined up-to-the-minute technical facilities with a lavish interior. By 1915, rising operating costs—and because most could not hold enough patrons hoping to see popular films—meant that smaller theaters were becoming increasingly uneconomic, and theaters like the Hippodrome were intended to be profitable by filling, and continuing to fill, their large volumes (5,200 seats in the Hippodrome). Stark economic reality thus drove the move to larger theaters. Nevertheless, many Americans still visited their neighborhood and second- and third-run theaters, and in 1915, storefront theaters seating up to 300 were still being built, whereas in 1916, the average capacity was 502 seats.

Movie palaces soon became distinct from earlier theaters, their façades extravagantly decorated and studded with electric signage announcing the program. Because performances were continuous, waiting crowds had to be accommodated in large lobbies, most more ostentatious than the auditoria themselves. Although orchestras, some as large as 100, often accompanied the silent film, "the mighty Wurlitzer" theater organ came to symbolize these palaces. Most of these were designed by a small group of specialist companies, with some providing a house style for particular chains, whereas others developed their own signature style. Among the first to be widely acknowledged was Thomas W. Lamb, responsible for New York's Regent (the first in the city to be built specifically for showing movies), Rialto, Rivoli, and Capital, all between 1913 and 1919.

Although Lamb completed these theaters for the flamboyant impresario Samuel 'Roxy' Rothapfel (sometimes Rothafel), he also worked for other impresarios and consortia on such cinemas as New York's Capitol Theater in 1919, the largest in the world with seats for 5,300. The opening night of the luxurious venue included a reception, a concert overture, a newsreel, a tone poem, a rendition of Gounod's *Mireille,* a travelogue, a Universal comedy performed by dogs, an 11-act revue, which included specially written music by Gershwin and

The Hippodrome, New York, ca. 1910. (Library of Congress)

songs by Mae West, and, finally, at 11:30 p.m., the film *His Majesty, the American* with Douglas Fairbanks.

Not all of the critics were impressed. In 1914, the *New York Times* theater critic, Victor Watson, had already expressed his displeasure at seeing "the finest looking people in town . . . going to the biggest and newest theater on Broadway for the purpose of seeing motion pictures." (Koszarski, 1994, 20) Critics of the Capitol opening were highly vocal in their criticism, complaining of the "unwarranted ostentation" and "misdirected talents." (Hall, 1961, 62) Fairbanks was displeased about the late showing of his film, and city fathers, critics, and audiences were unanimous in their condemnation of Mae West's suggestive act. The opening night problems were worsened by the management's no-tipping policy, prompting ushers to picket the auditorium, and the beginning of permanent Prohibition, while audiences began to tire of the three-hour performances at a time when the average was one hour. In a time of postwar economic gloom, $2.20 ticket prices were more than most patrons were prepared to part with, attendance slumped, and the theater subsequently came under the supervision of Roxy Rothapfel.

Despite these and other setbacks, movie palaces continued their apparently inexorable rise during the next decade, providing an environment where "for a small charge they [audiences] can be picked up on a magic carpet and set down in a dream city amidst palatial surroundings." (John F. Barry in Koszarski, 1994, 25) Absent in this florid depiction was the relatively minor detail that they could also watch a film, but to the impresarios of the period, films hardly seemed a prerequisite of the experience.

THE IMPACT OF LEISURE AND POPULAR CULTURE IN THE 1910s

The impact of popular culture during the decade on an America moving from a predominantly agricultural, rural, or provincial society to a highly industrialized, mechanized, and urbanized culture was immense. Reductions in working time, wage rises and more disposable income, and the desire to shake off the last traces of Victorian propriety meant that working and middle classes alike could participate in the new recreational activities (vaudeville, movies, amusement parks, dance halls, and popular magazines and comics), all areas that almost inevitably attracted the dismay of largely middle-class reformers who believed that the only way to remedy the inexorable slide into moral decline was to impose their improving diet of discipline, thrift, diligence, and moral rectitude. Caught out by the speed at which these changes occurred and the constant blurring of boundaries between high and low, or mass, culture, social commentators struggled to keep up with the distinctions between the two, whereas the debates among those critics anxious to maintain the critical distance and the elite status of high culture persisted until well into midcentury.

The early decades of the century were characterized by the commercialization of organized recreation and its rapid dissemination to the working and lower middle classes. Technological innovations, improved transportation, and mechanization enabled the masses to participate to an unprecedented extent, whereas the loosening of social protocols permitted modes of conduct unthinkable in an earlier era. As capital became aware of the vast untapped potential in supplying affordable and accessible entertainment to a rapidly expanding and enthusiastic audience, the market increased exponentially. Innovators began to realize that the real growth did not lie in the supply of hardware (e.g., film projectors); rather, they found that it was the software (i.e., products and commodities like films and phonograph records).

New, or improved, forms of leisure were created and grew at an apparently limitless rate. Vaudeville continued to provide the masses with performers whose popularity was perhaps only exceeded by that of movie stars, whereas the growth and consolidation of the circuits lent an air of luxury and respectability that encouraged family audiences to frequent neighborhood theaters and large and luxuriously appointed venues (e.g., Broadway's Palace Theater and the Ziegfeld

Follies). Immigration and the growth of a working class with increased leisure time and more money also provided a ready-made audience. Despite such innovations as "chasers" (projected moving images at the end of a show), the growth of cinema eventually led to the decline of vaudeville. Along with vaudeville, burlesque grew in popularity during the decade as this cruder form of entertainment, which depended on an almost exclusively male audience, became consolidated in much the same way as vaudeville. As its core audience migrated to vaudeville and the movies, however, the form became progressively more tawdry and suggestive, eventually resulting in "stock" burlesque, a form stripped to its essentials and, in terms of content, the limit of its acceptability to the authorities.

The liberating experience of growing numbers of (still racially segregated) dance halls—often in impromptu venues—for young men and women anxious to escape from parental and societal supervision caused concern among reformers about the easy access they provided to alcohol and sexual experimentation. Other factors (e.g., reductions in women's working hours and their increasing financial independence and confidence) contributed to the growth of an ever-more sexually explicit dance culture and more risqué dress styles. Legislative changes (e.g., restricted opening hours) inevitably followed.

Amusement parks, their numbers swelled by social changes, improved transportation, and technological innovations, provided young working and lower middle classes in urban areas with excitement as they loosened the moral restrictions of the 19th century, leading to legal and educational reforms in some areas in an attempt to constrain and "improve" the moral health of the patrons. Despite this, the changes did herald a tentative beginning to the replacement of 19th-century moral rectitude and a working class that deferred to their "elders and betters" with a modern, inclusive, and democratic mass culture where "new" Americans could participate in American society on a different footing. Nevertheless, amusement parks began a long, slow decline toward the end of the decade as other forms of entertainment (e.g., movies) began to appeal more to an expanding middle class.

The decline in vaudeville and amusement parks was counteracted by massive increases in the audience for popular films. After its early appeal as a novelty, exhibitors competed strenuously for a potentially vast audience hungry for entertainment and moving images. Impromptu venues gave way to nickelodeons, renting became the norm, and moviegoing became part of people's weekly entertainment diet. Film programs started to change more regularly and, with multireel programs, films became longer. Capitalizing on the intrinsic cheapness of the form, nickelodeons soon began to overtake vaudeville, thus opening up the medium to a mass audience, which began to include women on their own, children, and families.

The inclusion of live acts broadened its appeal and moved the culture away from its association with the working classes and cheap, uncomfortable theaters.

Full-size theaters and those located in suburban neighborhoods were part of this initiative, whereas lavish and immense movie palaces began to appear in larger cities later in the decade. Growing concerns regarding morality among industry reformers resulted in the 1915 National Board of Review replacing the Board of Censorship, whereas the introduction of copyright protection in 1912 regularized revenue sources. Films became longer still, more narratively complex, and were often based on classic sources. Live acts started to disappear as musical accompaniment to silent films was increasingly the norm.

With regular changes to film programs, filmmakers produced more films, and, as moviegoers became more familiar with regular appearances by their favorites, a star system evolved with the consequent appearance of the first fan magazines. The restrictions imposed by an East Coast base where poor winter light and adverse weather limited year-round filmmaking prompted a shift in the base to Hollywood. With the move came expanded studios and such technological improvements as lighting, indoor studios, and back lots, where filmmakers could replicate almost any location.

As European filmmaking declined during World War I, America rapidly achieved global domination, and budgets increased to take account of the expanded market, with consequent improvements in sets, costumes, equipment, and special effects. As stars were exposed to wider audiences and the consequent emergence of a celebrity culture, their salaries also grew. Features became the staple of movie production, and the industry became consolidated along the lines of other mass production manufacturers, organized with the labor divided like a production line. Animated films also became popular during the decade, a period that can be seen as a transition between early cinema and the technologically sophisticated and complex machine of the 1920s and 1930s, an era dominated by the classical Hollywood cinema whose birth can be seen in the 1910s.

In the transition from a production-centered economy to one based on consumption and leisure, 19th-century values like industriousness, financial moderation, respectability, and self-discipline combined with 20th-century technology, which resulted in the proliferation of commodities and the consequent growth of a developed mass market to consume them. The decade was characterized by attempts to cultivate that market. Technology, and its increasing application to leisure activities from amusement rides to movies, was explicitly designed to expand the audience for those commodities and entertainments. In this drastically changed climate, traditional and outworn virtues and the advantages they were assumed to confer (e.g., social mobility and the anchor of the family) meant little as new opportunities promised more rapid gratification. This was to lead to still more radical changes in the following decades as popular culture became a more passive form of entertainment and recreation was increasingly premised on the amusement of the masses.

Historians' Debate:
Highbrow, Middlebrow, Lowbrow

In 1953, when the critic Clement Greenberg noted that "highbrow, middlebrow, and lowbrow are terms of brutal simplification" (Kammen, 1999, 100), he was merely continuing a debate that had gone on for nearly 100 years in America and elsewhere, emerging and re-emerging from time to time. The terms *highbrow* and *lowbrow* originated around 1875 when the pseudoscience of phrenology, the mid-19th-century preoccupation with cranial capacity, began to become popular. In this racist perspective, the former is distinguished by high intelligence, whereas the latter is equated with highly restricted intellectual ability.

The Progressive sociologist and advocate of nativism Edward A. Ross persisted with these categories when, in 1914, he attributed a lowbrow intellect to immigrants from southern and eastern Europe, and the terms have almost always been used pejoratively in the sometimes acrimonious debates around high and low culture. One of the early uses of "middlebrow" (i.e., neither high nor low) was in the mid-1920s, when it was used to describe those aspirants in the middle who hoped to get used to whatever it was that they ought to like; however, the issue has been further complicated in the conflation of "low" with "mass" or "popular" culture.

There is some debate, however, about the term *popular culture,* a phrase used pejoratively throughout the last decades of the 19th century and all of the 20th. Dwight Macdonald believes that it should more accurately be termed *mass culture* because "its distinctive mark is that it is solely and directly an article for mass consumption, like chewing gum." (in Guins and Cruz, 2005, 39) The term is frequently used in opposition to *high culture,* which, as Macdonald observes, is sometimes, though rarely, popular.

Popular culture developed in part from folk art or culture, which, at least until the Industrial Revolution, was the people's culture; however, Macdonald (in Guins and Cruz, 2005, 40) argues that whereas folk culture evolved from below, formed by people's needs, popular culture is largely imposed from above on passive consumers whose options are restricted to the alternative between buying and not buying by profit-motivated commercial concerns. High culture is the art (in its widest sense) of the establishment, made for (and sometimes by) the wealthy and powerful. It exploits the most exclusive material assets and the abilities of the most notable exponents for the gratification and enrichment of the privileged and is often intended to exhibit the power of those subsidizing it.

BIOGRAPHIES

Theda Bara, 1885–1955

Actor

Theda Bara, the highly popular silent film actor and one of cinema's earliest sex symbols, was born Theodosia Burr Goodman to Jewish parents. Her early career was as a stage actress, including her Broadway debut, *The Devil*. Beginning with her role as "The Vampire" in *A Fool There Was* in 1914, Bara made almost 40 films by 1919, her success contributing to that of Fox Film Corporation. Third only in popularity to Chaplin and Pickford, Bara made $4,000 per week at the height of her fame. She was best known as a "vamp," but in the 1916 films *Her Double Life* and *Under Two Flags,* she did attempt to transcend typecasting in more virtuous roles. She also played Juliet in a version of Shakespeare's *Romeo and Juliet.*

Most of Bara's early career was spent on the East Coast, before film production moved to California, but she relocated there in 1917 to star in *Cleopatra,* one of her biggest successes. During World War I, she joined the war effort, but after 1919, her career declined once her promotion by Fox began to wane, and such subsequent films in the 1920s as *Madame Mystery* and *The Unchastened Woman* were commercially unsuccessful.

Famous for promotional photographs portraying her in risqué costumes, Bara was also depicted as enigmatic and elusive by the studio, with several entirely fictitious personae attributed to her. Although publicity stills have survived, Bara is also distinguished for having a higher percentage of lost films than almost any other star of the era. Of her entire output, only three survive completely intact. Along with others like Rudolf Valentino, she is also one of the best-known stars of the period never to have made a sound picture.

Irving Berlin, 1888–1989

Composer

Irving Israel Berlin was one of America's most prolific and best-known composers and lyricists. His catalogue of ballads, dance tunes, novelty tunes, and love songs was to define American popular music for most of the 20th century. Born Isidore Baline (sometimes Bellin) to a Russian Jewish family who emigrated to the United States between 1891 and 1893, following the death of his father, Berlin busked on the street before beginning work as a singing waiter in New York's Chinatown. A request by the owner to write a song for the café led to Berlin's first published song. Because his name had been misprinted as "Berlin" on the sheet music, his professional name was decided. Moderate success with sheet music, songs for vaudeville, and as part of stage shows followed, but "Alexander's Ragtime Band," which was actually a march, in 1911 initiated his career as one of Tin Pan Alley's most successful stars, selling more than 1 million copies in a few months.

After this success, in 1914, Berlin wrote *Watch Your Step,* his first full-length stage musical work, for the dancers Vernon and Irene Castle, and one of the first shows to make extensive use of syncopated rhythms. He followed this with *Stop, Look and Listen* in 1915, but in 1917, he enlisted in the U.S. Army, staging a musical with a cast of 350 members of the armed forces. Along with the hit "Oh! How I Hate to Get Up in the Morning," the work is now remembered mainly for "God Bless America," a song left out of the original show, but which, when released years later, was so popular that it was suggested as America's national anthem. Following demobilization, Berlin opened his own theater, the Music Box, as a venue for annual revues that included his latest songs. An astute businessman, Berlin was a co-founder

Irving Berlin, perhaps the most prolific songwriter of the 20th century, responded to changing times and tastes with Main Street language and down-home images in such irresistible melodies as "Alexander's Ragtime Band" and "White Christmas." (Library of Congress)

of the American Society of Composers, Authors, and Publishers (ASCAP) and founder of his own music publishing company, Irving Berlin Inc.

Berlin's first marriage, to Dorothy Goetz in 1912, ended with her premature death from typhoid. His subsequent marriage, to the writer and heiress Ellin Mackay, was the subject of some controversy because Berlin was Jewish and Mackay was Catholic. Unable to read and write music beyond the most perfunctory level, while his piano playing skills were limited to the key of F-sharp major, Berlin nevertheless wrote thousands of songs, including "White Christmas," "Easter Parade," and "There's No Business Like Show Business," and was one of the few Broadway composers to write both music and lyrics for his songs.

Douglas Fairbanks, 1883–1939

Actor

Douglas Fairbanks was one of the leading actors of the silent era, as well as a director, producer, and writer for both screen and page. He was born Douglas Elton Ullman—"Fairbanks" comes from his mother's name from an earlier marriage—in Denver, Colorado, and acted in various minor stage roles from an early age. He moved to New York in the early 1900s to further his acting career, held various small-time jobs until his Broadway debut, and married Anna Beth Sully in 1907. Along with their son, Douglas Elton Fairbanks (Douglas Fairbanks, Jr.), the couple moved to Hollywood in 1915. Fairbanks had a relatively limited reputation as a stage actor and moved into films, making *The Lamb,* which proved to be a critical and commercial success.

Fairbanks was then teamed with writer Anita Loos and director John Emerson. There followed a succession of popular light comedies and action films in which Fairbanks was often cast as an affluent character at a time when many films depicted working-class protagonists, achieving his dreams through a combination of charm and almost acrobatic agility. The films were highly popular with an audience craving escapism. By the end of 1916, his salary had risen to $10,000 per week, and he was ready to establish his own production company along with Loos and Emerson.

Other films in a similar style followed until 1919, when, in an attempt to take control of the financing and distribution of his films—then masterminded by Adolph Zukor—he co-founded United Artists. Costume adventures like *The Mask of Zorro* would last throughout the remainder of the silent era and propelled Fairbanks into the ranks of Hollywood's highest paid stars. Films like *The Three Musketeers* and *The Thief of Bagdad* were among the most profitable of the silent era, and his final silent film, *The Iron Mask,* exhibits the attention and expense that he indulged on all his productions, unrivaled by any of his competitors of the time.

Concerns regarding the propriety of his affair with Mary Pickford and that it might affect their box office popularity led them to attempt to keep it secret, but their subsequent marriage only seemed to make them more popular with a public fascinated by the idea of marriage between "Everybody's Hero" and "America's Sweetheart." The couple collaborated with others in establishing the Motion Picture Relief Fund. In 1917, Fairbanks began to publish a series of eight volumes on popular philosophy. Titles such as *Profiting by Experience* and *Initiative and Self-Reliance* were intended to inspire a sense of his own apparently boundless optimism in his audience.

The end of the silent era was also effectively the end of Fairbank's movie career. The couple's first talkie together was poorly received, as were the sound films that Fairbanks made thereafter. This, and declining health, as well as a deterioration in his ability to perform the athletic feats for which he was once famous, led to Fairbank's retirement from moviemaking in 1934.

D. W. Griffith, 1875–1948

Film Director

The influential director David Llewelyn Wark Griffiths—better known as D. W.— is widely acknowledged as a pioneer of film technique and grammar, but his innovations have been overshadowed by the controversy surrounding his best known film, *The Birth of a Nation*.

Griffith became an actor after an unsuccessful start as a playwright, and between 1908 and 1913, he was the director of 450 short films for the Biograph Company. Looking for locations in California, Griffith came across Hollywood, then a small village, and thus, with *In Old California,* became the first director to film there. Convinced that feature-length films could be financially viable, Griffith produced *Judith of Bethulia,* one of the earliest feature-length films to be made in the United States. Biograph, however, remained unconvinced and Griffith left the company, taking with him the stock company of actors. As the David W. Griffith Corp., he produced *The Clansman* (1915), subsequently renamed, *The Birth of a Nation*.

Although the film was extremely popular (e.g., it was the first to be shown in the White House, to Woodrow Wilson), it aroused considerable controversy because it expressed the then widely held racist views that African Americans were inferior and depicted southern pre–Civil War slavery in a largely sympathetic way. *Intolerance,* which illustrated several different examples of humankind's intolerance, was made the following year, in response to the accusations of racism surrounding *The Birth of a Nation*. The film, which was enormously expensive, was commercially unsuccessful and bankrupted Griffith's Triangle Studios. He then went to Artcraft—part of Paramount—then to First National, simultaneously co-founding United Artists. His involvement with United Artists was short-lived, however, and Griffiths made only one further film in the decade, *Broken Blossoms*. His films of the 1920s and early 1930s were largely unsuccessful.

Despite the controversy, Griffith is still remembered as a pioneer of film technique. Although it is now believed that few of his innovations were entirely original, he was instrumental in establishing the codes that became part of studio system production, particularly cross-cutting (the use of editing between simultaneous events to heighten suspense), as well as the close-up and methods of temporal and spatial manipulation.

Mary Pickford, 1892–1979

Actor

Mary Pickford—"America's Sweetheart"—was an early silent movie star, who, as one of the founders of United Artists, a producer, and a pioneer of autonomy for independent producers and improved salaries and conditions for other filmmakers, became one of the most important figures in motion pictures. As one of the earliest stars whose international fame was generated by an entertainment medium, she is also a prototype for the cult of modern celebrity.

Born Gladys Louise Smith in Toronto, Canada, she performed as a child in stage melodramas. Following six years of touring the United States as part of a family act, in 1907, the young actor—still under her original name—landed a supporting stage role on Broadway. Changing her name to Mary Pickford at the suggestion of the producer made little apparent difference to her ability to win parts as she was out of work after the role for around two years until a meeting with D. W. Griffith led to a screen test. Although this proved unsuccessful, Griffith subsequently contracted Pickford at the then unprecedented rate of $10 per day at a time when most Biograph actors earned $5 per day. She quickly became Biograph's most prominent performer and the nickelodeon era's favorite star. Following the trend for relocating to the West Coast, Pickford traveled to Los Angeles in 1910, and after several films including *The One She Loved* and *My Baby,* in *Tess of the Storm Country*—the film that cemented her reputation as a star of motion pictures—she took advantage of the industry's move toward longer feature films.

A first marriage was short-lived and she became involved with Douglas Fairbanks, who she subsequently married in 1920. Together at Pickfair, the Beverly Hills mansion they bought in 1919, the couple, by then referred to as "Hollywood Royalty," seemed to epitomize the optimism of the era. Her fame was such that when she appeared in public, fans would try to touch her hair and clothes, incidents that occasionally resulted in near-riot conditions. During World War I, the couple promoted the sale of Liberty Bonds and afterwards became involved in the Motion Picture Relief Fund, an organization set up to provide financial assistance to impoverished actors.

Pickford's central economic role in the development of the motion picture industry distinguishes her from the majority of silent movie stars. By increasing salary demands, she both increased star salaries and production costs generally and also established a precedent that would change the whole industry. During the 1910s, she worked for Adolph Zukor's Famous Players, moving to First National in 1918, where her reputation gained her more creative control and the then unheard of salary of $675,000 for three films. This, added to a guarantee of 50 percent of the profits, would eventually result in a salary of $1 million a year. Pickford was acknowledged as the financial expert of United Artists, but film releases slowed in the 1920s. Unable to play the roles that had brought her fame in the nickelodeon era or to adapt successfully to the sound era, her acting career stalled in the late 1920s. She finally gave up acting in 1933 to concentrate on production, and even though she married Charles "Buddy" Rogers in 1937 after she and Fairbanks divorced in 1936, Pickford gradually became a recluse, remaining almost wholly at Pickfair.

Bert Williams, 1874–1922

Actor

Bert Williams was the foremost African American vaudeville entertainer of the era, the peak of his career paralleling that of vaudeville. He was born Egbert Austin

Williams in Antigua and, following his family's relocation, spent his early life in Riverside, California. Better educated than most African Americans of the time, Williams finished high school and enrolled at Stanford University. Early performing success, however, encouraged him into show business playing in minstrel troupes. Although he attempted to become a serious singer, setbacks forced him back into minstrelsy. Small-time minstrel shows turned into big-time vaudeville after Williams paired up with his long-term partner, George Walker, and the run of successes, which included popularizing the Cakewalk and a Broadway musical, continued until 1909 when Walker's illness forced his retirement.

Williams then pursued a new career as a stand-up comedian, joining Ziegfeld's Follies and performing with such stars as Eddie Cantor and W. C. Fields. In 1915, he produced, directed, and starred in the films *Fish* and *Natural Born Gambler* (1916) for the Biograph

Bert Williams was an early-20th-century African American actor who often performed in blackface. (Library of Congress)

Company. Williams also recorded his own songs on wax cylinders and early phonograph records. Further appearances with the Ziegfeld troupe continued throughout the decade, but heavy drinking, chronic depression, and overwork extracted a heavy toll. Williams died in 1922 after collapsing on stage.

His triumphs as a central player in the evolution of African American music and the first African American performer to achieve a major Broadway role masked both his own demons—W. C. Fields called him "the funniest man I ever saw, and the saddest man I ever knew" (Cullen, 1996, 125)—and the irony of working in blackface at a time of increasing racial prejudice. Although Williams claimed that blacking up liberated him, it also became something of a straitjacket, as did the exaggerated language of the minstrel show—"as much a foreign dialect as that of Italian," he later observed. (Cullen, 1996, 123) Even though he was a star onstage, he was forced to comply with the dictates of segregation off it. Returning to his luxury hotel with Cantor, Williams commented on the irony of being forced to use the back door: "It wouldn't be so bad, Eddie, if I didn't still hear the applause ringing in my ears." (Cullen, 1996, 125)

Adolph Zukor, 1873–1976

Movie Entrepreneur

Born Adolph Cukor in Hungary, Zukor was the founder of Paramount Pictures and one of the earliest movie moguls. He emigrated to America in 1889 and by 1903 had enjoyed considerable success as a furrier and lived comfortably in New York's affluent German-Jewish area. Zukor became involved in motion pictures when, that same year, he began operating a penny arcade featuring moving pictures on 14th Street at Union Square, New York City. The Automatic Vaudeville Company soon branched out into other cities, with fresh capital from the furrier Marcus Loew, later the president of Loew's Inc., the parent of Metro-Goldwyn-Mayer Pictures.

Following an unsuccessful enterprise where moving pictures were shown in small theaters simulating traveling railroad carriages, the cars were converted into nickelodeons, then increasing in popularity. Zukor resigned from Loew's Enterprises in 1912 and interested the Broadway producer Daniel Frohman in exhibiting a feature-length film. They obtained the American rights to *Queen Elizabeth* starring Sarah Bernhardt, then one of the world's most successful actresses, and the film—considered America's first feature-length film—was shown in the Lyceum Theater and subsequently around the country.

Zukor and Frohman founded the Famous Players Film Company, to produce, so the company motto claimed, "famous plays with famous players," producing first *The Count of Monte Cristo* and others like *The Prisoner of Zenda*. A merger and later consolidation with other smaller companies to form the nationwide distribution and production concern, the Paramount Pictures Corporation, followed.

A skillful director and producer, Zukor transformed the film industry by organizing production, distribution, and exhibition within a single company. Unlike other more flamboyant and temperamental moguls (e.g., D. W. Griffith, Samuel Goldwyn, and Louis B. Mayer, who became almost as celebrated as their stars), Zukor was a self-effacing and businesslike entrepreneur who nevertheless revolutionized the film industry.

REFERENCES AND FURTHER READINGS

Adams, Judith A. 1991. *The American Amusement Park Industry*. Boston: Twayne Publishers.

Allen, Robert C. 1991. *Horrible Prettiness: Burlesque and American Culture*. Chapel Hill: University of North Carolina Press.

Belton, John, ed. 1996. *Movies and Mass Culture*. London: Athlone Press.

Cullen, Jim. 1996. *The Art of Democracy: A Concise History of Popular Culture in the United States*. New York: Monthly Review Press.

Denning, Michael. 1996. *The Cultural Front: The Laboring of American Culture in the Twentieth Century*. London: Verso.

Gans, Herbert J. 1974. *Popular Culture and High Culture: An Analysis and Evaluation of Taste*. New York: Basic Books.

Hall, Ben M. 1961. *The Best Remaining Seats: The Story of the Golden Age of the Movie Palace*. New York: Bramhall House.

Heathcote, Edwin. 2001. *Cinema Builders*. Chichester, West Sussex: Wiley-Academy.

Holmes, Sean P. 2005. "All the World's a Stage! The Actors' Strike of 1919." *Journal of American History* 91, no. 4 (March): 1291–1317.

Kammen, Michael. 1999. *American Culture, American Tastes: Social Change and the 20th Century*. New York: Basic Books.

Kammen, Michael. 1997. *In the Past Lane: Historical Perspectives on American Culture*. New York: Oxford University Press.

Kasson, John F. 1978. *Amusing the Million: Coney Island at the Turn of the Century*. New York: Hill and Wang.

Kessler-Harris, Alice. 2003. *Out to Work: A History of Wage-Earning Women in the United States*. Oxford: Oxford University Press.

Koszarski, Richard. 1994. *An Evening's Entertainment: The Age of the Silent Feature Picture, 1915–1928*. Berkeley: University of California Press.

McBee, Randy D. 2000. *Dance Hall Days: Intimacy and Leisure Among Working Class Immigrants in the United States*. New York: New York University Press.

Macdonald, Dwight. 2005. "A Theory of Mass Culture." In Raiford Guins and Omayra Zaragoza Cruz, eds. *Popular Culture: A Reader*. London: Sage Publications.

Nasaw, David. 1999. *Going Out: The Rise and Fall of Public Amusements*. Cambridge, MA: Harvard University Press.

Nassau County Museum of Art. "Old New York and the Artists of the Period: 1900–1941." http://www.tfaoi.com/aa/2aa/2aa662.htm.

Peiss, Kathy. 1986. *Cheap Amusements: Leisure in Turn-of-the-Century New York*. Philadelphia: Temple University Press.

Thompson, Kristin, and David Bordwell. 1994. *Film History: An Introduction*. New York: McGraw-Hill.

Wilmeth, Don B., and Christopher Bigsby. 1999. *The Cambridge History of American Theater, Volume II: 1870–1945*. Cambridge: Cambridge University Press.

World War I

OVERVIEW

Described variously as the First World War, the War to End All Wars, or, at the time, the Great War, the global conflict that engulfed most of Europe and the rest of the world had profound and enduring consequences on world history and geopolitical configurations thereafter, acting as a hinge between the old 19th-century order and the new, technological modernity of the 20th century. America's active involvement began on April 2, 1917, when President Woodrow Wilson asked Congress to agree to a declaration of war on Germany, followed by the signing of the declaration on April 6, when it was passed by both houses.

Well before this, however, America had been involved with the Allied war effort as financier, supplier of arms and materials, and mediator between the belligerents. Although non-interventionists (e.g., Secretary of State William Jennings Bryan) counseled complete non-involvement, Wilson's hopes that America's wealth and moral stance would encourage the Allies toward a settlement, followed by a democratic world order, gradually diminished as Germany renewed and intensified submarine warfare and the war of attrition in the trenches paralyzed Allied attempts to break the stalemate.

Although Wilson approached the situation from an ethical perspective, believing that America's moral stance could reverse declining European standards and exert power through the nation's vast resources, Americans viewed the war more pragmatically. After an initial period when the State Department disparaged the expansion of loans and credit to combatants and it became clear that the war might continue for some time, the government realized that such an embargo would have a dramatic and devastating effect on trade with America's prewar mercantile associates. America's part in bringing the war to a conclusion without the involvement of millions of fresh troops, when it might have been extended by at least a year, was as much economic as military and political.

The figure of Woodrow Wilson overshadows every aspect of America's involvement: it was his determination to redeem Europe from its own foolishness through a combination of moral and ethical principles and economic opportunism; it was his decision to reverse his hitherto neutral stance and go to war; and it was Wilson who determined the conditions of the declaration and the progress of the war through to the negotiation of the Fourteen Points and the Armistice with the German chancellor in 1918.

TIMELINE

1914   Austria-Hungary declares war on Serbia. Russia mobilizes.

Germany subsequently declares war on Russia and France.

Germany invades Belgium. Following the invasion, Britain counterdeclares war on Germany.

President Wilson offers to act as intermediary, later urging neutrality "in fact as well as name."

U.S. government allows commercial loans to combatants.

1915   Women's Peace Party founded with Jane Addams president.

Commercial Agency Agreement between J. P. Morgan and British government.

Germany proclaims "war zone" around British Isles. Wilson announces Germany would be held accountable for submarine action.

Following the sinking of the *Lusitania,* Wilson sends three notes to Germany, culminating in the final note, which states that further sinkings would be regarded as "deliberately unfriendly."

U.S. Secretary of State William J. Bryan resigns in June, denouncing the trade in arms and the financing of war and Wilson's failure to soften the ultimatum.

British merchantman *Arabic* sinks with loss of two American lives.

Anti-Preparedness Committee founded. Wilson calls for expansion of armed forces.

1916   Limits on submarine warfare declared after torpedoing of *Arabic*.

Germany orders U-boat captains to sink armed merchantmen.

French steamer *Sussex* torpedoed, followed by pledge to discontinue unannounced submarine attacks.

National Defense Act includes agreement on expansion of U.S. Army.

Naval Act sanctions new battleships and destroyers.

Council of National Defense created to coordinate industry and resources for national security purposes.

Wilson re-elected and attempts mediation by requesting peace terms from belligerents.

1917   "Peace without Victory" speech by Wilson. Unlimited German submarine warfare resumes.

United States severs diplomatic relations with Germany. Wilson authorizes arming of U.S. merchant ships. After torpedoing by U-boats, three merchant ships are sunk.

Cabinet advocates U.S. declaration of war.

Following Wilson's request, both houses agree to declaration of war.

Lever Act, also known as the Food and Fuel Control Act, allowing emergency powers to regulate food and fuel supplies passed.

U.S. Food Administration established, providing legislation to assure the supply, distribution, and conservation of food during the war; facilitate its transportation; and prevent monopolies and hoarding.

General John J. Pershing appointed Commander American Expeditionary Force.

Draft registration commences.

First Liberty Loan announced.

First U.S. troops arrive in France.

Government raids on IWW halls begin.

U.S. and Allied military activities coordinated by creation of Supreme War Council.

Railroads appropriated by federal government. U.S. Railroad Administration established.

1918   Wilson presents Congress with the Fourteen Points address.

Bernard M. Baruch appointed head of War Industries Board.

Sedition Act passed by Congress. Overman Act passed, increasing and reinforcing president's war powers.

First significant active combat for U.S. troops. Alongside Allied forces, 300,000 U.S. troops involved in Aisne-Marne offensive, marking a turning point on the Western Front.

"Slacker" raids net thousands of suspected draft evaders.

U.S. soldiers take possession of St. Mihiel salient and embark on Meuse-Argonne offensive.

German chancellor requests armistice derived from the Fourteen Points.

Kaiser Wilhelm II abdicates and armistice becomes effective on November 11.

1919   Paris Peace Conference opens.

After Treaty of Versailles is signed, it is endorsed by Germany and subsequently submitted to Congress by Wilson.

Wilson collapses on nationwide tour, later sustaining a stroke.

Senate rejects Versailles Treaty.

THE WAR

Causes

America's entry into World War I in 1917 had been preceded by three years during which Wilson had attempted to maintain U.S. neutrality in the face of mounting and unprecedented Allied losses and the gradual coagulation of their forces in a war of attrition. Several factors demonstrate the connection between America and Europe from the outbreak of hostilities in Europe in 1914: American commodities, as well as fiscal and political policies, took on an increasingly pivotal role in the development of the war; America's governmental, economic, and cultural conventions and institutions, as well as the majority of its population, had their origins in Europe, and these compelled politicians and, eventually, the American people to realize Europe's significance in America's past, present, and future. This mix of sentiment and economic and political pragmatism provided the context for American diplomacy between 1914 and 1917.

A significant factor in Wilson's 1916 re-election had been his insistence on neutrality; however, America's freedom to trade was challenged by the British blockade and retaliation by German submarines. By 1915, Germany had abandoned the traditional code of practice of alerting ships before attack so that passengers and crew could disembark into lifeboats and adopted a policy of attacking merchant ships without warning, presenting a severe challenge to the policy of neutrality. Economically, American agriculture, manufacturing, mineral reserves, and financial institutions quickly became critical to the Allied war effort, and the blockade of the German merchant fleet effectively ruled out trade with the Central Powers. After initial uncertainty, the economy, boosted by exports to Europe, flourished and Americans were united in the desire to maintain profits from the war trade with a profound reluctance to join the conflict.

Along with the importance to the Wilson administration of continuing economic expansion through trade and loans came Wilson's own growing conviction that America should act as a moral force by bringing about an end to hostilities, both diplomatically and by the power that America could exert through its resources. Ambivalence between adopting the moral high ground while still supplying munitions and inciting international conflict grew in these years, however, as such dissenters as Secretary of State William Jennings Bryan and other politicians and newspaper editors denounced the trade in arms and the financing of war. The torpedoing of the *Lusitania* in May 1915, with the loss of more than 2,000 passengers and crew, including 128 American citizens, nonetheless brought about a shift in Wilson's avowedly neutral stance and the issuance of what was effectively an ultimatum stating that the United States would regard any subsequent sinking as "deliberately unfriendly," a veiled hint at the termination of relations and possible belligerency. Failure to soften the ultimatum led to Bryan's resignation and, with his departure, the disappearance of the most powerful non-interventionist voice.

The sinking of the British merchantman *Arabic* three months later followed by that of the French steamer *Sussex* in March 1916 prompted a pledge to discontinue unannounced attacks, but these promises were not motivated by any sense of fair play; rather, they were driven by the acknowledgment that if America were to enter the war at that time, German submarine numbers were insufficient to counter an American offensive. German submarine production was thus stepped up, but without this information, the Wilson administration continued to attempt to reconcile economic return with nonbelligerency and moral leadership. After late 1916, however, there were growing demands to ready America for war and, following the resumption of unlimited German submarine warfare, attempts to break the blockade. These factors, however, alongside a growing awareness of the bloody stalemate paralyzing Europe, meant that

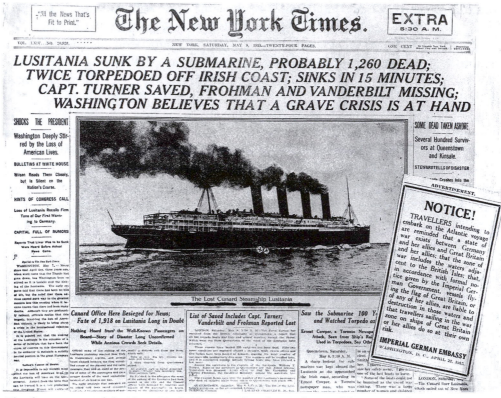

The front page of the New York Times *after the sinking of the ocean liner* Lusitania *by a German submarine, along with a notice printed within from the German Embassy in the U.S. warning against trans-Atlantic travel, May 8, 1915. (Bettmann/Corbis)*

balancing these conflicting tensions was impossible. Diplomatic relations were severed, and on April 2, 1917, Wilson requested that Congress declare war.

The years 1914 to 1917, then, were characterized by considerable diplomatic tension and political and public ambivalence. In large part, these were caused by Wilson's attempts to maintain neutrality in the face of the increasing realization of the scale of European casualties; immigrant (particularly those of German provenance) loyalties divided between their country of origin and their country of adoption, against a sense of isolation and physical remoteness and the knowledge that the choice of America as a new home colored any nostalgia they may have still felt; the desire to profit from the trade in war, coupled with an equal determination to stay out of the conflict; and the belief among dissenters from the prevailing isolationist and economically motivated orthodoxies that simultaneously adopting a high-minded *and* a mercantile stance was no longer morally sustainable.

Immigrant Culture under Siege

Immigrants and immigrant culture came under increasing pressure during the period of American neutrality and escalating tension. Calls for the restriction of immigration had gone on throughout the 19th century, but increases in immigration from southern and eastern Europe after 1880 and publication of the Dillingham Commission report in 1910–1911, as well as the Americanization campaigns and nativism among some parts of the American population, had led to a cumulatively hostile climate for immigrants. The entry of America into the war in 1917 provided a focus and a catalyst for this animosity.

Because German agents had perpetrated acts of sabotage and attempted to incite labor unrest on the East Coast to impede delivery of materials to the Allies, and because some acts of radicalism were carried out by foreign-born extremists, concerns regarding the role of immigrants and their perceived loyalty in a neutral America were not without foundation. Wilson's attacks on hyphenated Americans during the annual message to Congress attracted enthusiastic applause, and in a country where one in three of the population was foreign-born or had at least one parent born abroad, xenophobia reached hysterical levels with America's entry into the war. There was a contentious provision to censor the press included in a program of legislative measures intended to thwart espionage and treason following Wilson's request for a declaration of war.

The Foreign-Language Press during Wartime

Amid petitions to delete that section, support for its retention came from the ethnic and foreign-language press. Aware of their vulnerable position, certain publishers were keen to deflect accusations of disloyalty by capitulating to censorship. Congress removed the provisions from what became the Espionage Act, more so the press would be available for factional criticism and not because of any close ties with the foreign press. The Act was subsequently used by the postmaster general, Albert Burleson, against ethnic groups dependent on the mail to circulate news to members, among others. Foreign-language publications were later monitored by bilingual readers for potentially subversive material. In 1917, Congress extended the powers available to the postmaster general in the Trading-with-the-Enemy Act, which required foreign-language newspapers to submit English translations of articles, referring to a broad sweep of subjects in advance, effectively delaying and even curtailing publication. Although verifiably "loyal" publications could be exempted, many became unconditional and even excessive supporters of the government, whereas others simply ceased publication. Table 7.1 illustrates the number of papers in foreign languages between 1910 and 1920. Although most foreign-language newspapers still maintained their circulation figures after the war, German-language papers are obvious casualties.

Table 7.1. Number of Papers in Foreign Languages in the United States, 1910–1920

Language	1910	1915	1920
Albanian	—	—	4
Arabic	3	11	8
Armenian	6	9	—
Belgian-Flemish	—	—	3
Bohemian	51	55	51
Bulgarian	1	1	1
Chinese	6	7	7
Croatian	8	16	9
Dutch	21	19	13
Finnish	15	18	22
French	34	45	46
German	634	533	276
Greek	8	10	15
Hebrew/Yiddish	21	38	39
Hungarian	12	21	27
Italian	73	96	98
Japanese	9	16	15
Lettish	—	4	2
Lithuanian	11	18	16
Persian	—	—	1
Polish	51	68	76
Portuguese	8	12	18
Romanian	2	2	4
Russian	4	8	11
Scandinavian	139	134	111
Serbian	1	9	7
Slovak	16	19	28
Slovenian	7	10	14
Spanish	55	73	100
Ukranian	1	7	10
Welsh	2	2	2
Total	1,198	1,264	1,052
Total Less German	564	731	776

Source: Adapted from R. E. Park, *Americanization Studies: The Immigrant Press and Its Control* (New York: Harper and Brothers Publishers, 1922), 318; King, 2000, 112.

Anti-German Sentiment

As Americanization programs became more established and animosity more virulent, immigrants were subjected to a widening range of civic and legislative measures, ostensibly intended to facilitate assimilation, but which effectively deprived ethnic groups of their original identities. Gerstle (in King, 2000, 27) discusses how extensive "cultural coercion" had become in northeastern and midwestern American cities swelled and transformed by the prevalence of "ethnic and racial minorities." Many of his comments that during the 1920s "millions of ethnics felt culturally besieged . . . mandatory Americanization programs, and immigration restriction were coercive measures designed to strip immigrants of their foreign languages, customs and politics" could equally be applied to post-1917 America.

Anti-German feelings were evident almost from the start of the war in Europe, but Germans were singled out for fresh outbreaks of xenophobic hostility following America's entry. The excesses that had characterized 100 percent Americanism began to contaminate those who had demonstrated a more tolerant attitude before the war. Patriots declared that allegiance required the complete elimination of German culture. The teaching of German, taught in schools until 1914, was forbidden in many places; German opera and music were ostracized; German place, building, street, and personal names were Anglicized; sauerkraut became liberty cabbage; and hamburgers became Salisbury steaks, or liberty sandwiches. Focusing hostility on Germans meant that censure for other sectors of the foreign-born population was, for the time being, reduced; indeed, the desire for national unity went some way toward removing the barriers between them and older Americans.

Americanization Programs

Teaching immigrants to become American was already underway when America joined the war. Education initiatives originated in two apparently incompatible sources. The first considerations for the American Union Against Militarism and the Committee for Immigrants in America were to encourage education and to safeguard immigrants against exploitative employers and agents. The other initiative was a loose alliance between old-blood Americans whose anxieties for the abiding dominance of their status and values led them into a coalition with businessmen seeking to control a potentially uncooperative and diverse workforce. The latter advocated allegiance based on compliance. The war pressed these two into an alliance that at first seemed biased toward the more liberal approach. Collaboration between the Committee for Immigrants in America and the Bureau of Education led to the "War Americanization Plan" that underwrote English and citizenship classes in schools, community centers, and factories. Despite such liberal sentiments, homogeneity rather than pluralism was the ambition of most reformers and educators.

As American involvement in the war escalated, enlightened education gave way to more repressive tactics concerning preparedness and forced assimilation that partly stemmed from anxieties about America's ability to survive in a hostile situation. Some thinkers, most notably Horace Kallen and John Dewey, argued against Americanization. Kallen believed that "it would require the complete nationalization of education, the abolition of every form of parochial and private school, the abolition of instruction in other tongues than English, and the concentration of the teaching of history and literature upon the English tradition" (King, 2000, 29) and that homogeneity would be counterproductive. These arguments had their advocates at first, but they gradually fell from favor as Americanism and anti-Communism increased after the war. Many immigrants were themselves highly resistant to complete Americanization and antagonistic to the loss of ethnic characteristics. Because the majority of immigrants were trapped in the working class, Americanization meant consent to their subjugation.

By the end of the war, the 100 percent tendency prevailed, with advocates petitioning for state authority of repression and exclusion. The passing of the literacy test for potential immigrants in 1917 and the subsequent ending of unlimited immigration endorsed the nativist spirit the war had reinforced and accelerated.

The Call to War

Wilson had initially expected that the American contribution would be comprised largely of financial aid, materials, and munitions, but circumstances conspired to thwart these beliefs.

Following the declaration of war, the government ratified a multitude of unprecedented measures that included building shipyards and munitions factories, taking over railroads, controlling prices for staple goods, creating new agencies, and imposing tough penalties for undertaking formerly legal transactions. These measures, which penetrated almost every aspect of private life and were intended to mobilize America, combined compulsion and the willingness of the people to participate in what some felt was "state socialism." (Zieger, 2000, 57)

Despite the widespread adoption of power, voluntary methods, appeals to patriotism, and massive publicity were felt to be preferable to unequivocal force. Even though legislation enacted conscription, military enlistment depended more on men's readiness to declare their eligibility for the draft. More than 1 million American soldiers were in action against Germany by mid-1918, and, influenced by Britain's experience and internal factors, Wilson used conscription to mobilize manpower. Britain relied on volunteers at first, but the casualty rate among the young and mostly well-educated men was catastrophic and deprived the army both of manpower and those with leadership qualities, whereas the many skilled men who volunteered would have been better employed in war industries than in the infantry. Moreover, America's own unhappy experience of elite-

The draft board begins the second draft of World War I in 1918. Secretary of War Newton Baker draws the first number, 246, from an urn. (National Archives)

enlisted volunteer forces in the Civil and Spanish-American Wars convinced Wilson to adopt conscription.

In a climate of racial, social, and doctrinal divisions and tensions—and because America was not vulnerable to physical attack—it was at first thought there may be resistance to the draft, but the 10 million men who registered exceeded all expectations. Out of the 24 million who eventually registered, more than 4 million were selected, and almost 4.5 million served in the war. Eleven percent of those eligible, however, evaded the draft. By mid-1918, increased requirements exposed the coercion below the surface of the government's early dependence on patriotism and obedience when federal agents, the police, and vigilantes swept up those reluctant to register.

African Americans were not permitted to volunteer and because occupational exemption was more readily granted to whites, the proportion of African Americans selected was higher. As the negligible army pay actually increased many African American family's incomes, many African American men were not entitled to exemption on the grounds that their families depended on them. Military prejudice resulted in fewer assigned to combat duty, while the exemption of aliens caused bitter resentment, although guarantees of accelerated citizenship did encourage immigrants to register. The comparatively short duration of

America's involvement in a period of breakthrough and ultimate victory, rather than the stasis and stalemate experienced by the other Allies, meant that the casual nature of U.S. conscription was never really tested, but the aggressive nature of government coercion and the patriotic blackmail resorted to by the press indicated the potential for violence and contravention of civil liberties had there been a recruitment crisis.

America already supplied munitions and goods to the Allies, but urgent French and British requests for the most pressing requirement—manpower—were refused by the administration, which planned an independent force instead —the American Expeditionary Force (AEF)—to be allocated its own zone and maintained by an obviously American supply chain. This decision was partly influenced by Wilson's neutral stance before 1917, so no plans existed for training and transporting a sizeable army. Accumulating such a force would necessarily delay the arrival of urgently needed manpower. Maintaining a large military campaign of its own would divert immediate assistance from the Allies as well as existing obligations to supply Europeans with materials. It quickly became clear that this diversion would be further exacerbated by outdated methods of procurement and weapons development and indecision on the extent of government involvement in private enterprise, or, indeed, whether the government should hold a monopoly for weapons and munitions production.

Food and the American Soldier
The chaotic and uncoordinated systems that characterized the army and the War Department between the declaration of war and January 1918 continued to have a paralyzing effect on America's ability to mobilize and equip an army for modern, industrialized warfare. The administration eventually responded to what had become a real crisis in manufacture and acquisition. The army ration had been improved before U.S. belligerence, with items added intended to improve the soldiers' diet, but the cost often exceeded the permitted ration allowance. In theory, American soldiers' rations were better than those of Allied troops; during training, the daily calorie allowance was around 4,000. However, in the field, the official ration, which included canned meat, bread, beans, potatoes, dried fruit, coffee, and sugar, was often replaced by canned tomatoes, canned salmon (known as "goldfish" and so ubiquitous that some soldiers could not face it for years thereafter), and powdered eggs. Soldiers were not allowed to light fires at the front, and logistical problems meant that many went hungry and thirsty, whereas German machine gunners picked off desperate Americans hoping to find water in streams or reduced to licking moist clay. Food piled up in depots behind the front, and contemporary diaries describe food shortages and the poor quality of that food, while recording soldiers' losses of more than 10 percent of their body weight since arriving in France. This reflected a feeling that poor nutrition may have contributed to a reduction in the effectiveness of the AEF.

The civilian situation also began to improve with the streamlining of war-related industries, coordination of the railroads, government intervention in agriculture, and the promotion of economy drives for the public. In food production, the government relied on the appearance of willing acquiescence that disguised the compulsory nature of the measures.

Propaganda

Galvanizing public support for the war demonstrated the government's ability to exploit the methods and terminology of commercial advertising to serve national unity and objectives. Because the threat of direct attack was minimal and the country was divided by racial and ethnic tensions in addition to wholesale antimilitarism and labor conflicts, the government acknowledged that deliberate endeavors would be needed to secure public support. In information, as elsewhere, it relied on the same combination of compulsion, acquiescence, and propaganda. More positive measures that enlisted the support of newspapers, cinemas, libraries, and education to promote war aims and programs were placed along with such legislation as the Espionage and Sedition Acts and widespread powers to subdue free expression.

The war overseas was only part of the war that the government fought. They also had to contend with public apathy and dissent. There were other organizations, both new and old, along with the official and highly visible Committee on Public Information (CPI), which was run by progressive reformer and long-time muckraker George Creel. These other organizations had the largely self-appointed role to secure loyalty or instill opposition to objectors. Geographic remoteness and the absence of any impending emergency meant that mobilizing public opinion was dependent on promoting or even fabricating prowar sentiment through appeals to emotion. Given the widely divergent allegiances of America's many ethnic communities and that Wilson's usual diplomacy had apparently been replaced by belligerence, loyalty was no longer a given. The concern that the country should be of like mind, always a strong thread in American life, was evident even before Alexis de Tocqueville had observed that "few countries displayed less independence of mind and real freedom of discussion" in 1830 (Kennedy, 1980, 46). The feeling that collective and uniform opinion was essential for stability could have been no stronger than in 1917.

Reformers, who were reluctant to attempt any imposition of enlightened opinion through expansion of government power in a country historically antagonistic to state intervention, believed that education and publicity should be the agents of social change instead. Wilson's growing skill in maneuvering public opinion to political ends was influenced by his unshakeable belief in appealing directly to the people; however, in 1917, a reversal on this scale, from a president who only a few months earlier had been re-elected on the basis that

The Committee on Public Information, a creation of the U.S. federal government, issued this propaganda poster during World War I. Four-Minute Men was a nationwide group of respected men who were trained by the government to give four-minute speeches promoting the war cause. (Library of Congress)

he had kept America out of the war, was a difficult sell. Wilson managed to consolidate apparently irreconcilable stances by promoting American belligerence as a fight for a democratic, liberal, redemptive crusade against the forces of barbaric militarism.

Along with the morality of using a combination of sales and public relations methods with Americanism and patriotism to enlist public support, there were also concerns regarding the activities of propagandists who often demonized the enemy and about materials that depicted harrowing scenes and racial stereotypes. The project with the highest profile and perhaps that which caused most concern was the "Four-Minute Men" program. By using local citizens to drive home patriotic messages supporting the war effort, an eventual total of 75,000 speakers delivered necessarily short speeches to captive audiences in movie theaters (a leisure pursuit particularly favored by the working class and foreign-born and thus an important target) at first in the breaks between reel changes, later expanding into schools, community centers, and factories.

Perhaps predictably, given that the speaker was required to present material in a concise, informed, and supposedly nonpartisan way, the orators were culled mainly from the more affluent middle and professional educated classes. Finding working-class speakers proved difficult, and the Four-Minute Men who went into factories and the leisure spaces of workers and immigrants often carried with them the prejudice that their audience was antipathetic or even hostile to the war effort. This campaign, along with those involving the successful mobilization of a vast array of resources, was ostensibly achieved by leaving underlying concerns and establishments intact and by emphasizing compliance, rather than compulsion. The repressive legislation, government-sanctioned vigilantism, implicit threats, and appeals to the more jingoistic side of patriotism, however, hinted at the potential for intimidation had the war lasted longer.

Few observers imagined that the government would produce unbiased and disinterested material—after all, the CPI was established for the sole purpose of presenting one version of the war—but scholars and historians employed to produce pamphlets that were often written in an intelligible yet academic style were often highly partisan and occasionally seditious. Wilson's ideological moral high ground was soon appropriated and misrepresented by factions anxious to manipulate the critical situation to their advantage, thereby corrupting public discourse and undermining credibility. It was distinctly at odds with Wilson's views that some of these academics were also advising the government about America's postwar role.

Schools were obvious targets for competing local and national groups anxious to impose their own patriotic agenda on a highly decentralized education system. In a climate of rabid anti-German hysteria, language and culture were expunged from the curriculum, and early attempts to maintain a routine program and a balanced perspective soon deteriorated as the Bureau of Education began to cooperate with the CPI in the circulation of "war study courses" to schools. Although these courses were intended to present a considered account of the government's war perspective, by selection and omission, and by disallowing ambiguity, complexity, or any negative connotation, they often depicted the conflict and the Germans in a simplistic, one-dimensional, racially stereotyped way, portraying them as the sole aggressors.

Those same features also distinguished prewar popular, and ferociously marketed, publications such as *Collier's* and *McClure's,* whose muckraking exposés of dishonesty and sharp practice in the highest echelons of business and government were notable mainly for inciting indignation, rather than for bringing about any reform achievements. Given that context, Wilson's choice of George Creel to control the CPI was indicative of his avowed intent to appeal directly to the people. A fervent advocate of Wilson and a progressive reformer before the war, Creel abjured compulsion and expurgation as "European," emphasizing the value of voluntarism and consensus in the battle for the "minds of men." (Kennedy, 1980, 61)

Through a campaign of millions of copies of pamphlets in several languages describing America's involvement, war exhibitions, and thousands of press releases to aid (and mold) newspaper reportage, the CPI's agenda gradually drifted away from its instructional vocation, assuming a blunt, propagandistic role. Advertisements urged readers to report anyone who spread antiwar sentiment to the Justice Department, whereas the Four-Minute Men were prompted to employ atrocity stories. Despite Creel and other reformers' belief in the sanctity of "the fact," the simultaneous Americanization campaigns and the activities of the 100 percent American movement soon meant that attempts to control how propaganda was used were increasingly unsuccessful.

The early phases of the campaign to Americanize immigrants through education were characterized by genuine consideration for immigrants' welfare (to protect them from a potentially hostile country). As antagonism to hyphenated Americans grew after the outbreak of war, however, that emphasis shifted to a feeling, rabidly expressed at times, that America should be protected from the potentially harmful immigrant. Creel also believed in assimilation through education, but he also felt that the "tendency towards segregation" (Kennedy, 1980, 66) should be replaced by integration and, thus, homogeneity, rather than cultural and ethnic diversity. In this, he differed little from even enlightened reformers whose aims, if not means, were the same as those who advocated forced assimilation.

Creel's sympathies for immigrants were surrendered in the pernicious wave of hostility and prejudice that, by the end of the war, had resulted in the triumph of the 100 percent tendency. His consideration for labor similarly succumbed to the same diehards. The CPI considered immigrants and workers largely interchangeable and emphasized the importance of both groups in every aspect of their propaganda because they were critical to the war effort. Capital and government determined to act on several fronts: to minimize labor's potential for disruption, to prevent workers from enhancing wages or conditions, to decrease the possibility of unionization, and to undermine the threat that workers would be attracted to socialism or, worse, pacifism. Although all these jeopardized the government's mobilization of industry campaign, employers viewed attempts by radical groups to recruit workers as a singular opening to stigmatize *all* labor unrest as treacherous.

Creel was aware of employers' attempts to use patriotism as a blunt instrument to ensure workers' loyalty and resisted such efforts. Creel instead believed that "the most important task we have before us today . . . is that of convincing the great mass of workers that our interest in democracy and justice begins at home." (Kennedy, 1980, 71) Creel opposed the lure of socialism by enlisting the president of the American Federation of Labor (AFL) and implacable foe of socialism, Samuel Gompers. He established a Division of Industrial Relations at the CPI, as well as a propaganda section of the Department of Labor, distributing posters and sending speakers to factories. Creel's other initiative (financing the American Alliance for Labor and Democracy) was intended to keep labor "industrious, patriotic, and quiet." (Kennedy, 1980, 72) These objectives were remarkably similar to those employers who rejected labor demands as disloyal, and the eventual outcome of labor in the war demonstrated how, in practice, welfare and loyalty were inseparable.

Newspapers and Magazines

Wilson's declaration in 1914 that America must be neutral in fact as well as in name seemed to reflect the mood of the American public fairly accurately. When the weekly magazine *Literary Digest* asked 367 newspaper editors on which side their sympathies lay, 105 favored the Allies, 20 favored the Central Powers, and 242 stated that they had no preference. (Wells, 2002) Although American participation in the war still seemed a long way off in 1914, it is evident in terms of propaganda that the British grasped the initiative in their attempts to influence American opinion from very early in the conflict. After Germany's trans-Atlantic cable link with America was severed by the British navy only days after the outbreak of hostilities, American newspapers were almost entirely dependent on British sources for news on the war. American war correspondents based in London were treated extremely favorably by the British propaganda operation, who were thus able to mold what was read by Americans back home and therefore ensure that the war would be seen "as if through British eyes." (Ibid.) Substantial quantities of war-related material was also sent to American newspapers and libraries who, given the appetite for news, were pleased to receive it. In contrast, German attempts to influence American opinion were largely regarded as ineffectual. Since Germany merely had to maintain American neutrality while Britain had to alter American opinion, German objectives were rather more limited. Nevertheless, American opinion was swayed by such policies as unrestricted submarine warfare and the execution of Nurse Edith Cavell, which was widely reported in the American press, in marked contrast to the subsequent execution of two German nurses, which went almost unreported. The U.S.-based German propaganda effort was centered in New York because it was believed that provincial papers would follow the lead of the more prominent and influential newspapers there.

The Allied cause was undoubtedly helped by the increasingly active preparedness lobby, whose views became more prowar and more stridently interventionist as the war progressed. One of the lobby's more vocal advocates was former president Theodore Roosevelt, whose inflammatory rhetoric (which argued for the outright banning of the German language in schools and that women who did not raise their sons to be soldiers were unfit to live in America) in newspaper editorials matched the more extreme opinions of conservative business interests and the National Security League. The CPI's Division of News published two newspapers (the *Official Bulletin* and the *War News Digest*) as well as press releases and a Division of Syndicated Features, which originated war material for inclusion in the feature sections of Sunday papers for those readers who did not read headline descriptions of the war. The CPI, which was ceaselessly active in influencing newspaper coverage of the war, also established a Foreign Language Newspaper Division to overlook the content of those papers, as well as a Bureau of Cartoons to promote patriotic content in that area. A Division of Advertising was created to exploit the skills of the advertising industry, while ensuring that space donated by newspapers was used to maximum effect, and to assist the government in the writing of advertising copy.

Because the CPI had particular anxieties about the perceived loyalty of women, immigrants, and labor, the Division of Women's War Work targeted these domestic workers as part of a wider campaign to mobilize women by focusing propaganda efforts specifically toward them. The CPI attempted to invalidate

Activists Jane Addams and Mary McDowell demonstrate for a peaceful end to World War I. Addams was the first chairwoman of the Woman's Peace Party, a movement created to bring an end to the war. (Library of Congress)

the opinions of women activists by manipulating magazine content because women could make a significant contribution to the war effort through food conservation and, more importantly, because they had been active in the peace movement and were regarded as a potentially subversive threat to unity and stability—"unpatriotic, selfish, more pacifist than men, and excessively devoted to their sons." (Ibid.) The *Ladies Home Journal* had a particularly close relationship with the CPI, both in editorials supporting Wilson and outlining how women could and should assist the war effort as wives, mothers, and volunteers, and by the use of highly mawkish and jingoistic covers and articles on prudence and conservation and the difficulties caused by "sacrificing" their sons. In this way, magazines like the *Ladies Home Journal* created an important conduit for the national agencies to reach significant numbers of the population.

In addition to domestic newspapers, between February 1918 and June 1919, the U.S. Army published *The Stars and Stripes* for forces in France. Intended to provide a feeling of unity and a sense of their part in the war effort to a highly dispersed army, the weekly paper, which was printed in Paris and distributed by train and automobile, published domestic and sports news as well as cartoons and poetry.

Joining the Army

The reality of the draft, where significant inequities in the ethnic and class composition of draftees were exposed, demonstrated the inaccuracy of the assertion by political and moral leaders that the AEF constituted a new spirit of democratic egalitarianism. Although joining the army did lead to the amalgamation of men from diverse ethnic and religious environments, there was never the cohesion or the sense that it functioned as the melting pot that some claimed for it. Moreover, the discriminatory and prejudicial treatment of native-born African Americans contradicted American egalitarian conceits. The polyglot nature of the force was such that some Europeans denounced it as the "American Foreign Legion," whereas some estimates put the proportion of foreign-born draftees at 20 percent.

The army was comprised of heroic, pioneer-descended riflemen, keen to reestablish order and to liberate the sclerotic battlefields of France. That, at least, was the vision presented by the army to the population at large. Despite a grudging acknowledgment of the importance of the machine gun in modern warfare, the rifleman was thought to provide the core to the military effort; however, the reality was rather different because most men were unfamiliar with firearms and because of weapons shortages, so soldiers were not issued a rifle until departure. The 20 percent of foreign-born soldiers spoke around 49 different languages, making communication difficult at best. The recruits were found to be physically and mentally underweight, and around one-third were illiterate. Recently designed but racially biased IQ tests assessed that 47 percent of whites and around 90 percent of African Americans were under the mental age of 13. (Zieger, 2000, 87) The validity of the tests was disputed, however, when northern African Americans scored higher than Appalachian whites because this was inconsistent with racial stereotypes. Historians describe these tests as a prime example of the 1910s construction of racial hierarchies.

Making an Army

By September 1917, incentives in the construction industry resulted in some 32 new accommodation and training units for up to 400,000 soldiers. By the end of the year, one of the most comprehensive and costly construction projects undertaken in the United States was completed. Of the 200,000 officers required, almost half had to be recruited or promoted from the ranks and then trained, and after 90 days, they were meant to train new recruits who themselves often received little military training. American soldiers often learned little of Allied developments in coordinating tank, air, and infantry attacks, whereas shortages meant that many wore civilian clothes during basic training.

The lack of military equipment and weapons training that would equip recruits for modern warfare meant concentration on physical conditioning, whereas many were exposed to dental and medical care and a wholesome and varied diet for the first time. Nor was their moral and religious welfare neglected. Under the auspices of the military-sanctioned Commission on Training Camp Activities (CTCA), the Young Men's Christian Association (YMCA) and other organizations undertook entertainment, education, and religious programs designed to keep soldiers healthy in mind as well as body, and to avoid problems with the sexually transmitted diseases that afflicted European troops, which might impair their military efficiency. Cooperation between the CTCA and the War Department resulted in campaigns against vice and led to the establishment of vice-free zones around military facilities.

Ethnic and African American Recruits

No consistent policy for the induction of immigrants existed; some non–English speakers, along with those considered unsuitable for hostilities, were consigned to "depot brigades" to be allocated lowly tasks. Others felt that induction was an opportunity for Americanization, so the Army created "development battalions"—units for "substandard but remediable" recruits (Kennedy, 1980, 158) who would receive instruction in the English language and American history. Elsewhere, ethnically segregated sections were formed, overseen by officers acquainted with the relevant languages. Even greater ambivalence, conflating hatred and alarm, existed toward the militarization of African American recruits, the arming of whom constituted a threat for some. The army was thus strictly segregated on the basis of race, but several important problems were never satisfactorily resolved: Where would training take place? How should they be deployed (i.e., in combat or as service troops)? Should officers be African American? Should recruits be centralized in the South, or trained quickly in the North then sent immediately to France? Should there be a single African American regiment at each training unit? The War Department ultimately made no commitment to resolving the "so-called race question." (Kennedy, 1980, 159)

Racial violence in Texas precipitated the decision by the War Department to spread African American recruits throughout the camps, a decision that applied equally to the single African American combat division (the 92nd). None of the 14 officer-training units accepted African Americans, and on graduation, officers from the exclusively African American officer-training program at Des Moines, Iowa, were detailed to the 92nd, where the policy of white superior officers was maintained. Compared with around 66 percent overall of AEF troops who experienced combat in France, only 20 percent of African Americans encountered combat; as in civilian America, the majority worked in subservient assignments.

Conscientious Objectors and Draft Evaders

Conscientious objectors were defined only as those exempted on religious grounds because there initially were no concessions for ethical objectors or German Americans. They were often subject to arbitrary decisions because guidelines regarding which religious groups were exempt were imprecise and, therefore, many were unfairly treated. There was also no alternative to combat specified, so 20,000 were enlisted, only to experience substantial hostility. Many were subsequently "shamed" into waiving their objections. Although appropriate noncombatant pursuits were defined in 1918, protesters who were unable to convince the Board of Inquiry of the validity of their beliefs were still persecuted, as were "absolutists" whose refusal to comply with any military instruction often led to courts-martial and subsequent imprisonment.

As the war progressed, the initially tentative efforts to net draft evaders were stepped up with the initiation of so-called slacker raids, which trapped many thousands of draft-age men. Along with other such measures (e.g., the introduction of a classification system to grade the supply of registrants and the widening of eligible age limits), these were designed to expand those eligible for the draft and gave the lie to the pretence that the government simply chose from a pool of volunteers. Massive publicity measures were instigated to appeal to those newly eligible, suggesting that the government still preferred the voluntary route, but also that the limits of this approach were being reached now that the initial enthusiasm was beginning to wane. They also reflect the growing awareness by the military of a potential shortfall in manpower, and it is clear that had the war gone on any longer more rigorous measures would have been needed.

The 1917 Espionage Act gave the government sufficient power to suppress any opposition to the war, including $10,000 fines and up to 20 years imprisonment for those impeding military operations during wartime. The American Socialist Party, which was unambiguously committed to an antiwar position by 1916, provided the largest coherent group opposing America's participation in the war by 1917, declaring the war to be a crime against the people of the United States and advocating robust opposition to conscription, censorship, and restriction of labor's prerogative to strike. Government suppression of socialist opposition was thus given legal sanction in the Espionage Act.

Even though many reformers were ambivalent about America's involvement in the war, they along with medical professionals and government officials regarded the induction period as an opportunity to test and refine ways in which life could be improved. A new feeling of national pride, identity, and unity could be inculcated, they believed, while simultaneously familiarizing recruits with healthy, patriotic, and forward-looking influences. This thereby made them ideal ambassadors for distinctively American principles of ethical superiority, limitless optimism, and the values of their country's achievements.

In the Army

Despite initial concerns that neither training resources nor transportation would be adequate for large numbers of troops, a number of Allied setbacks in late 1917 and early 1918 led to the acceleration of inductions and shipments of American troops to France. Alongside increasingly desperate Allied entreaties for American troops, the continuing hesitancy over whether Americans should be amalgamated into Allied units led to confusion and indecision in the government. The commander of the AEF, General John J. Pershing, had no such doubts. He believed that American soldiers would be better deployed as a separate force on the Western Front. His uncompromising position was informed by several factors: that amalgamation would be unpopular with both the public and soldiers themselves; that American troops would be used to make French or British soldiers available for deployment elsewhere; that it would obstruct his main aim

IQ Tests

IQ tests were also called the Stanford-Binet test, so-called after Alfred Binet (pioneer of the procedure who originally designed the tests in the early 20th century with children in mind) and Stanford University (where the tests were refined and the term *intelligence quotient* was coined). They were promoted by the American Psychological Association as a method of filtering out the mentally unfit and categorizing army inductees by intelligence. They also had the added advantage of providing psychologists with massive amounts of data. Even though they were faced with huge numbers of recruits who had to be sorted into various army positions, the service was nevertheless initially ambivalent about the tests. By early 1918, however, all training camps had examiners who graded recruits "superior," "average," or "inferior." This supposedly allowed potential officer trainees to be identified and the rest to be dispersed throughout various units.

Examiners remarked on the degree of illiteracy revealed (between 25 percent and 30 percent) and the sparse educational background of recruits. The difference in years of education between native whites, immigrants, and southern African Americans was also notable in the figures (6.9, 4.7, and 2.6, respectively) (Kennedy, 1980, 188), along with how few had graduated from high school. "Native" or old immigrant recruits predictably tended to be classified "superior," whereas new immigrants were often classified as "inferior," among them Italian, Russian, and Polish recruits scoring particularly poorly. Although still more African Americans were categorized as "inferior" (around 80 percent) and had higher illiteracy rates, many questions tended to favor native whites. The value of such a crude and embryonic measurement tool is debatable. The widely disseminated test results merely reinforced the prejudices of those reactionaries looking for "proof" of African American and immigrant inferiority.

Table 7.2 gives examples taken from intelligence tests given to U.S. soldiers in "home" training camps. Contrary to claims that the tests measured intelligence, many questions were biased toward demonstrating a familiarity with mainstream American culture and educational background. The questions were included in the exam given to literate recruits. A checked box indicates responses that were considered correct.

The army remained highly skeptical of the procedure and ended the tests shortly after the end of the war in 1919, at which time they were enthusastically appropriated by the educational system.

(to bypass the stalemate of the trenches and mount an overwhelming assault on German forces); and that a separate American force was critical in any peace negotiations after the war. Pershing's resolution and his insistence on the use of the rifle, however, ignored the realities of modern technological warfare (long-range artillery and machine guns forced both sides into defensive positions)

Army recruiter administers an IQ test to an African American man, March 15, 1918.
(Bettmann/Corbis)

and that American officers were evidently ill-prepared to conduct a massive and complex military operation.

Pershing's insistence on a separate force eventually resulted in the co-option of America as a full partner, and despite its dependence on Allied artillery and transport, negotiations were completed with the British to supply shipping. Along with the streamlining of formerly chaotic supply and procurement channels in America, this meant that increasing numbers of American troops began to arrive in France by early 1918.

Battles: War Is Hell

Inspired by government propaganda that was informed more by 19th-century notions of Civil War heroism than the realities of 20th-century industrialized warfare, along with the highly romanticized and much-embellished tales of derring-do, the boyish expectation and eagerness that animated young recruits acted as an antidote to three years of news of day-to-day trench warfare and atrocities and the evidence on arrival that modern war meant long periods of boredom in often appalling conditions, interspersed by terrifying and bloody carnage. There were four major engagements involving American units, but the Meuse-Argonne

Table 7.2. Examples Taken from Intelligence Tests Given to U.S. Soldiers in "Home" Training Camps

Food products are made by
- ☐ Smith & Wesson
- ☑ Swift & Co.
- ☐ W. L. Douglas
- ☐ B. T. Babbitt

"Hasn't scratched yet" is used in advertising a
- ☐ Duster
- ☐ Flour
- ☐ Brush
- ☑ Cleanser

Nabisco is a patent
- ☐ Medicine
- ☐ Disinfectant
- ☑ Food product
- ☐ Tooth paste

The Dictaphone is a kind of
- ☐ Typewriter
- ☐ Multigraph
- ☑ Phonograph
- ☐ Adding machine

The Battle of Gettysburg was fought in
- ☑ 1863
- ☐ 1813
- ☐ 1778
- ☐ 1812

"Spare" is a term used in
- ☑ Bowling
- ☐ Football
- ☐ Tennis
- ☐ Hockey

Scrooge appears in
- ☐ *Vanity Fair*
- ☑ *The Christmas Carol*
- ☐ *Romola*
- ☐ *Henry IV*

Why are pencils more commonly carried than fountain pens? Because
- ☑ They are brightly colored
- ☐ They are cheaper
- ☐ They are not so heavy

Why is leather used for shoes? Because
- ☐ It is produced in all countries
- ☑ It wears well
- ☐ It is an animal product

Streets are sprinkled in summer
- ☐ To make the air cooler
- ☐ To keep automobiles from skidding
- ☑ To keep down dust

Why is wheat better food than corn? Because
- ☑ It is more nutritious
- ☐ It is more expensive
- ☐ It can be ground finer

If a man made a million dollars, he ought to
- ☐ Pay off the national debt
- ☑ Contribute to various worthy charities
- ☐ Give it all to some poor man

Source: Keene, 2000, 96–97.

countered Pershing's assertion that large numbers of enthusiastic troops could repel established and experienced German forces. Pershing's situation, exacerbated by insufficient supplies of food, water, and ammunition, was made worse by inexperienced officers, exhausted troops weakened by influenza, and the chaotic logistical state of supply chains behind the front that resulted in massive traffic jams where even the wounded could not be evacuated to base hospitals.

Progress was slow even though Pershing brought in fresh troops and resolved logistical problems. American dependence on French artillery support meant that their skill in this area only began to become apparent in the final stages of the war. Pershing's reliance on infantrymen also meant that the potential of the tank to effect the open warfare that he felt would be decisive was never fully realized. The battlefields of Aisne-Marne and Meuse-Argonne finally destroyed any illusions that American soldiers might still have harbored about chivalry, glory, and old-fashioned values. American troops told of poison gas, unburied corpses, and body parts in fetid pools; rats grown fat on human offal; lice that were impossible to eradicate; and the reek of excrement and decaying bodies.

Some cultural artifacts do go some way to giving an accurate depiction of the war, but the majority of these were not seen until after the conflict. Although there are many paintings that epitomize the horror and futility of World War I, two stand out. The first, William Orpen's *The Signing of Peace in the Hall of Mirrors, Versailles, 28th June 1919,* was perhaps the most important British painting commissioned of the war, and it cost £3,000 against the £300 for John Singer Sargent's *Gassed.* It was intended to record the roles of the leading Allied politicians, diplomats, and military in the defining moment as they demonstrate their unity and power in the signing of the treaty.

The location is the scintillating Hall of Mirrors at Versailles, Louis XIV's demonstration of his political power and wealth. Above the delegates' heads, the legend *Le Roy Gouverne par lui même* refers tellingly to the interminable disagreements as Germany claimed to be unable to meet the penalties imposed and the Allies could not reach a compromise. Orpen emphasizes the profligacy of the architecture, thus reducing the politicians to a subsidiary role. The apparent orderliness of their world is distorted and fragmented by the mirrors in which the artist's reflection also appears and, perhaps more significantly, no other audience. For Orpen, politics is reduced to superficial posturing, signifying that the political forces and personal conceit and arrogance that molded the palace still exist.

The second, *Gassed,* by John Singer Sargent, was commissioned by the British Government for the Hall of Remembrance for World War I. Sargent was given the theme of "Anglo-American co-operation," but was unable to arrive at an appropriate subject. While visiting a casualty clearing station at Le Bac-de-Sud, Sargent saw an orderly leading some soldiers blinded by mustard gas. He decided on this allegorical frieze as an explicit rejection of the implication of comradeship. Still used to exemplify the horrors of technological, chemical warfare and to challenge the morality of its use, this harrowing image depicts a game of football in the background, Shown in sharp contrast to the casualties, the footballers are physically and visually coordinated, demonstrating their indifference to a routine event.

Although machine gun emplacements inflicted terrible casualty rates, artillery barrages were worse because their source was unseen and survival was often the result of providence. Considering the short period Americans saw active combat, casualties were heavy: 60,000 died in battle and a similar number from disease, with many falling prey to the influenza pandemic that accounted for at least 20 million lives in 1918 and 1919. American wounded fared better than

Shell Shock

"Shell shock" or "war neurosis" proved to be more resistant to treatment. Shell shock was characterized variously by twitching, loss of mobility, debilitating insomnia, catatonia, hysteria, or extreme lethargy in a climate in which honor and willing dedication to duty were prized. Early victims were treated as shirkers or cowards and punished, sometimes with the death penalty. Others were exposed to such bizarre and gruesome "cures" as electroshock treatment or physical and psychological harassment. The inadequacy and barbarism of these methods had become apparent by the time America entered the war. Medical officers preferred rest and nutrition in more amenable surroundings, which were nevertheless still undertaken in military conditions to emphasize soldiers' responsibilities to the army and their colleagues and to speed the resumption of duties. Those failing to respond to treatment were isolated and given menial tasks that, it was hoped, would promote sufficient shame for the soldier to submit to more positive methods. Concern that some would use the symptoms to avoid combat prompted doctors to avoid the use of the term *shell shock* because it validated neglect of duties by relating it to a discernible cause.

Statistics of those suffering psychological breakdown are vague and inconclusive, but it is believed that 100,000 men were admitted with nervous or related ailments, almost half of which were given disability discharges; however, not all these were combat related because many thousands of men were discharged from training camps in America and France. The real effects of wartime experiences were often not felt until some years later, with victims often suffering for decades thereafter.

Allied soldiers, largely because of what American doctors attached to the British—whose standards were significantly higher than the French—and those who served as volunteers before U.S. involvement, had learned about wound treatment and the importance of antiseptic conditions. Well-equipped and trained American doctors had an excellent record treating casualties of the pernicious effects of modern warfare and combat conditions.

Despite the relatively brief period in which U.S. soldiers experienced active service, they took part in several conclusive campaigns. Their principal value did not lie in the actual performance of American soldiers; rather, it lay in the sheer numbers of reinforcements that had inundated the Western Front by July 1918, and that signaled the beginning of the end of German operations. Allied troops also attested to the bravery and willingness of Americans to submit themselves to potentially murderous situations. America's involvement was critical in ending the attrition of stalemated trench warfare, and, as Zieger observes, "the AEF's exertions in 1918 undoubtedly helped shorten the war by perhaps as much as a year." (Zieger, 2000, 114)

Coming Home

World War I ended suddenly in November 1918, yet the reversal of German fortunes that sent their troops into retreat and their subsequent capitulation belied the ambiguity of the situation. Despite Germany's victory in the east, they were defeated decisively on the Western Front. In addition, many critical territorial, military, and political issues remained unresolved on both fronts. Although most of northern France and parts of Belgium had been liberated, the German army remained active until November and Allied forces sustained heavy losses. Even after the formal cessation of hostilities, Germany remained in control of significant parts of Belgium, some of northeastern France, and almost all of Alsace-Lorraine. Even though France and Belgium had suffered enormous structural damage, Germany itself was paradoxically almost entirely unscathed. Despite Pershing's call for surrender and the wholesale rout of the German army, the exhausted Allies favored armistice. In October, Germany had requested an armistice based on Wilson's Fourteen Points, which he had presented to Congress in January 1918 and which emphasized the reconstruction of democracy, rather than retribution. Following a month of negotiations, the armistice was signed and became effective at 11:00 a.m. on November 11. The terms of the armistice and the subsequent Treaty of Versailles, however, were far from Wilson's Fourteen Points that German leaders hoped would exempt them from unsympathetic treatment.

For many American soldiers, the conflict had scarcely begun. During the brief period when American forces saw active combat, the average "doughboy" spent more time away from combat than at war, and despite the fact that around 1.3 million servicemen experienced enemy fire, almost none was exposed to the apparently endless awfulness, boredom, and terror that European forces underwent. The many letters sent home by American soldiers, and the journals and diaries they kept, record their ambivalence to an armistice that relieved them of the obligation to fight on set against their sense that their experience overseas had been an exceptional interlude in an otherwise ordinary life. Reflecting afterwards, many men commented on the beauty and history of the country away from the battle zones, while still perpetuating the myth of the contrast between the exhausted, even effete quality of France and the French against the sheer energy and can-do attitude of the Americans. Troops became tourists both during and after the conflict, although many were at pains to emphasize their more "manly" activities, rather than to dwell on less heroic visits to cathedrals or the Côte d'Azur. The soldiers' inability to respond to the grandeur and beauty, or indeed to their war experiences, in authentic speech was evident in many of these accounts, and overwhelmed soldiers often resorted to the vocabulary of tourist publicity or clichés from classic literature.

There was little evidence of soldiers' deference toward France in their feelings about the army, however; journals contain constant complaints about the food, the conditions, the physical and psychological constraints of military life, and, above all, the discipline, which sat awkwardly with entrenched notions of egalitarianism and independence. Nevertheless, more than a few soldiers commented on their wish to remain in France, partly because the end had come so quickly after the AEF had entered the war, and partly because relief at the end of hostilities was tempered by a sense that things would never be the same again: they would no longer be out in the open, in definitively male company. For some returning troops, America seemed to lack the color and romance of "Over There."

On their return, 450 parades took place, but initial fervor soon dissipated and many soldiers, discharged long after the armistice, returned to an apathetic society, impatient to forget the war. By mid-1919, more than 2 million soldiers had been discharged, and by the end of the year, enlisted numbers had fallen to a peacetime low of 130,000. Concerns were raised over the ability of industry to assimilate large numbers of unemployed soldiers quickly enough. Some companies and organizations (e.g., General Electric) re-employed demobilized soldiers in order of seniority, but many released great numbers of civilians employed in wartime production, thus destabilizing the economy, which was, in part, a contributory factor to the depression of the early 1920s. Other anxieties focused on the potential drain to the public purse; the economist and social scientist Thorstein Veblen grumbled about "a legion of veterans organized for a draft on public funds and the cultivation of a warlike distemper." (Veblen, 1922, 347) Notwithstanding public indifference, official acknowledgment of bravery was exhibited in the creation of several new awards by the War Department, but more material support was urgently needed for hundreds of thousands of the unemployed or wounded of displaced veterans.

Legislation to rehabilitate veterans and to aid readjustment was enacted during the later stages of the war and after it, providing government-subsidized life insurance and disability coverage, vocational training, improvements to pensions, and a $60 discharge allowance in recognition of military service. The situation for African American veterans was, predictably, less than satisfactory. Elements of both the 92nd and 93rd divisions had seen action on the Western Front, but because of inadequate training, lack of essential equipment in France, and poor leadership, neither division was able to realize their full potential. The 93rd accumulated an honorable record, receiving many awards from the French, including several Croix de Guerre, but the 92nd, after disastrous failures of (white) leadership, mishandling, and appalling discrimination, were cast as failures during a bungled mission in the Meuse-Argonne offensive in what the army regarded as an experiment in the use of African American combatants and the commissioning of African American officers. After the war, their commanding general, Charles Ballou, who had described the 92nd as the "Rapist Division," refused to allow photographers to document the awarding of medals to his men. The white 35th division was absolved in a postwar army report, whereas the

Members of the 369th Infantry pause after a battle in France during World War I. The 369th served with the French 4th Army and played a major role in the defeat of Germany on the Western Front. Two of the men, Private Henry Johnson and Private Needham Roberts, displayed exceptional courage under fire during a German assault and were decorated with the French Croix de Guerre. (National Archives)

conduct of the African American 369th under similar circumstances exposed the true nature of African American combatants. No African American soldiers were allowed to take part in the Allied victory parade in Paris.

If returning African American soldiers believed that their service overseas might have changed the situation back home, they were to be disappointed. The same pattern of rejection, deprecation, and contempt that characterized their treatment before and during the war greeted their return. Insufficient and inadequate housing and the worsening economic situation meant that African American veterans were forced to compete for accommodation and employment with African Americans migrating from the South as well as European immigrants returning from the war. These tensions inevitably increased racial and class antagonisms across urban America until, in the spring and summer of 1919, serious race riots broke out in 22 American cities and towns. Chicago experienced the worst of these.

Unlike the Revolution and the Civil War, where African Americans' key role had imposed enlightened revision of their status and employability, no significant improvements occurred as a result of World War I. After the war, and despite African Americans' growing confidence and their resolve to shake off subjection and their recognition of the manpower requirements of industry and the forces in the reconfiguration of urban and industrial realities brought about by the Great Migration, and the increasing power of civil rights organizations, the government hurriedly retreated from any resolution of race-related issues.

Women and War

The question of women's function and status in World War I was as contentious as either the "labor problem" or the "Negro problem," and was potentially more likely to jeopardize and undermine existing power structures. Although perhaps less likely to result in violence, the repercussions of any successful petition for equality in social, political, and personal realms challenged those structures as well as male authority in a period of rapid change when masculine identity and men's perceptions of "women's place" were already threatened by campaigns for female suffrage and women's advances into new occupations. Despite initiatives that acknowledged women's concerns and the support of President Wilson and others, establishment figures in the public and private spheres attempted to protect gender superiority from the new opportunities that war created for women.

In the popular press and in magazines, women were urged to sacrifice "selfish" maternal impulses in favor of patriotism, allowing their men to enlist without guilt, whereas activists and dissenters were charged with sedition and subversion. In the run-up to American involvement, it was evident that the vocally active women who dominated both sides of the pacifism versus preparedness debate were drawn from a privileged elite, rather than from economically and socially dependent working- or middle-class women who were mostly denied suffrage. On one hand, activists like Jane Addams transferred their support for women's rights to pacifism, whereas on the other, such organizations as the Women's Department of the National Civic Federation argued that only preparedness could defend America against aggressors. Both sides' roles were transformed by America's entry in to the war; several pacifist groups gave notional support to the Wilson administration, whereas advocates of preparedness undertook such practical tasks supporting the war effort as preparing first aid kits or promoting food conservation.

For the majority of women, though, supporting America's war effort meant either a military or quasi-military role for a small minority or civilian employment in an economy deprived of European immigrants and of men who had enlisted for the majority. Women in the navy were accorded equal rank with their male compatriots, fulfilling administrative tasks and thus freeing up men for combat duty. Although they were eligible for veterans' benefits after the war, none was offered the opportunity to continue after the war and no women attained the rank of officer. The army was less enlightened. Women, including nurses (whose status was ambivalent at best), administrative staff, and switchboard operators were not conferred military status, even though many served in France. Although many wore uniforms and were accountable to military staff, they were classed as civilians and were ineligible for veterans' benefits. Despite the obvious and urgent requirement for auxiliary and administrative personnel, the army was sluggish and erratic in enlisting women and in acknowledging their worth. Although an Army Nurse Corps had been created in 1898 and more than 21,000 women served in it during the war—half of them overseas—the army's hesitancy regarding their position and importance was an enduring problem for nurses and impeded their effectiveness. AEF nurses, who were often denied a direct role in patient care, had no formal jurisdiction, and routinely untrained male ward masters, for example, often controlled their access to medicines.

Many were unaware whether they belonged to the AEF or to such civilian bodies as the American National Red Cross, who had recruited and placed them. Despite these barriers, however, the performance of army nurses was outstanding. Hundreds served in special surgical units, nursing appallingly injured men behind the front line. Even though none died in combat, several were injured by enemy fire (in which circumstances, more than 200 were decorated for bravery), whereas more than 200 died from influenza and other diseases. Although the need for medical staff was compelling, the army prohibited the employment of Red Cross–trained African American nurses, although some were eventually allowed to treat African American soldiers in the United States.

Women in civilian employment fared little better. Despite the evident necessity that women should fill formerly unavailable occupations, many employers and male co-workers remained resistant and antagonistic. The authorities did make some attempts to rectify inequalities and discrimination in such essential industries as munitions, but these hesitant initiatives ended after the armistice, and women were displaced from occupations only briefly available to them in both military and civilian fields. Despite the apparent need for many more wartime workers, there was no dramatic increase in the actual number of working women; however, a radical restructuring of the configuration of paid employment did happen. Domestic occupations fell markedly, whereas office jobs and such activities as assembly-line work, semi-skilled operations, driving, and laboring, along with many occupations formerly the preserve of men (e.g., welding and track repair on the railroads) increased noticeably. Women benefited from the wartime trend for disproportionate pay level rises in these lower-paid and lower-skilled jobs, but, perhaps predictably, there were fewer opportunities and more barriers for African American women, who were often left with jobs that white women avoided.

During World War I, women took the place of men on the Great Northern Railway at Great Falls in Montana. (National Archives)

Opinion regarding changed roles and opportunities was mixed and often contradictory. Better pay and experience offered young women, particularly, more autonomy, but even though women were assailed from all sides with entreaties to enter the labor market, misgivings arose about women's susceptibility to sexual experimentation, on the one hand, and their effect on young men, particularly soldiers, on the other. Hostility from male co-workers often emerged over fears of loss of status and perceived dilution of standards by ill-trained women. Some employers were urged to exclude women, whereas unions were persuaded to petition state legislatures (successfully) to bar women from certain occupations. Some unions, however, adopted a more progressive policy toward women, and female membership rose during the decade. Women often took an active role in unions. They negotiated for better pay and conditions, and they participated in the 6,000 or so strikes during the period of U.S. involvement.

Government agencies established to address specific issues related to increased female employment often encountered hostility from employers who resented interference from officials—often women themselves—suspecting pro-union sympathies, whereas male workers suspected that officials would abet employers' efforts to erode wage levels and dilute skills. The furtherance of changes in women's roles and status provided by the war left many gender issues unresolved after the armistice. Many of the incursions into areas previously the preserve of men did not survive the return to peacetime working.

For America, participation in the war and involvement with the Allies did require some in the government, as well as some ordinary citizens, to confront racial attitudes as well as class and gender inequalities. There were few who did, however, and none of these issues was resolved because along with the disappearance of government agencies and the gradual weakening of rhetoric after the war, the administration shrank from its progressive, but uneven, attempts to deal with these issues. Nonetheless, the petitions by the working class, women, and socially excluded or subjugated minorities for better representation and fuller inclusion did not disappear, and women's suffrage, which was finally adopted in mid-1920, was but one example of the beginning of change brought about by the war.

HOMEFRONT/READJUSTMENT AND STRIKES

War Bonds

America's entry into the war was overshadowed by a debate over whether and by how much the state should resist the expansion of the private sector, which had gone on since the turn of the century. The decade 1910–1919, though, was one of heightened concern given the rapid growth of giant corporations and the progressive view that the state should support the public interest in the face of a private sector increasingly unconcerned and antagonistic to that consideration. Wilson seemed to favor regulatory control, but his indecision was in sharp contrast to antiprogressives, who opposed any interventionism. By 1917, matters were exacerbated by almost complete ignorance of just what the call on the American economy would be, the timescale involved, and even the extent of federal reserves.

The urgent need for a war finance policy and mobilization was brought into sharp focus by all these factors. The coordinator of the policy was Secretary of the Treasury William Gibbs McAdoo. McAdoo, who was moderately progressive, was himself uncertain of the scale of demand for funds. His solution was to reject counsel that the money should be raised from income taxes and advice from private bankers that the markets would be destabilized by loans of more than $1 billion at less-than-market rates (at that time, 4 percent) and to issue $2 billion worth of war bonds at 3.5 percent. That decision was supported by the *Wall Street Journal,* which argued that "it is not right that the present generation should bear the whole burden of a conflict fought for the freedom of our children's children." (Kennedy, 1980, 17) His decision was informed by his uncertainty over the extent of the demand and thus his ability to make future issues; his concern over large government debt; his desire to minimize the damage to an economy that had profited so handsomely from America's neutrality; and that, at lower interest rates, lenders would be less likely to divert funds from other investments, but would reduce their current consumption to purchase the so-called Liberty Loan. This and all four subsequent loans were substantially oversubscribed, but McAdoo's objective (to maintain the framework of private capital and to inhibit inflation by deflecting funds from current consumption) proved to be impossible to realize.

McAdoo's objectives were compromised by his anxiety that the low interest rate would itself hamper large-scale sales; hence, his decision to incorporate such compensatory features as tax exemption on interest, which favored the wealthy, despite his assertion that the bonds should be available to the widest constituency. The bonds never competed with the prevailing market despite interest rate rises on all subsequent issues. McAdoo's policy of reducing consumption was confounded in practice by massive bank borrowing. Debt led to the creation of credit (i.e., the creation of new money that increased the total

Poster encouraging the purchase of Liberty Bonds, ca. 1918. (Library of Congress)

money supply between 1916 and 1920 by around 75 percent and almost doubled the consumer price index). McAdoo further challenged his policy of diverting funds by encouraging the public to use bank loans to buy bonds, thus increasing inflation still further.

America's contribution to the war was thus enabled to a large extent by the creation of new money, and because there was little increase in production, inflation was the inevitable outcome. Nevertheless, money creation was probably more acceptable than higher taxation, and it left finite resources undisturbed, thus concealing the true cost of the war. Maintaining public support was an important factor. McAdoo capitalized on patriotism in a series of speaking tours and exhorted the people to support Liberty Bonds, while commissioning propaganda from artists like Charles Dana Gibson and James Montgomery Flagg and persuading such celebrities as Douglas Fairbanks and Mary Pickford to publicize the bonds. The necessity of such efforts was debatable because the bonds were oversubscribed anyway, and any attempts at criticism were countered by accusations of anti-Americanism. Jingoism was deliberately fostered to conceal the real costs of the war, and McAdoo's reluctance to depend on market rates or taxation substituted emotion for the economic sacrifice he would not ask the people to pay.

War Work/Retooling

Great Britain had ordered 400,000 rifles from American manufacturers at the outset of war in 1914. This was followed by the signing of the Commercial Agency Agreement between the House of Morgan and the British government in January 1915, and it initiated close collaboration between the Allies and American arms makers, a liaison facilitated by Morgan representatives. Morgan's export department supervised more than 4,000 contracts between then and early 1917, whereas Allied specialists counseled U.S. manufacturers in the building of new factories and retooling existing ones. Under the agreement, Morgan became the single largest global buyer of goods, 60 percent of which were munitions with the remainder being largely provisions, unprocessed materials, chemicals, and machine tools.

This trade was clearly highly lucrative and provided jobs for tens of thousands of workers. American manufacturers also enthusiastically filled the gap left by British finance and manufacturing interests that were diverted toward the war effort, and short-term profits ultimately led to medium-term economic dominance. Despite bankers' and manufacturers' desire to establish American economic hegemony, however, Wilson's concept of moral leadership rather than economic motives directed American policy.

The Lever Act was passed in 1917 and gave the president extensive regulatory power over food and fuel prices. Food Administrator Herbert Hoover and Fuel Administrator Harry Garfield succeeded in increasing agricultural and coal production, eliminating stockpiling and racketeering, and promoting conservation. Those powers allowed Garfield temporarily to close thousands of factories to extricate coal cars from the transport bottleneck. Nevertheless, administrators preferred coaxing to compulsion. Various inducements were offered to farmers because America had to feed an army as well as to compensate for shortfalls caused by loss of shipping and harvest failures. In this context, maintaining and increasing production levels was critical and the government was well aware of the tensions between "guns or butter," a term used by economists to illustrate the essential distinction between allocating scarce resources to the defense of the country while not overlooking the needs of its people. Because resources are necessarily finite, producing both in infinite quantities is clearly impossible. Under capitalism, the government is not in full control of this decision, but influences it through such measures as defense spending and fiscal and federal policies. Following the declaration of war, measures that were instigated by the government were intended to shift the balance of power between capital and state and would result, Wilson hoped, in a more stable and productive economy.

Hoover declined the option of food rationing and instead attempted to appeal to the public to observe meatless or wheatless days. Hundreds of thousands of "doorknockers" went from house to house, delivering pledge cards to enlist the patriotic participation of housewives in the campaign to conserve food. Hoover's "spirit of self-sacrifice" (Kennedy, 1980, 119) proved to be relatively ineffective, but compulsion disguised as voluntarism combined with propaganda led to greatly increased production. The war's abrupt end paradoxically resulted in the need to dispose of stockpiles of commodities.

Industrial Reconversion and Recession/Strikes/Steel

For some, "reconstruction" merely inferred the inevitable transfer of means from military to peacetime ends; for others, the realization of Wilson's hopes that America would assume moral and spiritual leadership postwar. Progressives wanted a return to post–Civil War radicalism (i.e., an expansion of communal practices, state control, and intervention). Socialists had seen power pass from capital to state and labor, believing that "capitalism will not come back unchallenged and uncontrolled." (*Survey* 41, Nov. 16, 1918, in Kennedy, 1980, 247)

This idealism overlooked the reality of America's war. The war had been sufficiently remote and brief that it did not cause any great displacement of American material existence that might lead to further change, and Americans were far from committed to rebuilding society along radical lines. Given that this commitment was unlikely to materialize in the aftermath of war, industrial reconversion seemed to be the most likely option, but no umbrella agency was established to oversee such pressing postwar concerns as demobilization, Americanization, industrial reconversion, labor, or foreign trade. Believing that businessmen and workers were unlikely to accept further intrusion, Wilson's already half-hearted interest in such an agency vanished with the Republican victory in November 1918.

In any case, because mobilization had proceeded on the basis that there should be minimal disturbance to the economic system, there was little need for any state intervention. Even by November, only about one-quarter of gross national product was committed to military requirements, there was no absolute restriction on any institution, and nonessential businesses were merely restricted, not eliminated completely. Because economic involvement had been partial, it followed that reconstruction should be relatively straightforward. Most wartime emergency agencies were dismantled quickly. Criticism that disregarding their potential for controlling unstable postwar markets was shortsighted and symptomatic of reluctance to confront business interests ignored the degree of voluntarism inherent in the run-up to involvement and the reality that government shortfalls and accumulated orders revitalized the economy for at least a year, rather than the reverse. Faced with the cancellation of orders caused by the abrupt end to the war, business was placated by generous terms and subsidies for investment in new plant.

Unions after the War

If there was any one group that harbored the wish that the aftermath of war would consolidate the gains made during the war, it was labor. Postwar economic revitalization brought with it increased unionization, wage rises in industries with the greatest levels of union participation (e.g., mining, manufacturing, and transportation), and the reduction of the working day to a national standard of eight hours. Circumstances were changing rapidly by November, however, and the president of the American Federation of Labor (AFL), Samuel Gompers, knew that the artificially restricted labor market would be loosened by the termination of government orders. Gompers also knew that the labor market would be swelled by returning servicemen and the resumption of immigration, and, therefore, his power would also increase. War had necessitated a kid gloves approach to labor relations. Interruptions to essential war production could not be permitted.

Faced with the choice between persuasion and coercion, the government chose appeasement in the form of generous contracts that indemnified employers against rising labor costs.

A high-wage policy based on voluntary agreements between government and labor was legally unenforceable. Even though uncooperative employers could be threatened with the withdrawal of contracts, in practice the combination of improved conditions—which nevertheless, stopped short of the closed shop—written into contracts, along with indemnity, resulted in cooperation from both sides. In some sectors (e.g., shipbuilding and munitions), however, the fragile balance between demand and supply was skewed by high wages and heavy demand for labor. Shortages were caused in some areas as employers, unconstrained by any maximum wage, lured workers away from other regions. Reluctant to follow the British example of compulsory restraints, the government relied on largesse, enabled by necessity during the war, and prosperity afterwards. The benefits of plenty could thus substitute for unionization and prevailing power structures could be maintained.

Such generosity met with mixed success. There were more than 4,500 strikes in copper mines, shipyards, and timber in 1917, the highest in American history. The President's Mediation Commission, commissioned by an uneasy Wilson, discovered that workers lacking the security of recognized unions were frequently exploited by the domination of ruthless capital. In a particularly bitter labor dispute in the logging industry of the Pacific Northwest, the Commission reported in favor of a moderate union, believing that the owners had forced the men to be targeted readily by the IWW. Forced by the need for vital timber to take decisive action, the government first of all raided IWW halls, held mass trials, and jailed its leaders, then stationed 10,000 troops in the Northwest to work as civilians in the timber industry and form the core of a new union, the Loyal Legion of Loggers and Lumbermen (4-L). Production was stabilized and conditions and wages improved for its 120,000-strong membership, but the organization, effectively a company union, was acceptable only because of the no-strike pledge members were obliged to sign and its moderate policies. Labor policy during the war was focused on achieving the greatest, undisturbed production, and that policy was epitomized by the 4-L.

Despite high wages and enhanced conditions, no radical redistribution of the balance of power was contemplated, either by government or by employers antithetical to independent unions, independence that an administration intent on maintaining wartime production was more than reluctant to grant. The rationalization of labor policies in early 1918 led to many anomalies (e.g., the right to collective bargaining), while still allowing employers the option of negotiating with a union of its own origination, thus stimulating the creation of company unions. In any case, because government policy indemnified employers against losses caused by rising wages, they went along with what little control there was. Unions were permitted, but they were effectively powerless.

Government reluctance to disrupt production meant that they also had little power until further labor troubles led to the May 1918 edict that the unemployed would be considered first in the draft lists. Assurances that strikers would not be deemed unemployed did little to comfort unions, and the reduction in strikes in 1918 from 4,500 to around 3,500 was evidence that there was greater reluctance to strike.

Encouraged by increased membership and indulged by an apparently still benevolent government, unionists determined again to confront the largest remaining and, so far, the most resistant, nonunionized industry: iron and steel. The majority of steel production, which was essential to a modernizing America, was centered on a few large, vertically integrated companies whose profits depended as much on the financial tactics of aggressive and astute characters (e.g., Andrew Carnegie and Henry C. Frick) as on iron and steel production. The industry was irreconcilably hostile to unionization and had a long and troubled relationship with labor; a quarter century of antiunion policies followed the Homestead Strike of 1892, during which mechanization had effectively reduced skills levels to the point where, in 1917, the industry depended on a largely unskilled, new immigrant–dominated workforce. Although steel was the most visible in the trend toward rising labor costs and government-subsidized procurement of new equipment, the war accelerated the tendency in most other capital-intensive, mass production–centered industries, and the unions saw unionization of steel, the forerunner in these advances, as critical in their survival.

Steel and After

The end of war meant an end to much of government control of industry, which, in the case of the steel industry, had been shaky at best. Unions were thus left to confront alone a steel industry more determined than ever to resist demands for the eight-hour day and collective bargaining. Steel workers had already voted decisively to withdraw labor if their demands were not realized, and despite Wilson's intervention, on September 22, 1919, 250,000 men walked out of the mills. Against a background of a potential strike in the coal industry, a general strike in Seattle, innumerable smaller stoppages over the whole country, the perceived threat of insurgency by foreign radicals, and now the steel strike, public concerns focused on the expansion of business interests on the one hand, and labor unrest among increasingly powerful labor organizations on the other.

The collapse of the October Industrial Conference, instigated by Wilson to debate the industrial situation and which resolved none of the issues uppermost in the minds of employers or labor, only served to make clear the growing isolation of the labor movement. The withdrawal of controls was quickly followed by rising prices, and production slowed as deferred domestic demand and exports were drawn from stockpiled goods. As a result, the purchasing power of the dollar fell dramatically and unemployment rose, in some industries such as

Strike leader at Gary, Indiana, advises strikers, 1919. (Library of Congress)

automobiles to 55 percent in 1920. The wage gains of the war period were gradually undermined by the continuing inflation of 1919. The right to collective bargaining became even less likely than it had been during the war now that popular opinion, unsettled by the apparently endless and innumerable strikes and by the Red Scare, became increasingly ill disposed to organized labor. The steel strike heightened public antagonism and also contributed to growing awareness among unionists themselves that even though employers were still prepared to use crude and violent measures (e.g., the use of armed federal troops to break the strike), they increasingly preferred to arouse public hostility and anxiety among strikers themselves, alleging radicalism and Bolshevism among their leaders.

Some justification came in the form of William Z. Foster, secretary of the National Committee for Organizing Iron and Steel Workers and a one-time Wobbly and founder of the Syndicalist League of North America, whose aims included worker control and the dismantling of capitalism. In the volatile and emotional climate of antiradicalism, however, the steel employers remorselessly manipulated public anxieties. Added credibility for this vilification was provided because the high proportion of new immigrants among their numbers exacerbated the public perception of the strikers, whose loyalty to America was already suspect. The deliberate and divisive hiring policy of the years before the war resulted in further scope for disruption when employers dispatched agents to foment hostility between native and immigrant workers and imported African American scabs whose presence was intended to provoke fear among unskilled whites, who were anxious that their jobs were threatened by African American workers. The strike had collapsed by January, and with it the anticipation of unionization among mass-production industries.

Western socialists had not had an easy war. Their ideological principles were confounded by the outbreak of war and by the undignified rejection by European socialists of working-class cohesion in favor of nationalism and a prowar stance. Despite the American Socialist Party's antiwar position, socialists in other belligerent nations were more equivocal, unsure whether to support the war and whether and how forcefully to demand labor's rights during such fraught times. The apparent proletarian victory in the 1917 Russian Revolution, however, had inspired socialists in America, and elsewhere, to announce the end of capitalist oppression. The events of late 1918 and early 1919 seemed to bear this out. The Seattle strike, unparalleled strike activity elsewhere across America, and bombings in early 1919 seemed to presage some underlying malaise that might mirror uprisings in Russia, Germany, and Hungary.

The discovery that at least one of those responsible for a bombing atrocity was an Italian immigrant anarchist reinforced the impression in the public's mind that radical (i.e., immigrant) extremists were culpable, and, inflamed by hysterical newspaper reports and rabid headlines referring to the "Red Threat," reactionary elements across the country embarked on an anti-Left terror offensive. In many of these, perpetrators deliberately neglected to differentiate between labor and radical organizations, targeting anyone perceived to be sympathetic to the Left. Some of the worst clashes occurred on May Day 1919, when parades in New York, Cleveland, Boston, and other cities, as well as the offices of socialist newspapers and organizations, were the focus for violent attacks. Violence continued throughout 1919. An attack on the local IWW hall in Washington, D.C., resulted in retaliation by Wobblies and a subsequent revenge offensive that resulted in the horrific killing of one Wobbly, Wesley Everett.

Private citizens carried out the majority of this violence, though often with the knowledge or active participation of police and public officials, and at no time did the president or the administration acknowledge or condemn these illegal attacks. In the hysterical and intolerant atmosphere of the immediate postwar years, civil libertarians believed that such draconian wartime measures as the Espionage and Sedition Acts, along with the Red Scare and anti-immigrant sentiment, had fomented such a lawless and bigoted environment. These measures, maintained by the administration throughout the war and postwar years, nurtured an enormous and unparalleled labyrinth of "domestic surveillance and control organizations to monitor and silence critics of the war, labor activists, and radicals." (Zieger, 2000, 197)

Corporate Hegemony

The consolidation of industry was the predictable outcome of government's relative inability and apparent reluctance to control increasingly large companies and the disappearance of wartime regulatory bodies. Apparent impotence in the face of the overwhelming power of the steel industry did little to gain support for a Democratic Party that might have benefited from working-class backing to resist the re-emergence of corporate power in the postwar period. It was particularly striking after 1918 how rapidly growth and change occurred. Several factors were significant in the dynamic expansion of business. Highly organized, standardized mass-production methods came into general use, often in new industries (e.g., such as automobile manufacture, whose significance was magnified because of the impact on other industries) that had emerged before the war, and which now developed and matured extremely rapidly. The wartime drive to increase efficiency in manufacturing and to conserve essential materials had made industrialists acutely aware of the economy of standardization. The increasing number of trade associations, which were formed as whole industries began to act together, changed the nature of competition itself. These associations promoted standardization, as well as the business-management and time-and-motion systems of the kind introduced by F. W. Taylor, as ways of reducing the necessarily high fixed costs in large-scale mechanized industries.

Industrial consolidation, which had slowed down after 1904, increased and took on new forms as concentration emerged in businesses concerned directly with the public, as well as those among the manufacturing sector. Holding companies took on additional significance, and, as stock ownership increased and methods of financing changed, speculative trading on unprecedented scales became common. The tendency toward mergers that began in the prewar years among banks, chain stores, the automobile industry, steel and oil, and almost all sectors of the American economy accelerated rapidly after 1918. The antitrust laws intended to regulate business and safeguard competition had been all but suspended during the war, as Wilson feared any disruption of industry, and were only mildly enforced afterwards.

Wilson had already demonstrated his unease regarding the growth of large, monopolistic concerns and the concentration of industrial control in the hands of a relatively small number of powerful individuals when Congress, on his recommendation, created the Federal Trade Commission in 1914. Numerous other attempts to prevent monopoly by legislation had also been attempted, and these were partially successful in restraining some of the more conspicuous examples of controlling markets or artificially maintaining prices. It was acknowledged, however, that enforcing unlimited competition while simultaneously constraining the efficiencies of the economies of scale was counterproductive, and in any case, size as such was not limited by legislation. As a result, the courts were allowed substantial discretion in their interpretation of such provisions as existed. For example, although the U.S. Steel Corporation had been created by a merger and commanded at least half of the country's steel production, it was judged by the Supreme Court in 1920 not to entail any unreasonable restraint of trade.

Moreover, there were important sectors of industry in which antitrust legislation was not applied (e.g., where monopoly entitlements were granted by patents or in utilities and railroads where prices were supposed to be under public regulation). Successful corporations, often in the newer industries, grew rapidly to immense size, partly as a result of reinvesting surplus profits and partly because the substantial capital investment required in these highly mechanized industries prevented or delayed the entry of competitors. The result was concentration of industry dominated by a few large concerns that, although notionally competitive, tended to pursue a pricing policy established by its most successful companies. As a result of all these factors, and despite the few legal efforts intended to prevent monopoly, concentration and consolidation continued almost unimpeded, initiating the age of corporate hegemony in the years after 1920.

The Impact of World War I on the 1910s

The consequences of America's involvement in World War I were far-reaching and profound. The changes in America were so complex politically, socially, and economically, and in some cases so ambiguous, that the only incontrovertible result was that U.S. intervention brought forward the end of hostilities in Western Europe by at least a year.

During this period, two predominant but opposing progressive elements directed American public discourse; America's experience of the war reflected both those tendencies. The first extolled the testing of cultural frontiers and commitment to notions of egalitarianism, ethnic difference, and fair play; the other demanded order, restraint, and commitment to social proficiency and the values of the old white structure. Both believed that the war would allow for the promulgation of their own agendas, resulting in, on the one hand, a healthier, better-educated society in which capital would defer to society, and, on the other, a society in which discipline would prevent the further corrosion of traditional standards.

In the end, control and restraint proved more enduring than liberal aspirations. The elimination of dissent, government propaganda, disinformation, and surveillance did not disappear with the end of the war. Conscription and the marshalling of public loyalty through appeals to patriotism became important

Historians' Debate:
Should America Have Gone to War?

The names of Woodrow Wilson and those that informed and influenced American policy in World War I, such as Henry Cabot Lodge and William Gibbs McAdoo, are seldom mentioned now in public debate, but the term *Wilsonian* still has some currency. Long after Wilson returned from Paris and the Senate refused to ratify the Versailles Treaty in 1919–1920, whether Wilson was justified in taking the country to war and the issue of America's role in the war were dominant in debates on foreign policy.

In 1917, Senator George W. Norris contended that America had pursued a "band of gold," an accusation that found some favor among revisionists like Senator Gerald Nye in the 1930s and one that was informed by a belief that an ingenuous and inexperienced president had been lured into an ill-advised war by arms manufacturers and their financiers. Some similarly felt that Wilson had been taken in by Allied propaganda that demonized Germany to fight in a war that had been caused by European folly and that would lead to the deaths of thousands of American soldiers and prolonged international hostility. Other historians, however, notably Charles Seymour, believed that it was the reactionary and pessimistic opponents of the League of Nations (e.g., Senator Henry Cabot Lodge and his Republican accomplices) who broke faith with the American public and fomented American isolationism that eventually resulted in the ineffectual response to aggression by the Axis Powers.

Nevertheless, there are those like Carl Parini and William Appleman Williams who dispute this view of postwar foreign policy, identifying the significance of foreign trade and finance to the American economy and that both Wilson and his opponents' objective was to increase American economic hegemony, which is itself dependent on a functioning foreign policy. Even though historian John Lewis Gaddis recognizes the importance of economic objectives, however, he singles out the strand of aversion to dogmas and antiauthoritarianism characterizing America and that the Wilsonian ideal has been maintained since then. As Noam Chomsky trenchantly observed, however, U.S. interests have been aggressively advanced behind a Wilsonian smokescreen.

In terms of domestic policy, there are those who believed that events during and after the war revealed terminal weaknesses in the beliefs of liberal progressives. For the antiwar progressive Randolph Bourne, who had counseled from the outset that authoritarianism, militarism, and bigotry would be the inevitable outcome of the war, the assumption that war could deliver social improvements by controlling business, establishing public health and welfare programs, and alleviating want and poverty was preposterous. Bourne derided John Dewey's assertion that circumstances during wartime would advance progressivism by extending regulatory powers over America's economy, thus reducing poverty and inequality.

Continued on next page

Historians' Debate:
Should America Have Gone to War?, Continued

Any move toward social reform was provisional, contingent, and compromised. Bourne's warnings and his antiwar stance had been repudiated by liberal progressives, including colleagues on the *New Republic,* but by the end of the war, many acknowledged that wartime expediency had masked repression and coercion.

---

tools in the government's promotion of national security. Immigration restriction and Prohibition would give further expression to the forces of control.

Experiments in labor and race relations and welfare programs, which were always tentative and hesitant, were rapidly terminated as government agencies were dismantled. Even though women's wartime contributions were recognized with the endorsement of the Nineteenth Amendment in 1920, as war ended and women resumed their traditional domestic roles, any wider consideration of their significance in an increasingly urbanized and industrialized society was marginalized. Corporate hegemony became even more firmly entrenched as controls on capital through such regulatory bodies as the War Industries Board were relaxed.

Although apparently voluntary, the mechanisms that were introduced to conscript 4 million troops (e.g., control of speech, publication, and public gatherings), all ostensibly because of wartime expediency, cloaked a more coercive and repressive agenda that was effectively the beginning of the National Security State. The war constituted the beginning of the period of the enormous U.S. military-industrial complex and the government agencies that underpinned it.

Convincing a so-far antagonistic or apathetic public of the rightness of these policies in the face of no discernible threat to their physical security was one of the major achievements of the Wilson administration. Although unprecedented initiatives regulating almost every aspect of life were not maintained after the war, they provided templates for the politicians and reformers of later generations, as did the liberal reforms in labor relations and racial programs and the mobilization of the economy.

For many Europeans in the aftermath of war, Wilson himself represented the country that had liberated them, also epitomizing their aspirations for a different world. Illness had undermined his judgment by this time, however, and he arguably failed to understand the scope of the difficulties he would encounter when attempting to realize his vision of a New World order. Americans, particularly, felt betrayed by Wilson's failure quickly to negotiate a peace settlement with the leaders of other nations whose agenda was not to create a New World order, but rather to ensure that Germany would never again attempt to subjugate Europe.

BIOGRAPHIES

George Creel, 1876–1953

Journalist

George Creel was an investigative journalist and politician, but he is perhaps best known as the head of the propaganda organization the United States Committee on Public Information during World War I. As a pioneer investigative muckraking journalist, Creel began as a reporter on the *Kansas City World* in 1894, before establishing his own newspaper, the *Kansas City Independent,* in 1899. Work on other mass-circulation publications, his role as a progressive reformer, and his support for Woodrow Wilson led to his appointment in 1917 as head of Wilson's Committee on Public Information, established to present the government's version of the war and instill loyalty and public support using a program of propaganda. Under Creel, the Committee distributed millions of copies of pamphlets in several languages describing America's war involvement, organized war exhibitions, sent out thousands of press releases to aid (and mold) newspaper reportage, and initiated the Four-Minute Men program, which used

Journalist and progressive political reform leader George Creel organized and directed the first federal government attempt to project a positive image of the United States abroad in the 20th century. (Library of Congress)

around 75,000 local citizens to deliver short patriotic speeches on topics as diverse as rationing, the draft, and war bonds. This was done first in cinemas between reel changes, and then later in schools, community centers, and factories.

Always outspoken, Creel attracted hostility from Wilson's more conservative critics, whereas his forceful campaigning for Wilson's Fourteen Points provoked U.S. home opposition and may have contributed to the eventual rejection in Congress of the Treaty of Versailles. (www.firstworldwar.com/source/versailles .htm) His memoir of his wartime experiences, *How We Advertised America,* was published in 1920.

Arthur Fields, 1888–1953

Vaudeville Singer and Songwriter

Born Abe Finkelstein, Fields was a professional singer by age 11, performing at a movie house in Coney Island and with a minstrel show. His first success came in 1912 with "On the Mississippi," whereas his most popular song as lyricist in the pre–World War I era was "Aba Daba Honeymoon." It was as a songwriter and interpreter of patriotic songs, however, that Fields enjoyed his greatest success. The lyrics of the 1914 "Stay Down Where You Belong," in which the devil encourages his son to stay down below to avoid the fighting up above, matched America's antiwar mood. Once America entered the war, Fields recorded such songs as "Let's Bury the Hatchet," the title of which belies the following line, ". . . in the Kaiser's Head."

For the rest of the decade, Fields cut songs reflecting the country's involvement in the conflict in Europe, e.g., "It's a Long Way to Berlin But We'll Get There," "When I Get Back to My American Blighty," and "When I Send you a Picture of Berlin." Under his own name as well as that of Eugene Buckley and, because his recording output was so prolific, other pseudonyms as well, he recorded songs like "K-K-K-Katy" and "Good Morning Mr. Zip-Zip-Zip," both of which were termed "camp songs" by his record label and both were highly popular with troops, as well as more explicitly jingoistic examples (e.g., "Huntin' the Hun"). Many of these songs remained popular long after the war was over.

In 1918, Fields's record label issued a catalog, which noted that his records for Vocalion included patriotic song-hits that he had composed and that he was a member of the 71st Regiment. The catalog also publicized the state recruiting campaign in which the songs had been featured. His recordings in 1919 as vocalist for Ford Dabney's band (e.g., "Johnny's in Town,") are among the earliest examples of a white singer accompanied by African American musicians.

James Montgomery Flagg, 1877–1960

Illustrator

Although the artist and illustrator James Montgomery Flagg produced a wide range of graphic art and paintings during a long career, he is best known for the World War I recruitment poster, "I Want YOU for U.S. Army." Flagg started drawing and painting early in life, and his work had been accepted by several leading magazines by age twelve. He was contributing to *Life* magazine by 14 and on the staff on *Judge* magazine by the following year.

In his early 20s, Flagg studied painting in Paris and London, but he supported himself with book illustrations, magazine covers, spot drawings, political and humorous cartoons, and advertising work. Shortly after America's entry into the war, the Committee on Public Information was established to gain popular support for the war effort. Under George Creel, the Division of Pictorial Publicity was created to get the war message to Americans who might not read newspapers or attend meetings. Creel chose the illustrator Charles Dana Gibson (at the time, America's most popular illustrator and a fervent advocate of the war) to assemble a group of artists to design posters for the government.

Illustrators—who like N. C. Wyeth, Joseph Pennell, and Flagg often donated the work without charge—produced 1,400 patriotic images to promote recruitment, food conservation, and the purchase of Liberty Bonds. Some images had already been used in different contexts: "I Want YOU for U.S. Army" (1917, Smithsonian Institute) first appeared on the cover of *Leslie's Weekly* under the title "What Are You Doing for Preparedness?" and was inspired by the British recruitment poster depicting Lord Kitchener in a similar pose. Flagg drew around 45 images for the Division, including "Wake Up America" (1917) and "First Call" (1917), a recruitment poster for the navy that also featured Uncle Sam.

Henry Cabot Lodge, 1850–1924

Politician

Henry Cabot Lodge was a Republican politician, statesman, and eminent historian. The great grandson of politician George Cabot, Lodge was born into one of Massachusetts' most prestigious families. He graduated from Harvard and returned there to take a law degree and a PhD in political science. After initially failing to win a seat in Congress, he succeeded in 1886, becoming involved in the protection of voting rights in the South. Following his entry into the Senate, where he remained until his death, he developed a close relationship with Theodore Roosevelt until the two disagreed over domestic policy. Epitomizing the reactionary faction of the Republican Party, Lodge contested Woodrow Wilson's progressivism by supporting high protective tariffs.

Although Lodge supported America's entry into the war, he was forthright in his criticism of Wilson's war policies. After the Republicans gained control of

Henry Cabot Lodge was originally an isolationist, but in the years following World War I, he became a proponent of American internationalism. (Cirker, Hayward, ed., Dictionary of American Portraits, *1967)*

both the House and the Senate in 1918, Lodge became chair of the Senate Committee on Foreign Relations and Senate majority leader and presided over the Senate's rejection of the ratification of the Treaty of Versailles, largely driven by his wish to protect American interests and his enduring dislike of the president. He was instrumental in obtaining the Republican nomination for Warren Harding in 1920, effectively ending Wilson's vision of America's postwar role. He was always a prolific writer, and his account of events during the ratification contest, *The Senate and the League of Nations,* was published posthumously in 1925.

William Gibbs McAdoo, 1863–1941

Politician

William Gibbs McAdoo was a U.S. senator, secretary of the treasury between 1913 and 1918, and the main author of America's war finance policy. He was also the first chairman of the Federal Reserve Board. McAdoo began as a lawyer in Tennessee, and then later New York. His leading role in the raising of funds and subsequent completion of the Hudson Tunnel in 1911 made him a popular figure, and his motto, "The Public Be Pleased," was a philosophy he brought to the issue of war bonds, believing that appealing directly to the public would encourage ordinary citizens to identify with the war effort. After working for the campaign to elect Wilson in 1912, he left business and became Wilson's son-in-law in 1914.

Apart from the examples provided by the Civil War and the experience of the Allies in financing a war, neither of which McAdoo chose to emulate, he had few, if any, precedents. His strategy of raising money from loans without resort to potentially antagonistic taxation or unsettling financial markets was successful in that it was vastly oversubscribed; however, the Liberty Bonds had the opposite effect to that which McAdoo intended in that they encouraged inflationary pressures by massively increasing the nation's money supply, thus provoking demand for goods in short supply.

After the war, McAdoo stood twice as a Democratic presidential candidate, losing both times, in 1920 and 1924.

General John J. Pershing, 1860–1948

Soldier

The soldier, diplomat, and commander of the AEF, "Black Jack" (a nickname he had acquired serving with an African American regiment in Cuba) Pershing was 56 when America entered the war in 1917. As the only American officer since the Spanish-American War to have commanded a large military group on active service and a diplomat whose tact was in sharp contrast to his main opponent, General Leonard Wood, Pershing was the logical choice as commander of the AEF for Wilson and Secretary of War Newton D. Baker. Pershing was educated at West Point in the 1880s when the strategies of the Civil War (early and complete destruction of the enemy and reliance on the infantryman) still held sway. He disdained Allied defense tactics, believing that the war of attrition that had paralyzed the Western Front could only be won by a strategy of open warfare and a separate American force whose overwhelming numbers would crush the Germans. In these tactics, and in his reliance on the rifle as the weapon of choice for American soldiers, he overlooked the realities of modern, mechanized warfare.

Nevertheless, despite Pershing's obduracy and criticism from Douglas MacArthur, among others, that he was a desk soldier supervising the offensive from well behind the lines, American soldiers under Pershing's command accelerated Allied victory and he was subsequently honored as the architect of that triumph.

The commander of the American Expeditionary Force during World War I, General John Pershing was the first great war hero of the 20th century. He was also involved in the controversial campaign launched by President Theodore Roosevelt in 1904 to gain control over the Moro region of the Philippines. (National Archives)

Oswald Garrison Villard, 1872–1949

Editor and Publisher

Born into a wealthy German family, Villard inherited a commitment to capitalism and the concept of 19th-century laissez-faire liberalism from his father, and his strict, austere moralism from his mother, the abolitionist and anti-imperialist reformer Fanny Garrison. After Harvard and a short apprenticeship on a Philadelphia newspaper, Villard joined his father's title, the *New York Evening Post*. He quickly assumed the editorship and, following the death of his father, became the owner and publisher.

Like his mother, Villard was a vocal anti-imperialist, believing that America's imposition of its imperialistic will and its waging of foreign wars were morally unjustifiable. Like her, he also supported the rights of women and championed the cause of minorities. Although he began by espousing laissez-faire economics, he departed from its conventions by defending the rights of workers to organize and to strike. As a committed pacifist, Villard opposed America's entry into World War I. In 1918, with patriotism at its height, the pressure on both Villard and the *Post* to attract readers and advertisers to a liberal newspaper with strongly anti-American views became financially untenable, and Villard was forced to sell the publication. Villard also attacked the Treaty of Versailles, declaring it to be unjust and a vindication of his views regarding the unjust nature of war. He also campaigned for the impeachment of the attorney general, A. Mitchell Palmer.

Although Villard had sold the *Post,* he retained ownership of its weekly journal of opinion, *The Nation,* an organ distinctive for its frequently independent and dissenting voice. Once he assumed the editorship in 1918, the journal quickly became a vehicle for Villard's own opinions. As a pioneer civil rights leader, Villard helped to found the American Anti-Imperialist League and donated space in the *Post* publicizing the meeting that was to lead to the establishment of the NAACP, for which organization he served as disbursing treasurer. Among his books are a 1910 biography of John Brown and *Germany Embattled,* 1915.

REFERENCES AND FURTHER READINGS

Bourne, Randolph S. 1964. *War and the Intellectuals: Collected Essays 1915–1919.* New York: Harper and Row.

Chomsky, Noam. 1969. *American Power and the New Mandarins.* New York: Pantheon Books.

EdSiteMent. edsitement.neh.gov/.

FirstWorldWar.com. www.firstworldwar.com.

Gaddis, John Lewis. 1993. "The Tragedy of Cold War History." *Diplomatic History* 17, no. 1 (Winter): 1–16.

The Great War Society. www.worldwar1.com/tgws/tgws2.htm.

Hacker, Louis M., and Helene S. Zahler. 1952. *The United States in the 20th Century.* New York: Appleton-Century-Crofts.

HistoryNet.com. www.historynet.com/wars_conflicts/world_war_1/.

James, D. Clayton, and Anne Sharp Wells. 1998. *America and the Great War, 1914–1920.* Wheeling, IL: Harlan Davidson.

Keene, Jennifer D. 2000. *The United States and the First World War.* Harlow: Pearson Education Limited.

Kennedy, David M. 1980. *Over Here: The First World War and American Society.* New York: Oxford University Press.

King, Desmond. 2000. *Making Americans: Immigration, Race, and the Origins of the Diverse Democracy.* Cambridge, MA: Harvard University Press.

Noble, David F. 1977. *America by Design: Science, Technology and the Rise of Corporate Capitalism.* New York: Oxford University Press.

Parini, Carl. 1969. *Heir to Empire: United States Economic Diplomacy, 1916–23.* Pittsburgh: University of Pittsburgh Press.

Ryan, Alan. 1995. *John Dewey and the High Tide of American Liberalism*. New York: W. W. Norton.

Seymour, Charles. 1921. *Woodrow Wilson and the World War.* New Haven: Yale University Press.

Soule, George. 1968. *Prosperity Decade: From War to Depression: 1917–1929.* New York: Harper and Row.

Veblen, Thorstein. 1922. "Dementia Praecox." *The Freeman* 5 (June 21): 344–347.

Wells, Robert A. 2002. "Mobilizing Public Support for War: An Analysis of American Propaganda during World War I," at www.isanet.org/noarchive/robert wells.html.

Williams, William Appleton. 1988. *The Tragedy of American Diplomacy*. New York: W. W. Norton.

World War I. www.teacheroz.com/wwi.htm.

The World War I Document Archive. www.lib.byu.edu/~rdh/wwi/.

Zieger, Robert H. 2000. *America's Great War: World War I and the American Experience*. Lanham: Rowman and Littlefield.

People and Events in the 20th Century

THE 1900s

THE 1910s

THE 1920S

THE 1930s

THE 1940s

THE 1950s

THE 1960s

THE 1970s

THE 1980s

THE 1990s

1910s Index

About the Author

Gordon Reavley is a part-time senior tutor in the history of art and design and visual and cultural studies in media. He teaches online and more conventionally at the University of Oxford, Newcastle University, and Nottingham Trent University. A mature student, he gained a B.A. in History of Modern Art, Design, and Film and a Master's in Architecture and Critical Theory. He is a widely published writer in journals and books on art, design, cultural, and social history, as well as film and book reviews in both the United States and the United Kingdom.